Eva Palmer Sikelianos

Eva Palmer Sikelianos

A LIFE IN RUINS

Artemis Leontis

PRINCETON UNIVERSITY PRESS

PRINCETON AND OXFORD

Published by Princeton University Press
41 William Street, Princeton, New Jersey 08540
6 Oxford Street, Woodstock, Oxfordshire OX20 1TR

press.princeton.edu

Library of Congress Control Number: 2018939875
ISBN: 978-0-691-17172-2

British Library Cataloging-in-Publication Data is available

Editorial: Anne Savarese and Thalia Leaf
Production Editorial: Ellen Foos
Text Design: Lorraine Doneker
Jacket Design: Emma J. Hardy
Jacket Credit: Eva Palmer Sikelianos, Delphi, 1930, photograph by Nelly's
(Elli Souyioultzoglou-Seraidary) © Benaki Museum Photographic Archive.
Production: Jacquie Poirier
Copyeditor: Kathleen Kageff

This book has been composed in Sabon LT Std

Printed on acid-free paper. ∞

Printed in the United States of America

1 3 5 7 9 10 8 6 4 2

Contents

Illustrations

Acknowledgments

Eva Palmer Sikelianos, the consummate networker, knew countless people in her lifetime. More than half a century after her death, she introduced me to many others whom she never knew.

The kernel of the book formed in a workshop in 2005 entitled "Eva Palmer Sikelianos: Past, Present, Future Directions" supported by the Contexts for Classics interdepartmental faculty initiative at the University of Michigan, with presentations by Ann Cooper Albright, Mary Hart, Vassilis Lambropoulos, Pantelis Michelakis, Yopie Prins, Eleni Sikelianos, Gonda Van Steen, and myself. The cross-fertilizations were rich and the speakers smart and unselfish. The conversation continued on a panel at the 2007 Modern Greek Studies Association (MGSA) Symposium, "Eva Palmer Sikelianos between Greece and America." At the close of the 2005 workshop, Martha Vicinus assigned me to write this biography. Eleni Sikelianos offered unconditional support. The kernel lay dormant while I tried to imagine how to undertake such a big research adventure. Answers came gradually in my brilliant writing group: Elizabeth Wingrove, Yopie Prins, Peggy McCracken, and Kathryn Babayan. For more than a decade, they have been offering rigorous truth telling and genuine goodwill. There would be no book without them. Does "thank you" cover so great a debt?

I found more goodwill in the libraries, archives, and museums that I frequented. Lia Papadaki handed me the (metaphorical) keys to the archive in the Benaki Museum Historical Archive (BMHA) and the Natalie Clifford Barney archive in the Bibliothèque littéraire Jacques Doucet (JD) and dropped hints about hidden letters in the Center for Asia Minor Studies (CAMS). At the BMHA, Valentina Tselika, Maria Dimitriadou, and Tassos Sakellaropoulos answered questions, responded to permission requests, and carried boxes up and down several flights of stairs. Kostas Bournazakis graciously gave me permission to read and publish parts of Eva Sikelianos's correspondence with Angelos Sikelianos. Nathalie Fressard obtained permission from François Chapon for my research in the Natalie Clifford Barney archive. I gained access to the trove of Eva Palmer's letters in the Melpo and Octave Merlier archives in CAMS with help from Ioanna Papadopoulou, the consent of Stavros Anestidis, and practical assistance from Varvara Kontogianni. Paschalis Kitromilides extended crucial support, and the executive board of the center formalized my request a few years later. I will forever praise the center for the cooperative, scholarly spirit that prevails and for its regularity of hours, even in hard times. Konstantinos Ghirtis and Efi Spyropoulou opened many other doors. Through Mrs. Spyropoulou, I met Eleni Dallas, niece of Konstantinos Psachos, who gave a detailed account of his relationship to Eva Sikelianos and copies of papers in the K. A. Psachos House Archive. Sokrates Loupas and Evangelos Karamanes shared materials directly from the Psachos Archive. The research staff at the Lillian Voudouri Music Library of the Athens Music Hall, the Hellenic Literary and Historical Archives (ELIA), and the Gennadius Library were all knowledgeable and helpful. Katerina Krikos-Davis facilitated permissions for the Seferis papers. Members of the Typaldos family gave a glimpse of the Sikelianos house in Sikya, now the Sikyon Resort Hotel, and a version of its story. A wonderfully hospitable resident of Delphi opened the door of the Angelos and Eva Sikelianos Museum, formerly the Palmer Sikelianos house at Delphi.

In the United States, my visits to libraries and archives, real and virtual, were equally well supported. Steven Slosberg, retired journalist, shared stories from Stonington, Connecticut, about the Palmer family's rise and fall. Ann Craig Befroy, director of archives at Miss Porter's School in Farmington, Connecticut, confirmed Eva Palmer's matriculation in the school and gave me information about the curriculum. Camilla MacKay, then head of Carpenter Library at Bryn Mawr College, with Lorett Treese and Cheryl Klimaszewski, assisted with my research visit in the College Library Collections. Michael Prettyman, nephew of Virginia Greer Yardley, introduced me to Yardley's correspondence in the Alfred and Mary Gwinn Hodder Papers in the Princeton University Library, and Dimitri Gondicas facilitated access. Mary Markey and Heidi Stover offered physical and virtual entry points to the Alice Pike Barney Papers in the Smithsonian Museum Archives. Bruce Tabb, rare books curator and public services librarian, University of Oregon Libraries, helped me locate an unpublished photograph of George Cram Cook. Librarians in the Sophia Smith Collection of Smith College, Special Collections at the University of Michigan Hatcher Library, and the Memorial Library, University of Wisconsin, all helped me make unexpected discoveries. Charles Perrier, the now retired assistant curator of the Jerome Robbins Dance Division, Library of the Performing Arts, New York Public Library, pulled boxes from the Ted Shawn Papers. Norton Owen, director of preservation, Jacob's

Pillow, handed me valuable archived audio, visual, and textual materials and talked to me about Ted Shawn's choreography. Susan Neill, vice president of collections and exhibitions, Atlanta History Center, shared correspondence related to Eva Sikelianos in the papers of Mary Crovatt Hambidge, and Bob Thomas, former residency director at the Hambidge Center for Creative Arts and Sciences in Rabun Gap, photographs.

Several invitations to present papers propelled the writing of book chapters. In chronological order: twenty-five years ago, before I knew much about Eva Palmer Sikelianos, I spoke on the Delphic revivals at Ohio Wesleyan at the invitation of Stephanie Winder; the lecture series "The Theatron of Hellas" at Yale University; and the "After Greece" faculty and student seminar in Modern Greek Studies at the Ohio State University. John Anton gave me a copy of *Upward Panic* to correct my errors. Years later, Vassiliki Kolocotroni and Efterpi Mitsi asked probing questions urging me to think about Eva Palmer Sikelianos among other women travelers. Dimitri Gondicas's kind invitation to address the Hellenic Studies seminar at Princeton University occasioned the presentation of my first archival research, relating to Palmer Sikelianos's musical collaboration with Khorshed Naoroji, which I later published as "An American in Paris, a Parsi in Athens" upon invitation from Dimitris Damaskos and Dimitris Plantzos and read from it in the Fall Reading Series of Emerson College organized by Maria Koundoura. I presented versions of the research on drama and dance in the Department of Classics at the Ohio State University invited by Gregory Jusdanis; a forum on heritage at the University of Michigan Institute for the Humanities organized by Daniel Herwitz; the workshop "Archaeology and Imagination—Archaeological Objects in Modern Fine Arts, Literature, and Science" at the Collegium Budapest Institute for Advanced Study, with Éva Kocziszky as the organizer and intellectual center of the workshop; the "Greek Drama in America, 1900–1970" John E. Sawyer Seminar on Theatre after Athens: Reception and Revision of Ancient Theatre, organized by the now deeply mourned Kate Bosher at Northwestern University; and Gennadius Library and American School of Classical Studies in Athens, invited by Maria Georgopoulou. My research on weaving and dress built on knowledge that Mary Hart presented at the 2005 workshop and MGSA panel in 2007, developed in dialogue with colleagues at the conference "Reimagining the Past: Antiquity and Modern Greek Culture" organized by Dimitris Tziovas at the Institute of Archaeology and Antiquity, Centre for Byzantine, Ottoman and Modern Greek Studies, University of Birmingham; the Department of Classics at the University of Florida, where I gave the Polopoulos Endowed Lecture at the invitation of Gonda Van Steen; the Department of Classical Studies Literature Brownbag organized by Ruth Caston at the University of Michigan; the Department of Classics at the Ohio State University, where I was especially honored to give the Thomas E. and Anna P. Leontis Memorial Lecture endowed by my late parents at the invitation of the modern Greek faculty; "Globalization and Heritage beyond 'Marbles Lost' " panel, 2011 MGSA Symposium, organized by Despina Margomenou; Classics Colloquium at Bryn Mawr College invited by Camilla MacKay, in conjunction with the "Colors of Greece: The Art and Archaeology of Georg von Peschke"; "Hellenomania International Colloquium" organized by the École française d'Athènes and Nicoletta Momigliano; "Antique Fashions" panel organized by the Discussion Group on Classical Studies and Modern Literature, MLA Conference, under the leadership of Stathis Gougouris; and UC Santa Barbara, where I gave the Argyropoulos Lecture at the invitation of Helen Morales. I presented my work on Sapphic performances in a seminar of the Modern Greek Program at Brown University organized by Elsa Amanatidou; and the "Eva Palmer Sikelianos Masterclass" of Karen Van Dyck organized by the Program in Hellenic Studies, Columbia University. I presented research on Palmer Sikelianos's English-language publication of Angelos Sikelianos's *Akritika* at the Mahindra Humanities Center Seminar on Modern Greek Literature and Culture at Harvard University organized by Panagiotis Roilos and at the 2017 MGSA Symposium. Finally, at the end of the writing process, Peggy McCracken, director of the Institute for the Humanities at the University of Michigan, gave me the opportunity to anticipate next steps with her invitation to speak on the panel "Archiving the Materials of Life." Parts of chapter 1 appeared in an earlier version in "Eva Palmer Sikelianos before Delphi," *Americans and the Experience of Delphi*, edited by Paul Lorenz and David Roessel (Somerset Hall, 2013); chapter 2 in "Fashioning a Modern Self in Greek Dress: The Case of Eva Palmer Sikelianos," *Hellenomania*, edited by Katherine Harloe, Nicoletta Momigliano, Alexandre Farnou (British School at Athens and Routledge, 2018); chapter 3 in "An American in Paris, a Parsi in Athens," *A Singular Antiquity: Archaeology and Hellenic Identity in Twentieth Century Greece*, edited by Dimitris Damaskos and Dimitris Plantzos (Benaki Museum, 2008); and chapter 4 in "Griechische Tragödie und moderner Tanz: Eine alternative Archäologie?," *Ruinen in der Moderne: Archäologie und die Künste*, edited by Éva Kocziszky (Reimer Verlag, 2010), and "Greek Tragedy and Modern Dance: An Alternative Archaeology?," *Oxford Handbook of Greek Drama in the Americas*, edited by Kathryn Bosher,

Fiona Macintosh, Justine McConnell, and Patrice Rankine (Oxford University Press, 2015).

My research and writing were made possible by generous support from the University of Michigan. The Hunting Family funded my residence at the Institute for the Humanities for the academic year of 2011–12, with its weekly seminars with faculty and graduate student fellows. The Institute for Research on Women and Gender; School of Literature, Science, and Arts (LSA) Associate Professor Fund; LSA Office of the Dean; Constantine A. Tsangadas Trust; Foundation for Modern Greek Studies Fund; and Bruce Frier Research Fund covered research and travel support. I single out two classical studies department chairs, Ruth Scodel and Sara Forsdyke, for the time they devoted to securing research leaves and funding. Michelle Biggs, Jeff Craft, Anna Moyer, and Sonia Schmerl offered invaluable office support. Sally Bjork, Nicholas Cullen, Sarah Kandell-Gritzmaker, Melissa Levine, and Monica Tsuneishi helped prepare images and permissions. I am grateful to the colleagues who taught, advised students, and served on committees in my absence and the students who discussed the project with me. Maria Hadjipolycarpou, Emily Lime, and Nicholas Cullen did outstanding work as graduate research assistants, and Sophia Christos and Alexandra Niforos were my undergraduate research interns. Dr. Nick Geller, an exceptional editor, and Emily Lime, sharp and well read, offered insightful comments on a penultimate draft. I owe words and references to them. William Stroebel, another brilliant reader, helped with the index.

I thank Anne Savarese, executive editor of acquisitions at Princeton University Press, for her confidence in the project and critical guidance. Three anonymous readers caught errors and asked crucial questions. Bob Bettendorf, Ellen Foos, Thalia Leaf, Kathleen Kageff, and Stephanie Rojas have seen the book through production.

Colleagues, students, friends, and kin from all over the world carried me further than I could have gone on my own. Without duplicating names, Anne Waldman spoke of her memories of Eva Sikelianos; Kostis Kourelis, Despina Margomenou, and Laurie Talalay, buildings, objects, alternative archaeologies, and heritage; Dinyar Patel, Parsis; Chris Apostoleris, Recep Gül, Peter Jeffreys, Yona Stamatis, and Pavlos Vasileiou, music; Maria Kakavoulia and Susan Van Pelt, dance; Linda Ben Zvi, the Cooks and Glaspell in Greece; Natalie Bakopoulos and Julian Anderson, writing; Martha Klironomos, the Seferis episode; Yiorgos Anagnostou, transnational networks; and Susan Allen, spies and philhellenes. Manos Eleftheriou sent valuable ephemera. Angeliki Evangelinos was my alpha reader. Vassiliki Leontis spent a week with me in the Benaki Museum Historical Archives reading correspondence in French. Suzanne Stroh appeared out of nowhere at a critical moment, and her interview on Eva Sikelianos, published on Natalie Clifford Barney's birthday, gave necessary visibility to the project. She continues to fortify me. I benefited from conversations with Sara Ahbel-Rappe, Roderick Beaton, Netta Berlin, Ali Bolcakan, Clara Bosak-Schroeder, Vangelis Calotychos, Anne Carson, Etienne Charrière, Yiorgos Chouliaras, Jim Cogswell, Anna Cornell, Samuel Dorf, Karen Emmerich, Edith Hall, Judith P. Hallett, Johanna Hanink, Michèle Hannoush, Maria Iliou, Vrasidas Karalis, Cassandra Langer, Byron MacDougall, Fiona Macintosh, Maria Mylona, Alexander Nehamas, Lisa Nevett, Penelope Papailias, Zeese Papanikolas and Ruth Fallenbaum, Ioannis Plemmenos, David Roessel, Francesca Schironi, Anastasia Psoni, Niki Stavridi, Bob and Susan Sutton, Giota Tachtara, Susan Van Pelt, Panos Vlagopoulos, Natalie Vogeikoff-Brogan, and Peter Vorissis. I received reinforcements beyond words from Achilleas Anastasopoulos and Eleni Gourgou, Efthymia Damaskou and Despina Pantazidou, Jennifer Howard and Johannes Foufopoulos, Van and Janet Gegas, Todd Gerring, Stacie Harris, Eliza and Gene Holland, Perry Katsikas, Neocles and Vassiliki Leontis, Melanie Mallin and Bill Loumbouridis, Panayotis Pafilis, Neni Panourgiá, Mahi Pantaki, Sophia Pavlatos, Sara Randazzo, Sophia Roumanis, Carolyn Steiner, Holly Taylor, Mike Vander Roest, and Katerina Michaelidou and Yiannis, Ellie, Maria, Nicole, and Vassileia Varvarigos.

On the home front, while I was working to revive Eva Palmer Sikelianos, life marched on. Despite my decade-long attachment to a dead woman, Vassilis Lambropoulos, my cherished husband, advisor, and bibliography service, is still by my side answering questions upon demand. Our dog Argos wandered off after nearly seventeen years, and Zeno wagged his way in. Meanwhile Daphne completed university and medical school, married her high school sweetheart, was resident then chief resident in pediatrics, and landed her first academic job, while she also cared for and lost three beloved grandparents. Doctor Daphne Vander Roest, I dedicate this book to you, our radiant daughter, so you may finally read about the woman who intruded on your young adult life through my long adventures.

Introduction

"Eva Palmer Sikelianos needs no introduction."[1] In 1934, this classic line was sufficient to introduce Eva Palmer Sikelianos (1874–1952) to First Lady Eleanor Roosevelt. A member of the New York social elite[2]—whose father, Courtlandt Palmer (from the large, pre-Revolutionary Palmer family of Stonington, Connecticut) was famous in his day for his defense of freedom of speech[3]—she had an international reputation for her out-of-the-ordinary creative activities. For decades, she attracted regular news coverage. In the *New York Times* alone, more than one hundred articles published between 1900 and the early 1930s tracked her transatlantic movements and theatrical performances (figure I.1). Eleanor Roosevelt required no further references from the woman who made the introduction: Beatrice B. Beecher, great-niece of Harriet Beecher Stowe and a member of another legendary American clan. The First Lady wrote directly to Eva Palmer Sikelianos, inviting her to talk at one of her press conferences on how to harness America's future creative power.[4]

Today, Eva Palmer Sikelianos has slipped into the footnotes of other people's stories. As Eva Palmer, she appears as the "first lover"[5] of the brilliant American salonist Natalie Clifford Barney, the ravishing muse of Renée Vivien's novel *A Woman Appeared to Me*, and the "miraculous redhead"[6] who performed with Colette in Pierre Louÿs's "Dialogue au soleil couchant." As Eva Sikelianos, she is remembered primarily as the wife of the Greek poet Angelos Sikelianos, who shared his cultural work by reviving international festivals of drama and athletic games at Delphi in 1927 and 1930, and as the sister-in-law of Isadora Duncan. Today, she needs an introduction. The renown that made her recognizable to Eleanor Roosevelt has faded, and Eva Palmer Sikelianos has become an ancillary player in the history of other personages.

I was myself introduced to Eva Palmer Sikelianos while leafing through books and magazines about Greece in my parents' library in the 1960s and 1970s. The name and pictures of Eva Sikelianos appeared in several highbrow magazines of contemporary Greek culture. In one, I found a close-up of her middle-aged face and torso in a Greek tunic, with fashionable people in Western dress visible in the background. I was mystified by

"There is a report from London that Miss Eva Palmer will go on the stage" (April 5, 1903, SM7).

LOOKED LIKE GREEK GODDESS: Miss Palmer Landed In Classic Costume (September 1, 19071).

MISS PALMER WEDS ANCIENT PHILOSOPHER: Angelo Sikelianos, Whom She Met in Greece, Followed Her Over Seas. CEREMONY AT BAR HARBOR. Society Bride Some Time Ago Adopted the Classic Garb of Tunic and Sandals (September 10, 1907, 7).

GREEK DRAMA TO BE GIVEN AGAIN AT ANCIENT DELPHI: An American Woman Will Produce Aeschylus's "Prometheus," With Native Talent, in Memory of George Cram Cook, Founder of Provincetown Players (October 11, 1925, X8).

DELPHI AWAKES FROM HER SLEEP OF 2,000 YEARS... (May 1, 1927, RPA3).

EVA P. SIKELIANOS HERE TO TALK ON GREEK ART: Weaver of Robes for the Delphic Festival Will Also Lecture on Byzantine Music (September 29, 1927, 17).

DELPHIC FESTIVALS BEGIN: Thousands See Aeschylus's "Prometheus Bound" on Mount Parnassus. (May 2, 1930, 8).

*GREEKS OPEN BIG THEATRE: 15,000 See Dedication Play at Huge Open-Air Structure in Athens...*designed by Mme. Eva Sikelianos (April 25, 1933, 15).

GREEK PLAY CHOSEN BY SMITH SENIORS: 'The Bacchae," a Tragedy by Euripides, Will be Seen Outdoors in June... under the direction of Mme Eva Palmer Sikelianos (March 18, 1934, N3).

BRYN MAWR GIVES PLAY AS GREEKS DID: "Bacchae" of Euripides Staged in Open Air, Chorus Keeping Time With Cymbals. INCENSE BURNS ON COLUMN 62 Students, Chosen by Mme. Sikelianos, Join in Chants – Audience Is Absorbed (June 2, 1935, 2).

*NEWS OF THE STAGE:...*Mme. Eva Palmer Sikelianos...has been appointed by the WPA to produce Aeschylus's "The Persians." Plans call for a large arena and a male chorus of fifty voices. (July 24 1938, 13).

'VISIBLE SONG': Eva Sikelianos Conducts an Experiment with Ted Shawn. Gravely Handicapped Tempered Scale Abandoned Renaissance Provided Mediums (06 Aug 1939: 8).

EVA SIKELIANOS 77, IS DEAD IN ATHENS: Widow of Greek Poet Won Acclaim for Revival of the Delphic Festival in '27 (June 5, 1952, 31).

FIGURE I.1. Headlines from the *New York Times* featuring Eva Palmer Sikelianos.

the caption: "High Priestess of Delphi."[7] The text around the picture spoke of her life with Angelos Sikelianos, and how she helped him to organize two revivals of the ancient Delphic Festivals in 1927 and 1930 as part of his plan to make Delphi an international center of culture and learning. Elsewhere I read that she had come to Greece in 1905 or 1906 (sources were inconsistent) with Raymond Duncan, brother of Isadora, and his Greek wife Penelope, after pursuing a life in theater in Paris for several years. She married Angelos Sikelianos, brother of Penelope, in 1907 and supported his poetic career with absolute dedication. Having spent all her money to produce the festivals, she returned to the United States to raise funds for Angelos's larger project, his Delphic Idea. She failed; then World War II interrupted the Delphic plan. Now impoverished, she stayed in the

United States. But, according to these sources, her love for Sikelianos never waned. In the last pages of a large volume celebrating her legacy, I found a photograph of an older Eva Sikelianos, in Delphi, near the end of her life, back in Greece to honor the dead Sikelianos. She was dressed in a Greek tunic again.[8] Always she was in her Greek tunic; her slight figure, penetrating eyes, plain face, and straight-lined dresses of natural fibers were an obvious display of fashion independence. Here, her tired body rested on the seats of the theater of Delphi. The same volume opened with a photo of a youthful Eva Palmer, fashionable and pretty, in the white satin tulle dress of her New York society debut.[9] In this way, it set up a contrast between her life before and after Greece to make the narrative point, stretched out over four hundred pages of exposition, that Eva Palmer, once a beautiful, rich American, sacrificed herself for the love of Greece and Sikelianos. Thus, the images of the Eva Palmer *before* Greece underscored the overwhelming philhellenic passions of Eva Sikelianos *after* Greece, who absorbed the lessons of Greek national culture to help realize the dreams of her husband, the noted Greek poet. Eva Palmer Sikelianos struck me as a temporal misfit: lost in the past, misapprehending contemporary Greece, and underestimating the force of its forward-moving currents.

Decades later, a Kodak No. 1 snapshot of 1906 caught my eye (figure I.2). I was drawn by its distinctly round shape, a charming by-product of the limited technology of the first roll film camera.[10] A crowd of some fifty people is gathered in a street in Athens. It takes time to find Eva Palmer (then still unmarried) in the crowd. She is slightly off center to the left. She is turned away from the camera, and she wears a sleeveless white tunic that exposes her arms, shoulders, and back. Her hair is gathered in a low chignon. She looks like an ancient statue. Her classicizing dress and pose echo the rhythms of the city's neoclassical buildings; but they collide with the appearance of Athens's residents. Though Greek, they do not wear Greek-style tunics. Some men have on business suits topped with fedoras or straw hats, and others wear the uniform of the servant (shirt, vest, and fez) or laborer (jacket or vest and fisherman's cap). There are child laborers present, perhaps also some street children. A woman dressed in the style of the Paris belle époque is carrying a baby. At least half the men are staring at her. An unidentified man has stopped to confront her. The focal point falls on the tense space of interaction between them.

Though hard to read, the photograph confirmed my impression that Eva Palmer Sikelianos was a modern anomaly, focused on living in the past. My initial conclusion was challenged, however, by the volume in

FIGURE I.2. Eva Palmer in Athens wearing a handwoven Greek dress, surrounded by Greeks in Western dress, ca. 1906. The photograph was taken with a Kodak No. 1, the first roll film camera, which created visual records in a distinctively round shape. Acc. 189, Eva Sikelianou Papers, No. 647. Benaki Museum Historical Archives.

which the photograph appeared. Entitled *Γράμματα της Εύας Palmer Σικελιανού στη Natalie Clifford Barney* (Letters of Eva Palmer Sikelianos to Natalie Clifford Barney), this Greek translation of 163 previously unpublished love letters caused a bit of trouble in Greek literary circles. The collection covered the years 1900 to 1909, with a few stray letters from later decades. Published in Greece in 1995, the letters were appearing in print roughly nine decades after they were written, and yet, prior to the book's appearance, no one in Greek circles publicly discussed Eva Palmer's love life. After its publication, protectors of Angelos Sikelianos's reputation scrambled to limit the book's impact. They marginalized its editor and translator, Lia Papadaki, a scholar with encyclopedic knowledge of Sikelianos's oeuvre. Suppressed in Greece and unpublished except in Greek translation, Palmer's letters gained limited notice.

Though partial and one-sided, the letters were sufficient to identify Eva Palmer as a crucial member of Barney's circle of self-identifying "Sapphics."[11] The young, upper-class artistic American, British, and French women formed a group in Paris in the first decade of the twentieth century and produced an "incredible Sapphic outpouring," in the words of Joan DeJean in her masterful study, *Fictions of Sappho: 1546–1937*.[12] DeJean and others have analyzed the parallelism that Barney and poet Renée Vivien drew between themselves and the Greek poet Sappho of Lesbos, with a view to making Sappho a "distant ancestor" of their free-loving, woman-centered social order.[13] The letters demonstrated that Palmer was another key player in this circle. Not only did her ties with Barney run deep; when she was a student at Bryn Mawr College in 1900, Eva Palmer introduced Barney and Renée Vivien to ancient Greek learning, laying the ground for their learned appropriation of Sappho.[14]

I noticed a distinct interpretive approach in Palmer's handling of the fragmentary corpus of Sappho, as represented in her letters to Barney. She immersed herself intuitively in the unreconstructed gaps, responding to the lacunae of lost words and meaning with creative restoration. Moreover, fragmentary poems allowed Palmer to experience a different flow of time: one that moves not progressively forward toward fulfillment followed by decay, but backward, into the holes of history, to recover a past that never was in order to suggest a future that will never be.[15] Willful anachronism was part of the group's creative practice. Palmer, Barney, and others frequently put on period costumes and photographed each other in carefully assumed poses that commented on, parodied, and transformed words received from the past.

Over the years, Palmer and Barney formed many love triangles. Indeed, they sought out love triangles quite deliberately as the building blocks of their sexual-social community. In this too, they were creatively reading Sappho. The pursuit of desire, the triangulation of love, the unbearable pain of jealousy and broken ties were running themes found in Sappho's work and repeated in Eva Palmer's love letters. The letters chart the evolution of her relationship to Barney: chilly to Barney's approach in July 1900, Palmer became her learned adviser, stage manager, and costume designer, and still later, her sidelined, humiliated lover. The tensions between Palmer and Barney became unbearable in June 1906, just after

Palmer, in a classicizing Greek costume, performed the role of Sappho's runaway lover in Barney's play *Equivoque*, a creative revision of several fragments in the Sapphic corpus. Palmer did indeed run away a few weeks later, to Greece, carrying the costumes she had made for *Equivoque* and another Greek-style tunic she wove while making the costumes.[16]

This last discovery stopped me in my tracks. Palmer's unconventional Greek dress was the most conspicuous element in the round Kodak No. 1 snapshot, and it was rooted in her prior life: it was either a costume or the by-product of her costuming for *Equivoque*. It represented both a continuity in her conception of herself as she moved from Paris to Athens and a transition to another way of life. Reading Palmer's correspondence from after her arrival in Greece, I gathered—and later confirmed when I read Barney's side of the correspondence—that Barney was outraged to learn that Palmer was wearing Greek tunics in the streets of Athens. She was incensed that Palmer would make public modes of dress with in-group significance. For Barney, this kind of dress was meaningful only in private, carefully controlled settings. She was especially provoked because Palmer was making her public display in Athens, a place of no interest to Barney, filled—in her view—with subaltern people who did not merit her interest. In a letter of her own, she rebuked Palmer's "performance of defiance."[17] Palmer did not protest. She wrote of the freedom she felt in Greece, and she never took orders from Barney again.

From that moment, Greek-style tunics would become Palmer's daily habit, part of a broader drive against the forward movement of modern time that aspired not exactly to "make it new"—the modernist slogan read for the value it assigns to novelty—but to make it *old*: creatively to change the direction of modernity by implicating it in the revival of the inherited past.[18] Palmer's return to old styles and forms was not a misunderstanding of the present. The fact that the first tunic she wore in Athens's streets was a costume from a Sapphic performance in Paris showed me that her inhabitation of the past was an act, but it was also a piece of what would become a lifetime commitment to making herself different through imitation of the Greeks: a continuation, in other words, of her modernist engagement with missing elements of Sappho's universe.

I became curious to trace this continuity: to follow what happened to the Sapphic modernity of Eva Palmer as she crossed into modern Greek society to become Eva Sikelianos.[19] How did her former performance history of Sapphic roles in the circle around Barney inform creative activities such as her mastery of weaving and study, patronage, and composition of

Byzantine music? By what genealogy was Eva Palmer, the performer in theatricals that made Sappho a model of emulation for a protolesbian movement, connected with Eva Sikelianos, the director of the Delphic Festivals and other ancient revivals?

As I learned more about Palmer, the photograph of her standing in the midst of an Athens crowd became less a confirmation of what I thought I already knew and more of an invitation to consider the opportunities and challenges of an archive. Here was just one artifact from her archive: one of thousands of photographs and tens of thousands of unpublished letters, texts, musical compositions, woven dresses and costumes, and other materials. I was accustomed to reading photographs as witnesses, even though they are static products of technology, shot with intent, then printed and saved in fixed media that may or may not survive over time. Photographs often outlast the lives they document, which move and breathe, reach their biological end, and dematerialize. They involve conscious interventions and manipulations; in some cases, they are elaborately staged. To produce the snapshot of Eva Palmer on a street in Athens, the unidentified hand of someone accompanying her one fine day in 1906 set up a camera on a second-floor window overlooking the street. Palmer was a studied performer. She was wearing a costume, and although the street was not a stage, she took her place as if it were blocked. The hand steadied the camera's focal point just to the right of Palmer's head. A crowd gathered. A man stepped forward, and she reached toward him. The invisible hand pushed a button on the side of the camera, freezing Palmer's gesture in an instant amid a circle of gaping strangers. The photograph was developed and printed in its distinctively round shape, and copies were made. One was archived, then selected almost ninety years later and reprinted in the Greek translation of Palmer's letters. I bought the book and opened to the picture of the Greek-dressed Eva Palmer.

Observing the Athens photograph in a collection of love letters of Eva Palmer to Natalie Clifford Barney helped me to understand that Palmer's 1906 passage from Paris to Greece was shaped by several commitments. I was left with the question of how to read artifacts with traces of her life: what more could a photograph of Eva Palmer in ancient Greek dress in a street surrounded by modern Greeks tell me about Palmer's interactions and projects? In whatever way that I chose to unravel the complexity of the scene, I recognized this photograph—every photograph and artifact of Palmer's past life discussed in this book—as an act: part of her lifelong "performance of defiance" aiming to produce a different understanding of the present.

When she was young, Eva Palmer, an avid reader and performer of scenes from books, submerged herself so deeply in myths that her mother called her simply "my little myth."[20] Entering adulthood at a time of rapid technological change and social flux, she was conscious of society's loss of traditions, as modern life became more mechanized and alienated from an older order. To remedy what she saw as a loss, she became a kind of settler on the frontier of the Greek past, using it to build symbolic connections between present practices and past learning. In her relationship with Barney, for example, Palmer introduced Greek myths and props to give meaning to daily acts. Her animations of Greek culture followed a gendered intellectual practice of classical literacy, identified as "ladies' Greek" by Yopie Prins[21] and associated with women such as Janet Case, Virginia Woolf, and Edith Hamilton, who distinguished themselves by translating, performing, and embodying Greek letters. Yet Palmer's practice of Greek extended the scope of interest. She collaborated with living Greeks, who regularly debated the contours of their national identity in relation to the ancient Greek language and texts. Which variant of the Greek language was the most classical? Was Byzantine or Western classical music closer to the lost music of ancient Greek? These seemingly erudite questions were matters of concern in the public arena, and Eva Palmer entered forcefully into contemporary debates relating to musical sounds, habitual practices, and performance aesthetics. When she discovered that Greeks were losing traditional modes of expression with the penetration of Western mass-produced goods, she gained expertise in handicrafts to revive techniques of making that might offer an escape from "the dreadful routines of the growing monster of the mechanical world."[22] She asked Greeks to return to older models to pursue a freer life. Palmer, the "little myth," performed old Greece, restoring meaning to ancient poetry, weaving cloth using traditional methods, investigating non-Western modes of music making, directing revivals of Greek drama, and translating the poetry of Angelos Sikelianos. Her knowledge was wide ranging, creative, and deeply researched.

An actor who worked under the direction of Eva Sikelianos in the Delphic Festivals summarized the uncanny effect of her daily performance:

"She was the only ancient Greek I ever knew. She had a strange power of entering the minds of the ancients and bringing them to life again. She knew everything about them—how they walked and talked in the market-place, how they latched their shoes, how they arranged the folds of their gowns when they arose from table, and what songs they sang, and how they danced, and how they went to bed. I don't know how she knew these things, but she did!"[23]

How indeed! How *did* she know the things she did? What was her special brand of knowledge? How did she cultivate it, and how did she deploy it? What were her activities, practices, and techniques? The tribute expresses appreciation not only for Eva Palmer Sikelianos's total mastery of a set of arcane matters (how the ancients walked, talked, latched their shoes, and so on) but also for her "strange power" of replicating unknowable processes and bringing them into present life.

Her "strangeness" was an integral part of her performance, and it caused in those who observed her wearing ancient Greek dress in her daily life a degree of "nervousness,"[24] as Simon Goldhill observes. The importation of lost Greek ways into modern life signaled a distinct "untimeliness"—to borrow an idea used by Nietzsche to express the will to act "counter to our time by acting on our time and, let us hope, for the benefit of our time."[25] Like Nietzsche, whom she read all her life, Palmer immersed herself in Greek traditions to try to develop an oppositional aspect. Like him, too, her oppositional stance via the Greeks placed her in familiar ideological currents of twentieth-century modernity.[26] As an antimodernist who felt the spirit of the times diminished, she moved from individualism to collectivism, modernism to traditionalism, white Anglo-cosmopolitanism, anti-Semitism, and protofascism, to anticolonialism, antifascism, progressivism, internationalism, and possibly communism. With varying degrees of explicitness, she projected on the Greeks the dissonant perspectives of each succeeding decade. Whereas Nietzsche's oppositional stance was an art of living expressed through ironic, philosophical critique, however, hers was a daily creative act. She worked physically to embody another self from a different temporal standpoint, and her daily staging of the Greek life was transgressive and deeply unsettling.

Life was the dominant medium of Eva Palmer Sikelianos's work, and life writing is simply the most appropriate form to introduce her.

Life writing covers a wide range from autobiography to biography and the many creative and scholarly forms these may take.[27] This book, a cultural biography, leans toward the scholarly. Based on life-historical research, it follows the trajectory of Eva Palmer Sikelianos's adult life as she adopts ancient Greek models, simultaneously transforming them and being transformed by them. It puts her adaptations in a sociocultural context to pursue a set of questions. In much of the modern period in the

West, classical models offered precedents for personal constructions of dress, behavior, and identity in addition to cultural heritage.[28] While ideas of Greece took monumental, seemingly timeless forms in many of their neoclassical manifestations, they were quite "liquid" in their passage through the lives of people.[29] I ask: What new shapes did Greek textual and material fragments take when they inhabited Eva Palmer Sikelianos's daily life? What became of both the ancient ruins and the modern person? How did she incorporate them in her daily activities? How did they script her life? What associations, memories, and meanings did they inspire? How did her intense investment in finding the latent life in ruins change over time to become increasingly an art of life? What extant works, re-creations of ancient things, are the remnants of her art, and what is the history of their reception?

I consider the book's biographical mode to be vital to its contribution. In relating the story of a woman whose work in Greece was fitted to the procrustean bed of patriarchal, nationalist, and heteronormative discourses, I honor several decades of biographical writing that studies the gaps in recent histories for clues of women invested personally in the study of Greece who had nontraditional careers. A few made inroads into men's terrain.[30] Some were even celebrated, such as Jane Harrison, a professor of classics at Newnham College, Cambridge.[31] Most worked quietly, quite literally in the margins of the field, on archaeological excavations or philological puzzles.[32] There they may have interacted with local populations, who treated ancient ruins as their national remains, and with craftsmen, poets, or artists such as Eva Palmer Sikelianos who offered alternative perspectives.[33] They also connected with each other.[34] The importance of this kind of recovery work for classical studies cannot be overstated. It expands the history of scholarship to include a cross-section of missing figures while bringing into view the impact that class and gender exclusion criteria have played in shaping the profession. It also highlights creative practices happening in contact zones where local inhabitants and nonexperts cultivated other ways of knowing.[35] Moreover, it opens a space for a critical engagement with classical learning that considers how the field—through its complex layering of discourses of privilege, class, race, nation, sexuality, power, freedom, and resistance—empowered people to reinvent their place in the modern present even as it marginalized them.

My ambition to make sense of Eva Palmer Sikelianos's ongoing staging of the Greek life placed a subject at the center of my interest who bisected so many histories and operated in so many different communities that it offered a tactic for dealing with the abundant, diverse, and richly layered twenty-first-century archives of modern receptions of Greco-Roman antiquity.[36] These exist in countless sites. They relate to many institutions and occupy different languages. They touch on different classes of people and their activities. They accumulate in many media and materials. In the past three decades, they have taken additional, digital forms. While scholarly research on the afterlives of ancient literary or dramatic works tends to bring into focus a set of materials relating to a carefully circumscribed topic, researching Eva Palmer Sikelianos's life became a way to sample a broader range of archives in order to tell a wider, richer, more complex story about Greece's presence in the modern world.[37]

Just as one artifact of her life—the Athens Kodak No. 1 snapshot—set me on my path of inquiry, so too the discovery of multiple collections containing her extant things extended the course of my research. The search started in the Benaki Museum Historical Archives in Kifissia, a suburb of Athens, where her possessions in Greece were deposited. Here was her official archive. To begin, I read the accounts of the papers' archiving to develop a sense of what they were and why they existed together in that place. In her papers, I found correspondence from her many collaborators. I listed the correspondents and their letters' dates. I scoured databases on the internet and sought out conversations with archivists and researchers who knew something about those people. I tracked down collections of their work. I visited houses, libraries, and repositories on two sides of the Atlantic. I found thousands of textual and material artifacts belonging to her and to people who knew her. I sought out the interconnections. I looked especially for understudied archival materials to unsettle the claims made on her memory by official sources. The archived items helped me trace not only her life and work but also the power, interests, and desires that shaped assumptions about her.

While life was the primary medium of her work, her response to Greek texts and materials manifested itself in different media. The proliferation of media in the archives is in tension with the singularity and immediacy of the Greek idea that she sometimes expressed, for instance, with her statuesque pose in a sleeveless white tunic in that 1906 snapshot. No doubt it seems problematic now, as it was then, for a wealthy white American woman to pose like a Greek statue amid people laboring in the streets of Athens. How perfectly representative of the Eurocentric appropriation of the Greeks that idealized the classical and made it a symbol of white northern European superiority and an excuse for domination of people everywhere, including modern Greece! Specific manifestations of her life performance may indeed reflect commonplace notions of the classical—

though they are rarely as simple as they first appear. Even her most reflexive notion of the Greeks was part of a lifelong effort to complicate Western constructions of Greek antiquity by introducing contrasting strains—non-Western musical traditions, for example—in order to make appreciable the vitality of lesser-known perspectives. Thus, she moved from one medium to the next or folded one into another. The multiformity of her body of work aligns with her effort to keep moving continually against the currents of modern time.

The chronology I created does the work of locating Eva Palmer Sikelianos on a temporal continuum. It maps her historical coordinates from birth to her death and burial followed by the contestation of her life's remains. It also connects her to cultural currents and events and to people with whom she interacted. A cast of characters appears at the end of the book for ease of reference to the human players in the life story.

Each chapter is devoted to one medium or cluster of media and set of cultural artifacts containing traces of her activities and interactions, as the chapter titles denote. The focus on media and materials seems particularly appropriate for a subject who insisted so adamantly on materiality. The chapters cycle through her engagements with Sapphic performance, weaving and dress, music, revivals of Greek drama, and writing. In chapter 1, several unpublished photographs, a buried pile of letters, a newspaper story, and Barney's play *Equivoque* locate Eva Palmer at the center of a performance revolution that turned Sappho into a cult figure and contributed to gay and lesbian reappraisals of the Greek past. In chapter 2, her loom, dresses, more letters and photographs, and a posthumously published lecture span the years from 1906 to the early 1920s, when Eva Palmer Sikelianos practiced weaving to shape her life in Greece and eventually to agitate for women's emancipatory role in the Greek national body. Chapter 3 tracks her activities in a different performance medium, music. An organ named for her (Evion Panharmonium), records from a school of Byzantine music where she taught, two lectures, and more letters and photographs structure an inquiry into her collaboration with three subaltern musicians—Penelope Sikelianos, Konstantinos Psachos, and Khorshed Naoroji—and her patronage of non-Western traditions of music making to stave off the European instruments and sounds that were invading Greece. Chapter 4 uses letters, drawings, photographs, musical scores, and records of the Delphic Festivals and of her collaboration with Ted Shawn to relate Palmer Sikelianos's direction of Greek drama from 1905 to 1939 to moments in the history of modern dance. Chapter 5 follows her life to its end. It reads the manuscript history of *Upward Panic* (a work written by Eva Palmer Sikelianos between 1938 and April 1941 and published posthumously in 1993), personal correspondence, the published English translation of a poem of resistance to the Nazi occupation by Sikelianos, and hundreds of letters concerning American interventions in Greece to follow the political aspect of her oppositional stance.

The chapters unfold not in a single narrative line, but as intertwining threads. One thread follows her life and the other, vital developments in the cultural-political arena. Lives are messy, moving targets, changing course according to day-to-day occurrences, adjusting fixed ideas. Eva Palmer Sikelianos was always on the move. Her mode of living depended on the people she attached herself to, and those people kept moving and changing. Thus, the narrative may circle several times around a single event—as, for example, Eva Palmer's entry into Greece or her direction of the Delphic Festivals—which the reader can view from different cultural perspectives. Each narrative loop follows a facet of Eva Palmer Sikelianos's pursuit of the Greek life and allows me to explore the many faces, voices, interactions, and currents running through her archival materials.

In the epilogue, an account of the contest over her belongings gives occasion for me to follow the highly politicized assemblage of her legacy. Relating my encounter with the archives, I reflect on gender asymmetries, nonspecialist cultures of reading, structures of power between Greece and the West, and reuses of ancient sources in the practice of life matter in contemporary reappraisals of the classical legacy.

To set the story in motion, I turn to two photographs in which Eva[38] uses the camera pose as a mode of classical reception—a way of transferring classical learning to new audiences—to introduce the puzzle: how did she practice the Greek life before she came to Greece, when she was Eva Palmer, and after, when she became Eva Sikelianos. Consider the photograph in figure I.3. It may have been taken in London in 1903 to promote Eva Palmer's work in the theater. Her presentation of the Greeks is theatrical. The pleated tunic is a costume, the fluted Doric pedestal a prop, and both are signs of her temporary submission to a dramatic role outside her. The photograph reaches beyond the theater into the visual arts to borrow from the pictorial vocabulary of fin de siècle aestheticism. The pallid face, dilated eyes, enigmatic look, and attentively loosened hair recommend her for the part of a dreamy lover while also staring down years of British and French decadence. The photo shows that Eva Palmer was keen on playing the Greeks before she ever visited Greece.

FIGURE I.3. A portrait, labeled "Eva Palmer c. 1900," found among Alice Pike Barney's papers at the time of her death and deposited in the Smithsonian Institution Archives by Laura Dreyfus-Barney. It may be a record of Eva's theater audition in London in 1903. Acc. 96-153, Alice Pike Barney Papers, No. 6-188, SIA2018-072681. Smithsonian Institution Archives.

Another photograph (figure I.4) taken almost fifty years later, in May 1952, when Eva Sikelianos made her last trip to Greece, represents persistence and change. It is the one I saw long ago in the last pages of the volume celebrating her life.[39] It depicts Eva Sikelianos again in a Greek pose and tunic. This time she is offstage: a member of the audience, not the cast, resting her tired body in the seats of the theater of Delphi after viewing a performance. Her female companions, Greek friends of many years, shower her with concern, as if they were members of a chorus and she the tragic hero. Against their 1950s Western dress, her white tunic highlights her chronological cross-dressing, and their sharp features, dark hair, and medium-toned skin contrast with her pale face and faded hair. She is performing not a theatrical role but the role of a lifetime lived in dialogue with the Greeks, modern and ancient. Even more than her dress, her body language sets her temporally apart from her companions. The placement of her limbs, her slouched torso, her tilted head, the world-weary gaze of her eyes through the camera to a place infinitely beyond capture a spectral moment. A look of prophetic anticipation has replaced the lovelorn dreaminess of the youthful photograph. She might be reflect-

FIGURE I.4. Eva Sikelianos in May 1952 seated with Greek friends in the ancient theater of Delphi at one of four performances of *Prometheus Bound*, part of the "Greek Home-Coming Year" tourist campaign. Unknown source, reprinted in EOS, p. 384, with the caption "Mega Konitsa."

ing back on her production at Delphi or looking ahead to the future that will unfold without her.

The comparison of the two images confirms her lifelong obsession with Greek ideas and hints at the story I will tell of how she made Greece a source of cultural value in her daily habits, seeking to master the practice of a Greek life. She needs an introduction for many reasons, not least of which is that for a tumultuous half century she was steely willed, talented, dedicated, and eccentric enough to strive to realize this untenable idea.

Chronology

1865   Courtlandt Palmer (b. 1843 New York) marries Catherine Amory Bennett (b. 1849 Boston) at Calvary Church in Stonington, Connecticut (October 5).

1871   Courtlandt Palmer inherits one-fourth of his father's estate of more than $4,000,000. Additionally, he has a private fortune of $250,000.

1874   Eva (Evalina) is born to Courtlandt and Catherine Palmer (January 9), the last of five children (after Robert; Rose, who dies young; May; and Courtlandt).

1876   The Palmers live at 117 East Twenty-First Street, a block west of Gramercy Park in New York City. Natalie Clifford is born to Albert and Alice Pike Barney (October 31).

1882   Penelope is born to Ioannis and Harikleia Sikelianos in Leukas.

1883   The first meeting of Nineteenth-Century Club, a debating society, is held at the Palmer residence with Courtlandt presiding (January).

1884   Angelos is born to Ioannis and Harikleia Sikelianos in Leukas (March 15), their youngest (after Hector, Menelaos, Eleni, and Penelope).

1885–88   Eva sporadically attends Gramercy Park School and Tool House at 104 East Twentieth Street.

1886   The Palmers travel to Europe to consult specialists for Courtlandt's kidney problems (May 9). Eva attends Mesdames Thavenet and Taylor's School in Neuilly-sur-Seine. Between 1885 and 1891 she attends seven different schools in France, Germany, and the United States.

1887   Oscar Wilde jokes about Courtlandt Palmer's debating society in London.

1888   Courtlandt Palmer dies of peritonitis at Lake Dunmore House near Brandon, Vermont (July 23). His property, consisting mostly of real estate, is put in trust for the lifelong benefit of his heirs.

1888–91   Eva attends and graduates from Miss Porter's School in Farmington, Connecticut, a girls' preparatory school.

1891 Catherine Palmer marries Robert Abbe, a surgeon at St. Luke's Hospital, and becomes Catherine Abbe (November 15). The family moves to 11 West Fiftieth Street.

1893 Eva's makes her debut into New York society (December 5).

1894 Courtlandt Palmer Jr. makes his piano debut in the Madison Square Garden Concert Hall (March 3). Catherine Abbe and her children reportedly rent the "Italian Villa, Eden Heights" in Bar Harbor (July–August). She and Eva visit George Vanderbilt at Asheville, North Carolina (December).

1895 "Miss Eva Palmer" is praised as "an artist of rare gifts" for her "rare elocutionary interpretations of poems" at the Female Senior Evening School No. 13 closing exercises (February 27). Looking back thirty-five years later, Eva indicates that Barney entered her life at about this time.

1896 Eva meets Martha Carey Thomas, President of Bryn Mawr College (spring); she passes exams and gains entrance into Bryn Mawr (October).

1897 Catherine Abbe is a founding member of the City History Club of New York (April). Eva plays Pollie in Frank Daniels's "The Idol's Eye," an operetta by Harry B. Smith and Victor Herbert, at the Broadway Theater (October).

1898 Dr. Robert Abbe purchases "Brook End," a summer cottage in Bar Harbor. Eva produces and plays Rosalind in *As You Like It*, the freshman class play presented to the Bryn Mawr College class of 1901 (March 13). She is caught doing something strictly prohibited and is forbidden the right of residence for a year by President Thomas (May 28). She travels abroad with Courtlandt Jr.

1899 Eva returns from Europe. Catherine Abbe has her portrait painted by Cecilia Beaux.

1900 Eva is in Bar Harbor with the Abbes (July–September). Her first extant letter to Natalie Barney is dated July 28. She performs a tableau of Sappho in a fund-raiser for the Bar Harbor hospital (August 29). She invites Renée Vivien and Barney to stay in her residence at Bryn Mawr College (fall).

1901 Eva follows Vivien and Barney to Paris and takes acting lessons with Madame le Bargy of the Comédie Française. She meets Sarah Bernhardt. Renée Vivien ends her relationship with Barney.

1902 Catherine Abbe becomes president of the City Club of New

York. She hosts artist William Frederick MacMonnies in Bar Harbor (July 27), who paints a portrait of May Palmer. Barney receives a substantial inheritance following her father's death (December). Freed from his scrutiny, she begins living an openly lesbian life. Eva lives between New York and Paris.

1903   Eva and Barney share an apartment at 4 rue Chalgrin (April 1–summer 1904). Eva begins her affair with "Baby" (Bébé) Marie de Hatzfeld, princess of Hohenlohe (1903–5). She auditions with Mrs. Patrick Campbell in London and is offered opportunity to perform with her but does not accept her conditions (July). She travels to Spain with May. Raymond Duncan marries Penelope Sikelianos in Greece. With his sister Isadora, he begins construction of their "palace of Agamemnon." Isadora Duncan stages the chorus of Aeschylus's *Suppliants* at the Municipal Theatre in Athens (November–December).

1904   Dr. Abbe introduces the practice of using radiation therapy for cancer treatment in the United States. Eva and Barney move into neighboring houses in Neuilly-sur-Seine, with Eva at 56 rue de Longchamp and Natalie at 25 rue de Bois de Boulogne (summer). Eva travels to Bayreuth with Renée Vivien to attend the Wagner Festival. Barney follows and leaves with Vivien for Lesbos, where they briefly plan to create a Lesbian community. Eva leaves Bayreuth with "Baby" and travels to Venice, then returns to Paris (August–September).

1905   Barney holds a garden party in Neuilly with Colette and Eva performing Pierre Louÿs's "Dialogue au soleil couchant" (June). Eva leaves for Bar Harbor (July). She prepares an open-air performance of Swinburne's *Atalanta in Calydon* with a Greek chorus at the cottage of Anne Mills Archbold (September). She plays Romeo in *Romeo and Juliet* at Alice Pike Barney's "Evening at Studio House" in Washington, DC (December 28). *Life* magazine reviews her performance of Romeo and announces that she will play Melisande with Mme. Sarah Bernhardt in Maeterlinck's *Pelleas and Melisande* (December 30).

1906   Eva leaves New York for Paris with playwright Constant Lounsbery (January). She meets Raymond and Penelope Duncan and invites them to stay in Neuilly (April). They build a loom and learn to weave together. She plays Timas in *Equivoque* by Barney (June 6), with her own costumes and props, and music and dance by the Duncans. She follows the Duncans to Greece, dressed now in a Greek tunic. She meets Angelos Sikelianos (August). She travels with Penelope to Leukas (December).

1907   Angelos takes Eva around Leukas, then leaves for Paris, Rome, and Egypt (January). May visits Eva in Leukas. Angelos returns and travels with Eva in the Peloponnese (spring). Eva takes Angelos to Neuilly, hoping to repair relations with Barney. After Barney insults Angelos, Eva delivers all her love letters to Barney's doorstep (summer) and sails for the United States with Angelos on the *La Lorraine* (August 26), causing a national stir with her "goddess-like" dress. She and Angelos marry in an Episcopal ceremony conducted by Rev. Stephen H. Green in French at Bar Harbor (September 9). They return to Leukas. She continues to correspond with Barney.

1908   Eva is living between Leukas and a house on Serifou Street in Athens. She begins overseeing her husband's publications, ordering a luxury printing of his new poem Ἀλαφροΐσκιωτος (The seer) on Italian watermarked paper of Amalfi with leather binding (released spring 1909). She meets Konstantinos Psachos, professor of Byzantine music at the Athens Conservatory (October).

1909   Eva sends Barney two letters asking her not to write again (January 1). Barney moves from Neuilly to 20 rue Jacob (January). A son, Glafkos (March 27), is born to Eva and Angelos. Raymond and Penelope Duncan travel to the United States for a series of performances (fall).

1910   Eva purchases beachfront property in Sykia on the Gulf of Corinth. In the United States, the Duncans organize a protest of Richard Strauss's *Elektra* at the Manhattan Opera House (January), then perform their version of Sophocles' *Elektra* in the open air Greek Theater at Berkeley (April 12). Eva travels to Aix-les-Bains to vacation with her mother, seeing her possibly for the last time (May 29). Eva's brother Robert, an alcoholic and an inmate of Bloomingdale Asylum, is declared insane and incompetent (July 9). Angelos's father, Ioannis, dies (October 14).

1911   Alice Pike Barney paints *Evalina Cortland Palmer*. Raymond and Penelope Duncan establish the Akadémia Raymond Duncan in Paris. Eva tours Italy and France with Angelos and Glafkos.

1912   Eva performs the part of Chrysothemis in Raymond Duncan's *Electre* at Châtelet and Trocadero in Paris. Penelope is Elektra,

Eleni Sikelianos Pasagianni is Klytaimnestra, Dionysos Devaris is Orestes, and Raymond is Aigisthos and the chorus (February). Eva reportedly ends her sexual relationship with Angelos and encourages him to take up relations with his cousin Katina Proestopoulou, the household manager.

1913   Eva and Glafkos remain in Athens and Sikya while Angelos serves in the Greek army in the Balkan Wars. Raymond and Penelope Duncan move to southern Albania to care for Greek refugees in the region. Penelope contracts tuberculosis.

1914   Angelos meets Nikos Kazantzakis and travels with him to Mount Athos (November–December). Eva inherits $25,000 from her aunt, Ann Mary Palmer Draper (December 19).

1915   Eva begins construction of a villa in Sykia, reportedly designed by Angelos. She oversees publication of his Πρόλογος στη ζωή (Prologue to life), released in 1917. Raymond Duncan, again in Athens, campaigns for Eleftherios Venizelos's election (May) and helps settle Greek Orthodox refugees from the Ottoman Empire. Nikos and Galateia Kazantzakis visit Sykia (August–September). Angelos begins an affair with Nausika Palama, daughter of poet Kostis Palamas (September). Isadora Duncan visits Athens with her manager, Maurice Magnus, to try to set up a dance studio. Magnus escorts Penelope, terminally ill by now, to the Sanatorium Schatzalp in Davos, Switzerland (October).

1916   Eva enrolls in the Athens Conservatory as a student of Byzantine music. She meets Dimitri Mitropoulos, then a student of piano and composition, later a world-famous conductor.

1917   Eva funds the publication of Psachos's book on Byzantine musical notation. Penelope dies at Davos (April 22).

1918   Kalypso Katsimbali, sister of George Katsimbalis, confesses her love to Angelos, who spurns it. He contracts the Spanish flu but recovers.

1919   Eva addresses the Lyceum of Greek Women, calling on urban women of Greece to take up weaving and reform their dress (May 17). Angelos's brother Hector dies (summer). Angelos writes the "Delphic vision," his first articulation of a Delphic Idea (July–October). Psachos resigns from the Athens Conservatory (October 20) and establishes the Conservatory of National Music, where Eva teaches beginning Byzantine music and music theory.

1920   Kalypso Katsimbali, still madly in love with Angelos, commits suicide (March 13). Angelos is saved from near drowning in the Gulf of Corinth (April 24). Catherine Abbe dies (September 25), having suffered terrible grief after her son Robert Palmer was committed. Mary Crovatt Hambidge, an American in Greece with her partner, designer Jay Hambidge, studies weaving with Eva (1920–24).

1921   Eva lectures against luxury (National Women's Conference at Parnassus); on Byzantine music (Lyceum of Greek Women and the Hall of the Archaeological Society); on Greek fashion and local craft industries (both in the Hall of the Archaeological Society) (February). She publishes "Three Lectures." She heads a committee to raise funds for a new pipe organ with an expanded keyboard of forty-two keys to the octave for modal music. Angelos writes to Kazantzakis about his idea of a secular monastic community (December).

1922   Angelos publishes his "Open Letter to His Majesty," a letter anticipating that King Constantine I would lead Greece to a new era of dominance (March). George Cram ("Jig") Cook, founder of the Provincetown Players, and playwright Susan Glaspell, his wife, arrive in Greece (March). They spend the summer on Mount Parnassus near Agoriani, where Angelos is also in retreat. Psachos suspends the work of the Conservatory of National Music to supervise construction of the new pipe organ for Byzantine music in Germany. The Asia Minor Catastrophe leaves Angelos in shock (September). He spends the winter in Delphi, where the Cooks are also staying. Kazantzakis cuts his ties with Sikelianos (December).

1923   Glaspell publishes "Dwellers on Parnassos" in the *New Republic*. Angelos is working out his utopian idea of an international brotherhood of elite centered in Delphi. He organizes twenty lectures on Delphi at Athens's Law School (January). Glaspell, Cook, and Cook's daughter, Nilla, spend a month with Eva and Angelos in Sykia (May–June). Fourteen-year-old Glafkos falls in love with Nilla. Cook in Agoriani stages two plays with shepherds of Kalani (June). Returning to Delphi for the winter, he announces the creation of the "Delphic Players" with villagers from Delphi.

1924   Eva spends one million drachmas to build the pipe organ, now named after her: Evion Panharmonium. Cook dies of glanders and is buried in the cemetery of Delphi (January). Eva travels with Angelos to the Steinmeyer factory in Germany, then continues alone to Paris and visits Barney. She meets Khorshed Naoroji, a student of piano at the Sorbonne University (February–June). Members of the Writers' League of Athens organize the George Cram Cook Club and plan to reinstate Delphic theater performances in his memory (April). Eva and Khorshed launch the Byzantine pipe organ in Germany (late June). The organ never leaves the factory. Eva brings Khorshed to Greece (July 4) and hosts her in Sikya with Dimitri Mitropoulos, who composes music for several Sikelianos poems. Angelos formally announces his Delphic Idea (October 16). Eva, Khorshed, and Angelos visit Epidaurus, Mycenae, Olympia, Delphi, and the Acropolis in Athens. Khorshed returns to Paris (October–November).

1925   Eva lectures on *Prometheus Bound* to the Lyceum of Greek Women in Athens (January). Angelos gives speeches on the Delphic plan (April–December). In a house in Phaleron, Eva weaves costumes and trains the chorus in preparation for the Delphic Festival. She builds a house in Delphi. She travels with Angelos and poet Kostis Palamas to Leukas to commemorate the centenary of Aristotelis Valaoritis at his grave in Madouri (June 8). Glafkos leaves Greece for the United States in pursuit of Nilla Cook and stays with Mary Hambidge. She enrolls him in a preparatory school, but he is asked to leave for undisciplined behavior. Khorshed, now in Bombay, sends Eva the design for a "yoga garment" for a role in *Prometheus Bound* (September 16). The *New York Times* reports that Greek drama will be revived at ancient Delphi "with native talent, in memory of George Cram Cook" (October 11).

1926   Eva wins the gold medal in the Decorative Arts at International Exposition in Paris for her weaving. She and Angelos move to Delphi. Harikleia (mother of Angelos) dies and is buried in the cemetery of Delphi next to Cook's grave (January). Richard Strauss and architect Michael Rosenhauer visit Delphi and talk to Eva and Angelos about plans to build a music hall on Philopappos Hill in Athens (May). Eva meets with heads of the foreign schools in Athens to ask for help in promoting the Delphic Festival. Rabindranath Tagore visits Athens and is decorated with the Order of the Redeemer by the Greek state (November 25). Invitations to the Delphic Festival are extended to him, Gandhi, Edouard Schuré, Gabriel Boissy, Mario Meunier, and other international dignitaries. The publishing house Estia prints two hundred copies of Angelos's "Delphic Idea."

1927 Angelos oversees the construction of roads and paths and the installation of water pipes in Delphi at Eva's expense. She mortgages the houses at Sykia and Delphi to cover the expense of hosting international guests. The Delphic Festival takes place (May 9–10), with a performance of *Prometheus Bound*, athletic games, and Byzantine and folk music in the ancient site and exhibition of handiwork in the modern village. The festival receives positive international coverage but is a financial failure. Only the exhibition makes money. A film by the brothers Gaziadi, "Δελφικαί Εορταί" (Delphic Festivals) is shown at the "Dionysia" theater in Syntagma Square (May 26). The *New York Times* reports that Nilla Cook's marriage to Nikos Proestopolous, cousin of Angelos, is an "outcome of the Delphic festival" (August 31). Three years later, Nilla leaves Greece for India and is renamed Mela Naghini Devi by Gandhi. Eva is in New York City to give a lecture entitled "Talk on Greek Art" (September 29) and raise money to continue the Delphic project. She lectures on the Delphic Idea and Greek Music at museums and colleges and at the meeting of the American Institute of Archaeology at the University of Cincinnati (December 30).

1928 Eva invites journalist Alma Reed to move into her seventh-floor apartment at 12 Fifth Avenue near Washington Square in New York. They create the "Ashram," a salon paying homage to Gandhi's nonviolent activism, with the "Delphic Studios," a gallery promoting Mexican muralist José Clemente Orozco and other artists. Orozco paints a portrait of Eva. Eva's stepfather, Robert Abbe, dies, leaving an estate of $400,000 and willing $25,000 to a Stone Age Museum in Bar Harbor (March 28).

1929 Antonis Benakis asks Eva to return to Greece to organize the second Delphic Festival with funding from private donors and a loan from the National Bank of Greece. Back in Athens, she becomes a member of Association for the Preservation of National Music founded by musicologist Simon Karas. Preparations for the second Delphic Festival occupy her. The Academy of Athens bestows on her and Angelos "silver medals" honoring them as the "Phoebus-inspired couple" (March 25). Poet and diplomat George Seferis visits Angelos at Delphi with Édouard Herriot, former prime minister of France (April 21). Glafkos marries Frances LeFevre and settles in Greece (July). Despite financial troubles, Eva rents a place at 38 Odos Filellinon, Athens, for Angelos (December).

1930   Brastias (Mark) is born to Glafkos and Frances Sikelianos (March 7). The second Delphic Festival (May 1–3, 6–8, and 11–13) takes place with three performances each of *Prometheus Bound*, the *Suppliants*, and Pythian athletic games, followed by Macedonian war dances and torchlight processions. The music is by Psachos, and costumes, choreography, and direction are by Eva. After the event, Psachos breaks ties with Eva. Angelos and Eva Sikelianos meet with government officials, and Eva and Antonis Benakis meet with Prime Minister Venizelos to secure the future of the festivals. A "Lottery of the Delphic Festivals" is announced.

1931   Eva loans costumes to people in Komotini in northeast Greece and attends the "Pythian Games" there with Angelos (June). She disclaims any artistic connection to a performance of *Prometheus Bound* in the Panathenaic Stadium in Athens directed by Linos Karzis, which Angelos supports (August–September). Lawyers and creditors arrive at Sykia to take inventory of the house (August 22). Angelos publishes an article in *Eleofthero Vima* on "the problem of music and dance in ancient drama," dedicated to Penelope Sikelianos, who, he claims, inspired the direction of the Delphic Festivals (October 20–21). Eva writes to Ethel Earle about her plan to make a living staging Greek theater in the United States and asks for help with university contacts (December 27).

1932   Angelos completes the play Ο διθύραμβος του ρόδου (*Dithyramb of the Rose*; June 9).

1933   Eva directs two performances of *Dithyramb of the Rose* in a wooden open-air theater she has constructed on the western slope of Philopappos Hill in Athens. Between fifteen thousand and one hundred thousand people present ridicule the performance (April 24). Distraught by financial and personal strains, Eva leaves for America (August). An agent who promised her work in the Greek Theatre in Los Angeles backs down. She arranges to direct Euripides' *Bacchae* at Smith College. Eva, with Mary Hambidge's help in her home in Greenwich, Connecticut, begins weaving costumes for the *Bacchae* (November). She leaves Greenwich for New York (December).

1934   Eva directs the *Bacchae* at Smith College in a large outdoor athletic space with a few props and original costumes using her own choreography and musical compositions (June 15). She writes an article on modal music and plans to teach Greek modal music in New York City. Frances Sikelianos, still in Sykia, worries about Eva's health (November). Meanwhile, the situation with the mortgaged houses remains unsettled. Frances relates a rumor that Angelos is trying to sell the house in Sykia to the Ministry of Tourism (December 27).

1935   First Lady Eleanor Roosevelt invites Eva to the White House to speak about her work (January). Eva is offered fifty-five undergraduates to produce the *Bacchae* at Bryn Mawr College (February 25). She begins a fifteen-year correspondence with Edith Hamilton on the translation and performance of Greek drama (May). The *Bacchae* is performed twice at Bryn Mawr (June 1, 3).

1936   Eva publishes a manifesto on the Delphic center (January). She applies to the Federal Theatre Project (FTP) with recommendations from college presidents and professors. She receives her Letter of Instructions from the FTP, with Eugene O'Neill as her assignment officer (May 8) and is appointed to produce Aeschylus's *Persians* with a male chorus hired by the FTP. She writes music using the translation of Joan Vanderpool. She exhibits her costumes at the Metropolitan Museum of Art and gives a lecture on ancient dress (June–August).

1937   Eva presents her detailed plan for an alternative, Greek design for an outdoor theater to the director of the 1939 World's Fair (March). She recovers her American citizenship (April 21). While preparing to stage *The Persians* (Aeschylus), scenes from the *Peace* (Aristophanes), and Psalms, she is dismissed by the FTP without explanation (August). She tries to borrow money from her sister May to help Glafkos and Angelos. Angelos informs Eva about his renewed efforts to organize the third Delphic Festival with a performance of the *Oresteia*, supported by the Metaxas dictatorship. He asks her to return to Greece (October 30).

1938   Eva befriends Elsa Barker. She contracts double pneumonia
        (March). Mary Hambidge arranges for her care at the Sara-
        toga Sanatorium. She is released from Saratoga (April 21).
        While recuperating, she begins writing *Upward Panic*. Ham-
        bidge moves to Rabun Gap, Georgia, to create a craft com-
        munity. Eva returns to New York. She is invited by Grant
        Code, a curator at the Brooklyn Museum, to organize an ex-
        hibition on the Delphic Festivals but declines (May). She visits
        her old friend Lucy Donnelly at Bryn Mawr to seek advice on
        the manuscript of *Upward Panic* (November).

1939   Glafkos and Frances return to the United States, where Glafkos
        works in a shipbuilding yard. They divorce. Angelos writes to
        Eva about his new love, Anna Karamani, and asks her to sanc-
        tion the relationship (March). Eva sees Barney in New York
        (May). Katherine Dreier, an artist and patron of the arts, in-
        troduces Eva to Ted Shawn. At Jacob's Pillow, Eva teaches the
        first chorus of Aeschylus's *Persians* to Shawn's dancers, and
        their work is showcased at a Friday afternoon concert (Au-
        gust–September). Eva's manuscript of *Upward Panic* is rejected
        by Macmillan Publishers (September 1); she revises it several
        times. She moves to Eustis, Florida (October), Shawn's winter
        studio, to weave costumes for his company. Shawn pays for
        publication of Angelos's *Dithyramb of the Rose* in Frances
        LeFevre's English translation and sends it as a Christmas card.

1940   Shawn and his Men Dancers perform pieces he and Eva cre-
        ated together in Carnegie Hall (February 20–23). Angelos mar-
        ries Anna Karamani in a small church in Eleusis (June 17). Eva
        has not yet annulled their marriage. Italian forces invade
        Greece (October 28) and are defeated (October 28). Angelos
        recites his tragedy *Sibyl*, about the Delphic Pythia's rejection
        of Nero in 59 CE, and sends Eva a copy, asking her to translate
        and produce it.

1941   Barton Mumaw performs solo dance "Hellas Triumphant" in
        Carnegie Hall to honor Greek victory over the Italians, with
        help from Eva (April 16–17). Eva reports her disagreements
        with Shawn and moves to Rabun Gap, where she stays for
        three years. Joan Vanderpool asks Eva to collect money to feed
        hungry children of Greece (November 15). Eva's sister May
        Suydam Palmer dies unexpectedly in New York (December
        27). Eva returns temporarily to New York.

1942   Glafkos marries Miriam B. Tryon, with whom he has four children: Chris, Jon, Melitsa, and Poppy born in 1943, 1945, 1948, and 1951 respectively. Eva's translation of Angelos's *Sibyl* is rejected by Macmillan (May 18). Eva is invited to support the Greek War Relief in response to the humanitarian crisis (July). She returns to Rabun Gap and sends copies of her essay "What Is Great Theatre?" to acquaintances, asking for Relief support (summer).

1943   Angelos's eulogy for Kostis Palamas's funeral in Nazi-occupied Athens inspires crowds to sing the outlawed Greek national anthem (February 28). Eva writes an article on Angelos. Eva publishes an open letter, "For Greek War Relief," drawing parallels between Greece and the United States to inspire American support for Greece (April). Her article on Angelos is published by *Athene*, a literary and cultural magazine (December). She is asked to join the progressive, antifascist, antimonarchy League of Greek-American Progressive Men of Letters and Intellectuals.

1944   Frances LeFevre marries John Waldman and has two more children: Anne and Carl, born in 1945 and 1948 respectively. George Seferis, now a diplomat in Greece's government in exile in Cairo, secretly sends Eva a copy of Angelos Sikelianos's Ακριτικά, a collection of poems of resistance, asking her to translate and publish the collection (March 22). Eva moves back to New York to begin work on the publication. She holds a book launch at the Stanhope Hotel and reads two poems from the translated collection, *Akritan Songs* (June). She is interviewed on the "People to Remember" weekly series on WINS, a CBS affiliate in New York (August 20). Eva is invited to direct *Prometheus Bound* for the "Theatre of All Nations." She consults with Edith Hamilton about using her translation and writes music for the choral parts. She considers Paul Robeson for the part of Prometheus (September). Eva sends a letter, "On the Greek Situation," to President Roosevelt and other politicians (September 9). She delivers the lecture "Greek Music" at the Present Day Club in Princeton, New Jersey (November 29). She writes an open letter to Edward R. Stettinus Jr., secretary of state, and Henry A. Wallace, vice president of the United States, to express frustration with American policy in Greece (December).

1945   Edith Hamilton expresses regret that Eva will not produce
        Prometheus Bound (January 4). *PM*, a New York daily tabloid,
        reports that Eva Sikelianos has sent at least two thousand let-
        ters to educate Americans about Greece (January 12).

1946   Henry Miller and Eva draft a letter nominating Angelos Sike-
        lianos for the Nobel Prize in Literature, which is submitted by
        Anders Österling to the Swedish Academy. (Angelos is nomi-
        nated nine times between 1946 and 1950.) Eva becomes a
        member of the Progressive Citizens of America.

1947   Eva writes to Eleanor Roosevelt on the Greek civil war, de-
        nouncing the Greek monarchy.

1948   The House Un-American Activities Committee lists "Eva Sike-
        lianos" as part of the "communist 'peace' offensive."

1949   Eva makes amends with Courtlandt, after years of fighting.

1950   Eva moves into an apartment in Courtlandt's building at 64
        West Twelfth Street. She and Angelos are invited by the Amer-
        ican embassy in Athens to direct the "Home-Coming Year,"
        part of the "Return to Greece" tourist campaign supported by
        the Economic Recovery Program (Marshall Plan). She applies
        for a visa.

1951   Eva learns she was denied a visa because she called the royal
        family fascists and is considered a communist threat. She re-
        fuses to sign a retraction (April). Angelos dies of accidental
        poisoning (June 19). Courtlandt Palmer Jr. dies, leaving Eva
        $250,000 in trust (December).

1952   Eva is issued a visa and plans her return to Greece. She visits
        family and friends to say goodbye. She has a ticket to sail on
        the *Homeland* (April 12) but books a flight when the boat does
        not arrive. In Athens, she stays with friends, then travels to
        Delphi to attend events celebrating the twenty-fifth anniver-
        sary of the Delphic Festivals. She suffers a stroke after the last
        of four performances of *Prometheus Bound*. She dies in Evan-
        gelismos Hospital in Athens (June 4). The next day, she receives
        a state funeral in the Cathedral of Athens, then is transported
        to the cemetery of Delphi for burial between Harikleia Sike-
        lianou and George Cram Cook. Richard N. Crockett, the
        Palmer family lawyer and executor of the Eva Palmer Sikelia-
        nos estate, declares that Eva's property must remain in Greece
        according to her stated wishes (June 25). When inventory is
        taken, five of fifteen cases in Eva's bill of lading are reported

missing (June 25). Anne Antoniades and Angeliki Hatzimihali are issued power of attorney by Glafkos to deal with Eva's things and ask that the remainder of Eva's effects in the United States be sent to Greece (October).

1953–57 Frances expresses hope that Eva's things will be offered to the Benaki Museum. Antoniades tries to publish *Upward Panic*, but the project is dropped.

1959 One of Eva's costumes, "a chiton and a chlamys," is donated to the College Theatre of Bryn Mawr for performances of Greek drama.

1960 The Benaki Museum receives forty-one costumes made by Eva for the Delphic Festivals and puts them in storage in anticipation of the resolution of issues surrounding Eva's estate.

1965 The American Hellenic Union organizes an exhibit dedicated to Eva's work. The Benaki Museum receives her papers (December 22, with additions in June 1966) with a promise by Octave Merlier to microfilm them.

1969 Merlier visits Barney in Paris and brings to Greece over six hundred letters from Eva's correspondence, promising to microfilm them. The letters become part of the collection of Eva Sikelianou Papers deposited in the Center for Asia Minor Studies.

1992 *Ιερός πανικός*, the Greek translation of *Upward Panic*, is published by John P. Anton.

1993 *Upward Panic: The Autobiography of Eva Palmer-Sikelianos* is published by Anton under this title.

1994 Glafkos dies in California (November).

1995 A selection of Eva's love letters from Barney's papers in the Bibliothèque littéraire Jacques Doucet is published in Greek translation by Lia Papadaki. 2017–18 Artemis Leontis documents, reorders, catalogs, and digitizes Eva Sikelianou Papers in the Center for Asia Minor Studies.

2005 University of Michigan "Contexts for Classics" organizes workshop exploring the subject "Eva Palmer Sikelianos: Past, Present, Future Directions."

2017–18 Artemis Leontis documents, reorders, catalogs, and digitizes Eva's early correspondence in the Eva Sikelianou Papers, Center for Asia Minor Studies.

Eva Palmer Sikelianos

CHAPTER 1

Sapphic Performances

In the summer of 1900, Eva Palmer was reading the lines of Sappho in the company of her friends Renée Vivien and Natalie Clifford Barney, preparing for a series of Sapphic[1] performances in Bar Harbor, a summer island resort on Mount Desert Island off the coast of Maine. Of the three women, Barney and Vivien (who was later christened, in a portrait, "Sapho 1900")[2] are well known as formative members of a Paris-based literary subculture of self-described women lovers, or "Sapphics." In a period that scholars have identified as "pivotal" in delineating modern lesbian identity,[3] they interwove the fragmented texts of Sappho in their life and work, making the archaic Greek poet Sappho of Lesbos[4] the quintessential figure of female same-sex desire and Sapphism, or lesbianism. They appear in the history of gay and lesbian sexuality as the women who contributed substantially to the turn-of-the-century decadent rewriting of Baudelaire's lexicon of the sexualized woman.[5]

Eva Palmer is largely absent from this history. She has made cameo appearances as the "pre-Raphaelite" beauty with "the most miraculous long red hair"[6] who performed in two of Barney's garden theatricals in Paris. Yet Eva's correspondence, along with such sources as photographs and newspaper coverage, indicate that she participated in many more performances. From 1900 to the summer of 1907, the years when she moved with Barney between the United States and Paris, she developed a performance style that complemented the poetic language of Vivien and Barney by implicating Sappho in the practice of modern life. Eva's acts helped transform the fragmented Sapphic poetic corpus into a new way of thinking and creating, before her differences with Barney propelled her to move to Greece to live a different version of the Sapphic life.

"Implicate" is a good word to think with as I begin to track Eva's involvement with Sappho's poetry.[7] The word is rich in associations of braiding, twisting, weaving, and folding in its Greek and Latin roots (πλέκω, to weave; πλόκος, lock or braid of hair; πλοκάμι, tentacle; *plico*, to fold; and *plecto*, to fold, wind, coil, wreath[8]). It calls up the body of the reader together with her mind. To study how Eva's reading of Sappho "implicated" or involved her in Sappho's poetic corpus on both a physical and literary level, I pay attention to Eva's hair, dress, and gestures; the photographs for which she posed; the letters she wrote; and the ways in which these different media delivered the pain and pleasure of Sappho's effects. I look at how she folded Sappho's extant words into her life, simultaneously living through her readings of Sappho and shaping Sappho's meaning through her life to turn her life of art into an art of life.

THE IMPLICATIONS OF READING SAPPHO

Signs of Eva's involvement with Sappho's poetry are subtly coded in an early twentieth-century photograph (figure 1.1). Eva, viewed in profile, is seated in a leather, cushioned chair. She holds a book upright on her lap, and a wall of books appears in the background to her left. She is elegantly dressed, with a white fur stole falling over her white lace dress, and her hair loosely braided and collected in a low chignon. While the picture represents an upper-class white American woman reading in a Victorian home study, the Greek prototype is suggested by the hair. The hair's styling combines with the whiteness of the dress to give a feeling of being Greek.[9] This elusive Greekness then transfers to the reading pose. Eva is holding the book as if it were a scroll. She is posing as both a woman reading Greek and a Greek woman reading.

The pointedly Sapphic connections appear when the photo is set next to a line-drawn rendering of an ancient female reader painted on a fifth-century Attic red-figure vase (figure 1.2). At the turn of the century, Eva would not have seen the original vase, as it is displayed in the Greek National Archaeological Museum, and she did not travel to Greece before 1906. But she would have seen the line drawing reproduced in several books in the late nineteenth century.[10] A likely source was *Long Ago*, a collection of Sappho-inspired poems with explicit references to erotic attachments between women, published under the pseudonym of "Michael Field" by Katharine Bradley and Edith Cooper, who were aunt and niece as well as lovers. Eva, Renée Vivien, or Natalie Barney would likely have owned a copy of the 1889 edition, which included the line drawing in its front matter. The three women sought out books with references to Sappho. Might Eva be holding this book (which, at 10 cm × 21 cm, is just about the right size) in the photograph?

FIGURE 1.1. Eva Palmer reading, ca. 1900. Acc. 96-153, Alice Pike Barney Papers, No. 6-156, SIA2018-072680. Smithsonian Institution Archives.

FIGURE 1.2. Eva Palmer reading, alongside line figure of Sappho, also seated and reading, on a vase in the museum of Athens, as rendered in Albert Dumont and Jules Chaplain's *Les Céramiques de la Grèce proper* (1888), p. 358, and labeled, "Sapho et ses compagnes.—Hydres a figures rouges du Musée de la Societé archéologique d'Athènes" (Sappho and her companions.—Red figures from Hydra in the Museum of the Archaeological Society of Athens; 360).

In the drawing, a seated woman, also in profile, directs her eyes downward to a scroll held upright on her lap, while a lyre is handed to her by a standing figure. Beneath the lyre, the first three letters of Sappho's name, ΣΑΠ, form the arc of the reader's line of vision. What does the name of Sappho identify: the woman reading, or the author of the scroll she is reading? Is this an image of Sappho or of a woman reading Sappho? It is impossible to decide. This is just one of the drawing's many gaps, one of the troublesome lacunae of lost materials, context, and meaning. The photograph represents Eva's performance of the image of the woman reading under the name of Sappho—a performance that revitalized the ancient image by playing with its ambiguities. Eva holds a book as if it were a scroll, like the ancient woman reading. The lines of her body, and even the table with the vase and flowers in the foreground, perfectly reflect the shape of the drawn figure. The table cuts the view of Eva's lower limbs exactly where the ancient artifact is broken, where a piece of plain terracotta fills in the empty space. The photograph makes us see the negative space as a table. Thus it draws attention not only to the fragmented image but also to the many latent possibilities offered by the image. Eva might be playing the role of Sappho, or of a woman reading Sappho, or she might be making herself into a modern work of art in imitation of the vase painting, or she might be codifying her same-sex eroticism. These are all possible readings.

The play of the photograph with a classical image of Sappho was not an obscure allusion. The name of Sappho was known to people in the high society in which Eva traveled: wealthy vacationers such as the J. Pierpont Morgans, Pulitzers, George Vanderbilts, and Barneys, who all had homes in Bar Harbor. They were ferried from the mainland to Mount Desert Island on a steamboat improbably called the S. S. *Sappho*.[11] And when, in the previous spring, Barney had published *Quelques Portraits-Sonnets de Femmes* (Some portrait-sonnets of women), a book of traditional sonnets dedicated to her female lovers (whose identities she hid behind initials such as "P.M.T." for Pauline Tarn, aka Renée Vivien, and "L." for Liane de Pougy), a tabloid article in her hometown of Washington, DC, exposed the same-sex love interest of the book with an article entitled "Sappho Sings in Washington."[12]

What connotations did Sappho have for Eva and her friends and all those wealthy Americans? "Sappho" is the proper name attached to a collection of fragments of poetry dating from 630 to 570 BCE. In antiquity, Sappho was nearly as legendary as Homer.[13] Her name identified an exceptional poet of verse in Aeolic Greek who happened to be a woman from the island of Lesbos. So great was her poetry and so symbolic was her female gender that the ancients called her the tenth Muse. Yet little is known about her life. Contradictory stories circulated among ancient Greeks and Romans, who drew on her poetry to shape her biography and introduced new legends into her corpus. Some said she was a good lyre player, daughter, sister, wife of a rich man, mother, and homemaker. Others featured her unrequited love for a man named Phaon, which sent her hurling in a suicidal leap from the White Rocks, a high promontory on the island of Leukas. Still others, associating her with a community of women on Lesbos, wondered if she wasn't "γυναικε[ράσ]τρια" (in love with women), hence "ἄτακτος . . . τὸν τρόπον" (irregular in her ways).[14] She became "*mascula autem Saffo* [masculine Sappho] either because she is famous for her poetry, in which men more often excel, or because she is maligned as a *tribas* [a woman who has sex with another woman]."[15]

Everything having to do with the transmission of Sappho is elusive to the point of being powerfully suggestive. No book of her poetry survives. Indeed, hardly a whole poem is extant. Counted together, Sappho's poetry totals just over two hundred remaining fragments, preserved as passages quoted by ancient authors and on scraps of papyrus recovered from trash heaps at Oxyrhynchus, Egypt. Paradoxically, the fragmentary nature of the work and critical attention to the eroticism of her poetry have kept Sappho's name in circulation.[16] In modern times, especially in the nineteenth century, the fragility of Sappho's words and reputation encouraged new uses of Sappho's name and the place name Lesbos.[17] Baudelaire's usage was especially transformative: he cast Sappho as the muse of his decadent worldview, and his poem "Lesbos" (1857) made Lesbos, Sappho's supposed homeland, the "Mother of Greek delights" and generated "lesbians," female companions of the "virile" Sappho, on the island of Lesbos, who looked at each other with non-procreative sexual longing. Meanwhile Sappho became the Victorian figure of the poetess, denoting femininity, sentimentality, and the inevitable fall into obscurity of the female poetic voice.[18] It has been said that Baudelaire invented the "lesbian" Sappho in the 1850s; British poet Algernon Swinburne imported her to Victorian England in the 1860s; H. T. Wharton assembled her corpus and translated it in equivocating ways in the 1880s; and Pierre Louÿs, with his literary spoof *Songs of Bilitis* (1894), a collection of female same-sex erotic poetry supposedly written by a companion of Sappho, renewed the shock value of the name of Sappho in fin de siècle Paris.[19]

It is within this context that Eva, in the company of Barney and Vivien in Bar Harbor, was posing for a picture after an image identified with

Sappho. I found the photo more than one hundred years later amid boxes of Natalie Barney's things deposited with the papers of Barney's mother, Alice Pike Barney, in the Smithsonian Archives. It offered a first glimpse of how Eva was reading Sappho's fragments in 1900: how she was animating those fragments with her body, costumes, and props to perform a new kind of art. The photograph she created after the line drawing of the ancient painting had several layers of meaning. People uninitiated in the secrets of Sappho's modern reception probably missed the reference to Sappho entirely. They saw just a picture of Eva reading. For Eva's female companions, however, who saw the photo from a standpoint of their growing intimacy and developing Greek literacy, Eva's pose drew lines of affiliation with the absent Sappho, adopting her as a powerful Greek prototype for living and making twentieth-century art. Indeed, her pose was so deeply implicated in their reading of Sappho's fragments that it is impossible to tell where the fragments ended and Eva's body and art began.

"OLD THINGS ARE BECOMING NEW"

But what was Greece to Eva? By what journey of intellect and desire had she come to embrace this particular Greek prototype?

A notion that the new world found creative ground in old things was integral to Eva's nineteenth-century upbringing. It aligned with the progressive ideas of her parents, both from prominent American families and advocates of well-reasoned social and political change to counter the effects of industrialization. Her mother, Catherine Amory Bennett, a member of the Amory family descended from Salem merchants and part of Boston's traditional upper class, was a classically trained pianist who dedicated herself to the arts and progressive causes such as women's suffrage. She gathered musicians in the family home to play in her small orchestra or to sing. Operatic divas Nellie Melba, Lillian Nordica, Emma Eames, Marcella Sembrich, and especially Emma Calvé were near the hearts of Eva and her siblings.[20] Eva's father, Courtlandt, claimed he was descended from a knighted crusader and an ancestor who came over on the *Mayflower*.[21] Trained as a lawyer at Columbia Law School, he spent his days "investigat[ing] for himself the questions, the problems, the mysteries of life. . . . No error could be old enough, popular, plausible, or profitable enough, to bribe his judgment or to keep his conscience still."[22] When he purchased a stake in Gramercy Park School and Tool-House (also known as the Von Taube School, after its originator and director, G. Von Taube), he supported its "new education" model of self-directed learning harmoniously combining theoretical and practical learning to prepare students for a business or scientific course.[23] Yet he also directed pupils to study "Greek, French, German and English systems of philosophy, following his motto, "old things are passing away; behold, old things are becoming new."[24] This was his willful misreading of the passage in 2 Corinthians 5:17 that reads "*all* things are become new."[25]

Old Greek things were deeply ingrained in the look and feel of the world that these Mayflower descendants had inherited. Greece entered America (as it did Germany and Britain) as a country of the imagination, a special locus of aesthetic and intellectual origins, practically from the country's founding moments.[26] Initially the founders filtered Greece into American self-governance through the guise of Roman republicanism, considered a more congenial model than Athens's direct democracy.[27] Then, around the turn of the nineteenth century and coinciding with the receding of fears of the "perils of democracy,"[28] American elites began drawing visible lines of affiliation that filled the gap between the new world and ancient Greece through a variety of Greek "revivals." "Greek revival" architecture, for example, was seen first in the Bank of Philadelphia (Benjamin Harry Latrobe, 1798–1801) and quite creatively in the capitol building in Washington (Latrobe, 1803–17, and Charles Bulfinch, 1818–26), then in an increasing number of banks, universities, churches, town halls, plantation houses, and even small urban homes and farmhouses across the expanding nation, until it became known as the "national style" of architecture in the United States.[29] The naming of more than one hundred American towns after cities in ancient Greek literature (Athens, Sparta, Corinth, Thebes, Delphi, Troy, Olympia) and even after a hero of the Greek rebellion against the Ottoman Empire (1821–28) (Ypsilanti) from the early 1820s through the 1850s expressed both attention to ancient Greek prototypes and sympathy for modern Greek independence,[30] another spectacular materialization of the Greek idea in which American philhellenes participated.

Eva's parents and then her stepfather, Dr. Robert Abbe, themselves enacted Greek ideas on a daily basis. A case in point is a story Eva told about her maternal grandfather at his deathbed. His attending physician was Dr. Abbe, the man who would marry Eva's mother after her father's sudden death from peritonitis in 1888. An accomplished surgeon with strong training in Greek and Latin[31] and a serious interest in archaeology,[32] Abbe knew of his patient's love of ancient Greek. When he saw that the old man was "sinking into the last lethargy," Abbe "started reciting a Pindaric Ode" in order to gain time so that the patient's daughter Catherine could arrive to say her last good-byes. The dying man "recovered consciousness and finished the passage."[33] Many years later, Eva's mother, now married to Dr. Abbe, worked with a small group in Bar Harbor[34] to construct a building of the arts that was "severely classic" in design.[35] The building opened its doors on Saturday, July 13, 1907,[36] two months before Eva would return from Greece to introduce her mother and stepfather to Angelos Sikelianos. According to one eyewitness to the building's opening, "its red-tiled roof, its marshaled columns, and its fine proportions" offered not just "a glimpse of some forgotten Grecian temple" but also "echoes of a shepherd's pipe" and "the flitting passage of a flowing robe."[37]

Such enactments confirmed the sense that America was rooted in Greek culture. Like Percy Bysshe Shelley's Britons, Americans were "all Greeks"[38] when they moved in and out of Greek revival buildings designed to inspire "the highest aesthetic and intellectual stimulation."[39] They were "all Greeks" when they decorated their homes using architectural pattern books with Greek-inspired designs. They were "all Greeks" when they played parlor games posing as Greek deities or joined Greek-lettered fraternities. They were "all Greeks" when they suffered diseases with Greek-inspired names and participated in democratic political processes.

A shift in the distribution of Greek learning across gender divisions impressed itself on Eva's youth. She was born into a world in which elite American males studied Greek sources as a "prerequisite for entry into public life,"[40] while their female counterparts, excluded from participation in governance, found ways to study Greek informally. Over time and coinciding with her coming of age in the late 1800s, changes in the value given to Greek learning broadened its social reach. Hellenism was proposed as an antidote to the crude anti-intellectualism of industrial society. It became a "platform for the perfection of the inner self."[41] Thus imitation of the Greeks moved from elite domains of scholarship and governance to popular spheres such as athletics—for example, when the American team competed successfully, dominating the gold medal tally in the first international revival of the Olympic Games, held in Athens in 1896. Imitation of Greek prototypes became a private occupation too when figures such as the tragic heroine Antigone were upheld as good models for women of the rising middle class.

During Eva's adolescence, as women began gaining access to higher education, they also took on leading roles in reforming American culture. In the public sphere, they actively sought to translate classical models for new purposes, which were as pointedly sociopolitical as they were scholarly. A case in point was the solidly humanities-based curriculum of Miss Porter's School in Farmington, Connecticut, which Eva completed in 1891.[42] As a day and boarding school, Miss Porter's adopted a Yale preparatory curriculum for girls in grades nine to twelve. Even more revolutionary was the classically grounded humanistic curriculum that Eva followed at Bryn Mawr College, a school promising academic rigor equal to that of Harvard and Yale. After passing stiff entrance exams in Latin to gain entry as a twenty-two-year-old adult in 1896, she took advanced Latin and beginning and intermediate Greek classes there.[43]

At Bryn Mawr, Eva would have encountered Sappho on many fronts. From the mouth of the college's president, M. Carey Thomas, who set the school's high-minded direction, she would have heard Sappho named "the greatest lyric poet in the world,"[44] an exception in history, a sign of women's as yet untapped genius, and call for the necessity of their solidarity.[45] Thomas was the same person who established the goal that work done in women's colleges should be "the same in quality and quantity as the work done in colleges for men."[46] Eva's courses in Latin and Greek put that principle into effect by requiring that female students acquire skills in the original languages. They had to know the sources and stay informed about archaeological discoveries, such as the unearthing of new papyrus scraps of Sappho's poetic fragments. Perhaps it was for them that "M. Maspero, the Director of Explorations in Egypt," included the detail that "he detected the perfume of Sappho's art" in those scraps in the sands of Oxyrhynchus.[47] In her Latin studies Eva would have encountered stories of Sappho's life in Ovid's *Heroides*, or lingered on Catullus's line about the young woman who made herself "Sapphica . . . musa doctior" ("more learned . . . than the Sapphic muse").[48] In Mamie Gwinn's course on the English essay concentrating on "Arnold, Pater and Swinburne,"[49] she would have read Swinburne's *Notes on Poems and Reviews* in defense of "the very words of Sappho."[50]

Thomas's message to students at Bryn Mawr College was double: that women's higher education should replicate the "quality and quantity" of men's colleges, on the one hand, and provide women students with prototypes such as Sappho who could serve as transformative models for women of the future, on the other. Indeed the twofold nature of Thomas's notions was written into the project of women's higher education. Specifically with regard to Greek learning, it was impossible for young women to embrace the discipline of philology in the neutral, unstressed ways of men, whose gendered lives as men were not changed by their access to Greek learning. At the very least, women made Greek learning a sign of their capacity for cultivation. This was no small matter, for by learning to read Greek at Bryn Mawr College as if they were men reading Greek at Harvard College, women showed their capacity both for doing what men were already doing and for assuming some of their roles. In this way, they were "invert[ing] the traditional privilege system that lends primacy to men."[51] They and their Greek books were implicated in a social transformation. "What didn't the Greeks have?" Eva would later ask Natalie Barney, making the point that the Greeks gave her everything she needed to live a transformative life.[52]

Eva embraced the contradictory directions given to her by Bryn Mawr College. Though no stellar student, she gained enough training in classical languages to understand the significance of gendered adjectival endings and pronouns (lost in English translation) and to recite Sappho's poetry in ancient Greek. Then, following Thomas's second line of argument, she made use of classical prototypes to invert social conventions. She was likely practicing some form of "inversion" in the sexual sense[53] in her dormitory room in Radnor Hall in the spring of 1898—perhaps testing Sappho's words of love on a fellow student. At least one female classmate, Virginia Greer Yardley, recalled having a devastating "crush on Eva Palmer"[54] and remained emotionally attached to her for years. In any case, Eva was caught doing something strictly prohibited, and President Thomas wrote her a stern letter "[forbidding her] the right of residence in the halls of Bryn Mawr College for one year from the 28th of May, 1898, to the 28th of May, 1899."[55]

It was commonplace to believe that women might grow "unwomanly" or excessively free if they got too close to Greek learning.[56] In Eva's case, her accession to classical studies did bear something in excess of the anticipated outcomes of a college education. When she and her female friends exchanged Greek words in private moments, they were not just proving themselves to be "as fully classical as men."[57] These women were using the classical to renegotiate old gender and sex roles, circumvent the attendant taboos, and express new desires. They were pushing old Western cultural models onto unconventional ground as an unwelcome "heresy."[58] It was for some such unspecified heresy that Eva was suspended from Bryn Mawr in the spring of 1898 and traveled to Europe with her brother Courtlandt, who was studying piano in Rome.

"CHARMING TABLEAU"

Eva returned to the United States in 1900 to spend the summer in "Brook End," the home recently purchased and remodeled by her stepfather, Dr. Abbe.[59] She had started spending summers at Bar Harbor with her sister May and brother Courtlandt sometime after her mother married Dr. Abbe in 1891, with evidence pointing to 1894—when she was twenty—as her first summer there and that year or the next marking the beginning of her friendship with Barney.[60] It is possible that she visited Bar Harbor in her adolescence, something she and Barney each recalled many years later,[61] but I have not found evidence to support this. In any event, she and Barney had not seen each other in Bar Harbor for several years. Now Barney was under the careful watch of her parents in "Ban-y-Bryn," the Barneys' twenty-six-room summer cottage down the road from the Abbes. Apparently, her mother and father, Alice Pike and Albert Barney, members of Washington's high society, were so shocked when they learned of the same-sex love content of Barney's *Quelques Portraits-Sonnets de Femmes* (Some portraits-sonnets of women), published in Paris the previous spring, that they fetched her from Paris to keep an eye on her.[62] But either the story is mistaken or the punishment was ineffective, for Barney sent a personalized copy of the book to Eva,[63] and she invited her lover Renée Vivien to come stay in her parents' cottage.

A crucial moment in the coalescence of Eva, Barney, and Vivien as a group of readers of Sappho was a variety show fund-raiser held on Wednesday, August 29, 1900, for the new Bar Harbor village hospital.[64] In the show, Eva, in fancy sandals and a golden headband, like a figure in the Sapphic corpus, played a small but telling part. Basic information about the event is found in the "Bar Harbor" column published in the *New York Times*.[65] "Bar Harbor" of August 26, 1900, anticipates the theatrical event; then "Bar Harbor" of August 30 reports on the previous day's entertainment.[66] From the reports, we learn that Natalie's mother, Alice Pike Barney, hosted the theatrical, and Natalie and her sister Alice Clifford (called Laura) wrote most of the script. Renée Vivien ("Tarn"[67]) played an opening "burlesque" role entitled "The Dream of Alice in Wonderland."[68] The evening's entertainment closed with four "charming tableaux" with the following roles: Eva's sister May played Helen of Troy and Sarah Bernhardt; Natalie's sister Alice Clifford (Laura) was Cleopatra; and Eva performed Sappho.[69] It is Eva's tableau of Sappho that concerns me here.

While it was likely the social weight of the "list of characters and workers" generated interest for the *New York Times* readership (for "the enterprise [included] the names of the most well-known people here"[70]), Eva's tableau of Sappho holds more than social interest. The evidence is thin; yet careful attention to the tableau's context, some guesswork on how the performance went, and consideration of some unpublicized activities around the time of the performance give another set of clues, beyond the photograph, of how Eva was performing the role of Sappho onstage and beyond.

The fact that she chose to stage "Sappho" as a tableau indicates her knowledge of the connection between women's study of Greek and tableaux more generally. It marks her performance as an instance of "ladies' Greek" in this respect: through women's entry into Greek learning in British and American women's colleges such as Bryn Mawr, "women imagined Greece on their own terms and within a female homosocial context."[71] "Tableau" (plural tableaux or tableaus) names an individual or group performance of a picture. Short for *tableau vivant* (or living picture), a tableau is a picture brought to life through the performers' poses, costumes, gestures, and props. Tableaux create drama through artistic imitation, turning the stage into a living performance of a painting, sculpture, or bas-relief, which may itself be an imitation of a literary or dramatic scene. Drawing on a tradition of women striking poses inspired by ancient art, they reach back to Emma Lyon Hamilton, who performed charade-like "attitudes" of mythical and biblical personae for the British embassy in Naples. These were based on artistic renditions and tested the knowledge of visiting artists, aristocrats, and collectors of antiquities.[72] In Eva's day, tableaux were used in performances of Greek drama or verse at women's colleges.[73] They illustrated still scenes accompanied by narration. The dramatic effect of the illustration of Greek letters that "looked like a picture"[74] lay in the animation of the dead letter, which affirmed both antiquity's passing and the possibility of its return.

Eva was familiar with a number of paintings bearing the name of Sappho from her yearlong stay in Europe following her suspension from Bryn Mawr. During that time, she forged what would become a lifetime practice of visiting art museums. She likely saw firsthand the Roman fresco at Pompeii depicting a woman with a writing tablet in her left hand, with a stylus in her right pressed thoughtfully against her lips. People identified this vision of a presciently learned woman with Sappho from the time of its discovery in the late eighteenth century. It aligned with the image of the woman holding a scroll inscribed with Sappho's name in Raphael's *Mount Parnassus*, a fresco painted on an interior wall of the Stanza della Segnatura in the Vatican Palace. Eva would have encountered these and some of the many eighteenth- and nineteenth-century artistic works representing Sappho as the singing, teaching, listening, fantasizing, loving, leaping, and dying poetess.[75] These visual sources combined with Eva's basic knowledge of Greek literature and several years' experience producing and performing drama[76] to give her the resources to develop a Sappho tableau that would resonate with the audience in Bar Harbor.

Eva's conflicted emotions in the months preceding the tableau added another dimension to her performance of Sappho. She had returned to Bar Harbor the previous summer after two years' absence. She was reportedly present at a "canoe club parade" on August 15, 1899, when the multimillionaire George Vanderbilt II with his new wife, Edith, were given a dinner welcoming him back to Bar Harbor after *his* long absence.[77] Vanderbilt was a bookish, learned aristocrat, like Eva. He knew many languages, even modern Greek. He and Eva were old family friends, or perhaps something more, as Eva had visited him at Biltmore Estate in Ashville in 1894, when she was twenty. Rumors went around then that she and Vanderbilt were engaged.[78] When she encountered Barney in Bar Harbor in July 1900, after years of separation, she was, in Barney's words, "unhappy because of an old love,"[79] perhaps for George Vanderbilt. Then Barney sent her the hand-inscribed copy of *Quelques Portraits-Sonnets de Femmes* with a dedication comparing the state of Eva's heart to the fading days of autumn. Eva distanced herself from "the lines" that Barney inscribed in the front of the book.[80] "For look," she wrote, "without knowing much about my life, you have chosen to say that my dead leaves outnumber my flowers, which is as true as it would be to write a sonnet to November in the full fresh woods of July."[81] In cool tones, she undressed Barney's poems to scrutinize their bare contents: "Take off the pretty clothes and what have you left but a denial that Beauty exists."[82]

Already in this first extant letter of Eva's and Barney's voluminous correspondence, the tensions are simmering. Tension would become a feature of the two women's relationship, pushing and pulling them in a drama-ridden dance of differing temperaments and badly synchronized emotions even as they traveled side by side for nearly another decade. Here she is distancing herself from Barney's decadent worldview. "Now I believe that even as there is a faith and a youth in me which you are not looking for and therefore do not see, so also in life there is a vitality, a freshness, an eternal strength which you deny because you have never gone on a quest to discover them. Isn't it true that you haven't hunted any longer for God's Magnificence than you have for my flowers, and have denied it quickly, ruthlessly?"[83] Eva would never fully give into Barney's decadence: her emphasis on artifice over nature; her disinterest in public, political life; her disdain for the lower classes; her persistent desire to publicize her private life; her linking of eroticism to domination; and her predatory stance. Barney's persistent pursuit of pleasure in the transient moment—and her effort to make it as theatrical and ornate as possible—contrasted with Eva's longing for an ideal order beyond her passions and desires.[84]

When Renée Vivien arrived as Barney's guest in August, Eva learned that Vivien and Barney were lovers. The discovery coincided roughly with the Sappho tableau and with Eva's sharing of her knowledge of Greek with Vivien. Together she and Vivien dedicated time to studying Greek, while Barney socialized and counted on them to communicate their Greek learning.[85] Although I have found no record of the poem Eva recited or the painting or sculpture she imitated in her Sappho tableau, a few extant details help recreate the performance. Barney left a verbal sketch, mentioning "faux columns" and an accompanying harp. In addition, she states that Eva's feet were "encased in white sandals with straps crisscrossing her legs," and she had "a gold band circling her forehead."[86] The binding elements of fancy sandals and a headband regularly appear in modern paintings of Sappho, evoking lines from Sappho's verse. The crisscrossing straps of those sandals also dress Eva's ankles in a risqué photograph that parodies Christian paintings of the Annunciation. Kneeling before a virgin-like Barney, who is holding a white lily while seated on a Corinthian throne, Eva, the angel bearing good news, hides Barney's frontal nudity with her crown of braids and a draped piece of lace covering her left arm but not her own bare back or bottom (figure 1.3).

The effect of Eva's classicizing tableau was probably convincing; it was most certainly arresting, for Eva had striking features, none more impressive than her hair. Whether she wore it coiled around her head or loosely falling over her body, it signaled a "medieval virgin"[87] beauty that bound her lovers to her.[88] Vivien fashioned the beauty of "Eva," the female figure she created after Eva in *A Woman Appeared to Me*, to be dazzling, while hard and distant, like a statue or icon: "Looking at her, I felt that divine and terrible trembling that a perfect statue inspires, a dazzle of radiant marble, a long-loved picture of infinite harmony."[89]

FIGURE 1.3. Eva Palmer kneeling before Natalie Barney, ca. 1900. Unknown source, printed in Jean L. King, *Alice Pike Barney: Her Life and Art* (Washington, DC: National Museum of American Art in association with Smithsonian Institution Press, 1994), p. 137, with other photographs from the Smithsonian Institution, gift of Laura Dreyfus-Barney and Natalie Clifford Barney in the memory of their mother, Alice Pike Barney. The archivist in the Smithsonian Institution Archives was unable to locate the photograph.

As in the photograph of her reading pose, in her Sappho tableau, too, Eva deployed her assets to produce a multicoded message. Once again, she tapped into Sappho as a popular figure of complex significance. To the broader audience of the Bar Harbor hospital fund-raiser, Sappho, alongside Helen of Troy, Sarah Bernhardt, and Cleopatra, signified an unconventional female figure of great prodigy and uncertain proclivities. Progressive women in the audience, including Eva's mother, would have appreciated the "exhumation" of talented ancient women that Eva and her sister and friends performed.[90] A few spectators probably caught the sequence's antibourgeois undertones. But to Barney and Vivien—who attributed homoerotic feelings to Sappho's broken voice—the performance was erotically charged. Eva's tableau implicated her alongside Sappho in her circle's "inverse" passion for one another.[91]

The first traces of Eva's erotic correspondence with Barney are exactly from the time of this tableau. From that moment on, Eva's performance of the woman-desiring female in sandals with crisscrossing straps becomes a running motif in her staged productions with Barney, as is apparent in the sexually suggestive photograph and in the more demure photographs from the 1906 staging of Barney's revisionary play *Equivoque* (see ahead to figure 1.7), in which Eva played the bride-to-be Timas (figure 1.8). Either before or just after her Sappho tableau, Eva undressed Barney again, this time literally, and declared her "foolish love."[92] She invited Barney to Duck Brook ("you know the one I mean where the boys sometimes swim") to read poetry ("You can bring my Swinburne that I forgot yesterday or any other book you please, so that it be poetry, I can't bear to read prose").[93] A series of Kodak photographs taken in Duck Brook stand as a record that she, Barney, and Vivien went to Duck Brook and undressed together.[94] Although their instrument was the brand new Brownie camera, rolled out just that year to facilitate the quick snapshot, their poses were carefully composed imitations of female nudes in high art and mischievously parodied historic representations of women. Through the substitution of the female photographer's eye for the traditionally male desirous gaze, and through their poses' playful distortions of a range of visual sources, they sought to free the female nude from the male gaze to make it available for female-female alignments.

As the days of summer began to fade, Eva invited Vivien and Barney to Bryn Mawr College to stay in her comfortable dormitory room in Radnor Hall,[95] which she maintained despite having been forbidden entry from 1898 to 1899. She would not complete her studies there. In fact, while she gave Vivien and Barney access to the Bryn Mawr campus, she seems to have removed herself. Thus, Vivien attended Bryn Mawr lectures to bolster her readings of Sappho with Greek learning, while Barney "played tennis"[96] and generally gave her attention to socializing. Nevertheless, the sequence of events I have reconstructed here represented a moment of coalescence. The women's meeting at Bar Harbor in July 1900; Eva's performances of Sappho at the end of August; the three women's nude photos in Duck Brook; Vivien's Greek lessons and Barney's contacts at Bryn Mawr facilitated by Eva that September: the confluence of all these events identify a critical moment when Eva's "ladies' Greek" follows an important turning point in the history of sexuality.

"GOING BACK WITH KNOWLEDGE"

Eva's and Barney's letters, their loves, and their dissection of their loves in their letters during the first decade of the 1900s suggest that they came together and eventually separated by "going back with knowledge" to fill in where Greek words broke off. In Barney's words, "We learn to love things in the past—the past is infinite for it contains the future—and what is it all *après tout* but a going back with knowledge?"[97] In their best moments, they found inspiration in the lacunae in the textual record of Sappho's corpus, as if the gaps in literary history represented deep, lost time from which the as-yet unlived future of alternative affective communities might unfold.[98] This "queer time," as critics call it today, moves not progressively forward in sequence but "wrinkles and folds as some minor feature of our sexually impoverished present suddenly meets up with a richer past, or as the materials of a failed and forgotten project of the past find their new uses, in a future unimaginable in their time."[99] Yet the theme of "going back with knowledge" to extract life from ruins recurred so often in their interaction that Eva balked at the feeling that forces of death and decay were guiding their relationship: "It seems you live for me as if you were looking at a pile of ruins and creating a beautiful poem."[100] Moreover Eva worried there was something in their blend of natures that was itself "broken": "The sun throws millions of jewels on the water, and the flowers make the air seem like your breath. But my hands cannot gather the jewels for you and my lips cannot touch the flowers. And I can only speak to you in broken sentences."[101] If "broken sentences" were building blocks, how could they inspire new work? What sort of muse was a "pile of ruins"? That was a question to which Eva would keep returning all her adult years, especially after she left Barney.

Traces of Eva's and Barney's "broken sentences" of love are far from scarce. During the years when they were together, they constantly corresponded.[102] They exchanged thousands of pages of handwritten letters from the time they became intimately involved that summer of 1900 until they mutually excommunicated each other in 1909.[103] Stacks and stacks of letters, calling cards, telegrams, notes, cards, pneumatiques, photographs, and a lock of Eva's red hair were all stored away for decades with old ribbons tied around them. Whether carefully preserved in their envelopes or tear- and mud-stained, these are the material by-products of their Sapphic love. The materiality of the letters is crucial, for they interweave writing and reading with physical effects of love. Consider Eva's words to Barney: "Your letter folds me as closely as your arms and touches me as marvelously as your lips, I am bound by it as though all your body were over me, held by it as by your eyes when they glitter like jewels in the sun. My poet, my mistress, my lover! I love you all ways tonight, but most of all for the grace of your lines."[104] Here we see Eva creating written lines to express bodily lines she viewed through Barney's recreation of Sappho's lines.

However, if we compare the large body of remaining artifacts of Eva's Sapphic love life with the few surviving lines of Sappho, we face an enormous incongruity. The Sappho whom Eva and the rest of us have been reading exists as a corpus of some two hundred tattered fragments of barely scrutable words or phrases, whereas the Eva over whom the traces of Sappho always "presided"[105] exists in many complete, highly legible love lines. Thus, while Sappho, with a highly attenuated record of writings that tends to fall apart, has been assuredly identified as the original "lesbian," Eva, with a substantial, legible, and rather complete body of writings implicating her in the circle of turn-of-the-century Sapphics, has been largely missing from lesbian historiography.

Her absence, together with the continuing existence of the large surviving body of her correspondence with Natalie Clifford Barney, is attributable to the fact that Eva, at a turning point in August of 1907, when she abruptly determined to marry Angelos Sikelianos, delivered to Barney all the letters she had saved, including correspondence with other female lovers. Eva explained, "If you care for me let our misery be between ourselves. Keep me now if you love me as I have kept you, keep my letters that I love above other things, keep yourself and believe this that the love I wrote to you about was you."[106] Barney responded with cruel sarcasm directed at Eva's replacement of her with Sikelianos, another poet. Alluding to Eva's fall in literary tastes, she gave her spiteful curse: "may this new love . . . learn to be nevertheless a simple, big sure thing, with less literature and more heart beats in it."[107] Barney did keep Eva's letters to the end of her life, even though she cut herself off emotionally from her—she even omitted Eva from her famous 1929 sketch of her guests in "Temple à l'Amitié," where she admitted practically *all* her past and present lovers and friends, whether significant or a trifling intrigue.[108] Much of the correspondence is now in the Bibliothèque littéraire Jacques Doucet, a library of the Sorbonne University where the papers of Natalie Clifford Barney were deposited after her death. I note the irony that Eva's letters landed in the library of Jacques Doucet, who made a fortune selling dresses. Eva's Parisian closets were once "full of dresses from Doucet."[109] When she left Paris in August 1907, she abandoned all those dresses together with her love letters.

While more than three hundred letters, notes, and telegrams stayed in Paris, an even larger stack comprising more than six hundred letters disappeared in Athens when in 1969, near the end of Barney's life, Barney and her housekeeper Berthe Cleyrergue received a visit from Professor Octave Merlier. A French acquaintance of Eva's who lived in Greece, Merlier asked Barney if she had anything of Eva's to show him. He was hoping to microfilm all her papers. Barney, who was beginning to lose some of her mental acuity, produced several stacks of Eva's letters for him to read. He read a few and said he was deeply moved. He asked to take them with him to Greece.[110] Cleyrergue heeded his request but stopped short of giving him the remaining letters, for reasons that are not clear. Today the letters that Merlier took with him remain in Greece, separated from the letters in the Jacques Doucet Library. They are cared for in the unrelated Center for Asia Minor Studies, an institute for research begun by Octave Merlier and Melpo Logotheti-Merlier in 1930 and operated since 1962 by the Greek Ministry of Culture in Athens in the old Plaka district. Access to the collection was officially forbidden until 2016,[111] in order to satisfy the wishes of Angelos Sikelianos's widow, Anna, who feared that the exposure of Eva's Parisian affairs might reflect badly on the Sikelianos family.

The effect of Eva's returning the love letters to Barney might be exactly what Eva wanted. Barney distanced herself from Eva, while she both preserved the letters and kept them hidden. For many years, only Barney and Eva knew of their existence, and hence the "misery" the two intimately shared remained their well-kept secret. Even after scenes implicating "Eva Palmer" in Barney's circle of lovers were mentioned in Barney's and Vivien's biographies,[112] they were hidden in plain view under Eva's maiden name and so remained invisible to scholars of modern Greek studies who attended to the afterlife of "Madame Sikelianou."

The specific question raised in Eva's dialogue with Barney about Sappho's surviving words was how women of the present era might insert themselves where Sappho's tongue "broke off." It is admittedly ironic to return to their dialogue at this point, more than one hundred years after their words of love broke off and nearly fifty years since their correspondence all but disappeared. Fragment 31, Sappho's most famous poem of female desire, in which the desiring subject breaks off while declaring her jealous love, was for them an implicit point of return. In the fragment, the first-person female speaker reacts to a scene in which her beloved, another woman, reciprocates the affections of a man. Sappho's almost clinical description of the body's reaction to the "god-like" interloper—Sappho's ancient reader Longinus, who preserved the poem by commenting on it, medicalized the reaction as "παθήματα" (symptoms), associated with "ερωτικαῖς μανίαις" (lovers' madness)[113]—lists symptoms of the senses gone awry in a counterproductive overdrive. Her flesh burns subtly, her eyes are blinded, the ears hum, her pores sweat. Finally, the tongue is both described as "breaking" ("γλῶσσα ἔαγε") and literally breaks off nonsensically: "ἀλλὰ πὰν τόλματον ἐπεὶ καὶ πένητα" (but all can be endured, since even a pauper). The Sapphic poem actualizes through syntactical breakdown the heart-pounding, sweat-inducing, tongue-tying, sense-depriving vulnerability of the jealous lover who cannot bear to see her lover give affection to a man. Through the centuries, the genders of the pronouns and adjectives have lent to this fragment an intriguingly problematic status, as the Greek clearly shows it is a female lover describing her jealous reaction to a female beloved in the company of a male lover. More than the genders, it is the poem's ellipses, the "snapped off tongue," that have extended its life in verse not just by "articulating . . . the Sapphic corpus"[114] as an integrally broken one in need of collection but also by inviting supplementary creations.[115] The poem's "broken tongue" invited Barney and Eva to think of not just the anatomy of women's same-sex love but its geometry and artistic media.

From the time Barney shifted her locus of operation from America to her pavilion in the Parisian suburb of Neuilly from the first years of the twentieth century until 1909 (when she moved to 20 rue Jacob on the Left Bank), she sought to occupy the place of the missing Sappho. Deploying her social dynamism, wit, and immense sexual appeal, she conquered ever more beautiful, talented, wealthy women, contributing to the expansion of an international circle of interinvolved female writers and performers. The geometry of the group was decidedly the love triangle.[116] Triangle upon triangle formed a multisided pyramid, with Barney posing as Sappho at its apex and Vivien, for a short period, then Eva as the longer-term "confidante"[117] occupying several planes of Barney's affection with other women and even a man or two.[118] Eva was with Barney on both sides of the Atlantic from July 1900 through August 1906, many more years than Renée Vivien, who shared Barney with other women from 1899 until she broke away in 1902, then briefly traveled with Barney to Lesbos in 1904 before finally breaking off ties. When in Paris, Eva and Barney stayed at first in hotels or rented beds in the apartment of one of Barney's male suitors at 4 rue Chalgrin. Then, in 1904, they moved into neighboring houses in Neuilly-sur-Seine, with Barney at 25 rue de Bois de Boulogne and Eva at 56 rue de Longchamp.

Barney's pavilion, with its expansive garden, became a gathering place. Women came and went, sometimes crossing paths and sharing in acts of love. Eva watched as Barney made love to others; or she made love while Barney or another woman watched her;[119] or she read what Barney wrote about her other lovers; or she pursued lovers and wrote about them to Barney. Barney, Eva, and the following women were connected sexually in ways that cannot be easily disentangled: Minnie, Marchioness of Anglesey;[120] Sarah ("Sarita") Bernhardt; Emma Calvé;[121] Colette; Olive Custance; Baroness Ilse Deslandes; Lucie ("Amande") Delarue-Mardrus; Isadora Duncan;[122] Princess Marie ("Bébé") de Hatzfeld Hohenlohe; Wanda Landowska; Georgette Leblanc; Lilian ("Lily," "Lil");[123] Constant Lounsbery; Marguerite Moreno; Liane de Pougy; Amélie Rives; Henriette Rogers; Nina Russel; Renée Vivien; Virginia Yardley;[124] and Margaretha Zelle ("Mata Hari"). Men with a strong interest in the literary and dramatic Sappho played decisive roles from the sidelines: Pierre Louÿs, for example, who visited Barney's pavilion on occasion, received a dedication from Barney for his inspiration of her "society of the future."[125]

Just what it meant to live under the sign of Sappho was a contested matter. Barney spelled out the order for a female erotic pedagogy in "Cinq petits dialogues grecs" (Five short Greek dialogues, 1902). Women were to relinquish ties with family, husband, children, and country for their desire for each other.[126] Moreover, women were to write. What really interested Barney was the revolutionary precedent of Sappho, the woman who made writing her art shortly after the Greeks introduced writing. As Barney saw it, by writing, women could invert power relations. She elaborated on this rule in a letter in which she simultaneously praised her own work and criticized Eva for her performing art.[127] Paradoxically, to make her argument, Barney relied on conventional gender dichotomies that privileged the work of great men while leaving no room for women to define themselves except after the example of these men or of the rare woman such as Sappho, "who was . . . essentially a man." For Barney, Sappho was the exception who proved a historical rule. Barney divided the arts into "virile" and "effeminate forms." According to her definition, artistic work of "the greatest virility, originality, genius—whatever you call it—is the most unadulterated," that is to say, "engendered by and through itself only," while "effeminate forms of art [are] . . . impregnated with the very élan of someone else." In the historical scheme of things, "real men" did the "virile" work of writing and composing. Women, if they did any creative work at all, took on "effeminate," reproductive roles. This happened in the past, and it was continuing in their day, Barney observed, when women such as Eva kept falling "instinctively into adaptation, criticism, copy of metres, or ingenious rendering of the works of others." For Barney, Sappho showed the path for women to gain control over their circulation in the arts and in human society by becoming "absolutely and originally productive" and "hold[ing] the highest place in art." Women had to follow Sappho, and to do so they had to "mentally change sex and become Lesbian or unlovely"; they had to compose or write.

While Barney and Eva proliferated love triangles in their lives, in writing, they boldly revised them. We see a revision of Sappho fragment 31 in this letter by Barney to Eva in February 1902:

> My sweet—How envious I am of both of you! You will be with me soon . . . and tell me all about it. I wish I could have seen you . . . and her face close to your hair, like a pale white flower with the sun for auriole— and I what have I rested my eyes upon and found joy in? In nothing but the imagining of it—yet how much more real than the touch of real hands and the look from real eyes that I do love.[128]

As in Sappho fragment 31, here Barney, the female lover, addresses the female beloved, Eva, who is giving her attention to another lover. But Barney makes some crucial substitutions. She identifies a woman rather than a man as the interloper. This alters the sight lines of the poem, making both Eva and her lover potential objects of Barney's desirous approach. And while Barney states her "envy" of Eva, she does not display any symptoms of a lover's jealousy. She does not make the scene vanish by shutting down her senses, as happens to the speaker in Sappho fragment 31. Instead she covets what the two women have shared. Through the store she places in the "man-force" of original writing, Barney confirms her power to call up her eyes' unfulfilled wish of seeing Eva with her female lover ("I wish

I could have seen you . . . and her face close to your hair"). This inversion of the power dynamics of Sappho fragment 31 that places Barney in control to insert herself in a triangle of lovers as its seeing, feeling, imagining, desiring, and desired subject makes the scene even "more real" than if it were present.

Barney's terms in this passage deserved comment, and comment Eva did. Eva produced a competitive revision in a letter she sent to Barney a few months later in the spring of 1902.[129] Here and elsewhere the contest in their correspondence is ongoing. Eva's letter returns to the exact configuration of Sappho fragment 31, with Barney the beloved approached by a man and Eva the lover standing in Sappho's place—precisely where Barney liked to stand. The sight lines are Sappho's, the potential for jealousy and misery the same. But Eva anticipates this version of events through a performative idiom: she uses writing to demand the scene's change.

> Je veux te voir danser!
>
> Je veux, oh comme je veux. Je t'adore quand tu danse. Raconte-moi tes mouvements, tes poses. Dis-moi ceux qui t'aiment le mieux et ce qu'ils te disent. Y en-a-t-il qui l'apprécient? Non! pas autant que moi qui de loin te vois danser et suis excitée, et qui de près te sens danser sur les pointes de tes jolis seins, sur ton ventre et le long de tes jambes avec mon corps pour ton parquet.
>
> (I want to see you dance!
>
> I want it, how I want it. I adore you when you dance. Tell me about your movements, your poses. Tell me who loves you best and what it is they say. Is there a man who finds you attractive? No! not as much as I when I see you dancing from afar, and I am aroused, and I feel I am almost dancing on the tips of your lovely breasts on your belly and your legs with my body as your floor.)[130]

A key feature of this passage is its dramaturgical approach. Eva writes as a director, not a poet or narrator, with an aim to dramatize in the present rather than to describe a past scene of dancing and lovemaking. The opening lines give the beat of the dance through the repeated words of desire (Je veux . . . je veux, oh comme je veux). Eva commands Barney to speak (Reconte-moi . . . dis-moi . . .), then orders the scene to stop (Non!) so that she, Eva, may replace the interloper. The scene's change brings Eva "from afar" closer and closer to her dancing lover. She introduces erotic words to help Barney experience sexual arousal with each rereading of the letter. The effect is to make music and dance a metaphor for the way she occupies Barney's brain in something approaching the ecstasy of Dionysian "madness," as suggested by these lines from Barney:

> you are like a dance in my brain trampling all thoughts and filling me utterly with wild music of utter madness. It takes possession of my whole body and every nerve beats to the rhythm every motion falls into the harmony of it until all of me is like a lyre rent under the feet of a dancer— Desire sweeps up and down like a throb of drums and the ecstasy of it breaks me—stretches each chord into the inarticulate inversity of a perfect (terrible so human is the founded and varied and blended joy of it) silence.[131]

Barney liked to dress up her lovers in an "erotic embellishment of lesbian play."[132] She had experience assisting her mother, another social dynamo, with theatricals in Bar Harbor and Washington, DC. In Eva now she found a splendid stage manager, producer, designer, actor, and artistic director, who played an instrumental role in shaping her culture of "theatrical display."[133] Eva brought to Barney's burgeoning movement several years' theatrical experience and a lifelong attention to stage management. Barney relied on Eva for all her theatrical skill, especially her brilliant resourcefulness in hairstyling, costuming, and props (figure 1.4). Barney would give Eva an assignment, for example, to stage a photograph depicting the mirroring sameness of a loving same-sex couple in the style of a conventional portrait, and Eva would produce the costumes or props and hair styling to materialize Barney's ideas, as seen in a photograph (figure 1.5) from a series of pictures pairing Barney with Lucie Delarue-Mardrus as look-a-like lovers.[134]

As much as Barney relied on Eva to dress up her crowd, she did not tire of dressing her down for her submission to "effeminate" performing arts. Barney conceded that these "have their place in art and are indispensable just as women are to the making articulate of that which is engendered in them."[135] Nevertheless, she argued, they "are by nature subjective, less purely creative, secondary."[136] She was especially harsh in her criticism of musical performance, something that mattered a great deal to Eva. She compared "the rendering of music" to "a woman who lends her pretty grace and patience to the thought of [others]."[137]

Eva disagreed. She granted Barney the superiority of her verbal brilliance, and she acknowledged that her musical and theatrical interests were of lesser creative power than Barney's writing. Moreover, she acknowledged her weaker character compared to Barney's dominant personality: "I am fluid, without initiative, because I shrink so from the winter wind of a difference with you that I catch at any agreement that seems to offer a chance shelter, only in the end to have you pin me in the teeth of the blast by saying that I am only an echo of the last strongest force I have come in contact with."[138] Yet on the more significant matter of her life's direction, that is, the value given to the media of artistic expression, Eva held her ground. She challenged Barney for returning to the single paradigm of Sappho, the poetic mentor and muse of women's same-sex desire. On one particular occasion, she pinned Barney into a corner. In a letter to Eva, Barney defended her tendency to endlessly impersonate the Sappho model: "You humble me by seeming to suppose that just because you have seen me do more or less adequately the role of—who shall we say? a Sappho? I am an impersonation of her, capable and admirable be it ever so little in this one. Instead, I would have you believe that I am open to any of the reality."[139] Barney's defense of her constant return to her Sapphic model of the virile female writer was that her "surroundings were so lacking in suggestion." They offered her no strong alternative. But Eva saw another way. She reminded Barney of an article of her faith, the "belief in inclusiveness"[140] against the tendency of the world to exclude minorities. This was the principle she wished to follow. That is to say, she tried to find a point beyond Barney's binaries of masculine creative versus feminine procreative arts to justify women's work as singers, actors, dancers, and performers.

To do this she broadened the Greek canon. Her greater learning made many more Greek sources available to her than Barney could even imagine. No one else in Barney's circle of Sapphics could append the pre-Socratic Parmenides, for example, to the list of a young woman's required readings. Of special interest to her was the Parmenidean *plenum*—the "impossible 'One'"—a container rather than a divider of opposing things:

> the impossible "One that is in all things and also in nothing . . . that is a whole . . . that has neither beginning, middle, nor end . . . that cannot be in anything . . . that cannot be in time at all . . . that cannot be many . . . cannot have parts," and yet which "has parts and therefore is many includes differences has limits and extremes . . . therefore a beginning, a middle and an end . . . is both at rest and in motion . . . whose parts become older and younger, therefore the One which is both older and younger than itself, which is in all things and also in nothing, which is everything, and yet can never be anything that is."[141]

FIGURE 1.4. Eva Palmer in a lace dress, ca. 1904. Seated in a cushioned chair in a posture reminiscent of a woman in a *klismos* chair, Eva has accessorized her dress with an ancient Greek hairstyle and large, beaded necklace. Acc. 96-153, Alice Pike Barney Papers, No. 6-190, SIA2018-072682. Smithsonian Institution Archives.

Eva proposed this all-inclusive, indivisible One as a supplement to Barney's order of women writers after the model of the virile Sappho. Into the indivisible One she folded all the Muses' arts—and it is no accident that the words "music" and "drama" would become her Parmenidean containers later in life. Thus, while the Sappho whom Eva discovered in the interpretive community of Sapphics is tightly interwoven in the course of her ar-

FIGURE 1.5. Natalie Barney and Lucie Delarue-Mardrus in lace dresses in a photo by Pierre Sanitas, Paris, ca. 1904. The two women have nearly matching hairstyles and lace dresses, which also nearly match Eva's hairstyle in figure 2.4. Acc. 96-153, Alice Pike Barney Papers, No. 6-145, SIA2018-072679. Smithsonian Institution Archives.

tistic and personal life from Bar Harbor to Delphi, she is not Barney's "virile" writer but Eva's "effeminate" One: a Sappho "who lends her pretty grace and patience to the thought of [others]," in the service of the performing arts. One by one, Eva would work to master the arts of costuming and stage design, vocal performance, musical composition, and choreography, with a powerful feeling that what once existed had passed away, yet still inert ancient poetry could be made into a living dramatic art that would engage and transform modern life.

"IF I CAN EVER SING TO YOU"

The performance of ancient Greek poetry in song was an element of Eva's Sappho tableau. Song was a piece of ancient Greek poetry, whether epic, dramatic, or lyric: the most irretrievably lost element of Sappho's art. For Eva, song was part of a complex tangle of relations. There were musical tangles, for the question of how to excavate the music in Greek poetry was and remains unanswerable. In Eva's time, it was not just scholars of Greek antiquity but composers of new music and even philosophers who were drawn to the puzzle of Greek poetry's missing sounds.[142] What did the music of poetry sound like when it came from such archaic psychic depths? By what technical means might one push the poetry of tragedy, for example, into the realm of music so as to shake the complacency out of modern audiences? What were the qualities of a specifically "Greek" music, and how did they intersect with Western musical theory? These were questions that would occupy Eva for decades to come.

There were personal tangles too: a mix of family complications arising from her intimacy with Barney, some quite traceable, others suspended in archival vagaries. Eva's comings and goings with Barney caused Eva's mother and brother deep distress. Her mother disapproved of her intimate relationships with women; she especially disliked Barney, who reportedly told Eva's mother that "the only way to treat [Eva] was like a dog."[143] Eva's brother Courtlandt, whose music making she described as part of her core being ("I am what Cory's music has made me," she once told Virginia Yardley at Bryn Mawr),[144] became hostile when he discovered that Barney was Eva's lover. He dished out verbal abuse, then stopped speaking to her.[145] This was a pattern he would repeat throughout their adult years: Eva's correspondence from 1900 to the end of her life bears witness to a pattern of harsh recriminations followed by long periods of aggressive silence—especially for her choice of partners, regardless if they were female or male (he despised Angelos too), and other choices as well. He never spared her feelings, contrary to his claims,[146] but served her large doses of pain.

On one occasion Eva worked especially hard to win back Courtlandt's love. She was studying classical vocal performance in New York City from 1901 to 1902 as a step in her goal to achieve the Parmenidean plenum.[147]

As a slightly less ambitious aim, she determined to sing "Liebestod" from Richard Wagner's *Tristan and Isolde* for Courtlandt. The Palmers were a musical family with many musician acquaintances. Catherine, Eva's mother, was a gifted pianist and conductor of a small chamber orchestra. She entertained world-class musicians in their home, as mentioned above. Courtlandt, also a pianist and a student of Ludwig (Louis) Breitner and Ignacy Jan Paderewski, was "suspected of being a genius," a child prodigy,[148] though he retreated from live solo performance after receiving mediocre reviews for his lack of musicianship. Eva studied violin with Madame Ludwig Breitner in her youth, but she was much too interested in performing poetry and drama to ignore vocal performance. From the age of fifteen, when she attended Miss Porter's School, she began to experiment with ways of reciting poetry to push language in the direction of music. Classical opera, choral music, and art song were forms she knew well from her earliest years; so it makes sense that she turned to studying them when she first tried to cultivate her voice's dramatic potential as a young adult. The music of Richard Wagner, the most influential composer of her era, had a special resonance. Eva, May, Courtlandt, and their mother were all Wagner enthusiasts. When Eva planned a pilgrimage to the Bayreuth Festival in August 1904, her mother and sister May both wrote letters anticipating her journey, and Courtlandt wrote after the fact to inquire about the festival.[149] Eva later recalled the powerful effect of Wagner's "strange" harmonies on Courtlandt in his early childhood.[150]

It was near the end of the first of Courtlandt's long cooling periods, in March 1902, after two years' separation, that Eva determined to sing for him: "Music is the only thing that could bring us back together."[151] An aria by Wagner was just the thing, Eva figured. She imagined progressing far enough in her voice studies to perform "Liebestod" (German, "Love death"), the very difficult final aria from the sepulchral last scene of *Tristan and Isolde*. By singing this particular piece of music—with its trochaic feet recalling Greek lyric poetry—she thought she would bring herself closer to Courtlandt. To Barney, she described her goal in a way that she thought Barney was "surely imaginative enough to see."[152] The provisional plan she laid out in her letters suggests both how far she had gone in her voice studies[153] and how closely she attended to musical drama's emotional effects. Thematically "Liebestod" is a strange choice of music for winning back an estranged brother, for the nearly seven-minute song is one of the most sustained musical expressions of erotic love. Kneeling before her dead lover Tristan, Isolde sings phrase after phrase without harmonic resolution until she reaches "höchste Lust" with the corpse of Tristan in her embrace. At the moment of musical climax, Isolde has herself reached an ecstatic climax. She is almost out of this world. Imagining Tristan risen from the dead, she points to him: "Do you see, friends?" she cries, as if calling on an ancient chorus to confirm her vision.[154] Tristan remains lifeless, however, and as the orchestra plays the aria's only resolving notes, Isolde dies of grief. Neither the song's erotic content nor the scene's failed resurrection was lost on Eva. In her odd suggestion that Barney was "surely imaginative enough to see" the effect the song might have on Courtlandt, Eva recognized the seductive power of musical drama. Sung well, a song of love in death might not resurrect its heroes, but it could reignite "Lust."

Eva's lust for singing "Liebestod" was complex, perhaps as rich as the German word "Lust," the semantic field of which extends from delight and joy to an inclination, wish, or desire to sexual pleasure and lust. It was equally a means to reignite Courtlandt's love, who, in his angry dismissal of Natalie, performed as a competitor for something more than sibling love, and to pursue her new lustful longing for Barney. Eva used song to give Barney pleasure too, balancing with music the pleasure Barney gave to her with verse. Both saw their erotic union as one combining song and verse, the two elements of Sappho's poetry. "I will write, you will sing, and better than all we will live,"[155] Barney wrote to Eva. For Barney in her moments of amorous rapture, Eva was not just a singer. Her life was itself a song: "I am so glad that I have never carved a statue or painted a picture or produced anything as beautiful as yourself. Life has been your art—you have set yourself to music, your days are your sonnets."[156] Eva kept raising her musical expectations to try to please Barney. At first it was enough for her to recite or sing choral passages from literature.[157] The next step was "to be an artist" by mastering the art of song: "Ah dearest I shall be happy if I can ever sing to you if I can ever give you the kind of spontaneous yet lasting delight that your lines give me, I would be an artist for you as well as a lover, a beloved, a friend I would lift that side of me up to the line of my capacity for loving you."[158]

Over time Eva's wish to reconcile with Courtlandt was overcome by her desire to lift Barney to new heights of lust through and for song. She wanted Barney to experience music's seductive power on the grander scale offered by choral music. In vocal ensembles, Eva sensed an "invisible force" capable of lifting "the masses." She described this feeling late in 1901 after a Christmas Oratorio Society concert she attended at Carnegie Hall, where her father's friend Andrew Carnegie had invited all the city's popular choruses to join in song.

I wish you were with me yesterday, to see how great and beautiful that invisible force is on the masses, the small pawns, which you despise. . . . The performance of the oratorio was magnificent, all the people received it with enthusiasm, and in the end everyone stood and sang the "Halleluia Chorus," a great choral piece by someone, Händel, I think. I assure you it was grand to hear all those people on stage, in the hall, and the orchestra and organ playing, and playing so well. It gave me a feeling I wanted to share with you.[159]

Despite her best efforts to sing operatic music, Eva was not able to achieve her intended effects. By March 1902, as she was preparing to sing "Liebestod" to reconcile with Courtlandt, she sensed that her hard, disciplined preparation contained the seeds of the death of Barney's love. As we have already seen, Barney drew a dividing line between the arts that she considered worthy of her efforts and those too "effeminate" and secondary to be given her attention. While Eva saw in music something "so beautiful, so disembodied and universal that [she felt] for it as the man did for his country who said he was sorry he only had one life to give for it,"[160] Barney appreciated music's effects—she was herself a student of the violin in her youth—but she denigrated Eva's formal studies, giving value instead to "inspiration independent of technique."[161] Sensing the "'jangled strain'" between her musical efforts and their reception, Eva quoted Victorian poet George Meredith's "The Promise in Disturbance" (1862) to articulate a "mess where fruitfulness was meant." The relationship of sister, brother, beloved, and music had become a tangled mess. Eva was especially sensitive to Barney's judgment: "before you I have failed and broken faith, and been in all ways a poor miserable thing."[162] Her lust for Barney won out over her "Lust" for Courtlandt and his music. She ended her voice lessons without singing for Courtlandt, choosing rather to become Barney's oft-chided lover and Courtlandt's out-of-favor sister, as she pressed on to realize her performance ambitions.

"MY ORCHARD IN MYTELLINI"

At several major turning points in her life, Eva staged a theatrical departure just as she was about to make a real departure, with these performances uncannily prefiguring major turns in her life. She performed her Sappho tableau, for example, at a point when she was leaving behind one lover, perhaps a man, in order to dedicate herself to Barney. Eva's recitation of lines from Sappho while dressed in a Greek tunic and fancy sandals provided the opening frame of that Sappho-inspired episode in Eva's life. It initiated an intense dialogue with Barney on the consequences of their Sapphic love. Sappho fragments—especially the latent potential of the poetry's gaps—were the point of necessary return. Because they were fragmentary, Sappho's words encouraged a creative life: one of filling in where Sappho's tongue broke off so as to shape a world worthy of their love. Then, on June 25, 1906, Eva was given the opportunity to enact the part of Timas, a character barely mentioned in Sappho's corpus but given a substantial role in Barney's revisionist *Equivoque* as the lover of Sappho who was slated to leave her to marry Phaon, the man named in Sappho's corpus as someone unresponsive to Sappho's love.

Leading up to the performance, the dialogue between Eva and Barney was breaking down. One long-standing difference lay in the values they assigned to different artistic media. Another was their sense of the audience for their message of "freedom": Barney aimed to address "the minority"—of lesbians and otherwise "worthy" creative people—while Eva wished to do something more freeing for the entire world. She wrote, "I turn to your letter and find, 'the never ending defect of the minority weighs on me at times with the tons of disappointed centuries.' On me too, . . . only I can see no outcome except freedom for all. I can't see how with all the best will, the world would ever find the minority who are worthy unless all be first set free. There is enough earth, and enough air and enough food and enough houseroom for all who live."[163] After separating from Barney, Eva would try to reach this larger audience beyond her community in Neuilly.

Their third disagreement, the one leading to their ultimate break, was about the workings of Sapphic Eros. How should they read Sappho's representation of amorous desire, particularly the insertion in her poetry situating a third party between lover and beloved? How much infidelity should they tolerate? Barney thrived on serial infidelity. Eva was polyamorous too, but worn down by the endless triangles. For six years, she and Barney had been pursuing numerous short- and longer-term relationships that crisscrossed their affair. Moreover, according to Eva, Barney was making ever more complex demands on her. Barney regularly wanted her to playact and dress up to make herself desirable to Barney's new love interests.[164] Then, cold, hard, and suspicious, Barney would turn on Eva and accuse her of letting her tears of jealous love "[fade] into joy for another."[165] Barney's tasks were "like the fantastic demand of a fairy tale: to love [her], and lose [her completely], and yet to hold to her."[166] Eva wished "more for [her] tenderness and friendship."[167] As a young woman who had lived her adolescence and young adult years with only the memory of her father and the reality of her mother's marriage to a new husband, Eva was unable to navigate the complexities of romantic attachments. She was near a breaking point, though she did not yet know it.

Equivoque is a play about equivocation in the reception of classical texts. It plays on equivocation in the pronouns and adjectives used to translate Sappho's loves. It is itself an act of classical reception: a reiteration of Sappho's suicidal leap from the promontory of Leukas, and the uncovering of a cover-up in the inherited story. According to the received legend, Sappho fell in love with Phaon, an old ferryman who was given the gift of godlike youth when he transported Aphrodite in human disguise. So passionate was Sappho's love for Phaon that, when she learned he was to give himself in marriage to another woman, she hurled herself in desperation from the White Rocks on Leukas, the island name for the whiteness of those rocks (Gr. λευκός, *leukos*, white). The tradition handed down from man to man through the centuries made the man Phaon the object of Sappho's pure, white, unrequited love and the cause of her suicide. *Equivoque* raised the possibility of other endings.

The play sought to revive the "lost fleshliness" of Lesbos's "celebrated amours," to bring up from her "blue bed in the Aegean" the dead figure of Sappho in order to recast her erotic disappointment.[168] It did so neither to repeat mindlessly Sappho's suicidal leap nor to erase a tradition that lived on so marvelously in the visual arts. Instead it interrogated the reception of the story. It brought into view its equivocation. It pointed to missing pieces. Sappho's corpus is full of holes, and the story of her life is the most riddled of all. Anyone who has given thought to the story of her suicide should have wondered: Why didn't the patriarchal legend give Phaon's bride a name? Why did it not mention her fate? And what were the relations of Sappho and this woman? Where did Phaon's bride fit into other legends of Sappho, for example, the one that had Sappho coordinating a close circle of female friends, or singing of love and marriage at her friends' weddings when she was not "irregularly" (ἄτακτος τὸν τρόπον) courting female lovers?

One reader has called *Equivoque* a "scholarly tour de force."[169] Its special qualities can be seen in the way it carefully interrogates Sappho's verses. While taking nothing away from the classical legend, Barney scoured the received corpus to uncover what might have happened to the other woman. We recall here how the letters of Natalie Clifford Barney and Eva found their literary footing, as it were, on the ellipses where

Sappho's tongue broke off. The broken state of Sappho's corpus opened up for them creative possibilities for revising received notions of the past. In *Equivoque*, Barney exhibited a special philological flair, for the play uses evidence in Sappho's corpus to revise the received legend of her suicide.

Specifically, *Equivoque* assigns the other woman in Phaon's life a name, "Timas," from an extant epigram "On Timas" in the *Palatine Anthology* (158D), which is ascribed to Sappho and included in the Sapphic corpus. We learn from the poem that Timas was a woman who "died and was received in the dark chamber of Persephone before she married." She was so grievously missed by "all her companions" that they used a knife to cut "off their lovely hair from their heads."[170] By introducing Timas as Phaon's missing lover, the play points to the vagueness of the received tradition. Taking up where the legend left off, or perhaps better, where men's imagination historically could not penetrate Sappho's world, *Equivoque* places Phaon's bride Timas among the loving female companions of Sappho in a grove such as the one Sappho might have enjoyed, at least as Sappho's circle appeared in modern paintings and drawings.

A photograph from June 25, 1906, the most frequently published image from the event, renders an idyllic moment in the performance (figure 1.6). The scene plays out in Barney's garden at 25 rue de Bois de Boulogne, Neuilly. A section of a semicircular Ionic colonnade peeks through the foliage. A fluted pedestal and some props are barely visible on the left side of the photograph. There are props behind the pedestal to the left, while one on the right bears a statue of Aphrodite. The setting is calm, luxurious, separated spatially and temporally from the nearby city by its surrounding wall and the classical architectural features.[171] It is a *locus amoenus* so commonplace in its Victorian representation of Sappho's community of women that it is almost a playful cliché. Indeed, little in Barney's and Eva's performances from this period cannot be read as a playful recasting of contemporary tastes.

In the foreground, two tiers of women fill the scene, each woman skillfully wrapped in layers of richly draped fabrics, with fancy sandals covering her feet and elaborate headbands crowning her head—all this evoking a classical Greek scene. Six women are dancing around a makeshift altar, their linked hands raised in energetic same-sex solidarity. It is hard to determine who the dancers are, or whether this is the marriage scene or the "dance of the sea and of death" at the end of the play.[172] For although *Equivoque* is a much-cited point of reference for twentieth-century cultural history, its performance is underdocumented. The performers are listed in the published play, but there is no caption for this photograph.

FIGURE 1.6. Performance scene from *Equivoque*, June 1906. Eva Palmer is not in this photograph. Acc. 96-153, Alice Pike Barney Papers, No. 6-193, SIA2017-061364. Smithsonian Institution Archives.

Attempts to identify the performers have mixed up all the players, and even the most careful research tends to come up short. Is that Penelope Sikelianos playing Greek music on the flute and Marguerite Moreno as Sappho on the lyre? Who is the performer and female character standing above them?[173]

A different photograph, heretofore unpublished, shows Eva as "Timas" kneeling on a round altar she helped design before the cult statue of Aphrodite (figure 1.7). It represents Sappho's rule over the group of young women just as the group is separating. Timas is breaking away in marriage, something Sappho's companions are celebrating with one of Sappho's wedding songs, while Sappho distances herself from the celebration. And this is where the play gives its new reading of Sappho's suicide from the Leukadian White Rocks: it presents Timas rather than Phaon as the object of Sappho's love. Sappho steps away out of desperation for her abandonment by Timas, not Phaon, and leaps from the White Rocks while threat-

FIGURE 1.7. Performance scene from *Equivoque* with Eva Palmer as Timas (second from left) kneeling before the cult statue of Aphrodite. Eva Sikelianou Papers, No. EP77. Center for Asia Minor Studies.

ening to haunt every aspect of Timas's married life: her bed, her husband's kisses, his embrace, the cries from her lips in the pleasure of the marriage bed.[174] Timas then acknowledges that her love for Sappho is stronger than her love for Phaon. She follows Sappho's suicidal path to the Leukadian promontory and leaps into the Ionian Sea's sensual waters. Sappho's companions have the last word, mourning the death of Sappho.

A few weeks after she performed the role of Timas, Eva took her first steps away from Barney and her female companions, in the direction of the White Rocks of Leukas. Eva had been deeply involved in preparations for the performance of *Equivoque*; Barney relied on her to stage the play, and perhaps even to pay for the costumes and props.[175] Eva selected Raymond Duncan, brother of Isadora Duncan, to choreograph the movements, and Penelope Sikelianos Duncan, Raymond's Greek wife, to play authentically Greek music. Although she knew Isadora, Eva was newly acquainted with Raymond and Penelope Duncan. When she first met them, Penelope was singing a Greek church hymn in a mode that greatly moved Eva.[176] Eva then "adopted" Raymond and Penelope,[177] inviting them to stay in her pavilion on rue de Longchamp in Neuilly when a labor strike crippled the center of Paris on May 1, 1906. That was less than two months before the performance of *Equivoque*. During their time together,

FIGURE 1.8. Eva Palmer in her Timas costume for *Equivoque*, leaning against a column in Barney's garden, June 1906. Acc. 96-153, Alice Pike Barney Papers, No. 6-194, SIA2018-072679. Smithsonian Institution Archives.

Eva started learning to weave. It is likely that the three worked together to create the Greek costumes for *Equivoque*. A photographic portrait shows Eva as "Timas," wrapped to look almost like the fluted Ionic column she leans against, wearing a garland of flowers that crowns her head like a column capital and fancy sandals (figure 1.8). The portrait suggests just how very implicated Eva's body, hair, garlands, dress, feet, pose, gesture, demure expression—indeed, everything about her—had become in the performance of Sappho.

Barney had no special affection for Raymond or Penelope Duncan. She was jealous of the attention Eva gave them, especially Eva's attraction to Penelope, who, as an unwealthy southern European married woman, commanded behavior that was "strictly proper"[178] and was not the type of person Barney cared for. Yet unexpectedly, the much younger Penelope was rivaling Barney for Eva's affections. After the *Equivoque* performance, Barney told Eva she was going to Bayreuth and would meet her in Orange "en route pour Mytilene, Athens, etc."[179] Barney suggested that Eva and the Duncans follow her to "[her] orchard in Mytellini" (*sic*), the place she had visited two years earlier with Renée Vivien.[180] She pressed Eva for an answer that was not forthcoming and expressed her annoyance ("Eva, Eva"!).[181] Once in Bayreuth, she complained that Eva misunderstood her opposition to her choices: "You have decided that because I am opposed to the *voie* [way] you have chosen I am unfriendly."[182]

Eva, however, was following another "way" in light of Barney's opposition—exactly as she did when Courtlandt opposed her. Her decision to travel with Penelope and Raymond to Athens in July 1906 rather than with Barney to Bayreuth and then Lesbos reflected a change in her. It was not that she no longer loved Barney. She confessed, "my own detestable brain . . . still beats beats against your past tenderness."[183] Yet whereas once she belonged to Barney completely—"past, present, and future of my body had been yours, and . . . my heart and brain ever since I loved you had been yours, all yours; but . . . now this simple thing is no longer so and . . . whatever we do, however we turn it, it never will be again"[184]— Eva decided she would no longer allow her love for Barney to control her. "If we were to happen now to be together at one of the moments when you are 'capable of being mine in all ways!' I should refuse it even-though I loved you as much or more."[185]

Certainly Eva's new way pushed against her overwhelming passion for Barney. But it also turned on the material nature of Greece suddenly spreading before her when she arrived there. Here was another way of going back with knowledge to the Greeks. Almost immediately after Eva reached Kopanos, the hillside spot on the western slope of Mount Hymettos where Isadora and Raymond Duncan and their siblings had started building a home in 1903 (they modeled it on the "palace of Agamemnon"), Penelope dug up some terracotta fragments. "One decorated with figures and complete though broken,—the other almost whole," as Eva reported the discovery to Barney. Penelope "insisted there [were] many others sticking out of the earth in her spot . . . We're getting tools this morning and going on a raid this afternoon. We expect to find an ancient city, or at least a tomb."[186] Eva once had written that Barney looked at her as if *she* were a "pile of ruins."[187] Now she encountered ruins of the Greek past everywhere in her surroundings, and she used them to shore up her broken self.

Her Greek vision, once completely enveloped in the fin de siècle readings of Sappho, opened to take in new vistas. Besides the antiquities, she saw in the landscape the promise of a simpler life: the "donkeys," "Mityo—a shepherd boy" (with a name echoing the first two syllables of Mitylene), the shepherd's "flute," "the sea," the shore of the Aegean. On the Aegean shore, Eva "gathered beautiful stones all washed smooth and very small by the sea, and beautiful colours" and fit "about three hundred of them . . . in a tiny box, a little ancient box." Of special interest to her was the Greek sky "when all the stars are there."[188] The stars in Greece outshone Sappho's fair silver moon, beloved to Barney, Vivien, and other decadent Sapphics precisely when it "hid the bright face of the stars."[189] Sappho's literary moon had become "too white, too bright, too unfortunate with memory" for Eva.[190] In contrast, sleeping under the stars "made [her] well again." The pile of ruins of her old self that used to be Barney's artistic playground now came together in her hands: "I have now fitted together my buried vase," she wrote, "and it pleases me as it used to,—more than it used to. I love to be alone."[191]

Eva's new way implicated living Greeks, too. Eerily, Penelope was from Leukas (Lefkas or Lefkada in modern Greek, meaning white), the island with the promontory of White Rocks from which Sappho made her legendary leap. In August, Penelope invited her brother Angelos to Kopanos to meet Eva. In December, she and Eva traveled to Leukas to visit with Angelos, their parents, and several other Sikelianos family members. That was half a year after Eva performed in Barney's revisionist dramatization of the Sappho legend, which ended with Timas making her way into the Ionian Sea near the Leukadian promontory in pursuit of the dead Sappho. One after another, Eva's Sapphic performances, first of the woman reading and of Sappho in the "charming tableau" in the summer of 1900, then of Timas in *Equivoque* in June 1906, framed the periods of her waxing and waning love for Barney and made Sappho's broken corpus the medium of her affective, artistic, and epistolary life.

Sometime after Eva arrived in Leukas, possibly in January 1907, Angelos suggested that they take a "week's trip to Sappho's promontory."[192] In *Upward Panic*, the book she wrote decades later about her life and ideas, Eva recalled their excursion to "the very high ledge of rock":

From passing steamboats I had seen it looking shiningly white in the sun, and hence the name Lefkas, but from above it looked brilliant pink; we leaned over, or rather Anghelos [sic] did, and I crawled to the edge to look down from a really immense height over a wall that one could not see, for it was so steep it jutted inwards. There was nothing but the water below, a quiet little bay with bright red fishes swimming about. It was from here that Sappho is said to have leaped to her death; and she certainly chose a sure place to die.[193]

This reiteration of Sappho's suicidal leap, a veiled recollection of *Equivoque*, marks Eva's memory of the very high ledge from which she did *not* fall. In her account of that life-changing trip to Leukas, Eva came close enough to Sappho's promontory's edge to observe the contrast of the island's lifeless whiteness from a distant view and its luscious fleshy colors seen up close: the "brilliant pink" of the ledge of rock and the "bright red fishes swimming about" in the water below. She stood on a spot where ancient legend and the white hews of Western classicism gave way to present life. Clearly recalling Timas's choice between marriage to Phaon and suicidal love for Sappho, *Upward Panic* thus represents the choice she made to redirect Sappho's rule onto a less self-destructive path. Whatever the truth of this recollection, her self-implicating readings in the circle of self-described Sapphics had prepared her to beware of suicidal heights as she turned her attention to Greece's living bodies.

CHAPTER 2

Weaving

How did Eva inhabit Greece, the space where Greek ideas informing her Sapphic performances rubbed against Greeks' enactments of their national identity? When she arrived in Greece that summer of 1906 with Raymond and Penelope Sikelianos Duncan, she wore a simple, hand-woven silk tunic over her bare legs and sandals. She was testing the theory, put into practice by the Duncans in 1903, that this mode of dress was perfectly adapted to life in Greece. The tunic she wore when she moved about the streets of Athens was a by-product of her costuming of Barney's *Equivoque*. As daily wear in Athens, however, it was at odds with the dress of urban Greek women, who wore the high-collared blouses, ankle-length skirts, and short boots that were the rage that year in Paris. A Greek man, Kostas Pasagiannis, used the strange epithet "ελληνοφορεμένη" (literally Greek-worn, or Greek-dressed) to describe Eva's foreignness to his brother Spelios. According to him, Eva was "κάποια ελληνοφορεμένη Αμερικανίδα"[1] (some Greek-dressed American woman), as distinct from the French-dressed Greek women he and his brother preferred.

Shortly thereafter, Eva abandoned Western dress altogether. From this point until her death, she moved among the fashion-conscious urban elites of Athens, Paris, and New York in handwoven Greek-styled dresses. Already before she came to Greece, while in the circle of Natalie Barney, Eva modeled her performances on ancient sources. Both on and off the stage, she imitated the poses and dress of Greek sculptures and Greek vase paintings in carefully circumscribed performances. In Greece, she brought ancient prototypes into her daily life. Oddly, she did not wear the Greek style as high fashion, in the way that Lillian Gish, for example, wore a Mariano Fortuny pleated silk Delphos gown in 1920,[2] or Jackie Onassis the Valentino-designed "seafoam green silk one-shoulder . . . Hellenic *himation*" in 1967.[3] For Eva in Greece, Greek-inspired clothing was not luxury fashion but part of her daily habit: a quotidian production that turned her body into a manifestation of Greek culture and its relevance in an increasingly industrialized world.

To explore her fascinating shift from one stage to another as she left behind the fashion-conscious performance world of her Sapphic circle to try out a new role in Greek society, I return to Paris to observe her first attempts at weaving fabric for the Greek costumes of *Equivoque*. I retrace her entry into Greece, paying close attention to multiple levels of change: her attachment to Penelope, courtship with Angelos, decision to abandon Western dress, creation of new materials and techniques for dressing herself, performance of the role of wife and mother, and the gradual widening of her frame of interest and testing of nationalist ideologies. Eva's way into Greece was definitely her own; at the same time, it is representative of the way that certain Western women of Eva's era and class broached Greece differently from men: from the margins of scholarly disciplines and through "webs of practices"[4] bound up with social life. By breathing life into ancient practices, gradually she found her voice to propose counter-cultural reforms placing Greek women at the center of Hellenism.

"ONE HANDWOVEN DRESS"

By early 1906, just when Natalie Barney invited Eva to help her stage *Equivoque*, Eva was growing weary of the love triangles, fancy clothes, and other indulgences that were becoming encumbrances in her life with Barney, her neighbor in Neuilly-sur-Seine. She felt as if she were trying to squeeze herself into an "ill-fitting," "high-heeled" pair of shoes, she later told Barney, which did not allow her the kind of freedom she required to shape herself.[5] Barney's demands had grown, even as her affection had diminished. For example, on Eva's transcontinental journey, returning from visiting her family in New York that January, she reportedly transported for Barney's garden a live alligator with "a bracelet inlaid with emeralds and rubies" attached to a chain.[6]

The turning point came in April, when Eva met Raymond and Penelope Duncan at a friend's house. Raymond was, in the words of Eva's sister, May, a "Greek vision . . . walking magnificently . . . [in] a daring mass of beautiful soft grey drapery and sandals that scarcely touched the earth."[7] And Eva later remembered how Penelope, "simply dressed in white," embodied for her "the features of Michelangelo's Delphic Sibyl."[8] Penelope especially drew her attention. It was as if she matched some unarticulated vision in Eva's dreams. A few weeks later, Eva conjured a reason to bring her closer: the huge general strike announced for May 1,[9] which she feared would erupt into street fighting in the center of Paris and threaten "this woman whom I had seen exactly once."[10] She invited Penelope, Raymond, and their infant son, Menalkas, to stay with her in Neuilly, a neighborhood outside the strike zone.

At the time, Eva was studying the sculpted look of "Greek clothes . . . on statues, bas-reliefs and vases" as inspiration for the costumes she was designing for *Equivoque*. Already Eva had fetishized the folds of Greek dress in ancient statues. The challenge was to recover the vanished classical spirit, to replicate the windswept folds of hard, sculpted marble in soft, airy fabrics. But she was frustrated by the "difficulty . . . in making any modern stuff look Greek in the wearing."[11] The Duncans shared her frustration. Together the three set out to solve that problem.

They were not the only ones fascinated with the pleated folds of Greek sculptures and paintings. For more than a century, the look of richly draped fabrics indexed as Greek had been a fashion interest of French and American women. According to Caroline Winterer, a historian of American women's classicism, already in the late 1700s, the rich column-like drapery of fabric in three-dimensional Greek art, engineered into high-waisted Grecian dresses with a low décolletage, defined a sartorial language of "cosmopolitan taste" with a "tasty" dash of "libertinism."[12] In Eva's day, an array of artistically and socially progressive women cultivated a Greek style as an alternative to street dress. Isadora Duncan sensationalized the style on the world stage. Her costumes were inspired by Tanagra figurines, the small terracotta pieces excavated in the 1870s from graves in the Boeotian town of Tanagra and displayed in major museums of Europe and the United States in the 1890s and collected by Isadora herself in her studio.[13] While her partially exposed body tested high society's tolerance of seminudity (it was "on the ragged edge of exposé," reported a family friend to Eva's mother),[14] Isadora's free-flowing folds made the classical look seem deliciously "modern."[15]

The fetishistic power of the Greek fold was not lost on fashion designers. At the very moment when Eva was discussing with Penelope and Raymond Duncan "the difficulty of making modern stuff look Greek," designer Mariano Fortuny Madrazo was on the verge of patenting a secret process that would permanently iron hundreds of narrow folds into silk velvet or charmeuse to give women the pleated look of a Greek-styled liberation.[16] Fortuny's "Delphos robe," first produced a year later in 1907 in imitation of a fluted column, used that process. It had more than twelve hundred pleats, reminiscent of the *chiton* on the bronze Charioteer of Delphi.[17] It was meant to be worn by women "without any corsetry and, ideally, with only the bare minimum of undergarments."[18] Instantly Fortuny's dresses and accessories became objects of desire for taste-setting women. Isadora Duncan was one of the first to wear them,[19] followed by dancer Ruth St. Denis, screen actor Lillian Gish, salonist Marchesa Luisa Casati, and Clarisse Coudert, the style-setting wife of Condé Nast. More than a hundred years later, Fortuny's Delphos gowns still retain both magical figure-hugging pleating and value as collectable items.[20]

The figure of the Greek-dressed woman also generated artistic images of liberation. Nineteenth-century art found excitement precisely in the tension between the flowing transparency of the well-pleated look and the hard surfaces that produced it. In ancient prototypes such as the Venus de Milo (raised from the waters of the Aegean Sea in 1820 and put on display in the Louvre a few years later) or the wingless Nike of Samothrace (a discovery of 1863 acquired by the Louvre in 1884), artists imagined that the body wrapped in well-pleated fabrics all but liberated itself from a block of stone. The sculpted folds had a latent potentiality, as if containing the memory of ancient movement and anticipating its return. In the seemingly free-flowing folds of classical sculptures, their modern eyes saw Greek bodies taking steps toward freedom, either as sensually or as politically liberated subjects.[21]

Eva was familiar with several nineteenth-century sculpted or painted figures in Greek-styled dress bearing the allegorical weight of liberty. An immense, Greek-robed lady with spectacularly indented bronze-cast folds, the Statue of Liberty, graced the harbor of her hometown; and when she attended the Chicago Columbian Exposition in 1893, she could not have missed seeing the sixty-five-foot-tall Statue of the Republic, another enormous neoclassical sculpture of woman symbolizing freedom—this one in gilded, pleated dress, recalling the lost cult statue of Athena in the Parthenon. In Paris, *La Liberté guidant le peuple*, a painting by Eugène Delacroix commemorating the July Revolution of 1830 in which Charles X fell, was prominent in one of the grand rooms of the Louvre Museum, which Eva frequented.

The painting featured Marianne, another well-pleated lady,[22] who leads the people of France forward to liberty over the bodies of those who have fallen. She is endowed with topical accessories of the July Revolution of 1830. Yet Greek elements are coded in her luminous whiteness, her classical profile, and her breasts bared by the loose dress in windblown free-fall—directly recalling the Venus de Milo in another room in the Louvre. Above all, the spiraling folds over Marianne's bare feet fill the painting with its rush of monarchy-toppling energy. *La Liberté* carries the message of liberty especially in its classicizing effects. Its revolutionary neoclassicism recalls the radically participatory political order of classical Athens, whose subjects poured their newfound freedom—verging on anarchism—into their seminude or nude creations. Marianne's neoclassical dress pushes against the carefully contained, tailored look of women's nineteenth-century fashions. It is airy; it is free; it is fallen. Like the dresses of Greek statuary, it "appears purely as a foil for nudity."[23] Marianne's body, hair, and feet are loosened almost to the point of being excessively exposed and charged with sensuality.[24] In her extreme freedom, she becomes a point of cathexis, attracting the gaze of the body politic as it experiences the shock of authority's loosened reins.[25]

The same sense of looseness was just as essential to Eva's project, as she sought to free modern materials of their undrapable stiffness. Since ready-made fabrics were too tightly woven, she and the Duncans decided to weave their own cloth in the style of the ancients, even though they had no experience with weaving. Raymond built a loom, drawing on his memory of looms in village homes he had encountered when living in Greece. They bought yards and yards of thread and spread it out in Eva's garden. "Rains came, cats and dogs also," Eva later recalled.[26] Barney's emerald-braceleted alligator probably ambled through it. The thread got tangled. They cut it shorter and wound it around the loom's beams. Penelope then recalled details of the loom's setup "in a peasant's house when she was a child."[27] She threaded the warp through "heddles and the reed" and got them started.[28] Together they made many trials to produce cloth with the kind of heavy draping they observed on Greek sculptures, eventually settling on a technique of throwing fine silk weft thread (the thread carried by the shuttle from selvage to selvage) across heavy white wool warp thread (the lengthwise thread stretched over the loom).[29] They wove enough fabric to make a wool and silk dress for Penelope, a linen tunic for Raymond, and a silk tunic for Eva.

This was the lightweight Greek dress Eva carried into Greece in the summer of 1906. Although burdened with a complex of ideas associating Greece with greater personal freedom, in physical terms Eva traveled light. She left behind all her French-designed clothes, bringing with her that "one handwoven dress" together with "a few straight dresses made with stuff from Liberty's or Vantine's, one or two from Barney's garden party."[30]

"BEAUTIFUL, STATUESQUE GIRL, HEROINE OF TWO SOCIAL CONTINENTS"

After she reached Athens, Eva took up residence in the goatherd's hamlet of Kopanos on the slope of Mount Hymettus opposite the Acropolis. The Duncans had laid the foundations of their "palace of Agamemnon"[31] there in 1903. Raymond, Isadora, and their mother and siblings had traveled to Greece as a family, wishing to be present in "holiest shrine of art."[32] Among other anachronisms, they replaced their "degenerate garments"—directoire dresses and knickerbockers—with "the tunic of the Ancient Greeks,"[33] following dress reform ideas that they were pursuing a more natural life by wearing things less binding to their bodies and nearer to the sensuality of the Greeks.[34] Isadora adopted the short diaphanous tunic or the longer crisscrossed toga and bare feet as her costume. This became her signature dance dress, the sign of the more natural, earth-bound, archaic movements she hoped to revitalize.[35] Raymond went more "completely Greek"[36] when he met and married Penelope Sikelianos, possibly in Leukas—the family's first stop in Greece—or in Athens, where Penelope's sister Eleni was staying.[37] Although no record of their first meeting is known to me, it is certain that she adopted *his* Greek habit after they met, for her dress was European in the town of Leukas where she grew up. Dressed in Greek tunics alongside her American husband, she registered in Greece not as a Greek but as an eccentric foreigner or as the wife of an eccentric foreigner; in Paris or the United States, she became a "native Grecian"[38] After Isadora left Greece, Penelope and Raymond stayed on to continue building the unfinished "palace of Agamemnon." Thus, they spent their first months of marriage in Kopanos until they ran out of money and Raymond took her to Paris to see if he could find work.[39] Now, three years later, they were hosting Eva Palmer in the still unfinished "palace," reciprocating hospitality they received from her in Neuilly and passing on to her some of their archaizing habits.[40]

Eva tried out her Greek dress in and about the Duncans' house. Soon she wandered in the countryside, testing various Greek poses (figure 2.1). Then in the company of the Duncans, she made her way downhill through the village of Pangrati into Athens to withdraw money from a bank. It was a bold move for Eva, a private, inward person who did not like to draw people's attention when she was offstage. Did she consider Greece an outdoor stage: a vast extension of Natalie Barney's garden in Neuilly with real classical artifacts and mistakenly costumed fellow actors? She drew a

FIGURE 2.1. Eva Palmer in Kopanos, posing in her handwoven dress, August 1906. In the background is the Duncans' "palace of Agamemnon" on the slope of Mount Hymettus. Eva Sikelianou Papers, No. EP80. Center for Asia Minor Studies.

crowd of gawkers as she passed through the streets, as captured in the Kodak No. 1 snapshot discussed earlier (see back to figure I.2).

Greek-styled dress, though fashionable for elite women to wear indoors, or for dress-up celebrations or the stage, was not conventionally worn outdoors in Greece or anywhere else. Catherine Abbe reminded her daughter of this in a stern letter she sent from Bar Harbor after she learned that Eva was walking about in public wearing a tunic and sandals. She challenged Eva's argument that her dress was artistic—an argument lost to us except in her mother's rephrasing:

> I fail to see what discarding worldly clothes has to do with life for art's sake. If you were making Greek clothes for Greek plays, and used them

for that purpose, or in the seclusion of your own home, I should think well of what you have done—but I do not like you to do things which make you conspicuous or to defy the conventionalities in the street. It seems to me that there is an element of selfishness in it that sooner or later is bound to react on you and on whatever you choose to do. I believe that you must be original and you have been, but why not try to reason with yourself that you are hurting others when you drive your eccentricities to extremity.[41]

Later in her life, Eva recalled straining to understand why her mother and other family members and friends took issue with her "eccentric" dress,[42] or why crowds in Athens made her conspicuous, when she felt a correspondence between her new outfit and "a simple and unaffected attitude toward life . . . free from strain."[43] At the time, though, even if freedom of self-expression might have been on her mind, her thoughts were not so lucidly rationalized, but an untidy mix. She was still brokenhearted from her affair with Barney. In her words, "I have no great heart to change my clothes, and no great funds to buy others and I love the south."[44]

People in Greece confused Eva with Isadora Duncan, whom they remembered walking through their streets as if she were an ancient Greek. Now another beautiful American was walking quite literally in Isadora's footsteps.[45] When they nicknamed her "Miss Duncan," there was quite possibly some genuine confusion. In large part, however, it was mischievous misrecognition. The attitude persists even today. In the past decade, I have heard several Greeks say that Eva Sikelianos dressed "à la Duncan,"[46] though her Greek dress evolved over her twenty-five-year stay in Greece into something more layered, complex, and ultimately more influential than Isadora's dance tunic.

When Penelope invited Eva to Greece, she sent word to Angelos to visit Kopanos. Many years later, Eva recalled the photogenic, Apollonian Angelos revealed to her in their first meeting.[47] At that later date, she made him the torchbearer of her "dreams and hopes and efforts, and [her] father's and [her] mother's hopes and dreams,"[48] ready to carry the light of her family's idealism to the twentieth-century archaeological site of Delphi, from their first moments together. Her earlier writing from their first meeting shows that she thought he had "une rayonnance, une transparence."[49] But he did not illuminate her path: he was a protean figure. In her eyes, he resembled first Percy Shelley ("qu'il ressemblait un peu à Shelley"),[50] then her Bar Harbor friend Weyman Cushman, then her brother Courtlandt— the latter because she knew that Angelos, like Courtlandt, was ready to deceive her ("il me trompera de la même façon).[51] Then she heard Natalie Barney in his every word.[52] If in *Upward Panic* Eva made out Angelos to be her eternal soul mate, her correspondence from 1906 to 1907 suggests that she had trouble imagining herself close to him; she wished to find new footing away from Barney;[53] and she wore her Greek tunics in defiance of friends, family, and even of Angelos, who did not especially like her dress.[54]

It is likely that Eva's growing attachment to the Duncans through their shared search for Greek forms of expression became a piece of a plan by Eva as well as Penelope to put distance between Eva and Barney. Eva, still in love with Barney, needed a diversion, possibly a permanent change, and Penelope offered her an entrée to a world outside Barney's realm of influence. For her part, Penelope, a free-spirited but protective personality, recognized that her talented but impractical youngest brother, Angelos, needed a source of income,[55] and she conceivably found a patron in Eva Palmer.[56] She encouraged Eva to redirect her affections to him in a time of weakness.

Barney suspected that the Duncans were manipulating Eva.[57] From half a continent away, she began sending scornful missives criticizing Eva as soon as the report reached her that Eva's dress had mixed her up with Isadora. Her words infantilize Eva, as if Eva were exhibiting a childish rebellion against her, and suggest also Barney's high level of anxiety, perhaps because she feared she was losing Eva: "What you are doing is both sterile and valueless—If it amuses you to 'rough it' as one might in Bar Harbour [*sic*] from a love of freeness . . . and pure air while mountain walking all very well, but as a continuous performance of defiance to the passer by I think you worthy of better things."[58] I will return several times to the remarkable phrase, "performance of defiance." A shift in metaphor follows, and Barney identifies Penelope, Raymond—and Angelos—with the web-weaving spider, master of the most cunning of hunting techniques, and warns Eva to beware: "You are—or were—complete. Don't let the Duncan fad ruin you, nor the brother of Penelope . . . ! Like the spider let us weave our own ruts, but not fall into those of others."[59]

Eva gradually moved into the Sikelianos family's realm. She traveled with Penelope to Leukas in December 1906 and was introduced to the parents. She visited the surrounding villages, where women invited her to weave. She ordered a loom of homegrown walnut. Outside the door of the Sikelianos family home, she modeled a new handwoven piece that she added to her still very small wardrobe (figure 2.2).

Angelos was in Leukas, too, and he took Eva around the island before he left for a short trip to Paris, Rome, and Egypt. They probably visited

FIGURE 2.2. Eva Palmer (first standing figure at left), in a columnular Greek-styled tunic, before a house in the town of Leukas, ca. 1907. Acc. 189, Eva Sikelianou Papers, No. 323. Benaki Museum Historical Archives.

Sappho's promontory that January 1907.[60] After his return from Egypt that June, he and Eva secluded themselves in the family's beachside hut on the islet of Agios Nikolaos. Then they journeyed to Delphi, Olympia, Mycenae, Epidaurus, Sparta, and Mystra. They were seen in various places alone together. People spoke of a growing "ἔρωτα" (love)—a word Eva understood from reading Sappho's fragments. Observers speculated. Was there an engagement? An approaching marriage?

Angelos, at twenty-one, was no guileless youth. Already he had a reputation for ruining young Greek women. Falitsa Pasagianni, sister of Kostas and Spelios Pasagiannis, had spent time alone with Angelos in Leukas in 1903, and she traveled with him and her two brothers to Mount Taigetos in 1905.[61] She was in love with Angelos and full of hope that they would marry. For the stretch of the thirty-some years when Eva was married to Angelos, exceptional young women were forever falling at his feet, desperate to make him exclusively theirs. Nausika Palama, daughter of Kostis Palamas, the national poet, entered into a relationship with Angelos in 1915 that lasted at least a decade.[62] Kalypso Katsimbali, sister of George

Katsimbalis, Henry Miller's "colossus of Maroussi," pursued Angelos in vain from 1918 until March 13, 1920, then threw herself to her death from the balcony of a Paris apartment where her family had sequestered her.[63]

Like Natalie Clifford Barney—and like the polyamorous Eva Palmer, to a degree—Angelos loved many women and was faithful to none. By late spring of 1907, when it was suspected that Sikelianos might marry Eva Palmer and fellow poets in Athens were marveling at his good fortune, Kostas Pasagiannis, Falitsa's brother, expressed relief. He was the man who identified Eva as "Greek-dressed." There was more, for Kostas's brother Spelios was married to Angelos's sister Eleni, but she had just left him to move to Paris. So Kostas poured his disdain for the Sikelianos family into his letter to Spelios: better that the "εϱίφης" (cunning) Sikelianos should marry "κάποια ελληνοφοϱέμενη Αμεϱικανίδα ή Βϱετανίδα" (some Greek-dressed American or British woman) than "ruin our sister Falitsa's life."[64]

In this Greek social circle, the free-flowing folds of Eva's dress took on a new significance. She was an American—or was she British? Certainly she was not Greek. In any case, she was a foreign woman dressed like an ancient Greek, so probably she was liberated in her lifestyle—or loose enough, anyway, to tolerate Angelos's infidelities. And if she suffered from Angelos's philandering ways, it did not matter. She was no man's sister in Greece.

While Eva did not actively resist being drawn into the Duncan-Sikelianos web, following two events, she threw herself in all the way. During the summer of 1907, she traveled with the Duncans and Angelos back to Neuilly to see if they and Barney might all be friends.[65] Barney had made it clear she did not like Eva's style of dress, as she thought it to have nothing "in common with real freedom," which was for Barney "a mental attribute" not expressed through "independence of costume or change of circumstances."[66] To avoid clashing with Barney, Eva put on "proper clothes" upon arrival.[67] But Barney, keen on drama, changed the subject. She had been dismissive of the "ridiculously affected"[68] Angelos when he introduced himself to her while passing through Paris a few months earlier. Now she was much more openly hostile. Intending to hurt him, she revealed to him a letter in which Eva declared undying, passionate love for *her*. Then, to win Eva back after her indiscretion, she sent "beautiful flowers."[69]

Eva knew she was caught between "warring" factions, as she called them.[70] On one side was Barney, driving a wedge between her and Angelos. On the other was Angelos, in a frightful condition of "despair" because he was convinced of Eva's undying love for Barney.[71] We learn from Eva's friend Virginia Yardley, who traveled from the United States to visit Eva when she first arrived in Greece and witnessed Angelos's fainting episodes there, that "he has a way of going suddenly more white than the dead, & of coming to the very point of death, without any evidence of illness or unsoundness. Eva told me she thought she would never get him away from Paris alive."[72] For a few hours Eva "lived in an atmosphere of tragedy and suicide."[73] She consoled Angelos by telling him that Barney had lied about their love: she was jealous because Eva loved *him* more than she loved her.[74] Barney's "unkindness and discourtesy,"[75] rubbing finally against Eva's refined gentility and her feeling that Angelos's life was "worth saving,"[76] helped her to make her choice. She set sail for America on August 25, 1907, intent on "taking Angelo[77] to Brook End . . . perhaps [to] be married there."[78] Dressed again in her attire of sandaled feet and a loose, handwoven tunic over her uncorseted body, a cover for her "unbearable . . . misery,"[79] her Greek-clad presence, "startling in a breeze, . . . add[ed] to the gaiety of the voyage [for the other passengers] of the oceanliner La Loraine."[80]

Their disembarking six days later in New York Harbor was so dramatic that it made front-page headlines in both the *Washington Post* and *New York Times*. Many newspapers across the country picked up the story. They called Angelos an "ancient philosopher,"[81] though he cut a contemporary figure with his dark eyes, Roman-styled hair, and European dress (figure 2.3). But the onetime debutante Eva Palmer, Greek-dressed in the shadow of America's Greek-attired Statue of Liberty, "attracted more attention . . . because of her classic costume." Wearing just "sandals fastened on long bands of loose leather, and . . . [a] flowing gown of light material draped artistically, a three-quarter cape of the same material, and a Grecian,"[82] or, more precisely "Phrygian hat,"[83] she represented more liberty than Americans would tolerate.

Eva's defiance of conventions upon her arrival in New York meant that she exposed herself in an unprotected public space where people talked.[84] Eccentric innovations in dress became gossip as much as the "celebrated beauty" of Eva Palmer, and "gasps" were in order when the two collided.[85] As newspapers across the country ran the story, they exaggerated accounts of the "beautiful, statuesque girl, heroine of two social continents" who made her way from New York Harbor to the Buckingham Hotel at Fiftieth Street and Fifth Avenue.[86] The more newspapers wrote, the more scandalous Eva's appearance became. Now she "appeared cool and comfortable."[87] Now she was creating a "sensation" on Fifth Avenue, "trip-

FIGURE 2.3. Angelos Sikelianos, ca. 1907, at the time of his marriage, when he was twenty-three years old. Acc. 189, Eva Sikelianou Papers, No. 222. Benaki Museum Historical Archives.

ping up the awe-struck thoroughfare in undeniably bare ankles with only a Roman toga for a dress, no hat on her head, and arms bare to the loosely-draped shoulders"[88] Now she was advocating for a cult and for the "abolition of lingerie of all kinds."[89] From story to story, her attire became freer, the wind that blew her dress more provocatively squally, her undergarments from immodest to nonexistent, her nether limbs more exposed, and her attitude irreverent to the point of provocative, proving she was "rich enough to do as she likes."[90] In a Chicago newspaper, the photograph with her name printed beneath it bore no resemblance to her person (figure 2.4).[91]

So onerous was the press coverage of Eva's Greek dress that she briefly sought cover in a more secure outfit. To protect her family from the social weight of her too-loose garment, she put on a long-sleeved shirt and skirt as her traveling attire for her flight to Bar Harbor. Then, arriving at her

FIGURE 2.4. Two photos of a woman misidentified as "Miss Eva Palmer" in a fashionable costume and in "The Greek Costume." "Devotee of One-Garment Costume Who Startled Passengers on Ocean Liner," *Chicago Daily Tribune*, September 2, 1907, 5. Public domain.

destination, she changed her dress again for the "most unexpected and unannounced wedding at Bar Harbor," a private event generating widely divergent newspaper stories.[92] By one account, the service was conducted in French, the language Eva used with Angelos, in an Episcopalian ceremony, with Eva dressed in the "classic garb of tunic and sandals" that she had she adopted "some time ago."[93] Another newspaper reported that the "bridegroom . . . appeared in native costume," whereas "the bride . . . an American girl . . . wore a classic Greek tunic of purple and white and jeweled sandals beneath bare feet, while her hair, which reaches to the floor, was loosely braided and crowned with a Greek fillet."[94] By a third account, Eva took her vows "in Greek" wearing "an Eastern costume, consisting of a pale yellow tunic over a long gown of white, and . . . a wreath of chrysanthemums on her head. The bridegroom . . . showed the same disregard of Western attire as did the bride."[95] What the bride and groom actually wore and how they took their vows is lost in the cacophony of voices weighing in on Eva's too-liberated habits. Her march to free modern fabrics from undrapable stiffness now made her less a symbol of liberty than that of social anarchy.

Instead of stepping back to somehow extricate herself from the web she had a hand in weaving, Barney's hostility toward Angelos and the public's inability to accept Eva's loose attire pushed Eva to leave behind her previous life. She cut her American ties altogether, moving to Greece permanently, now as Kyria Sikelianou, Angelos Sikelianos's wealthy foreign wife, in love with "his country, his people, his language, and most of all his dreams."[96] She did not cross the Atlantic again for another twenty years, and she did not revisit Western dress. Only once, when she met her ailing mother at the therapeutic baths of Aix-de-bains, did she compromise, for her mother's sake.[97] On that occasion, her mother "begged [her] to bring along some ordinary clothes."[98] So as not to cause her mother further grief, she "bought a whole wardrobe" of "gowns for morning, afternoon and evening; hats, gloves, stockings, shoes and slippers in the latest fashion, coats, negligees, everything."[99] After they parted, probably for the last time,[100] as she boarded a train, she piled everything into a railroad sheet and threw the bundle out the train window. From that point on, she abandoned machine-made Western clothes forever. For nearly half a century until the end of her life, she wore clothing inspired by ancient Greek prototypes, products of her own hands and her idiosyncratic sense of what it meant to "go native"[101] in a country where only ancient statues appeared in Greek tunics.

THE "ANADROMIC METHOD" AND
EXPERIMENTAL REPLICATION

How exactly Eva should fashion herself for her new Greek life was the pressing question. By fashion, I mean both how she should dress and how she should govern herself to appear socially distinctive and identifiable as Greek: how she should walk talk, go about her day, and present her identity from within Greek culture, not superficially but in an integral way.[102] In practice she fell into many comfortable interactions that did not require high degrees of self-awareness for her to be present in Greek society. She wrote of one pleasurable day to Natalie Barney in her last extant love letter, dated "New Year's [1909]."

> This morning I read and worked a little, this afternoon I went to the olive grove with Sassa, a child staying in the house, a little twelve year old cousin who is amusing and intelligent and has most beautiful eyes. We ran and played together, I taught her to climb trees and dragged her into enormous caves under the mountain where she was afraid of finding robbers; and she always unconsciously teaches me Greek as she fortunately knows nothing else, and so great is my delight at having to talk that I find myself positively gabbling.[103]

In principle, however, her Greek self-fashioning was no simple matter. In this Mediterranean contact zone, most foreign visitors looked to Greece with antiquarian interests. They sought signs of a Greek life in the remains of the ancient past. To the degree that becoming Greek mattered to them at all, this required their active engagement with classical sites and literature. Living Greeks were engaged in a parallel search for ancient survivals in the wider gamut of their national culture. Most foreigners worked at ignoring the natives' parallel pursuits. To the degree that they observed modern Greeks at all, they saw them as a kind of "riddle":[104] if the Greek is an ideal exemplifying a bygone era, under what conditions could present life in Greece be Greek. What might the modern Greek look like?

It was into this tangle of questions that Eva Sikelianos entered as soon as she chose to "go Greek" in Greece. Her manner of dress—at first a costuming experiment for Barney's *Equivoque*, then a short pleated woven dress symbolizing her defiance of Barney's efforts to control her—now expressed her stance as the American wife of a living Greek poet. How she created new materials and fashioned herself became a careful balancing act between her long-standing antiquarian interests and growing personal investment in contemporary Greek society.

According to *Upward Panic*, Eva was ambivalent toward the disciplined, professional, archaeological recovery of ancient Greek materials. She read official reports, visited sites and museums, and attended to new discoveries. She happily received confirmation from archaeologists for her work in replicating ancient Greek weaving. She was especially proud when in the late 1930s she heard from her friend Joan Vanderpool that the director of the American School for Classical Studies in Athens had announced evidence proving "the theory of Eva Sikelianou" on the techniques of ancient weaving. She quoted Vanderpool's letter in *Upward Panic*: "It clearly showed the pattern of the weave: a heavy warp, and an almost imperceptible weft. . . . It not only proved your theory, as shown in the weaving of the Delphic Festival, but it showed that . . . this method was used for the same reason: to produce the richness of folds seen through Greek and pre-Greek vase painting."[105]

Yet Eva disclaimed archaeological expertise. She pretended to "know nothing about archaeology,"[106] or at least to forget everything she had read. Her work was "bristling with archaeological mistakes."[107] Nor was she was aiming to be "strictly correct."[108] Indeed, her work is full of anachronisms. For instance, willful violations of chronology permeate the costumes she designed and wove for her production of Aeschylus's *Prometheus Bound* for the Delphic Festival of 1927. Her description of the creative process, particularly her explanation for dressing the chorus of Oceanides and Oceanus in silk (when she knew the ancient Greeks did not have silk), is of special interest. Eva used silk for the elaborate dresses of the supernatural beings, who were "removed from human suffering,"[109] as distinct from the play's suffering mortals, Prometheus and Io, whom she dressed in coarser materials. This contrast also served to highlight the silk costumes of the chorus: Eva imagined the powerful effect on an audience if the costumes of the entire chorus "would look like the folds on a Greek bass relief" when they danced.[110] Adding to the effect of classical folds were elaborate border tapestries she wove, replicas of fish, octopus, sea flowers, seabirds, and coral figures on Mycenaean and Minoan vase paintings. The very un-fifth-century costuming of the Aeschylean chorus in amply draped silk decorated with Bronze Age designs of fish and mollusks did not trouble her in the least. "I knew that the ancient Greeks were supposed not to have silk, but I did not really care," she wrote. "I was not trying to be strictly correct, and I felt that if Aeschylus did not have silk he would have liked to have it for this particular play."[111] Eva embraced the creative freedom to ignore historical periodization and reenter the classical mode armed with an enhanced arsenal of contemporary tools.

This was not a chance development; it happened quite deliberately through her careful thinking about the course that ancient processes such as weaving had followed in their journey through time. She wondered how she might remount that course to recover lost time.

Αναδρομή (*anadrome*, ancient Greek for "running upstream") is a word capturing the effort of running against time's inexorable current. As a common word and as a technical psychoanalytic term in modern Greek, *anadrome* represents the work of dredging up memories of life erased by the passage of time. It is a backward-moving recovery of life, or, conversely, a forward-moving turn to the past. Eva never commented on the term's psychoanalytic meaning. But she did use the term to characterize Jean-François Champollion's method of recovering the lost language represented by ancient Egyptian hieroglyphs on the Rosetta stone through his comparative study of ancient ruins and modern Coptic. She called his work "anadromic," because its "going backward or remounting the current"[112] pivoted on "the rich traditions of a spoken language."[113]

In English, an anadrome is a word that forms a different word when spelled backward. The letters are all in the same place, but they express something different when read from the end back to the beginning than from the beginning to the end. Eva sensed that a thing's "com[ing] down to us from antiquity" is likewise different from the process of its recovery.[114] In the case of the "lost" arts—that is, the arts that decay immediately, such as song, dance, and other kinds of performance, or rapidly, such as clothing and costumes made from soft materials—their "coming down" has occurred over time through successive reperformances or the repetition of an ever-transforming process. Greek Orthodox Christian chant, for example, gives a new voice each time to ancient Greek words, which grow older even as they remain in use. Weaving uses new threads on old instruments to produce a fresh piece of cloth for a changing world. In other words, the current of a thing's "coming down" follows a journey forward through passing time.

For Eva, "remounting the current" meant tracing old forms in current methods and following their traces backward by comparing present- and latter-day practices with ancient sources. And while the mounting of current processes and materials might throw some light on a lost ancient art such as weaving—it might recover an analogous form, or even an "analogous emotion"—Eva argued that "we shall not be able to reconstruct a lost art in an archaeological manner."[115] By chronological necessity, Eva insisted, whatever is produced today "expresses another context" from what something similar might have expressed before.[116] The recovery of the past is grounded in present desires or needs, including the need to re-vitalize traditions. It is always, already, anachronistic.

Supporting her anachronistic approach was Nietzsche's enormously influential philosophy of untimely meditations criticizing the excessive historicizing of his era, calling on his contemporaries instead to act "coun-ter to our time by acting on our time and, let us hope, for the benefit of our time."[117] And alongside Nietzsche, we hear Wagner's booming voice insisting that the "German spirit" would achieve an "inmost understand-ing of the Antique . . . restoring the Purely Human to pristine freedom" not when it employed "the antique forms to display a given 'stuff'" but when it molded "the necessary new form itself through an employment of the antique concept of the world."[118]

As inspiration for her art, Eva collected what she called "συντρίμματα" (*syntrimmata*, broken things, literally "things rubbed together"). *Syntrim-mata* was the word she used to refer to fragments of various kinds, from pottery sherds to shreds of musical phrases or gestures or dance steps "showing the dynamism of Greek tradition."[119] She found these in the Greek countryside or in museums and ancient sites. As she studied these remains—including ancient drawings of human forms, gestures, looks, and dress—she "imagined how the cloth illustrated by a sculpture or vase might sit on the loom."[120] Inspired by such acts of the imagination (they were imaginative because they came from her experience of making cloth rather than from careful historical study of the era of their invention), Eva worked out a plan to replicate the ancient garments. To execute her plan, to make new Greek clothes as beautiful as the old, she put into practice techniques that she learned by living beside Greek women. She used *their* materials, vegetable dyes, spinning and dyeing techniques, and horizontal loom (figure 2.5), rather than the warp-weighted vertical loom seen in ancient art, as a way of recovering ancient art.

Yet Eva's persistent attention to ruins is a reminder that she was not entirely disconnected from the work of archaeologists, no matter how much she protested that their activities were distinct from hers because "they distinguish[ed] science from the revolutionary passion of the heart," whereas she gave priority "to life."[121] Archaeologists use many methods to recover and analyze material data. In Eva's day, they were systematizing the work of excavating sections of the earth in strata and restoring arti-facts representative of more than one era to produce the feeling of a linger-

FIGURE 2.5. Horizontal loom of Eva Palmer Sikelianos. Photo by Artemis Leontis, courtesy of the Angelos and Eva Sikelianos Museum of Delphic Festivals, Delphi.

ing lost world. Excavation, stratification, documentation, restoration, and the presentation of artifacts were their most evident activities. While practically all the prominent archaeologists working in the field in eastern Mediterranean and Middle Eastern sites in the early twentieth century were European or American men, behind the scenes, in excavation headquarters and tents or village homes, a growing number of women were laboring. Some were trained to reconstruct and interpret past remains; others had come along for the ride and were learning the work on the spot. Few were institutionally funded. They found their way into digs either independently or as the wives or daughters of diplomats, scholars, archaeologists, or collectors, or as self-funded archaeologists. They worked in the field gathering minute data—for example, plant life. They sat in headquarters documenting shards of clay. They developed connections with local inhabitants and used diplomatic skills to draw out information from them. Or they made ethnographic observations of their household labor as a basis for historical comparison with past life. Some women operated on several fronts, developing multifaceted methodologies to support the experimental replication of ancient processes. For decades, in some cases more than a century, their activities were nearly invisible.[122]

Weaving was a process that attracted the attention of some women in the field, who had greater access than their male colleagues to relatively private women's quarters in village homes and learned to care about weaving as part of the fabric of human labor. Grace Mary Hood Crowfoot (1877–1957), for instance, a near contemporary of Eva and another unconventional dresser, came to Egypt as the wife of a classicist-diplomat. "Bored with the restrictions of life in Cairo," she took to photographing "men and women at work spinning, weaving and pottery-making" in the surrounding villages.[123] She then became "proficient . . . herself on present-day looms of the region."[124] While practicing weaving, she compared the activity as she came to know it to "paintings and models of weaving from Pharaonic tombs." Working experientially through ethnographic and archaeological evidence, she wrote speculative articles approximating the ancient technique of tablet weaving. Later archaeological discoveries "confirmed the correctness" of her reproduction.[125]

Crowfoot's weaving is representative of what is known today as experimental replication: the excavation not of things but of processes, which approximates the steps of a lost procedure.[126] This kind of work began happening early in the history of the discipline, but as "an eccentric sideline to the real study of archaeology."[127] It was "eccentric" not only because it was "not seen as an integral and necessary extension of archaeological research."[128] "Eccentric" women such as Crowfoot and Eva Palmer Sikelianos pursued it while occupying a space outside professional expertise. To be sure, Crowfoot and Eva differed in important ways. Crowfoot was working experimentally to approximate ancient techniques with confidence in the power of the archaeological record. Experimentation for her meant repetition of the same process toward an end of recovering the ancient art correctly. Eva's experiments changed each time to create a new design, and her goal was to produce new materials for present-day living. Yet the experimental work of both women drew on evidence comparing ancient source materials with living contemporary practices. And they and other women gained access to this kind of evidence because it lay outside the domain of archaeological excavation where men were dominant and in charge.[129]

The work of these women in the peripheries of archaeology follows a pattern of inquiry similar to what Bonnie Smith categorizes in historical study as "high amateurism." Smith's analysis relates specifically to women's nineteenth-century historical research. Yet the elements she finds common to that work are not far off the mark in characterizing Eva's experimental replications. According to Smith, female historians exhibited a keen interest in the details of the space of the past ("fabric, drapery, gardens, and works of art");[130] they attended to familial and social (over obviously political) arenas; and, most relevant to Eva's work, they "confronted the gulf between the living and the dead."[131]

Eva owed more than one debt when she embraced a creative, living spirit over "strictly correct" reconstructions of the Greek past—a spirit she insisted was more authentically Greek than rigid historicism (Aeschylus "would have liked" her anachronistic silk creations).[132] Surely she was building on the work of not just "eccentric" archaeologists but also the anthropologically oriented Cambridge University professor of Classics Jane Harrison. Harrison's interest in an archaic "web of practices emphasizing particular parts of life"[133] in which women were masters found uncannily literal fulfillment in Eva's designs. In particular, her work challenging exclusive, masculine, rationalist elements of classical culture[134] aligned in tangible ways with Eva's. Although it served the scholarly end of identifying elements of maiden-mother goddess worship at the origins of Greek rituals, the attention she gave to women's practices against male-centered abstractions of the classical era moved beyond scholarship. Her recovery of archaic practices with women as their agents was a utopian gesture. It imagined a future perfected on the basis of research that suggested a glimpse at matrilineal societies buried deep in the indefinite past. Although Eva never acknowledged a debt to Harrison, the professor's work was clearly in her line of vision when Eva identified archaic patterns in spinning and weaving activities in the present day.

Through her earlier Sapphic performances, Eva had learned to interweave lost archaic words with desires that had not yet found ground for expression. Before Greece, she operated in a "queer temporality," as discussed in chapter 1, which united the temporally disjointed "no longer" with anticipation of the "not yet present."[135] She placed herself in the threadbare remains of Sappho's poetry to perform a new kind of female desire and identity. Sappho's words were the fibers of her affective life, and Eva and her group of self-implicated readers shuttled themselves through those words to fashion new structures of belonging. Eva did not leave the lessons of her community of "Sapho 1900" entirely behind when she ran away from Paris. Her move to Greece, marriage to Sikelianos, and abandonment of Western dress all did deliberately express her break with Barney. Yet I see shades of her earlier Sapphic performances as I picture her picking through syntrimmata in Greece to find inspiration for her next day's dress. Now, however, she actually spun antiquity's lost threads. Experimental replication replaced self-implicated readings. The patient art of weaving softened the blows of Eros's arrows. Instead of being stuck in the web, Eva was now the one spinning it. Thus she found a way to strike a new pose for her Greek life.

"MY HAPPINESS HANGS ON A THREAD"

The idea that the loom might become an instrument for Greece's emancipation from dependence on Western markets did not come to Eva immediately after she married Angelos Sikelianos. For about a decade she wove cloth on her walnut loom to realize a personal, artistic goal of creativity and human freedom.[136]

To be sure, making cloth was a collective activity connecting her with the lives of rural Greek women. She found joy in those social relationships. There was a meaningful sociability to the event: "Spinning with a distaff is a most sociable occupation, especially when old women gather round their neighbor's fire-place to sit spinning and gossiping at the same time. . . . There is also the setting up of the warp which requires neighborly good will, for this is usually done in the village street, several women working together, and helping each other by turns: mine today, for instance, and some other day, Maria's or Ioanna's, when each one happens to have finished her spinning," she later recalled.[137] The spinning and weaving connected generations of village women, too, from daughter to mother to grandmother, reaching back many generations, many centuries. And as much as the thread of connection to antiquity mattered to Eva, increasingly what absorbed her was the notion of a "Greek tradition" found not in the "slavish copying of columns and statues and what-not which can never give any better result than the Romans and the French have reached—but a knowledge of the nobleness of the Greek spirit which one finds and understands better by living in the mountain village than by visiting an ancient temple."[138]

"Freedom and beauty" inhered for her especially in the ways she crafted materials to fashion herself. She filled her trunks with one-of-a-kind pieces of cloth. Every piece was of unfading, hand-dyed colors—shades of yellow, green, brown, red, gray, and blue—extracted from onion skins, beets, mussel shells, flowers, and weeds. She reveled in those natural dyes: the rituals of making them, their distance from the artificiality of the factories that

FIGURE 2.6. Eva Palmer Sikelianos in a simple, belted tunic dyeing threads in a vat under a roofed, pillared open gallery in the Greek countryside. Large skeins of yarn are hung to dry. Acc. 189, Eva Sikelianou Papers, No. 648. Benaki Museum Historical Archives.

she deplored (figure 2.6).[139] The uniqueness of the woven pieces also mattered: each piece differed from all the others in its width, length, weight, colors, textures, designs, border decorations, and the weight and composition of its threads. Because every piece remained uncut, Eva could restyle it freely for each new occasion. New creations added to the endless variety of her daily wear.

What she wore depended on the season, the place, and the purpose of the day. Her dress was generally modest. Not only had she left behind her Victorian crinolines and lace; she did not even replicate the more luxurious ancient *peplos*, the unsewn rectangle pinned at the shoulders and heavily draped to give the sculpted figures of ancient women their sumptuous look. On a warm workday when she was dyeing threads in the countryside or setting up the warp of her loom with other women, she wore a simple knee-length tunic. Designed after the ancient *chiton*, it was a tube made of two uncut rectangles of cloth stitched along the shoulders and sides and cinched with a belt at the waist. If the day was cool, she gathered her braided hair under a hat or in a scarf-like rectangle wrapped as a turban or bandana. She covered herself with an overlaying himation, a rectangle of heavier fibers worn as a cape or shawl. This was her travel dress when she walked from her house on Serifou Street in the northwest suburb of Patissia to the center of Athens or visited ancient sites (figure 2.7).

FIGURE 2.7. Eva Palmer among ruins at an unidentified site, ca. 1910. Acc. 189, Eva Sikelianou Papers, No. 485. Benaki Museum Historical Archives.

On a day of visits or public activities, she dressed in fancier tunics, brilliantly woven with embroidered designs punctuating the deep folds of the cloth's drapery. Posed photographs—for example, the one taken on the north porch of the Erechtheion (figure 2.8)—show how consciously her woven dresses interacted with Greek archaeological settings. Eva's Greek look extends from head to toe: from her "glorious bronze hair . . . wound over her brow like a coronet"[140] to her cinched waist to the position of her feet and hands. The dress's pleating imitates the rhythm of the Erechtheion's fluted columns. The folds and precise placement of Eva's limbs relate her to the sculpted figures of the Caryatids on the Erechtheion's iconic southern porch. The photograph captures on its surface the dress's deep linear folds and two-toned geometrical designs, replicating the look of folds and geometric patterns on a fifth-century red-figured Attic vase. It imitates the representational codes of a vase painting and the temple. It bridges the modern and the ancient.

Eva simultaneously became the Greek-dressed muse of Angelos's poetic calling, the guardian of his "purity," in the words of Eva's friend Virginia Yardley.[141] She looked after his publications. She funded his activities. She set up houses for him. And whenever Angelos traveled to solitary retreats to attend to his "truly vast reading"[142] or "read his poems to circles of

FIGURE 2.8. Eva Palmer in a beautifully embroidered dress on the north porch of the Erechtheion sometime between 1910 and 1920. Acc. 189, Eva Sikelianou Papers, No. 228. Benaki Museum Historical Archives.

adoring young ladies, who admire[d] him extravagantly and stroke[d] his long hair,"[143] Eva patiently wove. As with Barney, so now in her relationship with Angelos, she showed herself to be stubbornly devoted, almost grievously so. The contrast between her nonconformist Greek classical look and Angelos's ostentatious "Pythian Apollo pose"[144] enhanced her public profile. By assiduously turning the spotlight on him while remaining a mystery herself, Eva put *her* name on people's lips. Her demeanor, the entire package of her long-suffering attitude in classical attire, was not something people could interpret easily. Eventually they would resolve the puzzle by labeling her the support of her "Ἑλληνολάτρης ονειροπόλος" (Greek-worshipping idealist) husband, or herself "Ἑλληνολάτρης."[145] Before they settled on that epithet, however, they talked a lot about Kyria Sikelianou without knowing just how to place her.

Consider this description by Georgios Papandreou, who would become Greece's prime minister decades later (1944–45, 1963, 1964–65) and the father and grandfather of two prime ministers. When Papandreou found himself traveling with "a poet, Sikelianos," and his wife, "an American dressed à la Duncan," from Rio, near his native village of Kalentzi, to Antirio, on the north side of the Gulf of Corinth, in September 1910, he recorded his observations in a letter.[146] First he noticed Angelos: "His booming voice filled the boat and the sea with speech, song, and praises. He enriched my life." Then he turned to Eva. Her "στάσις" (attitude, pose, stance) impressed him—he used the word three times. This was "the thing," he wrote, "that taught me the most":

> It was the pose of absolute patience. There was something slightly grief-stricken (πένθιμον), sorrowful about it; her pose, her step, and her voice expressed the holiness of a liturgical prayer: of prayerful worship for the poet. Every so often she would glance up—she was reading non-stop—and her gaze had the ecstasy of a believer who burns incense as a suppliant to the All Powerful one. I asked Sikelianos about his married life. "Ευδαίμων (eudaimon, happy)," he said. "With her love, I have found confidence in my exceptional self . . . she lives to take pleasure in my happiness: she helps me, she gives me strength—and she never stands in my way. . . . [My] wish is her command."

Papandreou felt edified by Eva's pose, but he did not say *what* exactly it "taught" him, or how her apparent sorrow aligned with Angelos's happiness. He just conveyed her guise of mythical dedication. Eva might as well have been Penelope patiently waiting for her Odysseus.

Yet there really *was* something mythical in Eva's attitude. It was mythical first in the conventional sense of a meaningful piece of fiction. From the evidence that I have gathered of their conjugal life during those first years of marriage, she and Angelos shared a passion for ideas. "I have never once felt unexpressed when he was speaking," she later said.[147] For a while there was physical intimacy. There was emotional intimacy, too, as Angelos would return from long trips to "tell [her] stories, wonderful stories, *paramythia*, fairy-stories," with a winning smile in a language she absolutely adored.[148] Eva confessed her "love [for] Angelo" in her last love letter to Barney, when she asked Barney to end their correspondence. She was "happy," she said, though she felt things might fall apart: "my happiness hangs on a thread. I have worked against such odds in myself to make Angelo believe, his belief has come so hard, and now that I believe myself it would be too cruel to have him doubt again."[149]

In March 1909, less than two years after their marriage, when she was thirty-five years old and he was twenty-five, she bore Angelos a son. They named him Glafkos after "Glafke" or Glafkomata, Angelos's name for Eva. The name, which means "blue, grey, or green eyes: or eyes like the sea," featured in poems he wrote after their first meeting. Glafkomata appears in "Αλαφροΐσκιωτος" (The seer, 1909). There is also reference to Glafke in "Δείπνος " (Feast, 1909): "Η Γλαύκη, μεγαλόφωτη γυναίκα, / αναπαμένα στο μέτωπό της τα μαλλιά / πούχε σε δύο φτερούγες / χρυσές και πόφεγγε ήσυχα / το μέγα μέτωπό της" (Glafke, woman of great light / her two wings of golden hair / resting on her forehead, / her great forehead shining bright). When Glafkos was born, Angelos was not indifferent to him—though he would become so later. He took him to Paris a year after his birth to show him off to Eva's friends. ("The delightful adorable baby! I'm a little happier about Eva," Virginia Yardley confessed.)[151] Then, in 1912, Eva reportedly asked Angelos to end their sexual intimacy, and she agreed that he should take as his mistress his cousin Katina, a servant in their house.[152] She did not cease to satisfy his other desires. She supported him for the rest of his life, even when she was impoverished and forced to wash her own sheets by hand. She remained devoted especially to his poetic talent. The restless, itinerant Angelos stayed away for long periods. In the years when they were together, Eva's American acquaintances traveling in Greece commented on the distance between them,[153] but also on the pleasure Eva took in weaving and in "a thousand more practical activities, building, planting, sowing, . . . wine-making"[154] while he was absent.

Eva's "attitude" was also mythical in another important way. Eva emerged from a world in which American women, in much higher percentages than men, received training in the practice of mythic posing in their study of physical education and the performing arts.[155] "Mythic posing" was the production of "a bodily attitude imitating an ancient statue" as developed by the followers of Francois Delsarte.[156] Late nineteenth-century mythic posing can be compared to late twentieth-century music video voguing, the postmodern play of simulacra paying homage to statue poses in early advertising and silent film of Eva's era. Both voguing and mythic posing drew on Delsartean techniques. But the similarities end there. Though a representation of a representation, mythic posing was a piece of a somatic theory and practice that aspired to achieve not surface play but spiritual depth. Delsarteans believed in a human soul that was eternal, though covered with mortal flesh. Human flesh restricted the soul in space, time, and motion; yet the soul, the immortal, immaterial part of the human body, could raise bodily expression to amazing heights and nuances of emotion, reuniting the body with an undying life force under the right conditions. Delsarteans found in ancient artistic expression (especially Greek, Indian, and Egyptian myths) examples of human expression that united the material with the spiritual world. They trained modern bodies to work against the grain of the present day's too glib confidence in material progress, to ready themselves for a richer, more fulfilling self-expression through the study of ancient myths. By study, they meant bodily discipline: the careful replication of time-tested bodily poses, as exemplified by ancient figures from statues and vase paintings to Greek letters and Egyptian gestural hieroglyphs, as a means of reaching a more vital source of life. The historical trend of mythic posing linked Eva to Isadora Duncan, Ruth St. Denis, and Ted Shawn, all artists with whom she collaborated.

Eva's somatic practice of posing as a mythical Greek woman was visibly operative in her highly disciplined self-presentation. It was present in the "attitude" (στάσις) that drew Papandreou's attention and in the techniques that dressed her, following the anadromic method, which recalled the practices of a mythical past as a source of inspiration for authentic self-expression. We may identify it, too, in photographs for which Eva posed so exactly in imitation of sculpted figures, such as the Caryatids on the Erechtheion (figure 2.8), or some prototype of the patiently awaiting wife (figure 2.9) that they tempt viewers to play that nineteenth-century parlor game of guessing the visual source: "Viva la Penelope et Odysseus Louvre!" (figure 2.10).

While Delsarte's principles found their primary application in techniques for actors and dancers, in Eva's life they assumed a search for meaning beyond the stage. True to Delsartean ideas, her poses were neither ends in themselves nor confined to the theater or photographic studio. Eva concerned herself with mastering a set of tools for better living beyond the careful positioning of her limbs or the feel of the dress against her body. Specifically, her enterprise of replacing Western dress with handwoven tunics made of natural fibers "gradually came to mean more than just an indulgence in the sort of clothes [she] happened to prefer."[157] She tried to engage in a real "cross cultural enterprise,"[158] working with Greek women to reform not only their dress but themselves and the structures of economic relations that encouraged them to dress in European fashions.

FIGURE 2.9. Eva Palmer Sikelianos in a mythic pose, ca. 1920. The position of her torso and especially the feet suggest as a prototype Penelope and Odysseus of the terracotta relief in figure 2.10. Eva Sikelianou Papers, No. EP84. Center for Asia Minor Studies.

Yet it was not in her habit or perhaps her nature to adapt her mindset and work creatively with people on their own terms. Her tendency was either to impose her ideas, if she found fertile ground, or to leave others alone. Take her parenting of her son Glafkos. She raised him without formal schooling and with a great deal of freedom yet fashioned him after herself—especially when he was very young. She was happy that Angelos named him after her. His mythical prototype—Glafkos, "the fisherman

FIGURE 2.10. Terracotta relief fragment with Penelope and Ulysses, mid-fifth century BCE, from Melos, 18 × 15 cm. CA860 Photo: Herve Lewandowski. Located in the Louvre Museum, Paris, France. Image Reference: ART150161. © RMN-Grand Palais/Art Resource, New York.

who longed so for immortality that he leapt into the sea in order to reach the gods and . . . was received by them on Olympus"[159]—recapitulated Eva's dramatic role as Timas in *Equivoque*, merely replacing immortality for lost love as the desired object. A studio photograph of Glafkos and Eva taken when he was a toddler shows how uncannily duplication was Eva's

FIGURE 2.11. Glafkos and Eva Sikelianos, photographed by Boissonas Sey-mour, ca. 1911. This is part of a series taken with Glafkos dressed in a knee-length tunic tied at the shoulders and gathered at the waist, posing alone and with Eva. Acc. 189, Eva Sikelianou Papers, No. 308. Benaki Museum Historical Archives.

model of transmission on that occasion (figure 2.11). Mother and son pose in Greek tunics woven by her. His tunic is tied at the shoulders, with one strap sliding down to produce asymmetry mirroring his mother's one-shoulder dress. Their intense frontal stare focuses beyond the camera as if on the "longed for immortality" contained in Glafkos's name. The dou-bling of their poses, tunics, and eerie stares conveys the feeling of a moth-er's ego that did not quite know its bounds.

"THE KEY TO THE MATTER IS THE LOOM!"

The date and occasion when Eva called on upper-class urban women of Greece to lead the way forward to a manifest destiny of freer, more hu-mane living by weaving their own dresses may be located with precision.

On May 16, 1919, Allied powers authorized twenty thousand Greek soldiers to take control of Smyrna, a major cosmopolitan center on the coast of Asia Minor, in order to protect the city's substantial Greek community (219,647 by Ottoman count, 375,000 according to British statistics, as well as over half a million in the region), as powerful countries sparred over the Ottoman Empire's breakup into smaller territories.[160] The occupation was a trophy tentatively given to Greece by the Allies in the Great War as thanks for the country's cooperation. Greeks celebrated the entry into Smyrna as a *nike*, victory. For three-quarters of a century, Greek foreign policy had its sights on expanding the country's borders to include lands in Asia Minor where Greeks had resided for more than twenty-five hundred years. That was the Μεγάλη Ιδέα (*Megali Idea*, Great Idea): an irredentist vision of Greece of two continents and five seas devised in the mid-nineteenth century. On May 16, Greeks felt they had achieved their grand vision. Almost. *Nike* was within view.

On May 17, the jubilant next day, the still beautiful,[161] forty-five-year-old Eva, known as Kyria Sikelianou in Greek, appeared before the Λύκειον των Ελληνίδων (Lyceum of Greek Women) as a "vision of the venerable maternal ancestor . . . come down from a funerary monument in the Kerameikos cemetery."[162] She was facing the fierce headwind of Athenian high society as she tried to convince them to reform their dress. She gave a similar talk on "Ελληνική μόδα" (Greek fashion) a year and a half later on February 10, 1921, in the Αίθουσα Αρχαιολογικής Εταιρείας (Hall of the Archaeological Society),[163] just as the Greek army was consolidating its position occupying Asia Minor, while rebels of the emergent Turkish national independence movement secretly gathered a formidable force, ready to push back.

Eva opened by recognizing the significance of the Greek *nike*. Her repetition of this word, *nike*,[164] together with her deployment of the terminology of warfare, is a startling feature of her talk. For every person in her audience, *nike* suggested the all-male Greek army's conquest of Asia Minor. Eva did not deny her audience that vision. But a different, female figure of *Nike* was on her mind. (Recall that *Nike* of Samothrace alongside countless other συντρίμματα inspired her replication of ancient art.) According to her, victories in war brought brief but crucial moments of rupture. They rendered the occasion for a different kind of battle to be waged over new modes of living that could be pieced together from the ruins of the old. Those nonviolent battles over the new social order, though less obviously heroic than all-out war, were opportunities to renew the national body politic. For Eva the time was ripe. What she had in mind was a smaller-scale battle to be waged by female urban foot soldiers of Greece. With the right moves, their contest could produce a more secure *nike* for Greeks than any bloody men's war.

How might Greek women lead the way up from the ruins of the Ottoman Empire, Eva asked her audience of women to consider. The question of "how" gave focus to labor and process, against the stagnating tendency toward "intoxication, indolence and corruption,"[165] the hoarding of the loot of war that frequently followed military success. Two assumptions about human labor informed Eva's talk. Both were underpinnings of the arts and crafts movement of the late Victorian period and a reaction to the mass industrialization in England and the United States following the invention of mechanized weaving. The first assumption was that work is human, as human society requires labor; and a just, human society fights conditions of work that are inhumane. The second assumption was that work is noble; there is freedom in doing it; and a free society finds dignity in it rather than in wasting free time.[166] As Eva saw it, alienated labor was an overwhelming problem in the present world of fashion. Labor alienation happened at two ends of the process by which women clothed themselves. On one end, people labored like machines under inhumane conditions to create the latest fashions. On the other end, women mindlessly consumed machine-made products with rapid expiration dates, making themselves subject to the designs of others while handing away the opportunity to fashion themselves.

In the drive to fight against those two points of alienation, Eva singled out the potential of the unmechanized horizontal loom. "The key to the matter is the loom," she said.[167] She exhorted women to acquire a loom and learn to use it. By weaving, they would discipline themselves and recover the dignity of labor. They would "enlarge [their] consciousness through the development of [their] own creative capacity."[168] By weaving they would also effectively boycott the French fashion industry toward an end of silencing the textile machines that broke the backs of alienated workers.

Moreover, by weaving enduring pieces of cloth and crafting homegrown, traditionally made Greek materials into the next day's dress, they would also bolster their economy and contribute to the creation of a more classically Greek way of life. This last point contained the germ of Eva's idea of how urban Greek women's experiments in weaving would expand the destiny of Greece, the *nike* she referred to at the beginning of her talk. Her idea aligned Greek with other cosmopolitan searches for indigenous models that revolted against temporal ideas stranding individuals at the cutting edge of perennially ruptured time. It suggested a way of anchoring a swiftly passing present in time-tested, if endangered practices inherited from the past.

Her argument for the Greekness of handwoven dresses was multifaceted. On the matter of style, she concentrated on historically persistent dress lines. She reminded her audience that looms produce fabric with straight lines. Generations of women through "three, four thousand years" of Greek history had respected those straight lines. Women appeared in ancient Greek art wearing the chiton, peplos, and himation, all made of uncut, unconstructed cloth. The look of their dresses was airy and transparent because ancient Greek artists loved to depict women's nearly bare bodies as if in the summertime. Byzantine empresses and saints appeared with their bodies covered; this was deemed appropriate in their era. Yet the lines of the tunics remained unchanged. Byzantine women were as "classical"[169] as the ancients in their appreciation of uncut, straight-lined woven cloth.

The timelessness of the classical, which she equated with the Hellenic ("το κλασικό είναι Ελληνικό"),[170] was also expressed through the contrast of Greeks and Jews ("Εβραίοι").[171] She used the Hellenic-Hebraic opposition as an excuse to posit an anti-Semitic canard: Jews, who were distinct from Greeks in that they were "a people . . . without a homeland . . . [or] nationality,"[172] made all the decisions in Parisian fashion, that most ephemeral of industries. Moreover, a cadre of Jews (she listed "Paquin, Callot, Doucet, Worth, etc.")[173] profited by selling Greeks and others their immoral fashions. For example, it was Jews who promoted the color "Rouge Dardanelle" just after the Dardanelle Campaign, where one hundred thousand young men ("including Jews") lost their lives.[174] The virulent anti-Semitism of this passage, with its insinuation that Jews had stained their hands in addition to their fashions with the blood of Christians, is shocking. While anti-Semitism was a language cultivated and reinforced by members of Eva's American patrician class,[175] this is the single occurrence that I have found in her writings—though it is possible that I overlooked other prejudiced outbreaks. Nevertheless, it represents a rare occurrence. Eva came from an unusually progressive home, where "varied" people "were constantly dropping by" to converse with her freethinking father: "the atheist in a procession of Protestant ministers, Catholic priests, Hindu swamis, Jewish rabbis, anarchists, painters, politicians, poets, journalists, and musicians," as she would recall two decades later.[176] She was generally respectful of the value of other human beings and sought to demean no one. Why the anti-Semitism in this lecture? Why the verbal aggression?

Greece had a substantial Jewish population at this time. Indeed, the numbers had just increased with Greece's acquisition of Epirus, Thrace, and Macedonia—particularly of the city of Thessaloniki—following the Balkan Wars (1913–14). Although Jews in the newly acquired lands were given automatic citizenship and rights, ethnic Greeks derived a strong sense of identity through the contrast with Jews and frequently expressed sweeping suspicions of them. This was particularly true at the time of Eva's lecture, when pseudoscientific racism was introduced to Greece and a discourse of racism was evolving.[177] The interwar period has been called "among the most anti-Semitic in Greece's history."[178] She may well have believed what she was saying, and she was certainly trying to connect with her audience. Her anti-Semitic language was also a means by which to deflect her own alienness by aligning herself with a national idea. Against the alleged geographical and temporal uprooting of French fashions supposedly produced by Jews, she promoted national resistance through a native movement to reform Greek clothes. The notion of the Greek she was advancing conflated ethnic-national with ideational content. It was Hellenic and classical, as mentioned above: historically Greek and timeless, ethnically specific and universal. To become Greek-dressed, she insisted, was distinct from following Greek-styled trends. It did not mean duplicating a Greek look, whether Eva's own or any Greek style promoted as yet another fashion. That, she argued, would be un-Greek. The patriotically Greek thing to do was to become immune to the pressures of perpetually changing fashions by dressing "classically" against changing times.

It is instructive to compare Eva's advocacy of weaving to the Indian activist Mahatma Gandhi's introduction of the *khadi* program to the Indian peninsula in 1920: the movement to hand-spin and weave homegrown cotton threads as part of the national freedom movement against British colonialism. Eva's attention to the loom was not unrelated to Gandhi's advocacy of the spinning wheel as a tool for India's economic and political liberation. The Oxford-educated Gandhi had read the same books as Eva.[179] He carried similar ideas from the West into his adopted Eastern home. His arguments stood on the same philosophical underpinnings of the dignity of human labor and the political importance of self-reliance when he argued that everyone, rich and poor, should make simple clothes of homespun threads. But Gandhi directly linked the spinning wheel to the movement for Indian independence from overt British colonization. He challenged people of all classes in India to adopt the practices of the lower classes in order to make spinning both a tool to boycott Britain's marketing of machine-produced textiles and a sign of Indian solidarity. Although unsuccessful in his drive to lead a revolution in home spinning, he succeeded in making the image of himself at the spinning wheel a visible symbol of Indian independence from British colonialism.

Eva's intervention differed in that she called the members of a narrowly upper-class urban audience to arm themselves against an invisible force of domination. Most women of Athens did not count British machine-made textiles or French designs as subjugating forces. Their enemies were the Ottoman Turks, a power identified with a four-hundred-year historical occupation of Greek people and their lands. The present conditions of war between the Greek army and Turkish nationalist rebels concentrated their attention even more closely on that hostility. Over the triumphant news of the Greek army's occupation of Asia Minor (and the widespread belief that European Allies supported Greece's intervention), people could barely hear the call to arms against Western European cryptocolonialism led by the "Greek-dressed" Eva Palmer Sikelianos, whose cross-dressing into Greek antiquity never let them forget her foreign distinctiveness.

Even more elusive were the strains of Hellenism running through Eva's message. Hers was a Nietzschean reading of the Greeks suggesting that a Greek orientation was critical of modern life and ought not make people feel good about their current lifestyles. How many people could parse the distinction in her emphasis between Greek dress as a process and an objectified form? Who could tread the fine line she insisted on drawing between replication and duplication of ancient designs? How many people would even have believed that a change in dress practices was an effective step to reform?[180] Finally, what urban woman who had left village life a few steps behind would have felt the urge to return to a labor-intensive practice requiring observation, imagination, skill, endless trial and error, and the noisy, rhythmical threading, shuttling, shedding, picking, beating up, taking up and letting off, raising and lowering of the loom—to achieve a Greek *nike* as elusive as the flight of Nike of Samothrace on the Daru staircase?

The moment was not yet in sight when the picture of the Greek-dressed Eva Palmer Sikelianos working her loom would become a museum icon of Greek national culture. As time passed, a few upper-class women brought looms into their homes and made weaving a regular practice.[181] Eva began sharing the bond of weaving with other educated urban Athenian and American friends during the next decade. There was Angeliki

Hatzimihali, a trained folklorist who wrote ethnographies and tirelessly advocated for the preservation and exhibition of disappearing Greek crafts; Muriel Noel, an American student of Eva's in Athens who moved to Cairo to reteach native Egyptians their traditional crafts[182] using a Greek horizontal loom refunctioned with loom weights;[183] and Mary Crovatt Hambidge, another American, who discovered weaving in Athens in 1920 at the Υφαντουργείο S.E.N., a workshop on 38 Amalias Street in operation from 1874 until very recently. Hambidge claimed she found her life's purpose in that workshop. She stayed for a year to study weaving with "Madame Sikelianou"[184] before returning to the United States to sell her creations in upscale shops in New York City. Eventually Hambidge set up an artist residency program in the mountains of northern Georgia to encourage young women to relearn handicrafts. Late in Eva's life, she would work there. Meanwhile, in Greece, village women who taught Eva how to spin, dye, and weave continued to develop their art through their contact with her. They sensed the international value of their artisanship when Eva Sikelianos won a gold medal at the International Exposition of Decorative Arts in Paris in 1926 for a dress she made during the first years of her marriage.[185] Against urbanization and industrialization, they worked to enhance the prestige of handicrafts as expressions of a living Greek spirit. In other words, Eva and a few women in her new circle of friends "remounted the current" of traditions they themselves had a hand in shaping.

The prevailing response to Eva's call for liberation from French fashions, however, was one of humorous disdain, as captured in a newspaper article by Pavlos Nirvanas, a Greek fiction writer who made his living as a journalist. His satiric report, published in the newspaper *Estia* the day after her talk of May 17, reduced Eva's proposal to a labor-intensive instance of copying ancient Greek art. By his account, the Lyceum warmly congratulated Kyria Sikelianou for her patriotic embrace of Hellenism. But "no woman whatsoever ran up to the Erechtheion to ask the Caryatids for the name of their seamstress."[186] Instead, they rushed off to order new dresses in the latest French fashions. The American-born Eva couldn't even "manage to Hellenize her Greek husband, who continued to wear the latest style of vest, soft hat, and white spats, even though he was ever so Hellenically correct in his verse." For the time being at least, Eva "remained the only ancient Greek in modern Athens."[187]

CHAPTER 3

Patron of Byzantine Music

Eva's abandonment of Western dress neatly symbolized her dramatic entry into a Greek life that resisted the advancement of Western industrialized society. Of greater consequence to her critical aspiration, however, was her dedication to studying the Byzantine musical system, a non-Western form of music, in order to teach Greeks to use it again to recover their musical voice. During the same period when she became an expert weaver, she mastered this old musical system used for centuries in the Greek Orthodox Church.[1] Moreover, she became a valuable patron, supporting its study, performance, and the composition of new works against the invasion of European musical forms.

Eva was passionate about Byzantine music. She immersed herself in it completely. This was a reorientation in a double sense.[2] She was turning away from her training in European classical music—with its elaborate (and fully notated) structures built on precise pitch, harmony, and counterpoint—toward a richly melodic music improvising on a complex modal system of intervals that are not even in the Western tuning system. She was also positioning herself in the music of an Eastern Christian religion that she never made her own—and that made her conscious of herself as Other and of the Other in herself[3]—in order to lay bare the cultural effects on Greeks of their long-term Eastern contacts in their church and secular music. This music was of greater antiquity and geographical range than European music, extending into Persia and India, she believed. Eva felt she had found the ancient roots of Greek and non-European song. If properly promoted, it would not only help Greeks to preserve their musical heritage; it would reorient world music away from the dominating force of Western classicism.

Her commitment to Byzantine music was such that she agreed to help Angelos Sikelianos realize the Delphic Idea he was working through in the early 1920s only after he consented to her staging Aeschylus's *Pro-*

metheus Bound with new compositions for the tragic chorus in the Byzantine style by Konstantinos Psachos, professor of Byzantine music at the Athens Conservatory. But how Byzantine music became entwined in her revival of Greek drama, or even what it was for Eva, cannot easily be determined. Eva's account in *Upward Panic* draws diachronic connections of Byzantine music and ancient Greek drama. But this is a late recollection, written decades after her musical studies. It encourages an anachronistic reading that cannot do justice to the multivoiced, contrapuntal field Eva entered when she moved to Greece. Yet few primary sources from Eva's life are available from 1910 to the early 1920s, exactly the period of her musical studies, making it difficult to recover her voice during this time.

To make up for the paucity of primary sources from this crucial period, I broaden the frame of study. Digging into the sources of Greek music and theater in early twentieth-century Greece, I reconstruct two cultural conflicts in Athens a few years prior to her arrival. These two events brought music to the forefront of sociocultural concerns in ways that involved two of Eva's musical collaborators, Psachos and Penelope Sikelianos Duncan, and anticipate her bringing Byzantine music and ancient Greek drama together. The relationships Eva developed through her musical collaborations were an essential part of her Greek life. Following my exploration of the two contests, I trace her musical journey through Penelope, Psachos, and Khorshed Naoroji, a student of piano at the Sorbonne University from a prominent Parsi family of Bombay who came to Greece to study Byzantine music with Eva in order to help India recover its musical heritage. Each one of these figures shaped Eva's journey in a different way, causing her to change the orientation of her musical pursuits from an initial disorienting pleasure that beguiled her (Penelope), to an essential part of the curriculum of becoming Greek (Psachos), to the basis of a social movement (Khorshed Naoroji) and ground for staging the Delphic Festivals.

THE "MUSICAL QUESTION" AND THE *ORESTEIAKA*

Two cultural clashes shook up Athens in the first years of the twentieth century and created the conditions for Eva to study Byzantine music after she settled in Greece in 1907. Both events involved conflicts over musical practices, making the question of how to sing ancient Greek words not just an academic debate but a pressing "matter of concern":[4] a thing that separated people into parties, carried them into the streets, and mattered in the way that produced not only differences of opinion but material things to support one side of the cause or the other side. The public divisions began to shape a transnational field of Greek music with its own areas of interest. They made music a point of contention in the struggle of Greeks to repatriate Hellenism against the tendency of the West to claim Hellenism for itself.

The first was the μουσικό ζήτημα (musical question) confronting the Greek Church. At the heart of this debate was the issue of how to sing the ancient words of Greek Orthodox services: whether to preserve old forms of unaccompanied chanting or admit Western polyphonic singing.[5] The so-called musical question forced itself into the public domain in Athens in May 1902, when a rather obscure argument in the Church of Greece disrupted life in the capital city, setting the stakes for a structured set of oppositions and institutional interventions. The question turned on the style of music in Greek Orthodox services.

Music is an integral part of the services in Orthodox Christianity. Almost every word emitted in every service requires vocal performance. Scripture and prayers are intoned, not read. Petitions take the form of call and response. And services are filled with hymns sung in the tone designated for the specific hymn or for the day in the cycle of the church's musical calendar, following the traditional melodic patterns of an eight-tone system (οκτώηχος, *oktoechos*).[6] In the Greek Orthodox Church, the work of competently performing services in this complex modal system requires extensive linguistic and musical training over many years for the priest and ψάλτης (*psaltis*, cantor) in the company of more knowledgeable cantors.

The immediate event triggering the outburst in May 1902 was the discovery by a deputy in Parliament with an interest in church music, Nikolaos Levidis, that students of church music were taking their exams accompanied by a piano.[7] The matter of concern was the ύφος (style, musical system) of the music of the Church of Greece. In which musical system should it be sung? Should it imitate Western polyphonic choral singing in major and minor scales with piano accompaniment? Or should it remain true to the Byzantine style of single-voiced, unaccompanied chanting, with its richly embellished melodies in the eight-tone system?

On the one side, lead cantors and powerful lay members in the most prominent churches of Athens advocated the use of harmonized voices. They promised to de-Turkify church music by resetting ancient Greek words to Western diatonic scales and four-voiced harmonies based on the notes of the well-tuned piano. The future of Greece seemed to hang on the capacity of the piano keys to reign in the quavering pitch of Oriental singing.

On the other side, the majority of cantors, members of the Holy Synod, and even deputy Levidis countered that Western polyphony was itself a corrupting influence. It had invaded Greece as a foreign sound, assimilating a native elite into a foreign way of hearing music and shackling age-old Greek melodies in an impoverished tonal structure. Instead of the signature of the traditional tone prefixed to every hymn, it squeezed the hymns into major or minor keys. Thus, it broke the historical continuity of the transmission of Greek music, which reached back from orally trained cantors through generations of teachers to ancient times. Where was the age-old voice of Greece in the miscellany of sounds bearing the newest mark of foreign intrusion? "Κάτω η τετράφωνος!" they shouted. "Down with four-voiced (polyphonic) music. Down with serenades! Long Live Byzantine music!"[8] This became their slogan.

The uprising took on political dimensions. More than one hundred cantors and members of the clergy gathered in the meeting room of the Εθνική Μούσα (National Muse), a musical periodical, to protest the Westernization of church singing.[9] They filed a petition with the mayor of Athens, Spyros Mercouris (grandfather of the internationally known Greek actor Melina Mercouri), demanding that he end polyphonic singing in churches and establish an educational institution to train church musicians in Byzantine chant. A prominent member of the church hierarchy was replaced. The government of Greek prime minister Alexandros Zaimis fell. Georgios Nazos, musical director of the Athens Conservatory since 1891, was called to intervene in the crisis by hiring an expert to give new musical direction to the church.

Nazos was a Munich-trained musician dedicated to improving European-style musical education in Greece by "nurtur[ing] significant talent, mainly following [non-Italianate] European models."[10] In his first twelve years as director, he removed all the artists with Italianate training and shifted the instruction to German models, which he considered to be closer to ancient Greek.[11] Then in 1903, under pressure from higher authorities to work with the Church of Greece to raise the standard of church singing, Nazos grudgingly acknowledged the existence of non-Germanic music with Greek affinities. Having promised to hire a specialist to head a newly instituted School of Byzantine Music in the Athens Conservatory, he turned to the Orthodox ecumenical patriarch Joachim III of Constantinople to help him find the right person.

That person was Konstantinos Psachos, a dynamic, learned man, who would soon "[play] the most significant role [in Greece] both as an investigator and as a teacher of every kind of Greek traditional music, as well as Persian, Turkish, and Arabic music."[12] In Constantinople, he epitomized the Oriental Hellene. He was professor of religion and Greek music at the Metochion (Dependency) of the Holy Sepulchre and taught in the school of the Patriarchal Musical Association. An accomplished lead cantor, he was well trained in both the eight-tone system of the church and the *makam* (modes) and *seyir* (melodic progression) of Ottoman secular music. His commitment to fighting Western incursions was unrelenting. The patriarch could count on him to serve as a soldier in a holy war to fend off the invading European music.

Additionally, Psachos was trained in Western harmonic theory. Thus immersed in the musical system of both East and West, he was just the man to turn Byzantine chant into a subject of conservatory study in Athens: to systematize its instruction, scientifically establish its microtonal intervals, train voices, offer concert performances, explain the history of Byzantine notation to Western-educated musicians, and generally turn a body of religious learning into a field of study worthy of European attention.

This would have been what Nazos envisioned. The actual outcome was more than he anticipated. Under the order of King George I, a warship brought Psachos from Constantinople to begin teaching at the Athens Conservatory on September 23, 1904. His addition of Byzantine music to the conservatory curriculum increased the subject's value, placing it alongside opera and lieder, and opened its formal study to all students, female as well as male, international as well as Greek, thus making the study of Byzantine music under the instruction of Psachos available to Eva a few years later.

The second contest, the *Oresteiaka*, broke out over the staging of ancient Greek drama in the Royal Theatre on November 3, 1903. The protests ran for several days beginning on November 6. They were responding to a production of the *Oresteia*, a condensed version of Aeschylus's *Agamemnon—Libation Bearers—Eumenides* trilogy performed in modern Greek after a German production in the Burgtheater in Vienna with music by a British composer.

The Oresteiaka stands as a reference point in twentieth-century Greek cultural history. Nearly every history of modern Greece and Greek literature refers to the event as an extreme outbreak of the so-called language question (γλωσσικό ζήτημα), a long-standing battle over the proper form of Greek for current usage: whether καθαρεύουσα (*katharevousa*), the high, archaizing form "purified" of recent foreign accretions in the nineteenth century, or δημοτική (*dimotiki*), the demotic or vernacular language, best expressed the living continuity of the national soul. At the turn of the twentieth century, the language question was a matter of deep concern on which the deferred desire of the national body to embody its relationship to ancient Greece was projected.[13]

Yet the performance of the *Oresteia* raised more than the language question, as some scholars are now recognizing.[14] Almost every dimension of the production had a foreign connection. It was the first staging of an ancient dramatic work in the newly built Royal Theatre[15] subsidized by the Danish-born King George of Greece and Russian-born Queen Olga. The director of the play, Thomas Oeconomo, was a Greek-born man raised in Vienna and newly transported to Athens. He faithfully followed the production that he had seen in the Burgtheater under the direction of German actor and director Friedrich (Fritz) Krastel.[16] Using the stage instructions of theater critic Paul Schlenther, he created scenery and lavish costumes based on the discoveries at Mycenae of Heinrich Schliemann, a German businessman. The musical score was also from the Viennese production.[17] It included choral songs written by the Irish composer Charles Villiers Stanford, professor of music at Cambridge, who was known for Anglican liturgical music.[18] Rather than perform the play in ancient Greek, Oeconomo worked with Georgios Soteriades, an archaeologist on the faculty of the University of Athens, to translate the German adaptation by Ulrich von Wilamowitz-Moellendorff and Schlenther into a mixture of demotic and katharevousa. Oeconomo's production was essentially a re-performance of the Viennese production in a modern Greek translation of the German text. As Gonda Van Steen has summarily stated, "The Spirit of revival lay in the replication of European models."[19]

The one native element, a new prologue, "Το χαίρε της Τραγωδίας" (The greeting of Tragedy), written in demotic Greek by Greece's leading poet, Kostis Palamas, suggested that the opposite was the case: that this was an authentic Greek production. The director gave the prologue to Marika Kotopouli, then a sixteen-year-old actor making her debut performance. Over the next half century, she would become one of Athens's most popular actors. She played Athena in the production, and in the prologue she addressed Τραγωδία (Tragedy) in anticipation of the outright revival of Greece:[20]

Πάλε σαν πρώτα, απ τα βάθια του αμέτρητη σου τραγουδιού
Κάμε η Ελλάδα να υψωθεί

Σε Ανατολή και Δύση, που είναι του μέτρου η μουσική και της υγείας η
  βρύση
Η Ελλάδα χαμογέλα της αγέλαστε, κ'εσύ.

(Again as before, from the depths of your unending song [*tragoudi*]
In the East and West,
Raise up Greece, which is the musical standard and fountain of health,
Smile at her, you who do not laugh.)

This verse offered the audience a vision of Greece raised from the dead,
becoming again a source of both τραγωδία (*tragodia*, tragedy, from ancient
Greek) and τραγούδι (*tragoudi*, song, from modern Greek). The etymologi-
cal play of the two words, *tragodia-tragoudi*—the one an ancient word for
the Athenian performance genre, the other the word for music in the present era, both etymologically connected to τράγος (*trágos*, goat) + ἀοιδός
(*aoidós*, singer)—worked forcefully to suggest that Greece of today had
the power to revive the living, breathing, musical voice of tragedy.

A good part of the public accepted the connection of ancient tragodia
and modern tragoudi, perhaps even experiencing the performance as a
common cultural memory of ancient songs.[21] Either the enthusiastic audience did not notice that all the songs were made in Vienna, or, possibly, it
did not matter, since for most Greeks of the era, German compositions had
given ancient Greece new musical life. In the words of one critic, "Here
[on the stage] we are whole and completely alive, eternal and immortal.
Philosophers and Sophists. Immortal. In every way immortal."[22] Even
today, some people in Greece continue to refer to the work as a "virginal
performance of ancient tragedy."[23] The generally positive critical reception
of this production marks its success in presenting a work made in Austria
as indigenously Greek.

Yet another part of the public was furious. Almost as soon as the *Oresteia* opened, Georgios Mistriotis, professor of ancient Greek at the University of Athens and founder of the powerful Εταιρεία προς διδασκαλίαν
των Αρχαίων Ελληνικών Δραμάτων (Society for the Instruction of Ancient
Greek Dramas), which had monopolized staging of ancient drama in Athens for almost a decade, gave a scathing critique in a university lecture. He
resolutely accused the "vandals" who produced the play of subordinating
the original Greek play to foreign prototypes.[24] The use of modern Greek
was one of his primary criticisms: ancient Greek as the language of performance was one of his precepts. Mistriotis was critical of the music, too,
and of all the foreign prototypes. He believed that ancient Greek words

should be set to music in a manner as free as possible from European influence, based instead on Byzantine and Greek folk melodies.[25] Among his directorial choices, the most innovative (even if scholars consider it ultimately unsuccessful) was his collaboration with Greek composers.[26] As musicologist Anastasia Siopsi has described the contrast of Oeconomo's and Mistriotis's directorial choices, Oeconomo used a comprehensible living Greek language but otherwise foreign means, while Mistriotis used Greek musical compositions to put a "theory of historic continuity . . . into practice."[27] In different ways, each helped their audiences reimagine "the ancient world as something alive, both as an ideal example for modern art and as the most precious part of [the Greek] national inheritance."[28]

Inspired by Mistriotis's lecture, a group of students from the University of Athens gathered outside the Royal Theatre to vehemently protest the performance. "Κάτω οι μαλλιαροί!," "Κάτω οι χυδαϊσταί!" (Down with the vulgarizers!), they shouted. In the clashes that followed for several days, one young man died, and several were injured. While the rallying cry alluded specifically to the language question, as mentioned above, people's passions surged in the Oresteiaka over more than their disagreements about language.[29] The students took issue with the large number of production choices that denied, rather than affirmed, the connection of Greek antiquity and present life: the production's thirdhand translation; expensive sets and props with a "distinctly foreign flavor"; "eye-catching period costumes for the impressively large chorus . . . commissioned from artists and craftsmen based in Berlin or Vienna"; sponsorship by the foreign-born court; and foreign musical score.[30] Thus, a careful reading of the events shows that the protests also transferred the musical question from the church to the theater, where it bumped up against the language question and was reiterated thus: should Greek revivals of ancient drama render the chorus with European polyphonic music or try to convey the musical style of ancient Greek using Greek church and folk musical elements.

Both the musical and the language question were matters of pressing concern of the day. While the people's affective response to both questions registered the haunting insecurities of the Greek nation (in how many ways did Greeks have to prove their cultural legitimacy at a time when expansionist desires were swelling but military prospects were flagging!), they were distinct matters with distinct publics, until the Oresteiaka overlaid the one question on the other. Until this moment, the musical question, concentrating on the tone, intervals, and melodic lines of Greek, concerned church musicians who were invested in chanting Greek with attention to Byzantine-inherited systems. The language question, on the linguistic evolution of Greek, gathered around itself intellectuals and artists who saw "language and the nation as living organisms" and "believed that the language and culture of the rural population of Greece were the natural continuation of the ancient Greek language and culture."[31] By superimposing the two questions, the Oresteiaka jumbled ideological lines, permitting the creation of new responding publics, the mixing of musical and language questions, the jumbling of ideological positions, and the suggestion that Byzantine music might be the right style to give voice to ancient drama.

PENELOPE SIKELIANOS DUNCAN

Penelope Sikelianos Duncan was present in the Oresteiaka, newly arrived in Athens with her newly wedded husband, Raymond,[32] his sister Isadora, and the rest of the Duncan clan, all dressed in Greek tunics. As Isadora recalled the events, the students noticed the Duncans wandering about Athens. They "surrounded [their] carriage and acclaimed [their] Hellenic tunics and asked [them] to join their parade." The Duncans "did [this] willingly, for antique Hellas."[33] There is no direct record of Penelope's point of view. Indirectly, on the basis of her upbringing, education, activities, and interests, I surmise that she was ambivalent about the protests. On the matter of language, she would have sided with *Oresteia*'s use of modern Greek to deliver its dramatic content, against the Duncans' and other protesters' insistence on the ancient Greek of the source text. Given her musical interests, however, she would have felt sympathy for Mistriotis's stance that productions of Greek tragedy in Greece should use Byzantine and Greek folk melodies. In either case, she would have appreciated the difficulty of finding the right musical idiom to deliver ancient dramatic content to modern audiences.

Penelope came from a family of demoticists who believed in the antiquity of the living language and supported productions of ancient drama in demotic translations. Penelope's sister, Eleni, performed with the modernizing theater troupe Νέα Σκηνή (Nea Skini, New Stage), a competitor of the Royal Theatre.[34] Penelope would have seen the 137th, closing performance of Sophocles' *Antigone* by Nea Skini on November 2, 1903 (one day before the opening of the *Oresteia*), in which Eleni played Jocasta and her husband, Spelios Pasagiannis, was in the chorus.[35] That popular revival, like the others directed by the modernizer Constantine Christomanos—who previously worked in Vienna, like Oeconomo—had all the directorial signs of a German-inspired performance. It used Christomanos's demotic Greek translation and music by Felix Mendelssohn; it paid close attention to European stagecraft, visual effects, and the latest theories of acting.

The demoticist orientation of Penelope's family signaled by Eleni's choice to perform with Nea Skini was deeply rooted. Their father, Ioannis, was a university-trained high school teacher. His family had close personal ties to the popular demoticist poet Aristotelis Valaoritis, who modeled his verse advocating for the rights of the people of Leukas under British colonial rule (1810–64) on Greek folk poetry. Ioannis taught French in the Gymnasium (high school) of Leukas,[36] where Penelope's brothers Hector and Angelos received their secondary education but Penelope, a girl, could not attend.[37] Her mother, Herakleia, was from the affluent Stefanitsa family of Epirus, home of another strand of demoticism.[38] She had attended the privately endowed Arsakeion girls' school in Athens and was progressive in her pedagogical principles, giving both her daughters and sons opportunities to pursue deep cultural learning. Penelope's fluency in French, high level of literacy in Greek, and facility in playing the flute suggest systematic training in both letters and music.

Penelope differed from her siblings in that she pursued musical rather than literary or dramatic interests. Her close relationship with her nanny Maria, who recited popular folk and Cretan poetry,[39] exposed her to some of the prototypes of demoticist literature. Penelope's musical ear drew her to listen to the melodic, tonal, and rhythmic side of folk production. This was a dimension of folk culture that demoticists largely ignored. They generally upheld the vernacular language as a pure repository of the evolving Greek spirit but suspected that the musical traditions, particularly the ones evolving in the East, were corrupted by Turkish influences.[40] Even the demoticist composers of the Ionian School introduced folk poetry but not its musical themes in their compositions. It was not until poet Kostis Palamas speculated that melodies, like language, might bear the imprint of national character (1896)[41] and Italian-trained composer Georgios Lambelet, with his essay, "Η εθνική μουσική" (National music, 1901), invited fellow Greek composers to work folk melodies into their classical compositions that demoticists began to think about music as a national treasure.[42]

A portrait Angelos wrote in 1940, twenty-five years after Penelope's death, confirms that Penelope received "basic musical training."[43] Beyond this, the portrait emphasizes the learning Penelope received from people in the countryside. It specifies her pursuit of "lessons in the simple flute played by the lone cultivator of the earth, which she learned in the mountains and on the shores of Leukas, as she never yielded to the compromise of a musical pseudo-education, but instead was certain that authentic folk purity of expression is always superior to any musical virtuosity."[44]

Of special interest in Angelos's vignette is the insistence on "authentic folk purity of expression," in contrast to "pseudo-education" and "virtuosity." These are the same words Angelos would have used when discussing poets of the Ionian Island such as Valaoritis or Greece's national poet, Dionysios Solomos, both highly educated in the West yet wedded to the craft of folk poetry and averse to the so-called pedantry of katharevousa. This opposition—folk purity versus artificial learning—was the motor of demoticism, erasing every paradoxical sign of foreignness in its new canon of Western-theorized, folk-adulating, learned writing. Thus, Angelos's narrative absorbs Penelope's musical learning into the demoticist narrative of national, folk-inspired poetry by rejecting the "compromise" of formal study and extolling the search for "purity of expression" among illiterate villagers. "Purity" here is opposed to the artificial purification of katharevousa. Demoticism recognized that songs in the countryside performed many life functions while it also presupposed that people produced and enjoyed them purely, that is to say, with a knowledge that was implicit in the national unconscious rather than constructed, self-conscious, and rational.

Angelos's narrative gives weight to "authentic purity" as the thing folk artists possessed and learned city people lost, almost in a fall from grace. The rhythm of his story then adds a second major beat: the recovery of purity that happened when his sister Penelope worked most deliberately against the grain of formal training to recover more intuitive truths. The story rings true as a demoticist narrative but not as a summary of Penelope's life. Penelope's response to the Oresteiaka and the path of learning she took in the aftermath of those events belie this assertion. No matter what Penelope may have learned informally, the Oresteiaka taught her that to become an authentic Greek musician required *more*, not less, formal training. Evidence for this can be found in her response to the set of events that followed the insertion of the Duncans in the student protests.

Somehow Isadora decided she should stage the third stasimon of Aeschylus's *Suppliants*[45] following a dramaturgical course that aligned perfectly with Professor Mistriotis's made-in-Greece precepts: Greek tragedy performed in ancient Greek in a new musical composition drawing on

Orthodox church melodies and folk songs to recover the "tone of the . . . old Greek chorus."[46] The students helped her to procure the Municipal Theatre for her counter-*Oresteia* performance. Penelope's contribution to Isadora's performance was to offer the musical formula aligning the purist search for the antique with a search for purity in folk practices. She probably helped Raymond audition "a couple hundred ragged urchins in Athens"[47] to select ten Greek boys to sing the parts of the ancient chorus. And although Isadora does not make note of Penelope's presence, she most likely functioned as the intermediary who communicated with the Greek Orthodox seminarian (or priest or cantor; the sources are contradictory) from the Rizareios Ecclesiastical School in the center of Athens, whom the Duncans recruited "to square the words of the *Suppliants* to the . . . tunes" of Greek songs and teach the boys to sing.[48] The performance of the tragedy's third stasimon at the Municipal Theatre on November 28 dazzled the opponents of the *Oresteia*. Isadora danced, "accompanied by [the] nasal music tone (i.e. in a Byzantine motif) . . . sung [in ancient Greek] by [the] 10-member black-clad choir of boys, headed by a cantor,"[49] all in "multiflowing robes" (figure 3.1). The students applauded "in a delirium of joy."[50] But the performance, where Angelos was in all likelihood present and declared Duncan a "divine being,"[51] also complicated the Sikelianoses' sense of what was possible in demotic revivals of ancient tragedy.

Although her performance played well to certain Greeks, the lesson Isadora ultimately carried from her staging of the *Suppliants* was that her formula failed to recover the ancient chorus, because it "displeased"[52] the broader Greek audience on December 3 in the Royal Theatre and in the following weeks in theaters in Vienna, Munich, and Berlin. She thought the fault lay in the music, a "comic mélange of religious expression," as she described it.[53] She put an end to her experiments combining dance with Greek church music, returning to her older fusion of dance pantomimes with music by Glück, Chopin, Mendelssohn, Beethoven, Shubert, and Wagner: "The strains of Byzantine music grew fainter and fainter."[54]

Penelope drew a different conclusion, in Eva's assessment, confirmed through her decade-long study of Byzantine music in Greece and recalled in writing many years later: the Duncans' search for the "tone of . . . the old Greek chorus"[55] failed because they had done things backward. They had treated Greek music as a fossilized ancient product, just as the purists treated the Greek language, rather than a living compositional practice. Instead of fitting Greek melodies to the ancient words, they should have "made the ancient words the basis of new Greek melodies composed in a Method which the Greeks have always used."[56] But to achieve this end,

FIGURE 3.1. Isadora Duncan with seminarist and Greek boys' choir, Munich, ca. 1903. Elvira Studio. Public domain.

Penelope would have to study systematically this "Method," an utterly different system of music.

She did not do so immediately. First she met Eva in Paris and told her about Duncan's *Suppliants*. She and Raymond helped Eva render the music and dance of Barney's *Equivoque*. Then in August 1906, she introduced Eva to her brother. A few months after Eva married Angelos and moved permanently to Greece in September 1907, Penelope began attending lessons in Byzantine music with Professor Psachos in the Athens Conservatory at Eva's expense.

AFTER PENELOPE

Eva carried with her to Greece her own set of dispositions about music. One overriding influence was the long-term interest of Western artists and thinkers in recovering the lost schemata underlying ancient Greek music—the *melopoeia* of Aristotle or the mysterious *harmoniae* of Plato connecting scales and intervals to specific behaviors. What was the sound of this music, and how to revive it? This productive question had inspired many Greek-styled European compositions since the 1600s.

For most of Eva's early life, critics aligned Greek music with European classical music, in opposition to music of the Ottoman East. This alignment, although driven by Orientalist biases, was by no means settled. Indeed, the oppositional topoi, Hellenic West versus Ottoman Orient, kept generating new work that renegotiated the relationship and further complicated the scheme. The same year as Wagner presented *Der Ring des Nibelungen*, his most Germanic operatic drama, as the legitimate successor of Greek tragedy (1876), French composer Louis-Albert Bourgault-Ducoudray published his ethnographic collection *Trente mélodies populaires de Grèce et d'Orient* (Thirty Popular Melodies of Greece and the Orient).[57] The collection renders the score of the melodies in the European notational apparatus. The melodic line and lyrics in Greek with French translations appear on a treble staff, and below it on a second treble and bass staff is the piano accompaniment by Bourgault-Ducoudray. The composer also filled the collection with charts showing the equivalences of ancient Greek modal scales with the modes of the melodies of songs he recorded live from performances in Constantinople, Smyrna, and Athens.[58] Although a close look suggests that Bourgault-Ducoudray had little practical knowledge of the music he recorded, the collection nevertheless inspired the next generation's closer study of live performances of music in Greece and the Ottoman Empire. It contained "the seductive idea that there might be unified schemata (modal and rhythmic continuities) underlying ancient Greek, Byzantine, [and] 'folk' music"[59] in the Ottoman East. Among Greeks of Constantinople who were pursuing solutions to the musical question, the collection had the long-lived significance of "enhanc[ing] the prestige of folk music among Greeks" and encouraging new collections.[60] Psachos worked under its influence.[61] Eva would not have known this last bit of information about Bourgault-Ducoudray's connection with Greek musicologists before coming to Greece. Yet, as an admirer of the work on Greek dance by Maurice Emmanuel[62] and music by Claude Debussy, both students of Bourgault-Ducoudray who produced music in Oriental-sounding modes based on a limited knowledge, Eva was prepared to experience deep, ancient echoes in traditional Greek songs before coming to Greece.

Another influence on Eva was the public engagement of female contemporaries of her class in the ethnological study of subaltern groups. Eva's childhood friend Natalie Curtis Burlin was a trailblazer in ethnomusicology as well as an accomplished pianist, who collected the music and songs of Native Americans and African Americans using musical notation and an Edison cylinder recorder. She dedicated herself to the political work of restitution to such a degree that she absorbed the values she found in native societies and promoted them to reform American society. Eva learned about Curtis's turn to ethnomusicological study in letters from her mother while she was still in Paris. In 1904, her mother informed her of a talk Curtis had given on "the Indians and their songs"[63] in Bar Harbor. The lecture was a presentation of Curtis's highly anticipated book of musical transcriptions *Songs of Ancient America: Three Pueblo Indian Corn-Grinding Songs from Laguna, New Mexico* (1905), in which she reported on the underappreciated antiquity of Pueblo songs and of the "high order" of the Pueblo's ethos on the "primitive plane."[64] Curtis felt the urge to record the music because she sensed the destructive weight of her own people's influence on it. She wrote in her introduction to the collection, "Under the influence of white man, the art of the Indian—the making beautiful of common things—fast fades away, and the natural utterance of healthy people, the unconscious burst of song, is almost stilled."[65] Her principle of collecting was fidelity to the original, to restore in print what white man's imposition of power was erasing.[66] Yet Curtis was aware that a single white woman's notation could not deliver the beauty of lost melodies. In her words, "melodies are not always sung exactly alike by different readers, since there is no notation, and the songs, as an Indian so well expressed it, are held, not on paper, as with us, but 'all in the head.'"[67] Not even her determined hand could deliver the "quavering voice" of the native woman, with its "ring of old-time authority."[68]

When Catherine Abbe described Natalie Curtis's impossible mission to Eva in 1904, she knew that Eva's relationship to Natalie Barney was beginning to undermine Eva's confidence. Abbe would later "shudder" to recall her daughter's "slavish yielding" to Barney's will, calling this a very "low mission."[69] She always advised Eva to embrace a higher calling. On this occasion, she set before Eva the model of Natalie Curtis, who was everything the admittedly brilliant Natalie Barney was not: "earnest and serious and I think very gifted."[70] Her point was not to replace one Natalie with another in Eva's affections, but to pry Eva from her dependent state—to free her from an unhealthy emotional attachment to Barney and set her on a clearer social and moral path. In all her correspondence during the years when Eva chased after Natalie, then ran to Greece to escape her teasing affections, Abbe, addressing Eva as her "little run-away child,"[71] tried to convey to Eva the message that she should not stray, she should not wander so far as to lose her way, but turn herself around by embracing a more socially, spiritually responsible life.

The contours of that other life suggested by the example of Natalie Curtis, another runaway child who devoted herself to native American music, may have presented themselves to Eva in some shadowy form when she first heard Penelope singing a traditional church hymn in the house of Marie-Paul Hyacinthe Meyer in Paris in April 1906. Eva's oft-quoted telling of her first impression of Penelope is from *Upward Panic*. This is a very late memory. Shaped by Eva's vision of the trajectory of the life she had lived and the place of Penelope in it, the book gives a retrospective reading of how things unfolded. It is impossible to erase this now dominant account. Since it marks a pivotal point, and especially since it contrasts with an earlier, overlooked account, it is worth revisiting:

> When I entered there seemed to be only one person in the room, or, if you like, two. A woman, simply dressed in white, who had the features of Michaelangelo's Delphic Sibyl . . . [and] the child at her breast. . . . After lunch Hyacinth [*sic*] asked her to sing. She did not wish to; but finally she rose from her chair and sang two Greek Ecclesiastical melodies, the first quite slow, the second rather rapid. On me the effect was catastrophic. It was as if a wet sponge had been passed over a closely written black-board. I felt that I had heard music for the first time, heard a human voice for the first time. After singing, Penelope lapsed again into complete silence, except that before leaving she asked me to come and see her.[72]

This particular telling of Eva's first hearing of Greek church melodies places Penelope and her infant son at its focal center. It associates Penelope already with Delphi, making her a prophetic sibyl, as if she had foretold Eva's path. Her voice has the otherworldliness of a pure Platonic Idea, a form of sound "erasing" the poverty of all previously registered sounds for a split second. It breaks through the false notes of the world before becoming silent again. Penelope's invitation to Eva to visit her reopens the crack into that other world.

An earlier reminiscence appearing in a lecture by Eva, "Concerning Greek Music," delivered at the Fogg Museum in Cambridge, Massachusetts, in 1928, gives a different focus.[73] Penelope is a "Greek girl," not yet the "woman" or the named person of the later account. Moreover, she is just the vehicle delivering a "little ecclesiastical melody." In this earlier account, Eva even gives a sense of the musical qualities contributing to its strangeness. The "strange melody" acts as the catalyst appearing suddenly out of nowhere and propelling Eva into a kind of Heideggerian leap into being:[74]

> Suddenly one day in Paris, about a quarter of a century ago, I heard one little ecclesiastical melody, a *tropari* as they call it, sung by a Greek girl,

and in the space of about two minutes, all of my conceptions of music, everything that I had ever heard or thought about it was undermined. . . . Here were intervals which were certainly not those of the tempered scale, with something poignant in the melody that caught me like a magnet, something intensely true which made everything I had known until then seem shut in somehow in the stuffy atmosphere of theatres and concert-halls, whereas this seemed to have some mysterious relation with the open air. . . . From Paris, where I heard the song, I wanted to get nearer to the source of the strange melody, and I believe I first went to Greece more for that than to see the ancient ruins.[75]

While the agency of the transformation is located in the suddenly heard melody rather than in the reluctant Penelope rising from her chair to sing, the Platonic allusions are already present in the cavelike "stuffy atmosphere of theatres and concert-halls," in contrast to the "open air" of the music of Greece. I note in passing that the hierarchical distinction she draws between the "strange melody" and "ancient ruins" as signs of Greek life luring her to Greece falls away in her earlier (1921) discussion of syntrimmata—fragments of various kinds, especially snippets of musical sounds, gestures, and dance steps—as the building blocks of her art.[76] By this account, the tropari as a whole melody sung by a living Greek effects a magnetic conversion on her, pulling Eva out of her comfort zone in Paris into a Greece of strange melodies, Eastern religious rites, and unknown methods of composing music.

Was it Penelope or the melodic strangeness of her song that drew Eva to study Orientalizing Orthodox church music? How can we determine if Eva was attracted to the person or the music: to the embodied voice or the idea of Greek music or the opportunity to extract herself from Natalie's powerful draw by attaching herself to a self-transforming mission? How can we know the singer from the song? Is it possible to separate Penelope from her music making in Eva's imagination? By my reckoning, the personal and cultural investments informing Eva's disposition were too tightly interwoven to be divisible. She was always going after someone and something together. At the same time, the course Eva followed in her study of Greek music shows that Penelope was a kind of lodestone transmitting a complex field of force. Whenever Penelope was present, Eva hesitated. When she pulled away, Eva inched forward. And when Penelope left Greece for good in 1915, Eva would rush forward to take the place that Penelope had never really occupied in Greece. Eva stood in Penelope's shadow when the two of them made their initial contact with Professor

Psachos at the Athens Conservatory's School of Byzantine Music in 1908. The foreignness of the new vocal tradition was daunting, she would later recall.[77] Eva did not yet have adequate training in the Greek language to sing the church's ancient words fluently using the pronunciation of the present day. Additionally, the intervals of the eight-tone system were still foreign to her ear, which was trained to hear with great precision the tones of the equal-tempered major and minor scales. To be sure, the complex tonal system is also overwhelmingly difficult to learn.

Soon after Penelope's first meetings with Psachos, she, Raymond, and their son Menalkas crossed the Atlantic to promote Raymond's theories of music and dance. All across America—from Philadelphia, New York, and Boston to Portland and San Francisco—Raymond delivered lectures such as "The Seven Rhythms of Nature and Their Evidence in the Hellenic Music." Penelope, identified as the "native Grecian" by a reporter (figure 3.2),[78] sang to illustrate complex points such as "the three musical genders and the structure of the scales of the chromatic gender, together with their four systems of music and the master echoes and their plagals."[79] Her singing "proved to be of novel interest and [was] received with warm response. . . . Its unique tone coloring was both pleasing and artistic."[80] Building on her success, Raymond gave Penelope a theatrical part when they reached California. On April 11, 1910, she played the title role of Elektra in his production of Sophocles' tragedy at the open-air Greek Theater at Berkeley. Though "without singing numbers, [Penelope still] showed the range of her voice . . . through the intonations of her words," while Raymond's "lean limbs and besandled feet . . . tripp[ed] lightly over the stage"[81] in the roles of Aegesthus and the chorus. This was his counter-Straussian *Elektra*, which he billed as "the first correctly given performance in America"[82] because it was built on a Greek tonal system, in contrast to Richard Strauss's opera, against which Raymond had organized protests when it was performed in New York City a few months earlier.[83]

Penelope was abroad with Raymond and Menalkas for more than two years, between July 7, 1909, and November 11, 1911. Meanwhile, back in Greece, Eva took an active interest in supporting Psachos's research on Greek folk music. She must have asked her brother Courtlandt to write to Thomas Edison to secure a new "Edison" wax cylinder for Psachos, because in a letter to her mother she conveyed her gratitude to Courtlandt for his intervention and Psachos's anxious anticipation of it for his research: "Psachos asks me every few days if I have any news of it and is most anxious to hear. It will be a very great help to him in many ways in

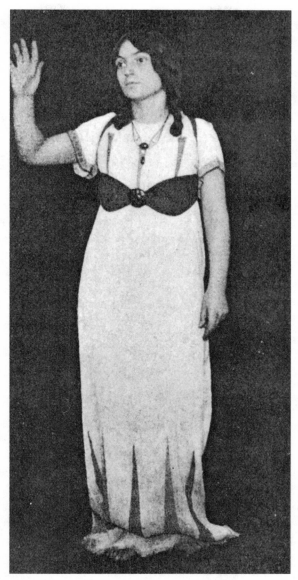

FIGURE 3.2. "Mrs. Penelope Duncan" waving to an audience during "Greek Music and the Folk Songs of Hellas," a lecture given by Raymond Duncan with Penelope offering song demonstrations, September 1909. The review praised her "natural talent for the vocal rendering of the music of her country, and for the exact intoning of the various modes and precise expression of the different rhythms." "Greek Music and the Folk Songs of Hellas," *Musical Times*, September 1, 1909, 579. Public domain.

the collection of national songs, for although he himself can immediately write any song he hears, others haven't the same facility, and his aides will need the phonograph."[84] Almost incidentally, she noted the good progress she was making in her studies of Byzantine notation:

> [Psachos] has started me working on the notation of songs and lyrics, or in fact anything one hears, and although it isn't a bit easy, I find that when he goes slow I can succeed in writing pretty well. I have had two lessons of this sort on both of which he wrote άριστα excellent and I felt so proud that I came home and showed it [to] everybody like a child who has brought a prize home from school.[85]

This letter may be read as a belated response to her mother's letters of 1904 praising the work of Natalie Curtis among the Pueblo Indians. The principle of gathering and recording native music with near absolute fidelity, which Natalie Curtis used to deliver to her compatriots a faithful repertoire of indigenous American songs, informs both Eva's desire to give Psachos the tools to support his "collection of national songs" and her own work on "the notation of songs and lyrics" of Greece. Eva's letter most proudly displays the professor's mark of "άριστα excellent." Herself a dedicated preservationist of the history and monuments of New York City, Eva's mother would have approved of Eva's course in parallel with Curtis's, despite the great distance that now separated her from her "little run-away" Eva.

When Penelope and Raymond returned to Europe, Eva again abandoned her studies, this time joining the cast of Raymond's *Elektra* in performances at the Châtelet and Trocedero theaters in Paris in February 1912. The Duncans had just opened their Akadémia (after Plato's academy) on the fifth floor of an apartment building on rue d'Alisia in the Montrouge district in January of that year.[86] Duncan's *Elektra* was the first of an announced series of Greek productions to "revive Greek Theatre in France!"—part of Raymond's "school of philosophy, of weaving, and of ceramics: in short A GREEK academy."[87]

"Une frise Grec," a series of three photographic tableaux published in a French review of the Châtelet performance (figure 3.3), shows Eva still chasing after Penelope. The photographs and captions sketch the two narrative lines of that performance. One is the mythical story of Chrysothemis and Elektra's encounter at a moment when the tyrannical rule of their stepfather Aigisthos is pulling them in separate directions. In the picture on the left, Chrysothemis, bearing the message of their mother, Klytaimnestra, is after Elektra to cease lamenting their fallen father, Aegememnon,

FIGURE 3.3. Photo series with caption "Une frise Grec: Mme Pénélope Duncan repentant avec sa soeur, la danse des choeurs de la tragédie de Sophocle; *Electre*" (A Greek frieze: Mrs. Penelope Duncan, remorseful, with her sister, the dance of the chorus of the tragedy *Elektra* by Sophocles), showing three moments in the play performed in the Théâtre du Châtelet on February 3, 1912, with Penelope Duncan as Elektra and Eva Sikelianos as Chrysothemis. RD, vol. 1, 28. Public domain.

lest Aigisthos send her where she will never again "look upon the sun's brilliance."[88] Chrysothemis adds a piece of advice in her own voice: even if Elektra continues to be filled with grief, she should at least appear to cooperate with the higher authorities in order to save herself. But Elektra observes that Chrysothemis's words are not her own; moreover, her actions are misguided. The middle frame shows Elektra's response. In a dramatic gesture, she rejects Chrysothemis's appeal to save herself: "I will fall, if need be, in the cause of my father!" In the frame on the right, Chrysothemis admits she is carrying Klytaimnestra's funeral libations to Agamemnon's tomb in order to suspend the vengeance of which night visions warn her. In order to soften Klytaimnestra's justifiable guilt, Chrysothemis heeds Elektra's plea to replace the libations with a lock of her own and her sister's hair.

The caption, "Mme Pénélope Duncan repentant avec sa soeur" (Mrs. Penelope Duncan, remorseful, with her sister), introduces a complex counterpoint. It mentions remorse and identifies the second figure as the "sister" of Mme Duncan; but Elektra, the figure whom Penelope plays, never exhibits remorse, while Eva, who plays Chrysothemis, Elektra's sister, is not Penelope's sister. The mislabeling of emotions and confusion of actors with characters invites another reading of the tableaux. Penelope's picture at the center is the pivot point. All eyes go to that central image first and are held by its near explosion of energy. Penelope has drawn in her arms, making a fist in a gesture of contraction, but extends her body. We anticipate an outcry of grief from the still closed mouth. The two outside frames feature Eva in pursuit of Penelope. She is after something Penelope possesses and has not yet given her: a sound, a tone, a lament, an "unconscious burst of song" (such as her friend Natalie Curtis wrote about) coming from a deep, archaic point of reckoning with the trauma of life. Penelope is leading her on to a new place, and Eva follows eagerly, one step behind.

The dynamic relationship between the two actors suggested by this series of tableaux serves as a reminder that Eva found motivation for all her artistic pursuits in and through affective relationships. She was always going after someone and something together. Her study of Greek music was especially bound up with Penelope. Penelope was that "young Greek girl" who first captured her interest with a different Greek sound. She replaced Natalie Clifford Barney, then the love of her life, who led her to produce queer theatricals, but who, as a person of the same economic and cultural background as Eva, kept bringing Eva back to a self she wanted to escape. In contrast, Penelope was foreign to her in almost every dimension: the dark hair and coloring, public breast feeding, language, education, class, and position in the world as a "full blooded Greek."[89] Indeed, she was so different that she represented something Eva had not yet imagined: a truly different self. Years later, Eva spoke of her musical pursuits as coming "after Penelope."[90] This coming after—with longing and desire and memory filling the space between them—is visibly asserted in the "Greek frieze."

After the performance of *Elektra* in Paris in 1912, Eva went back to Greece and anticipated Penelope's return. She wove as she waited, planning the development of the property she had bought with Angelos in 1910 in Sikya, a small promontory near Xylokastro on the Corinthian Gulf.[91] Three hard years passed. With the outbreak of the First Balkan War in 1912, Angelos enlisted, and Raymond took Penelope to London to start a new movement, which a contemporary reporter described as "for the immediate relief and repatriation of famine-stricken and homeless populations of Epirus and Macedonia, who have been ruined by the Balkan war."[92] From London they moved to Saranda (Ἅγιοι Σαράντα in Greek; *Santi Quaranta* in Italian) in the southern part of the newly established Principality of Albania to "restore villages shattered in war,"[93] in the words of another reporter; specifically, they worked to provide aid to Greek Orthodox refugees who had been displaced by Muslims fleeing the area of Epirus ceded by the Ottoman Empire to Greece. For nearly two years, they constructed buildings from stone ruins to house the refugees, worked to create a handcrafted industry of spinning and weaving to make them self-supporting, and even built schoolhouses to educate their children.[94]

Isadora Duncan briefly joined them in July 1913 as a kind of penance after her children died.[95] She left when she felt the living conditions were too squalid. Raymond remained enthusiastically committed, even after their eight-year-old son, Menalkas, became deathly ill. Menalkas recovered (figure 3.4); but Penelope's powerful lungs were failing. Upon their return to Athens in May 1915, while Penelope's health deteriorated, Raymond continued laboring for refugee settlement assistance, this time for eighteen thousand Greek Orthodox refuges of Ottoman Thrace "expelled by the Turks since the beginning of the [Great] war. . . . 'I'm sort of a Hercules,' he [said], that is, it's my task to go about the world cleaning up tasks that no one else will tackle.' "[96] He also worked on a political campaign. In fact, he introduced American campaign methods for the election of Eleftherios Venizelos, head of the Liberal Party. According to American reports, "he stumped all of Greece on behalf of the former Premier and organized a campaign by mail to enlist support."[97] In the election of May 31/June 13, Venizelos was victorious.

Then, on September 23/October 5, 1915, Raymond and Isadora, who was visiting Greece with her then manager Maurice Magnus, stood in shock as King Constantine I forced the resignation of Venizelos after Venizelos gave permission to allied troops of Great Britain and France to land at Thessaloniki in northern Greece.[98] Venizelos had discussed the policy with the Greek Chamber of Deputies and had the king's "approval."[99] Greece's observance of the 1913 Greco-Serbian treaty was on the line, as the allies were offering help to Serbia. But the king changed his mind.[100] Earlier that year, he had ordered that Greece should maintain neutrality, while Venizelos favored assisting the Allied forces in their Dardanelles expedition—in anticipation that the Allies, once successful, would compensate Greece with large territories in Asia Minor.[101] When Venizelos disobeyed Constantine's orders, the king dissolved Parliament and forced Venizelos to resign. The Allies had gone on to fight in the Dardanelles without Greece's support and were suffering huge casualties. Now the scene was repeating itself. Isadora staged a flamboyant dance in Venizelos's support. As Isadora "paused to sing the Marseillaise with a hundred enthusiasts,"[102] Penelope collapsed.

Magnus made it his mission to deliver Penelope to the Sanatorium Schatzalp in Davos, Switzerland (October 10–15).[103] He eventually paid the bills for her unsuccessful treatment.[104] From Davos, Penelope wrote to Eva on May 10, 1916: "A new wound was opening in my treacherous

FIGURE 3.4. Menalkas (left) and Raymond Duncan (center) with Glafkos Sikelianos (right) in 1915, when the Duncans returned to Greece and the cousins, Menalkas (about ten years old) and Glafkos (six), were reunited in Sikya. Aristides Pratelle, "Rescuing Epirus," *International Socialist Review* 15 (1914–15), 424. Public domain.

cursed lung, which made me choke at every minute."[105] Then, on June 7 to her mother: "Countless times I fall into deep despair when the idea of death overtakes me. My condition is changing so drastically from one minute to the next that it is impossible for me to describe it"; and on June 28 to Eva, "the fountain where I hoped to drink to cool myself disappeared from before me long ago."

Eva's determination to learn Byzantine music became rock solid as Penelope wrote of her painfully prolonged expiration. (Penelope died on April 22, 1917.) As if standing in for the now silenced Penelope, whose lungs were once so overpowering, Eva committed herself to the elegiac work of recovering the voice of her sister-in-law, who now became the sign of all the music in Greece threatened by the invasive forces of onward-marching Western influences. From this point on, she would work to empower Greek lungs: to give Greeks the tools to preserve and perform their own music; in her words: "to lift from obscurity this wonderful music composed in the past, and which has been preserved in writing from at least a thousand years, but whose tradition is without date in the memory of man. . . . to save the gift . . . [of] a musical literature as great both in bulk and in intrinsic value as the whole repertoire of European concerts."[106]

KONSTANTINOS PSACHOS AND THE FIELD OF GREEK MUSIC

Whatever it was exactly that moved Eva to follow Penelope in the study of Greek music, it is not obvious why she went so far as to pursue Byzantine church music with Psachos to the highest level, earning the title "Master of Byzantine Music," an honor never before granted by the Greek Orthodox Church to a woman.[107] The program of the School of Byzantine Music at the Athens Conservatory had a specific intended outcome: it prepared male singers to master the hymnal traditions in the Neobyzantine style so they would be skilled cantors in the Church of Greece. Its demanding curriculum converged on this end. The theoretical framework of the eight-tone modal system, Chrysanthine notation, and history of Greek music that interested Eva were interlinked with Orthodox liturgical subjects. Students worked through the books of the liturgical tradition to gain proficiency in the contents and sequencing of church services. They entered deeper into the complex aspects of each of the eight modes—their intervals, accidentals, and tonal attractions—as they learned the musical parts and substitutions of the many, many services: the matins, divine liturgy, and vespers, with their standard content cycling through the eight tones and following calendar variations; seven sacraments; sixteen daily observances of Holy Week from Saturday morning before Palm Sunday to the vesper service on Easter Sunday; and twelve major feast days. Eva was neither male nor a convert to Orthodoxy. She never intended to chant but rather was in pursuit of some notion of Greek music. To understand Eva's motivations, I will need to track down Professor Psachos, the man summoned to Athens to solve the musical question after its outbreak in 1902, to see how the field of Greek music was taking shape in and around the Athens Conservatory at the time when Eva dedicated herself to mastering Byzantine music.[108]

On the afternoon of Friday, February 4, 1916, Psachos could be seen running up Piraeus Street toward Omonia Square, late for a lesson at the conservatory. Aristos Kambanis, an ambitious journalist, aspiring poet, and critic (he had already praised Angelos's work[109] and received the poet's compliments[110]) was running after him, desperate for an interview. "Κύριε πρόεδρε" (Kyrie proedre, Mr. President), he cried. "I want to talk to you! Give me a meeting time!" "With pleasure!" Psachos replied. "Come to this address tomorrow at 4 p.m."[111]

The next day, Psachos, πρόεδρος (proedros, head) of his department in the conservatory, opened the door, and Mr. Kambanis discovered he had chased down the wrong man. He thought he was pursuing the former prime minister, Eleftherios Venizelos, πρόεδρος (proedros, leader) of the Liberal Party (figure 3.5), who had handily won parliamentary elections on June 13, 1915, with Raymond Duncan's assistance, and was forthwith deposed by King Constantine on October 5. Although Venizelos left Athens in December 1915, his political positions were a matter of deeply divisive public concern. By February 1916, newspapers were reporting that he was "so aloof from politics" that he did not even "read the reports in the proceedings from the chamber,"[112] while rumors were also spreading that he was intent on setting up a second, schismatic government in Thessaloniki. If the rumors were true, the Kingdom of Greece was facing its greatest constitutional crisis since its foundation: a conflict bringing to the fore the question of the power of the foreign-imported monarchy relative to the country's elected government and dividing the country into irreconcilable camps of royalists (anti-Venizelists) and republicanists (pro-Venizelists). What a journalistic coup it would have been for Kambanis—an anti-Venizelist writing for the antiliberal, national-populist demoticist newspaper Εσπερινόν Νέον Άστυ (Evening New City)[113]—to publish an interview with Venizelos! Instead here was Konstantinos Psachos, the "σωσίας"[114] (sosias, doppelgänger, double) of the protagonist of the moment. Psachos was like Venizelos in his "height, build, glasses, [and] the fire in his eyes"[115] (figure 3.6) and was eager to talk about his conflict with European musicologists over the historical continuity of Greek music.

Psachos not only looked like Venizelos: he also had Venizelos's polarizing personality. A man of "persistent enthusiasm . . . [with a] combative, fiery, volcanic temperament,"[116] he divided people for or against him. Like Venizelos, too, he knew how to keep his concerns in the news. On this occasion, his misidentification with Venizelos enhanced his public profile. Standing in the place of Venizelos precisely at a moment when Venizelos was the most controversial man in Greece, if not Europe, gave his words a political charge. So Psachos held forth on his musical theories, Kambanis took notes, and the newspaper published the entire story—the chase, mistaken identity, and conversation on music. All this took up the print space

FIGURE 3.5. Eleftherios Venizelos, September 5, 1919. Harris and Ewing. Reproduction Number: LC-USZ62-85047 (b&w film copy neg.), Digital ID: (b&w film copy neg.) cph 3b31585. Library of Congress Prints and Photographs Division, http://hdl.loc.gov/loc.pnp/cph.3b31585.

of a would-be story on the constitutional crisis, as if it was of vital national interest. The reason for this helps explain why Eva went as far as she did in her studies of Greek church music.

A careful reading of the interview reveals what was compelling about Psachos's musical positions at this moment in 1916. The political force of his argument makes itself felt, though it is not obvious. The country's geopolitical situation was quite complicated, and Psachos's notions of music mixed into it. World war was spilling into Greece, despite the country's official position of neutrality. King Constantine had handed over Fort Roupel, a new fortification on Greece's border with Bulgaria, to the Germans, who were allowing Bulgarian troops to occupy eastern Macedonia. Then at the invitation of Venizelos, Allied troops began disembarking in Thessaloniki, reaching four hundred thousand. Armed conflict in the region was portending to transform Greece's geopolitical alignment in Europe and Asia. People on all sides of the political divide sensed that the country was closing in on its national ambition to expand its borders to

FIGURE 3.6. Konstantinos Psachos, ca. 1929. K. A Psachos House Archive, Hellenic Folklore Research Center, Academy of Athens.

include formerly Byzantine lands in Ottoman Thrace and Anatolia. The stakes were high, but the uncertainties were greater. Would Greece finally enter the war, on which side, at what cost, and to what end? What would happen to the Ottoman Empire? Were the Allies or the Central powers more favorably positioned to Greece? And would the day ever come when Greece would be powerful enough to achieve its own ends without foreign interference?

Psachos's interview did not touch on any of these points directly; yet he struck a chord by giving voice to marginalized Near Eastern musical practices over European modes of composition. The thing at play was Greece's self-representation in relation to the Western view of Greece as the origin of European culture. In politics and culture, there was feeling in the air that elites were misrepresenting Greece through their fixation on the West. For Psachos, the Greeks themselves had forfeited their musical treasures to tone-deaf imitators of Europe. They needed to reclaim their native inheritance against the pressures to adopt Western ways. Psachos appealed to Greeks specifically to overturn their Orientalist biases so that they might recover the musical heritage of the Ottoman East.

In the earlier outbreak of the musical question, two antithetical topoi of Orientalism, Hellenic West versus Ottoman Orient, brought attention to the musical practices of the Greek Orthodox Church, where bona fide ancient Greek words sung according to time-honored practices sounded Oriental to Western-trained ears. The antiquity of the Greek words in the services, on the one hand, and their seemingly Turkish sound, on the other, called for experts to excavate the music to identify the system with the deepest roots in the lost ancient music.[117] While the hiring of Psachos as professor of music at the Athens Conservatory authorized Psachos to teach Byzantine chant in what would eventually become the officially recognized School of Byzantine Ecclesiastical Music of the Church of Greece (1936), it did not end the struggle for the legitimacy of the Byzantine system. The opposition, Western polyphony and Oriental modal monophony, kept the church's musical question alive, generating repeated efforts by Psachos's opponents to square Byzantine music with Western polyphony, while Psachos and his allies and competitors tried to prove the antiquity of Byzantine-style chant.[118]

The question was not just of Greek national concern. At an international Congress of Orientalists held in Athens in 1912,[119] Psachos had participated in a scholarly debate on the performance of Eastern church music relative to its transcription. The study of ancient Greek music had long been underway in the West, with European classicists and medieval musicologists working hard to recover the lost sounds by either analyzing ancient sources, which were theoretically rich but void of sound (classicists), or working backward through the wealth of ritual music still sung in ancient languages (musicologists). The prevailing European view was that Neobyzantine chanting was a Turkish corruption of the music of Byzantium and ancient Greece. As proof of the discontinuity, Psachos's colleagues pointed to the least European elements of contemporary chanting (the eight tones, irrational intervals, chromatism, melismatic ornamentations) and Chrysanthine Neobyzantine notation. They contrasted this with Byzantine music prior to the Ottoman conquest of Constantinople in 1453, as represented by medieval notational systems, which they read as European-style diatonic music. The revision of the notation system by Chrysanthus indicated to them that the music had submitted to Turkish influences.

Psachos, with his lifetime labor as a musicologist and cantor in the highest positions in the church, could not but have felt the sting of their judgment, which claimed ancient Greek music as European while bypassing the musical practice of living Greeks. He had deep knowledge of the material as a student, teacher, and performer and saw things in a way that the Western lens could not capture. To the journalist interviewing him, he made a studied contrast of his European colleagues' superficial knowledge—"They do not know how to decipher Byzantine notation"[120]—and his deeper reading based on a thorough comparison of "the old [medieval] musical manuscripts"[121] with present practice to make the point that Orthodox music of the Ottoman and present era, with its oriental sound and revised notation, was a continuation of an ancient tradition of Greek singing. To his studied eye, the notation of the Byzantine manuscripts was "a shorthand notation . . . [while] Neobyzantine notation [was] precisely an expansion of this abbreviated old notation system: an authentic elucidation"[122] of all the modal qualities in medieval music that were still audible in Neobyzantine chant and visible in its notation. The notation systems were different; but every stage in the musical practice of fifteen centuries' ritual singing of ancient Greek words was connected by generations of usage, as if by links in a chain.

Turning to another arena, the creation of new music in Greece, Psachos extended his accusations of ignorance to include Greek composers who ignored Ottoman secular music. The turn to Ottoman music happened in this way. Kambanis was pleased to discover that Psachos was not just a "theorist of Imperial music . . . but also a tireless researcher of folk songs (δημοτικά τραγούδια)."[123] Greek folk music would be a more familiar subject to his readers than Greek Orthodox church music, so Kambanis encouraged Psachos to expound on its qualities, to explain how it might inspire the creation of "καθαρώς ελληνική μουσική" (pure Greek music).[124] The turn in the discussion shows how easily the signifiers *Byzantine chant*, *folk music*, and *music composed by Greeks* lose their distinction under the capacious but ambiguous category of "Greek music." This slippery range is a striking feature of the field of Greek music that was just emerging. Resting on the multiple meanings of the Greek, "Greek music" could refer to the range of traditions of religious and ritual singing in Greek; the historical depth of those traditions; the geographical sweep of regions where self-identifying Greeks enjoyed music; the ideological charge of a national music; new compositions by ethnically Greek composers; and music in ancient Greece.

The idea that there might be a principle unifying all these referents began to take root in the period between Psachos's arrival in Athens and the present interview, with Psachos and Georgios Nazos, the conservatory director who hired Psachos, functioning as important agents. Between 1908 and 1914, Nazos required Psachos to teach Greek folk music alongside Byzantine music. During the same period, he, Psachos, and Armand Marsick, a French musician residing in Athens, worked in the field to record (using Eva's "Edison") traditional music of the Peloponnese and Crete.[125] Thus the musical establishment, once dedicated fanatically to European classical music, was gradually conceding a place to folk music. That same year Nazos hired Manolis Kalomiris, the German-trained pianist and composer intent on creating a Greek national school of music. That was two years after Kalomiris gave a conservatory concert performance of his "Ρωμαίικη Σουίτα" (Romeic suite),[126] a European-style embellishment of Greek folk songs composed for piano and voice, with the official program written in French and an unofficial one circulating in demotic Greek.[127] Attending the concert were some of the most prominent demoticists of the day: Kostis Palamas, Ion Dragoumis, and Eleftherios Venizelos, among others.[128]

Psachos may have been present at the concert, as he was connected to all these people.[129] But he was not a committed demoticist,[130] and he did not approve of Kalomiris's compositional practice. He had a different unifying principle in mind. To respond to Kambanis's question about the future of Greek music, Psachos completely bypassed the sentimental view of the Greek countryside, in order to bring attention to his publication in 1908 of Ottoman secular music under the title, *Ασίας λύρα, ήτοι συλλογή διαφόρων μελών της Ασιατικής μουσικής* (Asian lyre, or a collection of various melodies of Asiatic music).[131] The title word "Ασίας" (Asian) referred to Ottoman popular music sung in many languages,[132] and the collection comprised sixteen Turkish, one Arabic, and one Kurdish song, along with one improvisation on an Ottoman musical progression, or taxim.[133] Psachos recorded the lyrics in their original language and the music in Neobyzantine notation. "Asian" also stood as Psachos's marker of contrast with Europe. In a bold move that few Greeks in his day would have accepted,[134] Psachos was working to decouple Greek and European culture by identifying the Greek with the *makam* of Turkish classical music. In a lecture of November 27, 1905, entitled "The Transmission of Greek Music through Eastern Lands by Way of Greek Civilization," he had argued that Greeks should rid themselves of their fear of the Turkish element in Byzantine music, on the one hand, and their fixation on the major and minor scales of European music.[135] He also defended Ottoman vocal technique for singing Greek, arguing that Greek cannot be sung without nasal enhancements. Above all, he considered the corpus of Ottoman popular music an artistic masterpiece equal to European classical music in its compositional potential[136] and listening pleasures.[137] Now in his interview with

Kambanis he stressed the two-way flow of the equation: Greek music was Asian and vice versa. Asiatic music was Greek because it was traceable to music from Alexander's era in its "theories, modes, systems, scales, melodic formulae [μελωδική ἕλξις, literally melodic attraction], and myriad other matters."[138] And Greek music was Asiatic, because Ottoman secular music preserved the "modes, scales, and rhythms of ancient Greek music that even folk and Byzantine music lost."[139] In contrast, European music and its methods of composition were "utterly foreign to the music of Greece."[140]

Psachos's dismissal of his Greek colleagues' claims to know Greek music was as absolute as his rejection of European musicologists' claims to have understood Byzantine notation: their music was an anxious mimicry of something made in Europe. With this blanket criticism of his colleagues and his call for the reorientation of musical studies to feature Ottoman music, Psachos drew the interviewer's concluding praise. Kambanis ended the piece with recognition of the "scholarly method and precision" of Psachos and a call to "the well meaning Mr. Nazos" to give Psachos the resources he needed to establish a separate school of "δημοτική ελληνική μουσική" (demotic Greek music).[141]

This concluding phrase illuminates the symbolic power of Psachos's musical positions. From the beginning, Psachos's anti-Western rhetoric fed on a current of populist resentment of the West. Drawing on this energy, Psachos was staking his ground in a set of non-Western musical song types (Byzantine chant, traditional Greek folk songs, popular Ottoman music) to counter the forms that had entered Greece from the West. Yet the canon he was positing as an alternative to European music included ethnically Turkish, Kurdish, Arabic, and Armenian works that stood outside every notion of a Greek tradition. Here was a man in control of a huge repository of musical knowledge centered in the Ottoman East. He could hear the connections between these different song types on the basis of both their ongoing historical usage and the complex interactions of Near Eastern compositional systems. What the interview showed was the ease with which these parts could be collapsed under the ambiguous category of the Greek, to be made interchangeable signifiers of the continuous flow of the Greek spirit from antiquity to the present. Even Turkish songs might be imagined as Greek if their origins were located deep in the historical continuum.

The fact that a journalist writing for a national-populist newspaper would try to fit all the musical countertrends Psachos was describing under the umbrella of demotic Greek music indicated the availability of Psachos's ideas for appropriation by different strains of nationalism—in this case the anti-Venizelist, antiliberal demoticist cultural politics that was finding its voice at this critical moment. Psachos's interest in bringing to the foreground the sounds of the Ottoman East suited this national-populist narrative, even though Psachos was neither a demoticist nor an anti-Venizelos.[142] In Kambanis's retelling, his ideas were suggestive of "a real neo-Hellenic civilization" that would "coexist with the other nationalities and religions within the Ottoman Empire" until it eventually became dominant, not through armed Western intervention but as a matter of course, "because of its superiority."[143] The stake of Psachos's work lay in the belief that the region's music, if properly collected, notated, categorized, studied, and set alongside other forms of cultural expression, might help Greeks to reclaim the imperial Near East organically from the inside.

EVA SIKELIANOS IN THE FIELD OF GREEK MUSIC

The stake propelling Eva to devote herself to Psachos's School of Byzantine Music was not exactly the same. She sympathized with the desire of people in Greece to reverse the hierarchies of Orientalism: to repatriate Hellenism as a Greek tradition and a national heritage. She was also privy to the recent nationalist-populist drift of Angelos, the former aesthete. In 1912, when he enlisted to fight in the first Balkan war, he declared himself "τετρακάθαρα εθνικιστής" (literally, 4× pure nationalist).[144] He made the confession to Ion Dragoumis, the author, diplomat, and theorist of cultural nationalism whose complex interweaving of Nietzschean ideas with socialism and nationalism was attracting demoticist poets and intellectuals such as Angelos and his friend Nikos Kazantzakis to the nationalist populist movement. By "τετρακάθαρα," Angelos was playing on the more hyperbolic "πεντακάθαρα" (5× pure) commonly in use, as if to say that he was just one notch short of a perfectly pure nationalist.

As Eva threw herself into the study of Byzantine music after Penelope's departure in late 1915, she must have felt the tug of Angelos's anti-Western, Orthodox-pagan, demoticist-royalist, nationalist-populist attachments. But whatever ideological standpoints informed her study of Byzantine music (she did not articulate a political ideology until the last decade of her life, when she moved to the far left), she bore the weight of aspirations to reorient Hellenism differently from the Greeks. Hers was not the defensive pride of Greek nationals, who were struggling to position themselves in relation to powers invariably playing with their country's fate. While wholly sympathetic to Greeks' plight, she had the confidence of an

American female expatriate of a certain status and class, for whom Greece always already represented white Anglo-Saxon cultural pre-eminence. That she might enter it through the esoteric Eastern portal of the Greek Orthodox Church gave her access to elements of the Greek legacy that were unreachable by other paths. Beside the enticement of the church's continued use of ancient Greek and pious memory of Penelope, there was also, in Eva's words, "sensuous or spiritual delight" in the music's Oriental qualities.[145] The musical process had an exotically textured otherness in every aspect. In an open letter addressed to American music lovers in 1924, she would give emphasis to all the elements of difference that excited her: the names of the modes; their strange intervals; the notation; the manner of singing; the prayer books, feasts, and holidays; and the melodic development that used shifts in modes to mark changes in mood in the progression leading to Christ's Passion. Here was an utterly alien way of bringing language into music—in a way that her pianist mother and brother could only have dreamed of. For Eva, this was "all . . . so beautiful, so intensely musical," that it proved that the "creative genius of Christian Greek was worthy of their Pagan ancestors."[146]

While "sensuous and spiritual delight" attracted Eva to Greek Orthodox church music, it was her anadromic approach—her backward-moving approach to ancient sources that traced them in current methods and followed their traces backward through comparison with present practices, seen in her performative readings of Sappho's fragments and experimental replication of ancient dress—that structured her interest. Her prior work on ancient Greek materials not only reinforced her sense that she might replicate the processes of ancient singing by mounting the backward current of contemporary music; it also indicated the role she might play in building institutional support for this endangered musical tradition. In the exceedingly thin record of her epistolary output from 1910 to the early 1920s, a letter to her sister May of September 17–30, 1917, stands out.[147] It falls in this crucial period when the Eva's archive nearly dries up exactly as her commitment to Byzantine music deepens. Here I focus on her notion of the Greek musical tradition as it is mapped onto a pilgrimage to the Monastery of Damasta on Mount Kallidromo in central Greece in 1917.[148]

Eva wrote the letter while in Upper Agoriani, a village about thirty miles south of Damasta in a hollow of Mount Parnassus, the legendary mountain that rises north of the Gulf of Corinth exactly opposite Sikya, where she was now building a villa. To reach Damasta, she had already traveled two hundred miles across the Isthmus of Corinth through Attica into Boiotia. She was present for the celebration of the Nativity of the Theotokos on September 8, the feast day of the monastery and church, possibly to memorialize Penelope, who had passed away five months earlier. She stayed in Upper Agoriani for a few days before returning home.

"Greek tradition" is the leitmotif in the letter. Her account gives to this idea several of her by now familiar turns with an additional twist. Once again, her focus is on the gaps in ancient sources. As seen elsewhere, lacunae are the motor of inspiration. This time the lost arts of Byzantine fresco painting in addition to music making concern her. The letter refers to the "wonderful frescoes" of the Church of Damasta, "now most unfortunately restored." The poor restoration of the frescoes as well as the loss of what came before give Eva the impetus to imagine what is no longer there. Second, her interest lies not so much in how the things looked (she says nothing about the frescoes) as in the lost processes, which artists and scholars in the West were in Eva's day struggling to recreate. The letter refers to the fresco technique by Pierre Puvis de Chavanne, the French mural painter who, Eva reflects, "for all his beautiful work, didn't quite find the spirit of it" because he was studying Italian rather than Byzantine paintings. Eva is convinced that a new artist might "gradually invent" the "lost art . . . by inward instruction," by following the extant Byzantine paintings. This leads to the third of her signature ideas of Greek tradition: the emphasis on the "new life" that might be found in old, broken, or missing work. Her attention is on the potentiality of the recovered processes to produce new work.

In thinking about the church and its illustrated contents—the first item her letter mentions is the freestanding church icon of the Theotokos and child made of tempera on wood and covered in ornate silver work—the letter recalls another lost temple image. In passing, it refers to the massive chryselephantine (painted ivory encased in gold leaf) cult statue of "Olympian Zeus" made by Pheidias in the fifth century BCE and destroyed in late antiquity. Here again, the letter does not give details about the actual statue. It is the puzzle of the processes that matters. Reference is made to Antoine Chrysostôme Quatremère de Quincy, the French enlightenment architect and theorist, whose *Le Jupiter olympien, ou l'Art de la sculpture antique* (1814)[149] was more attentive to the lost processes of making chryselephantine art than to the lost object. How were ivory tusks cut to produce such large sculptures? What were the techniques of assembly? How did all the different materials (ivory, gold, precious stones, and the base of wood) mechanically and aesthetically coalesce? How did the fitness of these parts make evident the intention of the work? These were questions raised in Quatremère's study. While Eva does not enumerate them, her passing reference underscores a fourth, additional point: that the processes of making "Greek art and tradition"—even those traditions quite alien to Western tastes, such as the mixed-media painted cult images in ancient temple interiors (whether pagan or Greek Orthodox)—were based on what Eva considers to be "necessity": the absolute coherence of form and function.

The letter posits that such a unity of form and function could be found only by "building one's foundations on Mt. Parnassus"—that is to say, on a system worked out by Greeks through their study of the universe ages ago. Paradoxically, by "Mt. Parnassus," Eva is actually signaling the reorientation of "Greek tradition" away from Western classicism in two directions. One is the "mountain village," such as the one in which she was now staying, which demoticists such as Angelos extolled. Unfettered by book learning, it promised to reveal the secrets of the "bare necessities of life" that pedantic classicism overlooked. The other direction was the late antique, medieval, and modern reworking of Greek tradition in the imperial Near East. Eva mentions cultural critic Periklis Yannopoulos, who, some scholars say, "contributed, more than anyone before him, to the positive reappraisal of Byzantine . . . achievements."[150] Certainly, the idea of pushing the boundaries of Hellenism was not new. Already in 1814, Quatremère de Quincy's foray into the dark interior of an ancient temple with its glinting gold-encased-painted-ivory cult statue dared contemporary tastemakers to imagine classical buildings differently. Then from the late 1800s to the second decade of the 1900s, Byzantine sites in Greece and the Near East attracted growing interest.[151] New art and architecture in the West drew on its models. Eva would have been one of 1.4 million tourists who visited the Louis Comfort Tiffany Byzantine-styled chapel in the 1893 World's Columbian Exposition in Chicago.[152] Yet few people except the ethnic Greeks in whose company Eva now found herself thought that the Byzantine Empire linked modern Greeks with the ancients. Now in the decade of two Balkan Wars, the Great War, and the massive deportation and death marches of Christian minorities of the Ottoman Empire, just as the Greeks' pursuit of the Great Idea seemed to be reaching a critical stage, the idea of the development of a Greek national consciousness from the preserve of Byzantium was gaining a sense of urgency.

For Eva, in her reflections on the church of Damasta, with its silver-encased feast day icon and ill-restored frescoes, the remnants of Byzantium promised to yield the secrets of ancient artistic processes not traceable in Western art. She imagined extending her pilgrimage "in and out of the beaten paths [to] travel through Greece, Macedonia, Turkey, and Palestine . . . to see all the Byzantine churches still in existence and stop hanging on Italian art." Then, every facet in her notion of tradition is evident when she turns to music from fresco painting:

> In music I feel perfectly sure that its future power lies in the musical genius who will have the patience and the burning interest to learn thoroughly the Greek modes and be able to write in them, and to harmonize in the manner which Byzantine tradition permits harmony and that not because of any personal preference, but simply because the Greek musical laws are in harmony with the physical laws of acoustics just as the ancient laws of gymnastics and dancing are in harmony with the physical laws of health.

First, the missing sounds of the ancient music are the object of burning desire. The fact that they are missing feeds Eva's auditory imagination. Second, composition involves a replication of processes of harmonizing "in the manner which the Byzantine tradition permits harmony," through intense attention to present practice, mastery of which might lead to understanding ancient musical theory. Third, Eva's glance is turned persistently forward toward the "future power" of new music. Fourth, Eva locates the "Greek modes" in the Ottoman East, since her point of reference is the music of the Greek Orthodox Church descending from Byzantium.

Most important for grasping how Eva fit in Psachos's school is the point made here about the universality of the system. "Byzantine tradition," she writes, builds on "Greek musical laws [that] are in harmony with the physical laws of acoustics just as the ancient laws of gymnastics and dancing are in harmony with the physical laws of health." Eva's general statement of the foundations of the music is as slippery as Psachos's discussion of the connections between Eastern musical types. If Psachos's discourse ranged from Byzantine to Ottoman to folk music, as if these were interchangeable outcomes of an ancient Greek music, Eva moved between the cultural specificity of Greek church and folk musical practice and "physical laws of acoustics." In new terms, she was reiterating the *topos* of Greek exceptionalism—of the particularity of ancient Greek culture that stood as the cornerstone of civilization—which Western thinkers had been repeating since Winckelmann's day. Her stake in mastering Neobyzantine music under Psachos's tutelage was her belief that the music represented a system of greater antiquity and universality than European music. Perhaps the system extended into Persia and India. Perhaps in Byzantine music she had found the foundation for the study of a non-European world system for the production of song. If properly taught and promoted, it would not only help Greeks preserve their very old musical heritage; it would reorient world music.

PATRON OF GREEK MUSIC

The meeting ground between Eva and Psachos was their shared dedication to promoting Eastern modal music as the basis for musical production in Greece (Psachos and Eva) and the world (Eva). To this end, they recognized the need to produce technical intermediaries for the instruction of Byzantine music. Eva paid for the publication of Psachos's important book on Byzantine notation, *Η παρασημαντική της Βυζαντινής μουσικής* (The notation of Byzantine music, 1917, an elaboration of the theory of signs that he presented at the Congress of Orientalists in 1912),[153] while she was still Psachos's student. The evidence of her involvement is in Psachos's prologue, where he extends his "deepest gratitude . . . to the honorable Mrs. Eva Sikelianou, our dearest student, whose material and moral support has been as valuable as it is consoling, and whose contribution made possible the publication of this hard-earned product of my labor in challenging times."[154]

Now Eva was not an exceedingly wealthy woman, as people in Greece have long supposed. She did not possess wealth on the scale, say, of Natalie Clifford Barney, or of Romaine Brooks, Barney's new love since the outbreak of World War I (they were lovers from about 1915 until 1955).[155] Barney had inherited $2.5 million upon her father's death in 1902 and $1.5 million when her mother remarried.[156] The coincidence of the two transformative events, the death of a tyrannical father and Barney's coming into wealth of her own, taught her to protect her financial independence as the condition of her freedom. To this end, she exhibited remarkable discipline to the end of her life. Eva had neither Barney's sizeable inheritance nor her financial acumen. She and her three surviving siblings came into a shared inheritance of $1 million when their father died in 1888.[157] The money was held in trust by a bank, and she began receiving an annual income managed by the bank after she came of age. Additionally, they inherited property in New York City, which was managed by people appointed by the trust's executors.[158] She never paid attention to how her assets were handled. While living in Paris, the assets did not generate enough income to satisfy her tastes, which included paying for the costumes and sets of Natalie's productions. When she ran up debts, her stepfather would send her a statement itemizing the amount she owed, then offer to forgive the amount. "It seems a cruelly big sum—and I don't need it."[159] In Greece, she did not start running up big debts until she overspent on the Delphic Festival of 1927. Life was cheap, and her income grand by Greek standards, and she was relatively restrained in her personal expenses. She built two beautifully crafted, sensible homes, first the villa at Sikya, then another stone home in Delphi in 1925. She used surplus cash to satisfy Angelos's tastes, which, until the Delphic Festival, were within her means. She also supported other people's dreams. Family and friends benefited from her largesse. For example, when Nikos Kazantzakis was considering whom to solicit to support a new journal he was getting off the ground in 1922, he thought to ask "Eva Sikelianou to send us $100."[160] Her generosity suggested that she had unlimited resources, which was not the case.

She accepted a greater financial challenge when Psachos resigned from his position in the Athens Conservatory in 1919. He had been on bad terms with his superiors for some time, reportedly because he was criticizing the administration in the presence of students.[161] In October 1919, the board refused his demands for a raise and changes to the program. Psachos described his exodus from the Athens Conservatory as an "exile."[162] Manolis Kalomiris left the conservatory at the same time for similar reasons. They talked about starting a new conservatory together: an Ωδείο Εθνικής Μουσικής (Conservatory of National Music) offering a full curriculum of Byzantine, folk, and Near Eastern music (Psachos) and an Ελληνικό Ωδείο (Hellenic Conservatory) with a national school orientation (Kalomiris).[163] But Psachos refused to work under the umbrella of the Hellenic Conservatory as Kalomiris demanded. In any case, their ideas were incompatible and personalities too autocratic to succeed in a joint venture. Thus, Eva—who deferred to Psachos's authority most of the time—became his close collaborator in the new educational venture. The school opened in October 1919 with ninety-three students in the program of Byzantine Music meeting in a girl's high school from 5 p.m. to 9 p.m. each day. Eva taught first-year Byzantine music in addition to ecclesiastical music theory. Again, these details are not found in her archives but in the papers of Psachos (figure 3.7).

Besides offsetting the day-to-day expenses of the Conservatory of National Music, Eva's largesse made possible the construction of a keyboard instrument, an organ, designed to help Psachos promote the tradition of Byzantine music.[164] As Eva explained the project in a set of talks,[165] the idea was to invent an organ to give shape to Eastern modal music in the way that the piano shaped European music.[166] The instrument would fix

ΣΧΟΛΗ ΒΥΖΑΝΤΙΝΗΣ ΕΚΚΛΗΣΙΑΣΤΙΚΗΣ ΜΟΥΣΙΚΗΣ

ΜΑΘΗΜΑΤΑ	Δευτέρα	Τρίτη	Τετάρτη	Πέμπτη	Παρασκευή	Σάββατον	ΔΙΔΑΣΚΟΝΤΕΣ
ΤΑΞΙΣ ΠΡΩΤΗ							
Ἐκκλησιαστικὴ Μουσικὴ	5—6		5—6				Εὔα Σικελιανοῦ
Θεωρία Ἐκκλ. Μουσικῆς					5—6		» »
Θεωρία Εὐρωπ. Μουσικῆς		8—9		8—9			Κ. Σφακιανάκης
ΤΑΞΙΣ ΔΕΥΤΕΡΑ							
Ἐκκλησιαστικὴ Μουσικὴ	6—7		6—7				Κ. Ψάχος
Θεωρία Ἐκκλ. Μουσικῆς					6—7		» »
Θεωρία Εὐρωπ. Μουσικῆς		8—9		8—9			Κ. Σφακιανάκης
ΤΑΞΙΣ ΤΡΙΤΗ							
Ἐκκλησιαστικὴ Μουσικὴ		5—6		5—6		5—6	Κ. Ψάχος
Θεωρία Ἐκκλ. Μουσικῆς							» »
Ἱστορία Βυζ. Μουσικῆς							
Φυσιολογία τῆς φωνῆς						7—7	Μ. Παπαθανασόπουλος
Ὑμνολογία καὶ Μετρικὴ						7—8	Ἐμ. Πεζόπουλος
Θεωρία Εὐρωπ. Μουσικῆς		8—9		8—9			Κ. Σφακιανάκης
ΤΑΞΙΣ ΤΕΤΑΡΤΗ							
Ἐκκλησιαστικὴ Μουσικὴ	7—8		7—8				Κ. Ψάχος
Θεωρία Ἐκκλ. Μουσικῆς							» »
Παρασημαντικὴ, Τυπικὸν, Ὀρθογραφία, Μελοποιΐα, Συγκριτικὴ.					7—8		
Ἀχουστικὴ — Αἰσθητικὴ					8—9		Σ. Βραχάμης
Πρακτικὸν Διδασκαλεῖον	8—9						Κ. Ψάχος
Φροντιστήριον.			8—9				

ΣΧΟΛΗ ΕΛΛΗΝΙΚΩΝ ΔΗΜΩΔΩΝ ΑΣΜΑΤΩΝ

ΜΑΘΗΜΑΤΑ	Δευτέρα	Τρίτη	Τετάρτη	Πέμπτη	Παρασκευή	Σάββατον	ΔΙΔΑΣΚΟΝΤΕΣ
ΤΑΞΙΣ ΠΡΩΤΗ							
Δημώδη ἄσματα		7—8		7—8			Κ. Ψάχος
Ἱστορία ἠθῶν & ἐθίμων							Γ. Γαρουφάλης
Θεωρία Ἑλλην. χορῶν			«		«		
Φυσιολογία τῆς φωνῆς						6—7	Μ. Παπαθανασόπουλος
Ἀχουστικὴ. Αἰσθητικὴ					8—9		Σ. Βραχάμης

ΣΧΟΛΗ ΑΝΑΤΟΛΙΚΗΣ ΜΟΥΣΙΚΗΣ

ΜΑΘΗΜΑΤΑ	Δευτέρα	Τρίτη	Τετάρτη	Πέμπτη	Παρασκευή	Σάββατον	ΔΙΔΑΣΚΟΝΤΕΣ
ΤΑΞΙΣ ΠΡΩΤΗ							
Ἀνατολικὴ Μουσικὴ		6—7		6—7			Κ. Ψάχος
Θεωρία ἤχων & ῥυθμῶν						6—7	Μ. Παπαθανασόπουλος
Φυσιολογία τῆς φωνῆς							
Ἀχουστικὴ - Αἰσθητικὴ					8—9		Σ. Βριχάμης

Ὁ Διευθυντὴς
Κ. Α. ΨΑΧΟΣ

FIGURE 3.7. Program of Instruction, Ωδείο Εθνικής Μουσικής (Conservatory of National Music), for the conservatory's school of Byzantine ecclesiastical music, levels 1–4 (top) and school of demotic song (bottom). The name of Eva Sikelianou is given as the instructor of Byzantine church music and European music theory for level 1 on Mondays, Wednesdays, and Fridays from 5 to 6 p.m. K. A Psachos House Archive, Hellenic Folklore Research Center, Academy of Athens.

the microtonal intervals of modal singing, just as the tempered piano fixed the tuning of Western instruments. Symbolically it would stand for the difference between Eastern and Western music—against the critics of Psachos, such as the British musicologist H.J.W. Tillyard, who argued that Byzantine modes could be played on any modern keyboard.[167] Since the

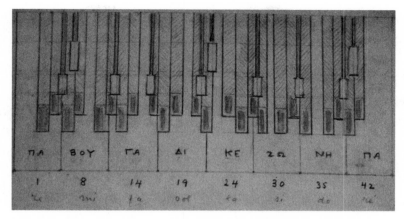

FIGURE 3.8. Drawing of one octave of the keyboard of the Evion Panharmonium. The Greek letters written on the white keys (ΠΑ, ΒΟΥ, ΓΑ, ΔΙ, ΚΕ, ΖΩ, ΝΗ) are the Neobyzantine equivalent of the solfeggio and follow the Greek alphabet sequence (Α Β Γ Δ Ε Ζ Η). The number under each white key indicates its place in the forty-two-interval sequence. Below these numbers are the sol-fa syllables. The black keys are the microtonal accidentals, something like sharps and flats on a piano keyboard. Acc. 189, Eva Sikelianou Papers. Benaki Museum Historical Archives.

intervals of the new organ were so many, with forty-two to an octave rather than the twelve of the piano keyboard (figure 3.8), Psachos worked with the mathematician Stavros Vrahamis to determine how to fix their frequencies, build a keyboard with the octaves within a hand's reach, and "have all the stops of the modern organ."[168] He and Eva agreed to include a "pianola attachment" to record the music as it was being performed, "in order that some, as many as possible, of the characteristic kinds of Greek music may be heard at once."[169] Psachos suspended the conservatory's operation in September of 1922 to personally supervise the assembly of the large pipe organ with two thousand pipes and of two portable pump organs (harmoniums)[170] at the G. F. Steinmeyer factory of Oettingen in Bayern, Bavaria, the maker of many German grand pipe organs.

Eva did not intend to pay for the organ's construction, which eventually cost her more than one million drachmas,[171] or $3,000, and bore her name (Evion Panharmonium). Psachos had presented the organ as a national instrument, so it did not seem right for a foreigner to assume the cost. Still she threw herself into the organ's promotion, never questioning whether such a project was practical or would ever catch on. This was one of many occasions when Eva's indefatigable idealism eclipsed any sense of practicality. As a member of the unsuccessful fund-raising committee, she explained why the project required Greek support in a lecture she gave on February 24, 1921, three days after her lecture on Greek fashion. This time she expressed her "aporia" that Greeks preferred to "imitate" European musical practices in the vain hope of winning European approval, rather than to play their own music,[172] while she, a foreigner, had thrown herself into their musical terrain. Thus, while she was struggling to learn Byzantine music—"the inheritance of all time, as Beethoven himself would have been the first to recognize"[173]—they were sending their children to conservatories to study the violin and piano and learn the great European composers but nothing of their own musical giants: "Petros of Peloponnesos, Grigorios, Iakovos, St. John of Damaskos; and they [were] not in a position to know that Byzantine musical notation is Greek Music and not Arabic letters."[174] Reading the lecture, I can almost hear Eva deliver the names of these giants of Byzantine music in her now fluent Greek, spoken with a beautiful sense of the structure, musicality, and rhythm of the language in her ineradicable American accent. There was just a little too much aspiration in the p's of Πέτρος Πελοποννήσιος; the gh's of Γρηγόριος were too hard; the rolled rh's were too guttural; and the clause "η Βυζαντινή παρασημαντική είναι Ελληνική Μουσική και όχι αραβικά γράμματα" (*ee veezantinee paraseemantikee eenai eleeneekee mouseekee keei ochhi araveeka gramata*)—emitted from a spot a little too far back in her throat and held too long in the mouth—added an un-Greek length to what should have been clipped "ees" and "ahs" thrust to the front of the palette and ricocheted over the tip of her tongue. Her point, so beautifully represented by her perfect Greek lexicon and American tonality, was about the disorienting impasse to which her pursuit of Greek music had brought her. The more deeply she, a foreign woman, became invested in finding a native Greek solution to "the musical question" (her words: "το ζήτημα της μουσικής"),[175] the more foreign she felt herself to be. With the new organ, which she called a "Greek piano,"[176] she was hoping to bridge the gap of foreignness between them: to offer a "rainbow bridge" (her words again: "η γέφυρα... το ουράνιο τόξο"—following Nietzsche's "rainbow bridge," the fantasy but not the impossibility of connecting the modern self to the Greeks)[177] to throw off the specter of her foreignness while helping to "free [her Greek interlocutors] from foreign influences so [they] might express [themselves] harmoniously again, not through ancient ruins, but according to the eternal necessity of the Greek Earth."[178]

LESSONS FROM INDIA'S DECOLONIZATION MOVEMENT

By 1924, Eva saw that the organ would have little Greek support. Now she was presenting it as *her* contribution for *world* usage. Her "Appeal to Musicians," an adapted English translation of her 1921 Greek speech, written for an American audience in the first months of 1924 in anticipation of the organ's launch that year, makes both points: "A new organ, with new intervals, is building in Germany,—a forest of pipes! I, an American in Greece, am telling its significance to musicians in America. . . . This organ is *my contribution* to the cause of Peace and Understanding *in the world*,—and my appeal to you is to . . . send a few musicians to hear it."[179]

The statement that the organ was *her* "contribution to the cause of Peace and Understanding *in the world*" brings attention to dialectical shifts in her three extant statements dating respectively from 1917, 1921, and 1924. Her letter of September 1917 addressed to May in Paris presupposes the international availability of the principles of Greek tradition. It locates Greek tradition on Mount Parnassus ("Montparnasse" is also a neighborhood in Paris famous for its artistic circles) as a symbol of the Western artist's search for fresh grounding in Greece to create new work. In a portion of the letter not discussed above, Eva writes: "[Greek] art is always based on necessity, and one feels perfectly at ease *whatever nation one may belong to* in building one's foundations on *Parnassus*."[180] Her February 1921 Greek lecture before the Greek Archaeological Society narrows the focus to the exclusively national community, calling on Greeks to recover their traditions. In this case, the audience was urban elites with a Greek national self-identification. So too the imagined collectivity was national and territorial, and her expectation that Greeks should "express [themselves] harmoniously again . . . according *to the eternal necessity of the Greek Earth*"[181] aligns itself with a form of environmental determinism that was emergent at this time in Greece, when the boundedness of national territory and its naturalized elements were increasingly linked with qualities of the Greek nation.[182] Eva's third document, the 1924 open letter, is an invitation to Americans to explore her new organ and the ancient method of singing that it was built to support.

Her changing audience only partially explains her shifting point of reference in the three documents. There is also a changed conceptual focus: from the individual (American, French) artist working to reinvent the lost arts of antiquity; to the Greek national collectivity seeking to expand its connection to "the Greek earth"; to American/world musicians seeking to extend the radius of aesthetic taste beyond the Western center for the sake of "Peace and Understanding in the world." Of special interest to me is her shift from the national to the "world" framework between 1921 and 1924.

More than the failure to secure Greek financial support for the organ was informing this reorientation. World-changing events had intervened since the day when she instructed members of the audience in the Greek Archaeological Society auditorium to rediscover the intrinsic value of their traditional music in February 1921. At the time when Eva gave her first talk on Greek fashion in May 1919, twenty thousand Greek soldiers took control of Smyrna on the west coast of Asia Minor, a sort of trophy given to Venizelos by the Allies of the Great War to thank him for his country's cooperation. Then Venizelos lost the election of 1920 under circumstances that aroused old divisions. King Constantine, who had been forced by the Allies to leave Greece, was returned to the country by plebiscite. His supporters in the military then dismissed experienced pro-Venizelist officers, just before initiating a major military campaign inland from Smyrna in hopes of defeating the rebels of the Turkish national independence movement centered in Ankara. Their goal was eventually to take Constantinople. Having pushed into Anatolia along two fronts, they were too badly stretched to counter the Turkish revolutionaries' fierce resistance. By September 1921 the Greek army was out of supplies. An appeal to the Allies for help met with indifference and, worse, the loss of support. Britain, France, and Italy decided to end their commitment to the postwar agreement with Venizelos. A stalemate followed. Then on August 26, 1922, came the full Turkish counterattack. Both the Greek and the Turkish armies enforced a scorch-earth policy as the Greeks rushed in mad retreat. By September 13, the villages with Greek population between Ankara and Smyrna were taken. Greek and Armenian quarters in Smyrna were burned and Christian homes pillaged. About half a million abject, panic-stricken refugees were crammed in the waterfront of Smyrna with no means of escape. An estimated 440,000 Armenian civilians and 264,000 Greek civilians were killed by Turkish forces during the Turkish War of Independence between 1919 and 1922, adding to a total of 3.5 to 4.3 million Armenians, Greeks, Nestorians, and other Christians killed by Ottoman regimes between 1900 and 1923,[183] while over fifteen thousand Muslims were killed by the Greek army. The Republic of Turkey emerged from the ashes.

On January 30, 1923, the Greek and Turkish governments signed the Treaty of Lausanne to end the conflict, settle their borders, and mandate the de jure denaturalization and exchange of approximately two million people (1.5 million Anatolian Greek Orthodox Christians and five hundred thousand Muslims in Greece) between them. Beginning with the Smyrna inferno in September 1922 and continuing through the end of the decade, the greatest wave of refugees ever to hit Greece's shores in the twentieth century descended on the country. The numbers were much greater than the eighteen thousand refugees Raymond Duncan was helping to settle in Athens in 1915 when Penelope's lungs gave out.

With the arrival of so many refugees came acute socioeconomic problems, while at the same time an ideological vacuum presented itself after a decade of almost continuous war. The ouster of Greek Orthodox Christians from Anatolia, coinciding with the violence that accompanied the end of the Ottoman Empire, would go down in Greek history as the Asia Minor Catastrophe, or simply *the* Catastrophe, because it marked both the end of the Greek presence in Anatolia and the failure of the Greek dream to retake Constantinople, which had fueled the national imagination for eighty years. This failure further fanaticized the populace. The old political parties could no longer derive legitimacy from the country's irredentist aspirations. Drawing energy instead from the old conflict of Venizelos and the king, people representing every region, institution, social sphere, and class were consumed by the continuous rehearsal of old scenes of political rupture—even after the monarchy was abolished and the second Hellenic Republic was established on March 25, 1924. In the meantime, the Communist Party of Greece (KKE) was formed from the Socialist Worker's Party. It drew support from the working class, although Greece's slow industrialization hindered its quick growth. Its broader effect was the unification of the bourgeois elites against it.

Angelos responded to the Asia Minor Catastrophe by entering a long period of isolation. A few months before the Greek defeat, he had publicly endorsed King Constantine in an open letter expressing his confidence that the king would make Greece strong again, while vilifying Venizelos for selling out to the West. When he heard about the disaster in Smyrna, he was spending the summer and fall of 1922 in Upper Agoriani, the same village visited by Eva after her pilgrimage to Damasta. Nearby was the camp of two Americans: George Cram ("Jig") Cook, founder of the Provincetown Players, and Susan Glaspell, the American Pulitzer Prize–winning playwright, who was his wife. They had abandoned their theater company to travel to Mount Parnassus for the proverbial fresh start. When the news reached them, Cook and Glaspell went immediately to Thessaloniki to witness "the sight of twenty thousand people from Smyrna, arriving in the middle of one night, in bravely-born misery."[184] Perhaps Cook expressed to Angelos his feeling after seeing that awful sight: "'The world is going other ways than ours. We must let it go, or we must lay down our lives to stop its going so.'"[185]

Whether actually uttered or unconsciously shared, these words perfectly expressed Angelos's idea that Western modernity's promise of progress had failed. The world was untethered; it was like a rudderless ship headed into troubled waters. Now, in the midst of crisis, it was up to him and Cook and the few other "ασύγχρονοι" (untimely) visionaries like them—people not disconnected from the problems of the present day but able to see past, present, and future all in one sweeping vision—to become the world's leaders.[186] Angelos spent the winter holed up in Delphi working to replace the Great Idea with his own big idea. For the time being, it was a "Balkan Idea" of encouraging Greece to pursue unity with its enemies, to take the place at the helm "amid the tempestuous cross-currents of our time."[187] Early in 1923, as the Treaty of Lausanne was being prepared for signature, he gave a series of lectures, "Ομιλίες μου στους Αρίστους" (My talks for the elite), addressing the elite of Greece.

Eva's response was different. A progressive thinker who had let go her sense of the superiority of Western civilization to embrace Greece's Eastern underside, she was now filled with concern that all of Greece, preoccupied with refugees and political infighting, had become too distracted to attend to her call to preserve its musical inheritance. Perhaps she was too myopically focused on the construction of the organ to notice that the Anatolian refugees reaching Greece's shore included musicians who were carrying old Eastern tunes, who had knowledge of the *makam* of Ottoman secular music. During the next half century, they would make the greatest contribution to Greece's musical reorientation along lines similar to what Eva was imagining. For now, the musical future of Greece looked dubious to her, and Eva needed allies. This was the moment in early 1924 when she expanded her search for collaborators outside Greece.

Eva and Angelos traveled to the Steinmeyer factory near Munich in January 1924 to supervise the final stages of the organ's production. A delay caused by problems with the pianola mechanical attachment[188] created an opportunity for a side trip. Angelos, who was now studying utopian visions that generated successful revolutions, tried to cross into the Russian Socialist Federative Soviet Republic but was stopped at the border.[189] He returned to Greece alone. Eva went on to Paris.

There she paid Natalie Clifford Barney a visit, possibly for the first time since 1909. She told Barney about the new organ and her plan to make the music of the East available to the world. Barney encouraged her to bring it to Paris for a performance.[190] As they discussed the organ, I wonder if they didn't think back on a letter Eva wrote in 1903 on a painting by Titian in the Prado Museum in Madrid that centers on an organ.[191] The letter was still in Barney's possession. Even if they did not recall it, I shall, in order to measure the distance Eva traveled after her breakup with Natalie. Here is Eva's description of the painting, which is entitled "Venus with the Organist":

> A woman lying on a beautiful couch and at her feet a man playing the organ; his left only resting on the keys as if he were just holding the base notes of the last accord, and he is turning toward her, the music finished, to see it taken up in the harmony of the color of her flesh. She is naked and he is dressed—and it makes no difference,—it is all quite natural. Her feet are pressing a little against him, just suggesting human nearness, and beyond them a beautiful near path of grass bordered with tall straight trees stretches off to the horizon and right near, yet not too near, a fountain splashing joyously. The place where they are is so broad and open, one sees so far in the distance, that it suggests somehow a world inhabited only by beautiful people, because they are thousands so unconcerned, so natural, and one feels sure that any one who walked up the great lawn toward them would be glad to see them there, and they quite unabashed at being seen.[192]

In all the paintings by Titian's studio with this title, a male organist turns from the keyboard to gaze longingly on Venus, naked on a luxurious bed. From one painting to the next, the organist disengages further from the instrument as he turns his attention more fully to the vision of Venus. This one in the Prado has the organist still connected to the organ, though just barely, as Eva observed: his left hand is "only resting on the keys as if he were just holding the base notes of the last accord,"[193] even as his gaze is totally absorbed in his backward glance on the goddess of love. The painting shows music turning into love, or sound becoming vision (both processes interested Eva), and the entire spectacle is rendered to "be seen" by voyeuristic viewers—both those looking at the canvas and those imagined on the other side of the window looking in. But what Eva's ecphrastic description captures best is the notion she had of music opening up a window to a "world inhabited only by beautiful people." Her phrase in 1903 is striking in its elitism.

How far had her "fifteen years in Greece travelling, listening, studying,"[194] taken her from the elitist aestheticism of that earlier moment, when she was captivated by the artistic vision that transformed music into the beautiful spectacle of love? At first, art for art's sake was her doctrine to compensate for the ill effects of modernity's mechanization. Gradually, Eva's sense of inclusion versus that of Barney's elitism became a major difference between them. After her move to Greece, through her absorption in musical matters of concern, she gained the confidence to express her inclusionist feelings more forcefully. Through contact with people outside the elitist circles in which she once traveled, she developed awareness that the world comprised not "only . . . beautiful people," yet the "thousands [of] unconcerned" were destroying the music she cared about: "The public schools are trampling it, European music is stifling it, educated people are laughing at it, and ten years' mourning caused by constant war has left the people little heart to sing."[195] With personal integrity, she had thrown herself into the field, grasped the stakes of different positions in musical debates, and adopted an anti-Western, conservationist stance. She had learned Byzantine music so expertly that she was authorized to teach it to aspiring male church cantors, even though she was neither Greek Orthodox nor a man. She had spent thousands of dollars on a book, a school, and an organ to encourage musical practices that could not be played on a piano keyboard. She had developed the social connections, linguistic and cultural competence, and Greek national rhetoric to question urban Greeks on their consumption habits.

Thus, Eva's break with Barney initiated a rejection of the elitism that Barney represented.[196] Moreover, it caused a seismic shift in Eva's center of interest from dead Greeks to living. Yet, despite these changes, as of early 1924, I do not think Eva had worked through the ideological dimensions of her ethnographic project: Who were the "Greek people" whose music she was trying to save?[197] By whose authority was she speaking on their behalf? By what mechanism was she intending to mobilize them and to what collective effect? And to what political positions might her project lend support?

Thinking about collective groups and how to address them came to Eva as a crash course that year in the person of Khorshed Naoroji, a student of piano and composition at the Sorbonne University.[198] She was the granddaughter of Dadabhai Naoroji, the first Indian member of British Parliament, known as the Grand Old Man of India because he "renounced personal fortunes and material comforts . . . to address the issue of Indian poverty."[199] His "simplicity and devotion to [his] fellow Indians" directly influenced Gandhi. In turn, Gandhi recruited Khorshed and her sisters into his noncooperation movement with the call that they should "return to a lifestyle of simplicity and positively contribute toward the constructive program for *swaraj* [self-rule]."[200] In Paris at the time of their meeting, Khorshed was still committed to her musical education, while also extensively connected with the Indian associations and publications from Paris to Poland to India.

Eva met her either by chance or by seeking her out upon hearing about the Anglo-Parsi pianist who "could play Beethoven quite well and Chopin really charmingly . . . but [could] not play the simplest Hindu melody on the piano."[201] My guess is the latter. In whatever way it happened, Eva found something she was looking for. There were obvious differences between them—of nationality, Khorshed's experience of racism in Europe, and other matters discussed later in this chapter. There were also important cross continental points of convergence. Like Eva, Khorshed was an educated, upper-class woman born into wealth and privilege. Her grandfather Dadabhai had made money in a commercial house for trade in cotton before he dedicated himself to politics. Eva's grandfather Courtlandt Palmer had humbler origins as a trader in hardware before he became one of the richest, most powerful men in New York City through investments in real estate. Khorshed's father, Ardeshir Naoroji, the only son of Dadabhai, was a physician, whom Khorshed lost while an infant.[202] Eva also mourned the loss of her father, a Columbia-trained lawyer and social reformer, in her youth. Khorshed exuded an air of aristocracy, like Eva. She was described as "an "aristocrat to her fingertips, highly Westernized, sensitive and sophisticated."[203] And through her grandfather's legacy, she enjoyed access to eminent people in India and Europe, as did Eva in America and Europe through her familiar and social connections. The successes of both women entered the public record from their youth.[204] Perhaps even more important than these convergences of birth and situation was the fact that both Eva and Khorshed were tired of Western civilization and its exploitation of the East, particularly the disastrous effect of European musical imports on traditional culture. At the time of their meeting, Khorshed wished to use her musical education to disrupt the economy of sound that was bringing "thousands of pianos and phonographs and small church harmoniums"[205] from the West, silencing native cultural expression.

Like Eva, too, Khorshed considered herself "peculiar,"[206] and she shared with Eva the will to "break down all barriers of convention."[207] Almost immediately, they were bound in a relationship of intimacy. Khorshed was "baby" to Eva's "mums" or "mummy," and Khorshed, in her tender moments, referred to Eva or herself in the third-person masculine pronoun:

"Mummy will not see his baby any more in silks and gold but he'll love him all the more. I've got rather mixed up in the gender."[208] They sometimes slept together in "the middle room in the other house"—the original in Sikya—when Angelos or guests were in the villa.[209] Khorshed expressed enormous affection for Eva and Glafkos but only once in her correspondence "included" Angelos ("My love to all of you, Angelo included").[210] She delicately referred to a "misunderstanding" surrounding him ("but the love and friendship between Angelo and myself has been a great misunderstanding from the very beginning")[211] and justified her decision to stay on despite unspecified "incidents"[212] "because [she] was very happy in [Eva's] love."[213] Was Khorshed subject to Angelos's advances? Were she and Eva lovers? Was she caught between them? Was the Sikelianos household, with its famed comings and goings of visitors and rumored orgies, a sexually threatening place? Some or all of these scenarios may be true.

Their path from Paris to Greece took them first to Oettingen to test Eva's new organ. A group photo taken outside the Steinmeyer factory (figure 3.9) offers us a glimpse of the festivities.[214] As Eva recalled the event to an American audience four years later, it was a test of the utility of Byzantine notation as a universal music writing system as much as the organ: "I had Korshed sing to [Psachos] when I was out of hearing, he wrote her songs and gave them to me. I read them to her from the manuscript, and we proved to her that Byzantine notation could write her music. She also found she could play her music on our organ and she was happy."[215] A performance for an audience followed. Eva proudly reported the concert's "huge success" in a letter to Barney a few days later.[216] The letter underscores just how valuable ("best of all") Khorshed was for Eva's endeavor to promote the organ as an international instrument. After her frustrated address to Greeks for support and failed appeal to Americans to come hear the organ, it was more than a small accomplishment that a "very good pianist" who was not Greek but Indian could both manage the new keyboard "with perfect ease" and especially play "Indian religious and popular songs as if she [had] been doing it all her life."

The photo bears witness to the European-dressed Khorshed beside Eva in her Greek tunic. She is standing to Eva's left from the camera's viewpoint. Both women are cross-cultural dressers—with the difference that Eva's Greek dress is anachronistic and a sign of her privilege as a wealthy white woman from the West, whereas Khorshed's European dress signals her modernization, success as a member of an elite colonized subgroup, and near alienation from India. Eva wears her most beautiful, ankle-length, white embroidered tunic and himation, which she has twisted around her

FIGURE 3.9. Group gathered outside the Steinmeyer factory in Oettingen, Germany, June 1924. In the front row (center left) are Eva Sikelianos, dressed a light-shaded Greek tunic, with her red hair braided in a crown on her head, and Khorshed Naoroji, in a dark-shaded Western dress, with her hair braided in pigtails and wrapped in two buns on the sides of her head. K. A. Psachos House Archive, Hellenic Folklore Research Center, Academy of Athens.

breasts so that it falls in generous pleats. Her hair, still long, thick, and "torch-light" red,[217] forms a massive braided crown over her head, setting off her pale skin, gray eyes (but they are shut), and white dress, which almost run together in the black-and-white photo. Khorshed's black hair is parted off center and worn in double-braided buns on each side of her warm-toned face. Her dark-shaded dress follows the European design of the day: straight lined, calf-length, elbow-length sleeves, with a ribbon marking the dropped waistline. A mid-length beaded necklace drapes below her breasts, and her feet are covered in dark leather shoes. The two women are a study in contrasts.

In a photo taken several months later in Greece (figure 3.10), however, the figures of Khorshed and Eva are more intertwined. On a tour of ancient sites with Angelos, an Englishman, and Khorshed's brother, they are posing inside the famous lion gate at Mycenae, with the plain of Argos behind them. Khorshed is again to the left, this time with some distance between her and the seated Eva. Now each exhibits elements of the other. The tone of their clothing is reversed: Eva is wearing the darker-toned dress and Khorshed luminous silk. Eva's tunic and himation, another of her remarkable creations, sets off her pale skin dramatically. Her hair is now parted off center and worn in double-braided buns following Khorshed's styling in the Oettingen photograph. The cabochon moonstone around her neck is from India. It was a gift from her mother, which she passed on to Isadora Duncan during her visit to Greece in 1915 when she sang the Mareillaise in Venizelos's support, and which Isadora returned to her in 1921, complaining that it had brought her bad luck.[218] Khorshed is wearing something Indian too. She has now abandoned Western dress for a luxurious sari. There's a modest blouse underneath, and the long rectangular silk cloth twisted around her body and up over her head has an embroidered ribbon border to signify her upper class Parsi identity. Her black hair is now center parted above the bindi on her forehead and falls straight over her shoulders under her partial head covering. She is wearing sandals on her feet, like Eva.

Khorshed changed into her "Indian clothes" when she reached Greece.[219] Thus between July and November of 1924, Eva was no longer "the only ancient Greek in modern Athens,"[220] as the snide Pavlos Nirvanas pointed out after her talk on Greek fashion in 1921. While no elite Greek woman heard Eva's plea to revolt against economic colonialism by replacing French fashions with her own Greek designs, now Khorshed Naoroji, an upper-class woman from one of the most renowned families in India, abandoned Western dress and was moving about Greece in the Indian equivalent of a himation.

Eva's and Khorshed's photograph in this prehistoric spot draws attention to their mirroring journeys. For both, the pursuit of a different music was a propelling force, as one woman with a strong attachment to Greece drew another of a vastly different background into her sphere. Like Eva's travels after Penelope, the singer of ancient hymns, Khorshed's trip to Greece found its impetus in Eva and the promise of her organ and Byzantine notation. The journey inspired also a change in dress. Like Eva, Khorshed removed her Parisian dresses in Greece to wrap herself in uncut cloth of natural fibers. This change in dress signified her turn away from Western culture. The divestment was a sign of a larger commitment: to labor for the recovery of the ancient cultural expressions that European imperialism was erasing, with Byzantine music as the technical means to achieve the desired end.

Eva seems in charge in this photograph. She almost gives the impression that she is directing Khorshed's Greek journey after her own. She has placed Khorshed near the center of the picture frame, while she sits to the side, her eyes lowered, as if to acknowledge Khorshed's transformation. Yet, despite the obvious parallels, the photograph also marks the different trajectories the two women had followed to reach this archaic location

FIGURE 3.10. Khorshed Naoroji (standing, left) and Eva Sikelianos in the lion gate at Mycenae, late fall, 1924. Acc. 189, Eva Sikelianou Papers, No. 355. Benaki Museum Historical Archives.

and the different turn each would take in the months ahead. Khorshed had come from the East to study European classical music. In Paris she gathered with groups of Indian students (the "Hindustan Association") to talk about the future of "Bharat Mati."[221] Her network extended to similar groups around the world and included formidable scholars (Prabodh Chandra Bagchi), poets (Rabindranath Tagore), journalists (Ramananda Chatterjee), scientists (Prasanta Chandra Mahalanobis), nationalist revolutionaries (Gandhi, her two sisters Moshi Captain and Perin Captain, and

Gandhi's supporter in France M. Romain Rolland).[222] Most of these people lived and breathed the decolonization imperative that was currently taking the shape of a mass movement.

Khorshed's journey to Greece was for her a crucial digression. Musically, it added just superficial knowledge of Byzantine notation to her arsenal, while teaching her to study ancient visual art with an eye to lost gestures and movements.[223] Politically it heightened a facet of her dual consciousness as a Western-trained woman and colonial subject, in a way that prepared her to alter her course.[224] To be precise, her friendship with Eva raised awareness that her European musical training—the necessary path to her cultivation as an upper-class cosmopolitan Indian woman—would never make her European: "I believe East is East and West is West," she wrote, echoing Rudyard Kipling. "Just as the panther cannot change his skin so however much we imbibe Western education and culture we are incapable of understanding the West and vice-versa."[225] Instead it both subjected her to an unforgiving measure of European cultivation and contributed to the erasure of native culture in India. There were moments when she just withered in recognition of all it would take to overcome the effects of British rule, and she wondered if she shouldn't just accept her subject position: "I'm just shrinking into space. I sometimes wonder if I couldn't be a . . . maid, I think there could be no argument in washing up dishes. I'd feel so happy if I was left alone and could amuse myself with a bowl of water, dip my fingers into the water and smile at my happiness."[226] Even on those occasions, however, she was moving to clarify her vision of a freed, reintegrated India and her place in it. She began to imagine herself teaching not European but "Indian national music"[227] when she returned to her home in the Europeanized city of Bombay.

Eva followed the evolution of Khorshed's thinking over the course of eighteen months from their meeting in Paris to her return to India and attempt to "work in Indian music with a view to a profession"[228] in September 1925, until she left Bombay to become a close associate of Gandhi in the North-West Provinces. The letters from Khorshed preserved in Eva's official archive in the Benaki Museum—eighteen written between the late summer of 1924 and September 1925 and several after 1936, when she was released from jail following years of noncooperative confrontation with British authorities—bear witness to Eva's lasting interest in Khorshed. What Eva wrote in reply is open to the imagination, since her letters do not survive in the archives I have studied. I assume she felt satisfaction when Khorshed personified Greece as "Mother," after "Mother India," and even convinced her "fellow countrymen" in Paris to "talk of Mother

Greece."[229] The analogy suggested that Eva had found an ally in Khorshed who might join India with Greece in the effort to decouple music—and civilization—from the West, to promote non-Western music, with Byzantine notation and theory as the shared pedagogical foundation.

But what did Eva understand of the discrimination Khorshed experienced as a racialized, colonized subject? In the warmth of the Greek sun, sea, and soil, the birthplace of democracy, which her grandfather had extolled,[230] Khorshed recalled serial experiences of racism and expressed her commitment to social justice:

> Mother Earth came out and made my sight her eyes see [sic]. It's not men that can show you nature but vice versa. You feel, my darling Mummy, that you haven't shown me your country. But Mother Earth (Greece) has shown herself to me, I have played on her breast. I have laughed and cried and I slept and worked. She has put [word?] and flowers in my life. It was all necessary. I have always felt her Mother love and protection, in the metro train in Paris, in the patronizing attitude of the Anglo-Indian women on the English train. In the foul language addressed to me by a Belgian in Brussels, in the ill health that I enjoyed in Italy. In the rotten eggs that abominable "a——s" of Germany and in the swearing I got last Thursday. Mummy darling, everything belongs to everyone and nothing belongs to anyone.[231]

Eva received this letter a few weeks after the Mycenae snapshot and just days before Khorshed left Greece. We know that Eva became a member of the Indian association in Paris that year and renewed her membership regularly. But what were her political commitments?

The photograph of Eva and Khorshed in the prehistoric citadel of Mycenae and another in the ancient theater of Epidaurus suggests to me that Eva drew a specifically civic and nationalist message from Khorshed's allegiances to make a commitment of her own. Eva's trajectory leading to this turning point in her life mirrored Khorshed's. She came to Greece from the West. She was supported by the accouterments of money, education, a large social network, and sociopolitical arguments reinforcing white privilege in the world. Greek culture had a special status in her social framework as an exceptional, universal prototype. In Greece, she discovered that its universality applied to certain people in the West but not to Greeks. Her sympathy for the Greek people—an effect of her attachment to the Sikelianos family and experience of the swings in Greek fortunes (the wars, high hopes, massive losses, and repeated mourning of the early twentieth century) and, I suspect, her immediate enchantment with the darkly melodic music of the church and countryside—all these things led her to advocate for Greeks to repossess Hellenism. Her advocacy took her deep into native Greek systems of knowledge that were distant from Western notions of the Greeks, and she experienced them like a sympathetic participant observer of living people whom she was studying.

Through her journey of eighteen years up to this point, however, she had not managed to connect her work to a larger social vision. Her passion for certain elements of Greek culture, particularly weaving and even Byzantine music, was seen as eccentric. Indeed, her advocacy for these things placed her in an awkward spot. On the one hand, as a Westerner telling Greeks how to be Greek, she was replicating the West-to-East flow of power and knowledge that she wished to reverse. On the other hand, the many Greeks who were ensconced in the trappings of Western classicism—who identified Western visions of the Greek as their national culture—could not understand why she would abandon the universe they aspired to inhabit. As noted earlier, Eva felt especially foreign precisely when she was telling Greeks to reclaim their non-European, Eastern musical heritage. Thus, she experienced a different psychosocial divided consciousness from that of Khorshed or other colonized, racialized subjects. Her Western skepticism, which encouraged her to test alien viewpoints and launch an investigation of non-Western practices, led her to go native in Greece in a way that Greeks did not recognize. This gave her the "sensation" (I quote W.E.B. Du Bois's terms in his "Strivings of the Negro People," with awareness that the conditions Du Bois was exploring do not apply) "of always looking at one's self through the eyes of others, of measuring one's soul by the tape of a world that looks on in amused contempt and pity."[232]

It was at this point in her musical journey—when, in the company of Khorshed, she could look at herself through the eyes of Greeks and sense their amused contempt—that Eva discussed with Angelos his Delphic Idea: to bring an elect group of individuals from around the world to the sacred ancient precinct of Delphi, where, through the unifying experience of revived Greek drama, sports, poetry, discussion, and song, they would gather primordial seeds of life to revitalize humanity. By 1924, when their conversation took place, a live production of *Prometheus Bound* in demotic Greek with new Greek music was part of his plan. Aeschylus's play was to stand as an allegory for the entire project. Prometheus in the esoteric philosophy and protofascist mix of Angelos's current thinking was the titan who saved the seed of fire of the gods in order to show humans how to face the naked brutality of nature's violence, discover a path of spiritual evolution, and dream of becoming godlike.[233] A production in Greek at

Delphi would represent the survival of the Promethean spirit in the present. It would both give the world a spiritual boost and make Greece stand tall among nations.

Angelos had already identified either Manolis Kalomiris or Dimitris Mitropoulos as the appropriate composer for the choral passages. Mitropoulos was Eva's friend from the Athens Conservatory.[234] Currently their houseguest in Sikya—together with Khorshed—he had just set several of Angelos's poems to original music, possibly Greece's first atonal compositions.[235] But he had also recently accepted a job directing the Symphony Orchestra of Kalomiris's Hellenic Conservatory. (He would go on to have an international career as a major conductor in the United States.) So Angelos asked Kalomiris, and he accepted.

Seated in the pine forest next to their house in Sikya, with Mount Parnassus in sight and Delphi hidden in its folds,[236] with Khorshed somewhere nearby, Angelos turned to Eva for help. Would she direct *Prometheus Bound*? Would she pay for the event? Would she be Angelos's collaborator and supporter? We know that Eva agreed on the condition that Kalomiris would step aside so she could recruit Psachos, a man with limited compositional skills, to write music for Aeschylus's choral odes in the Byzantine tradition. *Upward Panic* gives this retrospective explanation of the condition she set: she had studied with Psachos *in order* to learn how to compose music for Greek tragedy. The musical story I have outlined above offers another reason. Eva did not recognize Kalomiris's compositions as Greek, whereas she believed that Byzantine music linked present practice with both ancient Greek music and long-established musical traditions of the East, which were endangered by Western cultural invasions. The reenchantment of the modern world that Angelos was imagining required a musical reorientation.

This brings me to the more interesting question of why Eva agreed to render her labor and ultimately her inheritance to the service of Angelos's proposal, since it meant she would cancel her dream to found an international school of non-Western modal music to preserve traditions from Greece to India. Khorshed's ambivalent presence is crucial. No matter how excited Khorshed was about learning Byzantine music in Greece, her primary commitment was public spirited and national, concentrating on the revolt of India against British colonial rule. She imagined putting her musical learning to use to promote Indian self-rule. Barring this, she would "try yoga."[237] This eventuality came quickly, as she left for what she called "a yogi ashram"[238] (namely the Sabarmati Ashram, also known as the Gandhi Ashram, or Satyagraha Ashram) in the Northwest province, the heart of

Gandhi's civil disobedience movement, in September 1925. Eva, in the company of Khorshed in Greece in 1924, anticipating that she would soon lose her only international collaborator, imagined a parallel destiny for herself. By joining Angelos's Delphic effort, she would connect herself to a national movement, to promote a Greek cultural ascendancy. Moreover, she would become "the first woman to stage an ancient tragedy in an authentic Greek outdoor setting . . . on an archaeological site."[239] Most important for the movement's success, her work would have the signature of Angelos Sikelianos, a nationally recognized poet and charismatic leader. With Sikelianos as the festival's nominal head, she, the foreign wife, would finally collaborate with Greeks to put Greece on the map with a totally made-in-Greece revival: a tragedy performed by Greeks in demotic Greek, sung to melodies composed by Psachos in the tones of Byzantine music, and mobilized with the rhythms and steps of Greek folk dances.

CHAPTER 4

Drama

After centuries of silence, the open-air amphitheater at Delphi re-sounded with a performance of Aeschylus's *Prometheus Bound* on May 9, 1927. Three decades earlier, the fourth-century BCE theater was still underground, until archaeological excavations carried out by the École française d'Athènes (French School at Athens, an archaeological institute) unearthed it between 1891 and 1901. Restored as a ruin with broken benches, a despoiled *skene* (scene building), and a cracked dancing floor, the theater looked as though it had been standing forever. The performance of *Prometheus Bound* likewise signified antiquity's continuation, even though nothing like it was ever performed in Aeschylus's time. Eva's direction used modern Greek elements to convey the message that Greeks of her era were the heirs to a living performance tradition. Actors recited the play's lines in a demotic Greek translation.[1] Young women, selected from the daughters of the Lyceum of Greek Women[2] to form the chorus, sang music composed by Psachos. Their poses replicated gestures from archaic vases in the National Archaeological Museum. In just the right places, they brought these gestures to life with the rhythm and steps of Greek folk dances.[3] The entire cast wore costumes Eva had woven, using techniques she learned from peasant women. Actors and members of the chorus filled the circular stage with coordinated movements, giving form to Nietzsche's concept of a primordial unity, and drawing together a theater audience in what one critic described as a "single collective emotion" (figure 4.1).[4] The masks, the costumes, the singing and dancing chorus, and the cracked stage of the ancient theater nestled on the southwestern slope of Mount Parnassus all gave the feeling that Greek tragedy had never died. The Greeks were alive and once again performing their drama.[5]

While not everyone in attendance saw the revival favorably,[6] the positive reviews followed one of two lines of thought. From the standpoint of cultural nationalism, the festival created a sense of collective belonging.

FIGURE 4.1. Chorus of Oceanides in *Prometheus Bound*, 1927, seated around the circular stage of the ancient theater of Delphi in two semicircular formations. Posing in a gesture of mourning, they face Prometheus, who is chained to the rock-like set on the foundations of the ruined *skene*, ancient scene building. Acc. 189, Eva Sikelianou Papers, No. 374. Benaki Museum Historical Archives.

Koula Pratsika,[7] the principal of the tragic chorus of Oceanides, who spent two years preparing the group, expressed its collective effect thus: "We followed Eva's lead to discover an unknown Greece, the existence of which we hadn't imagined, a Greece of our own and for ourselves."[8] From an archaeological perspective, it filled a scientific void. Archaeologist Ernst Buschor, head of the German Archaeological Institute in Athens, reportedly said to Eva after the production, "'You have solved archaeological problems which we have been working on fruitlessly for years.'"[9] He was referring to questions about the elusive elements of the movement and sound of the tragic chorus, about which little evidence remained. In both of these assessments, Eva was seen to have excavated a missing clue as if from a void.

The Delphic Festival's dialogue with sources contemporary to it is a complex affair, especially as it intersects with Eva's recollection of her life. Eva wrote in *Upward Panic* (the book first drafted in 1938–39 and revised, tellingly, in 1941, as she was cutting her ties with American dancer and choreographer Ted Shawn, her last major collaborator)[10] that she had "left everything behind" when she moved to Greece in 1906.[11] She was referring specifically to her closet of Parisian dresses; but her account of the journey to and from Delphi dismisses almost every point of contact with her colleagues in America and France. It casts Penelope and Angelos Sikelianos as the ones responsible for Eva's escape from her old self: Penelope for wiping away Eva's ear for Western music with her singing that fateful spring day of 1906, and Angelos, whose Greek-speaking voice represented for her a "Schopenhauerian . . . 'thing-in-itself,' unattached and free."[12] The narrative of *Upward Panic* places Eva always following Penelope and Angelos; solving archaeological problems, it would seem, was never her goal.[13] In fact, by making her highly sublimated memory of Penelope the condition of her production of the Delphic Festivals, Eva suggested that she completely broke away from both her non-Greek past as well as her scholarly interlocutors. This was part of a pattern she developed of hiding behind masks and erasing facets of herself.

The revival of *Prometheus Bound* in the Delphic Festival of 1927, a production identified with its "aura of resurrection,"[14] has received ample critical attention from several angles: its dialogue with other choreographed stage events in Greece, Europe, and the United States;[15] Nietzsche's ideas of tragedy;[16] the tradition of European festivals responding to the utopian model of Wagner's Bayreuth;[17] and Angelos Sikelianos's broader sociopolitical vision.[18] Here I follow a different course, while building on these critical projects. I push against the notion that Eva's work in Greece was disconnected from her non-Greek past and indifferent to "archaeological problems." Digging deep into her papers and other sources dating between 1903 and 1940, I piece together Eva's dialogue with artists from Isadora Duncan to H. D. to George Cram Cook and Susan Glaspell to Angelos Sikelianos, who were all familiar with archaeological problems but standing at an oblique angle to them as they thought about how to stage the ancient Greek chorus. This transatlantic genealogy gives me occasion to reflect on how creative work happening near ruins yet outside the formal discipline of archaeology responds to the place, takes on the feel of archaeological discoveries, and generates further rounds of imaginative reworking. The same genealogy brings into view how Eva Sikelianos's efforts to revive the tragic chorus, having transformed Isadora's experiments, traveled across the Atlantic to inform the work of Ted Shawn. I use the episode to reflect on how archaeological problems enter nonacademic work and there generate their own set of investigations to become creative, contested ground. In this same period of fruitful artistic production, while Eva was working among the actual ruins of Delphi, some competing ideas and exigencies threatening the foundations of Eva's Greek life begin to surface.

ISADORA DUNCAN'S "MULTIPLE ONENESS," 1903

Isadora Duncan's encounter with Greece, the first moment in this story, has a surface resemblance to Eva's—although the ways Eva's staging of the Greek chorus differed from Isadora's will become clear when I describe the Delphic production. Like Eva's early work, Isadora's took shape in the museums of Europe from 1900 to 1902, where she and Raymond combed through the Greek collections, copying gestures from ancient Greek works and reproducing them with their bodies.[19] Isadora was a trendsetter in concentrating on the replication of classical gestures as a source for modern taste. But she was not alone. She emerged from a culture of gendered bodily exercise in the United States and Britain that codified the gestural theories and exercises developed for the theater by François Delsarte in France.[20] The popularization of the Delsartean system reformed women's education in addition to everyday matters such as their dress and comport, for it was put to pedagogical use particularly in physical culture exercises that helped women visualize and cultivate expressive assets.[21] For example, women in physical education classes were called on to imitate the poses of ancient statues in order to acquire "bodily eloquence,"[22] as if their bodies were the tools for writing ancient letters, and their accurate and expressive recovery of a pose proved their level of literacy. The question of how still poses, captured in material relics, might release their energy in a moving sequence, like the question of how silent Greek texts might sound again, then mobilized women in schools and colleges to stage amateur Greek performances. Outside of school, a Delsartean form of entertainment developed, in which "a series of statue-poses modeled after classic works of art" told a story[23] and sometimes occasioned a game of participation and recognition.[24] Hence it was not in a cultural vacuum that Isadora—who in the 1890s advertised herself as a "Professor of Delsarte"[25]—aspired to embody the Greek chorus.

Isadora did not learn Greek, but she studied books steeped in Greek learning. Among the influential books of her era was *La danse grecque antique d'après les monuments figurés*, a massive compendium of ancient poses and dance steps reconstructed from those poses, published in French by composer Maurice Emmanuel in 1896 and translated into English in 1916.[26] Emmanuel's motto, "ἐστὶ δὲ καὶ τὰ τῶν ἀρχαίων δημιουργῶν ἀγάλματα τῆς παλαιᾶς ὀρχήσεως λείψανα" (sculptures by ancient artists are the relics of old dance),[27] succinctly articulated an archaeological assumption: that material remains are signs of a lost but restorable ancient life. For archaeologists, restoration goes as far as recovering, ordering, assembling, cataloguing, and then endlessly rereading the record of carefully excavated material culture. For an artist such as Isadora Duncan, "the relics of old dance" offered themselves for the creative reconstruction of the movement gap, the translation of still images into kinetic energy.

Isadora pored over Emmanuel's and other books in the British Museum and Paris libraries to gather relics of old Greek dance, which suggested to her—as they did to Loie Fuller, another revolutionary American dancer of her era[28]—both a path to liberation from Victorian constrictions and the triumph of modern dance over associations with crude forms of exploitation in dance halls.[29] She adored Greek art's depictions of women's uncorseted torsos, unbound breasts, flowing tunics, and loosened hair captured in the midst of motion, with bare or sandaled feet in parallel position—not the turned-out position of ballet. She wanted to set those images free. She used her body as the medium of exploration to develop the argument that Greek poses "evolved . . . from the movements of nature": "Dancing naked upon the earth," she wrote of her experiments, "I naturally fall into Greek positions, for Greek positions are only earth positions."[30] Here we see the suturing of nature and culture in the idea that Greece was forever youthful—a common early twentieth-century figure of thought, present also in the belief of the Weimarian archaeologist Ernst Buschor, who praised Eva for her archaeological correctness, that archaic Greek culture represented the "youth of the world"[31] and the hope for future rejuvenation.[32] What is important is that women artists such as Isadora Duncan, whose bodies were taste-shaping weapons, used the trope of Greece's "earth positions" (with its assumption that relics from the Greek earth gave evidence of a culture both closer to nature and more highly cultivated than modern civilization) to blaze a path for women's physical, sexual, and social liberation.

Because she was a dancer with a powerful kinesthetic sensibility, Isadora found inspiration especially in the latent stillness of ancient drawings and sculptures. She wanted her dance to supply the lost movements uniting one pose with another. Her journey to Greece in 1903 gave her a feeling of that lost life, which existed in her imagination as a still, silent world. Her body's physical connection to Greece's imposing temple architecture became a source of inspiration, as her essay entitled "The Parthenon" suggests and the later Edward Steichen photographs of her posing in the entrance to the Parthenon in 1920 illustrate.[33] During the four months of her stay in Athens in 1903, Isadora studied the rhythms of the Parthenon. "Lifting my eyes to the rhythmical succession of Doric columns," she later wrote, she tried to "express the feeling of the human body in relation to the Doric column." Movement at first eluded her. She sensed that all she "had danced was forbidden in this Temple—neither love nor hate nor fear, nor joy nor sorrow—only a rhythmic cadence, those Doric columns—only in perfect harmony this glorious Temple, calm through all the ages." Intuitively, she paid close attention to the architectural refinements—the columns' gentle curves "from the base to the height, each one . . . in flowing movement, never resting . . . in harmony with the others." This gave her the spiritual inspiration—and the movement shown in Steichen photograph: "my arms rose slowly toward the Temple, and I leaned forward—and then I knew I had found my dance, and it was a Prayer."[34]

In the Theater of Dionysus on the south slope of the Acropolis, Isadora, bare-legged in her signature white tunic and sandaled feet, gave physical expression to Dionysian ecstasy—the other side of the Apollonian harmony she found in the Parthenon—and to the recesses of the unconscious elements it unleashed, the wisdom it conveyed. A series of photographs taken by Raymond Duncan in 1903 shows Isadora creating the impression of her body's freeing itself from the limits of the ego to become the site of rapture. She produced this effect by dancing with curvilinear movements emanating from the solar plexus, the complex network of nerve fibers and muscles connecting the abdomen and pelvis. In one beautiful movement, she contracted the muscles of the solar plexus to produce a graceful C-Curve.[35] In another, she extended those muscles, arched her back, and tossed her head to produce the backward bend, also known as the "Bacchic shiver":[36] a gesture of lost inhibitions found in Maurice Emmanuel's compendium of ancient images (figure 4.2).

For Isadora Duncan, the Dionysian dance was a step toward something greater than a powerfully expressive solo of liberation. It was a move to recover the artistic origins of the tragic chorus, a notion she conceived through her encounter with Nietzsche's *Birth of Tragedy* as it circulated among performing artists at the turn of the century. Isadora embraced Nietzsche's appreciation of the body, calling him "the first dancing philosopher."[37] She was especially inspired by Nietzsche's ideas about the tragic chorus, namely that "tragedy emerged from the tragic chorus and was nothing but the chorus"[38] and that "the chorus . . . produces the vision from itself and speaks of it with the whole symbolism of dance, music, and word."[39] As she translated these ideas into dance, she "conceived the dance

FIGURE 4.2. Illustrated "backward bend," also known as the "Bacchic shiver," described by Maurice Emmanuel as "one of the extreme moments in a character-step" (Emmanuel, *Antique Greek Dance*, 174, figure 427a). Public domain.

as a chorus or community expression."[40] She wanted to reinvent the choral entity in her own solo dance. She wrote, " 'I don't mean to copy it, to imitate it, but to be inspired by it, to recreate it in myself with personal inspiration; to take its beauty with me toward the future.' "[41]

Isadora's experiments in Greek dance included the revival of the third stasimon of the *Suppliants* performed in Athens in 1903 (see chapter 3).

She selected this play, with its chorus as the protagonist, because she considered it to be the earliest tragedy by Aeschylus. Influenced by trends in comparative musicology in addition to the insights of her sister-in-law Penelope, Isadora was convinced that surviving Greek musical traditions most closely approximated the lost music of ancient Greece. She therefore selected the ten Greek boys for the chorus and gave the role of *koryphaios* (chorus leader) to the seminarian from the Rizareios Ecclesiastical School. She made the Greek boys sing while she danced the part of the chorus of fifty maidens. According to Isadora's recollection of the performance, "I found it very difficult to express in my slight figure the emotions of fifty maidens all at once, but I had the feeling of multiple oneness."[42]

Despite her sense of inadequacy, Isadora initiated a process of redefining classical literacy for women in the first years of the twentieth century by reading ancient artifacts as sources of dance. According to Tyler Jo Smith's assessment,

> Isadora Duncan, and to an extent her family, did for Greek dance what [John] Beazley did for Greek vases. She elevated dance to a more noble art than it had been considered, and she was instrumental in the development that led to its being counted as among the hallmarks of women's education and refinement. Her dependence on vases, in turn, must have encouraged a popular perception of the importance of their imagery onto the world of dance.[43]

To this I would add that her impact went beyond dance and popular perceptions of ancient imagery. She endowed silent Greek texts and images with multimedia, moving three-dimensionality in ways that inspired contemporary American writers and artists such as Eva Palmer to pay attention to not just the lost words of ancient sources but their look, sounds, and movements. Her improvisations opened up paths for new imaginative work to mobilize ancient sources.

ATALANTA IN BAR HARBOR, 1905

Eva wrote about her relationship to Isadora in *Upward Panic*. She "had seen [her] dance quite often, and met her once or twice"[44] before she heard Penelope sing Greek music in Paris or visited Kopanos. Her earlier letters place her in Bayreuth at the Wagner Festival the summer of 1904[45] when Isadora danced the Bacchanale in Wagner's *Tannhäuser* with Dionysian ecstasy.[46] Inspired by that performance, perhaps, or by another theatrical dance giving movement to ancient statuary, Eva sought to animate the chorus of a Greek-style drama the following summer. Her stage preparation of Swinburne's *Atalanta* in an open-air setting in Bar Harbor in 1905 suggests itself both as a response to Isadora's *Bacchanale* and as one of her own hidden or forgotten works leading up to her *Prometheus Bound* in Delphi.

Upward Panic gives only the barest hint of this earlier theatrical production. It mentions Swinburne as the inspiration of Eva's earliest "dream" of staging Greek tragedy.[47] She "knew all the choruses of *Atalanta of Calydon* and of *Erechtheus* by heart" and engaged in a "continuous performance of recitation" for her "spellbound" classmates when she was a student at Miss Porter's School in Farmington, Connecticut. The book acknowledges that Mrs. Dowe, the headmistress of the school, was probably showing good sense when she put a stop to those recitations because she found them "too exciting"[48] for fifteen-year-old schoolgirls. Swinburne's hunt narrative is a wild exploration of women's sexuality. It would have been indecorous, of course, for *Upward Panic* to mention exactly how her recitation of Swinburne's poetry became a piece of her intimacy with Barney, something she wrote about in her more personal letters.[49] More inexplicable, however, is another omission. Eva states that Mrs. Dowe's "interruption" of her Swinburne recitations "was for me in a way, an end. My passion for Swinburnean choruses, for melody in words, from that time struck inward instead of outwards. As far as personal performance was concerned, it never came to the surface again, even in the few amateur plays which I directed, or in all the work I did in Paris for the stage."[50] Yet Eva's "passion for Swinburnean choruses" *did* strike outward again in a plan to stage *Atalanta* with amateur actors in Bar Harbor in the summer of 1905.

It is no accident that Swinburne's *Atalanta* was the work that brought Eva closest to directing Greek tragedy before she actually directed a Greek tragedy. Here was a tragic re-creation of a Greek myth by the premier English poet of the late Victorian period, a writer whose "mind and memory were more deeply immersed in the poetry of the ancients than that of any other English poet."[51] Even more to the point, Swinburne is a poet of strong affinities with Wagner[52] and Sappho,[53] two of Eva's points of entry into Greece.

The record of this production, which was planned but may never have been performed, exists in letters from Eva in Bar Harbor to Natalie Barney in Paris. The letters describe each step Eva took to stage *Atalanta* that summer. Several details anticipate her production of *Prometheus Bound* at Delphi in 1927. First, there was the outdoor stage. After returning from Paris to Bar Harbor to visit her parents in late July,[54] she approached Anne Mills Archbold, Eva's contemporary and a wealthy patron of the arts, who granted access to her terrace. Designed by architect Fred L. Savage in 1903–4, "Archbold Cottage" drew its inspiration from Tuscan villas. The terrace was its most unique feature, with a fountain at its center, "trailing vines and blossoms," and twelve supporting stucco arches overlooking a panorama of forest, mountains, and ocean.[55] Eva's decision to work in this open-air landscape, presaging her work in the open-air theater at Delphi, was not at all out of character. Found in much nineteenth-century art, the scene of women playing out their desires among "marvelous ruins of temples . . . [and] strange old gardens in warm flowering fields"[56] was an imaginary recreation of Sappho's Mytilene, as well as a fantasy that Eva, Barney, and other women in their circle[57] tried to reproduce in their garden theatricals. For example, in June of the same year, Eva performed with Colette in one of Barney's first open-air theatrical gatherings in Neuilly.[58] The experience of that event and the ideal she and Barney generally held of replicating Sappho's garden suggested to her the theatrical suitability of the open-air terrace of Archbold Cottage for *Atalanta*.

Then, there was the choreography. Eva planned to animate Swinburne's chorus rather than to stage it as a still tableau. For assistance, she invited "Mrs. Barker" from Boston, "a woman about forty-five, full of enthusiasm, and sincere love of good things . . . [who] spent most of her life making a study of dances, rhythm, balance, movement in general, and [knew] a great deal about the very sort of dancing that [Eva] wanted the chorus to do."[59] While it is hard to identify who Mrs. Barker was, or what exactly she knew about the dancing of the chorus as Eva imagined it, their minds probably met on ground prepared by women's education and contemporary performances of Greek drama. On one end, amateur and professional experiments in staging large Greek choruses before 1902 barely had any movement. The tendency was to mass the chorus members in still, harmonious, tableau-like groupings—like figures on a bas-relief—and then to have their carefully posed limbs and bodies sway.[60] As directors began to attend to choreography, some thought arose of modeling it on "the choral dances of modern Greek peasants."[61] On another end was Isadora Duncan, dancing alone, suturing the Apollonian classicism of a motionless temple with "menacing Furies and frenzied Bacchantes."[62] Eva and Mrs. Barker would have found common ground somewhere on the spectrum between stillness and mad frenzy in their combined effort to endow Swinburne's chorus with "the very sort of dancing" that would convey the driving force of the verse.

There were also costumes, of course, which were probably Greek in style, since the play's mythological subject is Greek, and recreating the "Greek clothes we see on statues, bas-reliefs and vases"[63] became Eva's lifetime obsession. To join the verse to movement, Eva stressed she was also "getting the Greek music."[64] This assertion is crucial. It shows that setting tragedy to "Greek music" was something that occupied her before she met Penelope—and that her production choices at Delphi followed some of her own earlier work, contrary to the story she told in *Upward Panic*, which put Penelope before her. Eva later claimed that before coming to Greece she had not been able to solve the "old platonic problem" of Greek music[65] or to find music that was "truly adequate"[66] to Greek tragedy. Already in 1905, however, she was not just wrestling with the idea of Greek music in theory. She was attempting to produce Greek pitch, tone, and rhythm to match Swinburne's Greek tragedy in English verse. Actually, she was arranging music all her life, whether in improvised recitations of Swinburne, or as melodies for the poetry of friends, or in carefully transcribed works she later composed in Byzantine notation for performances of drama she never brought to stage. Her direction of *Atalanta* in Bar Harbor was both a continuation of the knowledge of "ladies' Greek" she exhibited in her Sappho tableau in August 1900 and her first Wagnerian fusion of music, drama, dance, and theatrical effects.

One more point about Eva's direction of *Atalanta*: For that performance, Eva counted on the goodwill of wealthy friends and acquaintances to volunteer their time and space, while she covered the expense of costumes and props and dealt with the uncertainty of it all. Her Atalanta, for example, was not a professional actor but Mildred Barnes, a fellow New York heiress who, years later as Mildred Barnes Bliss, would donate to Harvard University her beautiful residence and garden in Georgetown, Washington, DC, creating "Dumbarton Oaks,"[67] a research institute dedicated to Byzantine and Columbian studies as well as landscape design. When Barnes dropped out of rehearsals, Bar Harbor's *Atalanta* fell through, and Eva had to turn elsewhere to try to stage the play.

Eva's commitment to amateur actors was a risky necessity, since she did not have an unlimited flow of cash to pay professional actors. Yet it was also an artistic choice. When Barney tried to woo her back to Paris during that same period—just as Eva was meeting with some kind of theatrical success on the East Coast, as "several New York women" had approached her to act in an "ideal theater" they were planning[68]—Barney made the counteroffer of another amateur theater in Paris: "come back and help in a new plan I have for starting a 'théâtre d'amateurs'—so many are talented that it seems a shame not to do something with them. My plan is to take a small theatre once a month and give just once or twice something exceptionally good."[69] She stressed the all-female cast: women like "Colette, Ilse, . . . toi, Russel, Isadora Duncan" (Colette, Ilse [Deslandes], . . . you, [Nina] Russel, Isadora Duncan). In terms of repertoire, Barney patterned the theater on Eva's experiments: it would concentrate on reviving classical subjects and classical or classicizing authors, "sometimes little Greek plays with music and dancing . . . sometimes we might have an act of Swinburne or Shelly—(the French care about good English verse more than the English) and an Idylle of Theocritus, Oscar Wilde's Salomé. . . . In time there is success in reviving really beautiful things and doing this well, and in the meantime there is the pleasure of it." The principle of an amateur women's theater proposed here aligned itself closely with Eva's interests. The use of amateur performers allowed her freedom from consideration of social expectations or business profits. It also opposed nineteenth-century bourgeois drama, not as "theatre of the people"[70] as Max Reinhardt would begin to use Greek drama a few years later, but as theater performed by and played for a self-selected group. It gave her opportunity to use singing and dancing to build a "Eutopia," as she once called the artistic union of "free" people who "are both generous enough, beautiful enough, to make a clear sustained poem of [their] . . . lives."[71]

Eva would later denigrate her theatrical activities in the United States and Paris as the work of "a rich dilettante, amateur smatterer on the outside fringe of the theater."[72] Yet the terms of her renunciation are not persuasive. Throughout her life she remained committed to the "amateur . . . outside fringe," where theater worked toward creating the feeling of a shared journey into another time. On a grander scale in the Delphic Festivals, she enlisted young women of the urban middle and upper classes for the choruses of *Prometheus Bound* and the *Suppliants* and regional lay talent for the festival's presentation of Pyrrhic dances, athletic competitions, folk art and handicraft exhibitions, and performance of Greek music. This was a continuation of a principle underlying her effort to stage *Atalanta* in Bar Harbor and indeed all her theater work.

DELPHIC VISIONS ON MOUNT PARNASSUS, EARLY 1920s

The "Delphic Idea," the zoning of Delphi as a divine *omphalos*, or center, and the use of its stage to revive modern spirits worn down by the crushing events of the early twentieth century, has been credited to Angelos Sikelianos. He first mentioned his "Δελφικό όραμα" (Delphic vision) to poet

Kostis Palamas in a letter from Moni Profitou Ilia, a monastery two miles west of Delphi, on September 27, 1919.[73] He started writing the "Δελφικός λόγος" (Delphic *logos*) in June 1921[74] as two talks "on prophetic forerunners, ancient and modern, and the idea of a global freedom and international brotherhood of all the peoples of the Earth," given in Athens in January 1923.[75] He published a new version of the essay in 1927,[76] with a nearly simultaneous translation into English.[77]

Prophecy and prophetic vision were themes in Angelos's earliest work. In 1914 Angelos met Kazantzakis and began to make pilgrimages with him to sacred pagan in addition to Christian religious sites. They traveled to the sacred peninsula of Mount Athos in November, then to Dafní Monastery, Eleusis, Kaisariani Monastery, Delphi, Epidaurus and other places in the Peloponnese, and finally to Jerusalem in 1921. Together the two writers developed a notion of creating a new "religion, everything ripe, to bring out whatever is most holy and deep within us."[78] During this same period, Angelos experienced a series of devastating losses. First, Penelope succumbed to tuberculosis in 1917. Then, in 1919, his brother Hector died of a heart attack. And in 1920, Kalypso Katsimbali, a young woman from a prominent Athenian family, in love with Angelos and driven mad by his refusal to reciprocate, committed suicide in despair. "Ο Σικελιανός νεοχριστιανίζει" (Sikelianos is being a new kind of Christian),[79] one critic reacted to his religious writings, unsure how to reconcile the Christian themes of new work with the neopagan dandy of the previous period.

The religious thought of Angelos was mystical and syncretic. He identified the abused body of Christ with Adonis, Orpheus, Prometheus—all subsumed under the inflated perspective of his poetic persona.[80] The suffering "Mother of God," conflated with Demeter and Alkmene, bears reference to his sister Penelope.[81] His large, prophetic ego reached beyond his poetry. First, he wanted to establish a "κοσμικό μοναστήρι" (worldly or cosmic monastery—the ambiguity in relation to religion exists in the Greek word) with Kazantzakis on Mount Penteli east of Athens,[82] after Nietzsche's idea of founding a brotherhood of educators in the castle of Flims in Switzerland and D'Annunzio's Italian Regency of Carnaro in the city of Fiume (1920–21). Gradually, Moni Profitou Ilia, the monastery near Delphi, and Agoriani on the far side of Mount Parnassus became his haunts. Eventually, Delphi drew his attention as the place to stage a renewal for the tired modern soul.

The idea that Delphi was a region "of mystery and magic, of religious affinities, of hidden, secret storehouses of revelation and inspiration and healing"[83] had several beginnings expressed almost simultaneously with

Angelos's Delphic vision (ὅραμα, 1919) or idea (ἰδέα, 1922). One other poet's vision in particular expressed intoxication with mythical figures, biblical images, and ancient writing. It is worth recalling, even though it probably had no direct bearing on Angelos's idea. It is the "Delphic vision" of the American poet Hilda Doolittle, better known simply by her initials, H. D. She was another Bryn Mawr student, like Eva, who did not complete her degree. The two women did not cross paths there, since Eva left in 1900 and H. D. arrived in 1905, yet they had commonalities. Like Eva, H. D. attended Bryn Mawr to study Greek and worked at "creating her own female Hellas."[84] She was truly steeped in Greek learning and had a very deep "Hellenic nostalgia"[85] driving her efforts to write works for "another mode of being."[86]

She visited Greece in 1920. In a hotel in Corfu, she reportedly saw a waking dream: "a head, a chalice, a lamp resembling the Pythia's tripod, and fluid picture of Nike, Winged Victory, climbing a ladder 'write themselves' on the wall" of a hotel.[87] There followed a "series of hallucinated dance 'tableaux' " (as H. D. called her spontaneous dance performances), including one of "a Greek mountain boy" and another of a lady in a tower with jewels " 'full of traditional occult power' and named, like the earth mother, Rhea."[88] That was in the spring of 1920, a few months after Angelos wrote his letter to Palamas telling of *his* vision (ὅραμα).

H. D.'s Delphic vision suggests the entangled density of the intertextual web within which Angelos arrived at the decision to organize the festival of drama, music, and games at Delphi. She makes a fleeting appearance here, though I have found no evidence that she actually met Angelos or Eva, because her vision introduces a feature that the Delphic Festivals eventually included, but which was not part of Angelos's original vision: the performance of "dance 'tableaux' " with a mythical subject. In both H. D.'s very spontaneously performed "hallucinated dance" in Corfu and Eva's actual revival of Aeschylean tragedy in the theater of Delphi, the element of a visually inspired tableau is present, bringing into movement and sound mythical scenes as part of a modern revival. The dramatic performance of myth in the divinely zoned ancient sanctuary became the anchor of the Delphic Festivals. Indeed, that was the piece of the festivals that received critical attention, while Angelos's broader, prophetic Delphic Idea of bringing together elite overseers in an ancient world center never caught on. But Angelos was not thinking about reviving Greek drama at Delphi when he first articulated his vision.[89] This element was missing from his Delphic Idea before the American theater director George Cram "Jig" Cook staged a play with shepherds on Mount Parnassus near Agoriani in the summer of 1923, then set about preparing to create a theater troop of villagers from Mount Parnassus in Delphi.[90] Jig Cook's Delphic vision laid out the theatrical ingredients of the Delphic Idea of Angelos Sikelianos.

Cook's journey to Greece in 1922, as recounted in *The Road to the Temple* (1926) by Susan Glaspell, his wife and fellow traveler, bears an uncanny resemblance to Eva's. An almost exact contemporary of Eva, Cook studied Greek at Harvard, graduating in 1893, while also sustaining an interest in music and drama. Although he pursued graduate studies in Germany and became a professor of English at the University of Iowa and then Stanford, his ardent Hellenism stood at an odd angle to the Hellenism of those male-centered scholarly institutions of learning. His was of a "democratic, quasi-socialist, political orientation,"[91] and he wished to create a "beloved community of life-givers."[92] He eventually left teaching for the theater. His big break came when he met several playwrights. With Glaspell, Neith Boyce, Eugene O'Neill, John Reed, Louise Bryant, visual artist Marsden Hartley, and a few others, he played out his idea to create a communal, political theater. Thus began the Provincetown Players outside a rented, ocean-view cottage in Provincetown, Massachusetts. The theater company found a growing audience there and in Greenwich Village in the winter. For several years, it continued meeting with unexpected success between these two settings. When after a few years Cook felt himself at a creative standstill, he decided to change course. "It's time to go to Greece," he reportedly said.[93] So he and Glaspell dropped everything and took the next boat. They arrived in Athens in April 1922. The next year, he abandoned Western clothing, replacing it with traditional shepherds' dress.

Cook and Glaspell probably met Eva in Athens that spring, while she was still teaching music at the Conservatory of National Music. They met Angelos in his retreat in Agoriani, where they spent the summer. The next spring, the couple and Cook's fourteen-year-old daughter, Nilla, from an earlier marriage, crossed the Gulf of Corinth to spend a month near the Sikelianos villa in Sykia. Nilla wrote about that visit in her memoir, *My Road to India* (1939). According to Nilla, George Cram Cook came to Sykia "to be near" Eva: Eva "admired Kyrios Kouk and his poetry, and he admired her and her weaving."[94] Nilla then spent the rest of the month holding hands with Glafkos. It is interesting that neither Glaspell's *The Road to the Temple* nor Eva's *Upward Panic* mentions the month-long stay. Glaspell and Eva both treat the interaction as if it never happened;[95] as if the three theater-loving expatriates never spent time together; as if the ideas that absorbed Glaspell and Eva were the exclusive property of their respective husbands and they themselves did not exist.

Despite their silences, intersecting lines of interest can be traced through a careful comparison of the two texts, pointing to subjects that may have been relayed. For example, Glaspell writes of Cook's fascination with the "ancient loom"[96] in a Greek village and his interest in the shepherds' dress.[97] Her book is filled with images of women spinning and of sheep crossing: signs to Glaspell and Cook of "something older than ancient Greece."[98] Even if Cook carried some idea of abandoning Western clothes before he traveled to Greece, surely he found in Eva's example the power of persuasion (as Khorshed would do a year later, when she too abandoned Western dress). By this time Eva had been weaving and wearing Greek dresses for fifteen years and spoke publically on the potential of the loom to lead the women of Greece anadromically back to their classical ancestors and forward to a freer life. We know that Cook adopted shepherds' clothes soon after their meeting (figure 4.3).[99]

Cook was also fascinated with Greek letters as a stimulation that "could take him into a world where he knew who he was."[100] His investment in ancient Greek as a foundation for self-knowledge betrays ideas circulating in elite halls of learning: places like Harvard and Bryn Mawr, where he and Eva had studied on parallel tracks. They were also places where revivals of Greek drama were regularly staged as a "typical embodiment of some permanent fact or aspect of life"—in the words of Daniel Dickey Hains, professor and head of the Greek department at Wabash College who directed Greek plays each year from 1908 through 1915 and reported to his profession in 1910, with some surprise, about how widespread the practice was in American colleges.[101] The idea that Greek held meaning for contemporary American life had a broader reach, too. Glaspell studied philosophy at Drake University in Des Moines, Iowa, a nonelite school, and did not have the opportunity to learn Greek; she felt quite alienated from the culture of Greek letters. Nevertheless, while in Greece, she wrote plays in dialogue with Greek prototypes that she read in English, and she discovered the peculiar pleasure of running her fingers over gaps in the stones of Delphi where Greek words were chiseled: "letters of old stone, into which were locked secrets from long ago. I felt the letters as a key,"[102] she wrote.

But how to unlock the secrets of Greek letters? How to bring the "permanent fact or aspect of life" to life? Glaspell's text reports Cook's long-standing interest in "strange Greek songs, whose scale is not our scale"[103]— something that fascinated Isadora and Eva alike from the turn of the twentieth century.[104] Like them, too, Cook harbored a long-lasting desire

FIGURE 4.3. George Cram Cook in shepherd's dress in the theater of Delphi, fall 1923, in a photograph by William J. Rapp. Acc. 604, William J. Rapp Papers, box 4. Special Collections and University Archives, University of Oregon Libraries, Eugene, Oregon.

to recover "dancing that is like sculpture."[105] He had experimented with the idea in his direction of Louise Bryant's *The Game* with the Provincetown Players in 1916. That production used the sculpturally inspired dance vocabulary of "Isadora Duncan, Ruth St. Denis, Maud Allen, and Vaslav Nijinsky."[106] Eva would have had much to discuss with Cook on this topic and also the utopian, communal aspect of the amateur theater, which the Provincetown Players had transformed into a serious popular form. And Cook, like Eva, was seeking an escape in Greece from a modern way of life that had worn him down. He and Glaspell saw ancient things in present Greek life. In the spinning women and avid political talk, the secrets of the past were half revealed. They made an appearance, too, when Nilla participated with villagers in the grape harvest and "danced upon the grapes with bacchanalian joy"; for Glaspell this "was as a festival: a day when sun and grapes, though unfermented, could make one drunk, and you believe this was the mountain of Dionysus": a convincingly related likeness to ancient practices.[107]

"The unwritten music in the words we speak"[108] was a source of dramatic interest for Cook, as it was for Eva from the time of her recitations of Swinburne. Cook enthusiastically studied modern Greek as an extension of the ancient language, a pivotal point for making nearly three millennia of Greek writing come alive. Surely they had much to say about the latency of it all, and perhaps also how to collaborate with Greeks to create a communal event.[109]

Collaboration in playacting was something Cook did enter into with villagers on Mount Parnassus. One day in the fall of 1923, he announced to Glaspell that he was creating the "Delphic Players"; several shepherds were helping to write a Cain-Abel play[110]—a ritualized festal spectacle after the prototype of the Oberammergau *Passion Play*. He also began translating one of his plays, *The Athenian Women*, into modern Greek. Then, suddenly he became ill and died in January 1924. Almost as soon as he was buried, the "George Cram Cook Club," consisting of Cook's friends from the "Writers' League of Athens," formed to honor his memory. The group suggested that stage performances and games should be reinstated in the Delphic theater, to be held once a year on Easter Monday, with the first festival performing Cook's play *The Athenian Women* in modern Greek translation.[111]

A few months later, Angelos Sikelianos announced his plans to produce the first Delphic revival with a performance of drama in the ancient theater and athletic games. Initially he publicized this as a "[memorial] to George Cram Cook, founder of the Provincetown Players."[112] As the festival neared, however, the dedication to Cook's memory disappeared from the publicity; Sikelianos erased the traces of competing visions, with the help of Eva, his uxorial "assistant."[113]

PROMETHEUS BOUND IN DELPHI, 1927

When Eva began directing *Prometheus Bound*, she found Isadora Duncan once again before her. She had been trailing Isadora for more than twenty years. In Paris in the early 1900s, they moved in the same bohemian circles.

Like Isadora, she imagined Greek antiquity as a source of liberation from the physical constraints of Victorian conventions. In the Louvre, she examined the same vase paintings and statuary. She read Maurice Emmanuel's *La danse grecque antique d'après les monuments figurés*. She followed Raymond and Penelope Duncan to Greece in the footsteps of Isadora. She stayed in their unfinished "palace of Agamemnon." She married the brother-in-law of Isadora. She studied the Greek church music to which Isadora had turned briefly in 1903 for the choral passages of the *Suppliants*. Isadora's brief visit to Greece marked Eva's path.

Eva was following Isadora's leads, but to further ends: making the study of music and movement a decades-long vocation in Greece with more sustained interactions with living Greeks and more systematic attention of the remains of the dead: the ancient ruins that inspired Isadora's movements in a general way but without the attention to archaeological distinctions that occupied Eva. The Delphic Festivals gave her opportunity to build on Isadora's experiments, or rather to correct methods she considered superficial or misguided. As noted earlier, Eva's final product received the nod of professional assent from archaeologist Ernst Buschor for its solution of "archaeological problems" that had troubled scholars "fruitlessly for years." Responding to those welcome words of praise, Eva disclaimed archaeological expertise. Her words as she later recalled them were sharp: "'I have read archaeological books only to forget them, and I have never thought of your problems. And besides . . . the performance was bristling with archaeological mistakes, but even you did not detect them, and you are not even conscious of them now. And that is because the place was moving around its own pivot; it was emotionally true, or almost true—and that was sufficient to make you feel that it was correct archaeologically.'"[114] Eva punctuated her disclaimer with this hard rejection of the very foundations of Professor Buschor's mode of enquiry: "There is no such thing as archaeological correctness. There is nothing in Greek drama except the emotional truth and consistency of the performers, and the immense responding emotion of those who are present."[115] This is how Eva records her response in *Upward Panic*. Regardless of whether the passage represents actual words exchanged or words that came to her a decade later, it suggests that Eva's dialogue was not primarily with archaeologists. Her interlocutors were people like Isadora Duncan, George Cram Cook, H. D., Susan Glaspell, Ruth St. Denis, Jay and Mary Hambidge, Khorshed Naoroji, Angelos Sikelianos, and other artists, too, whether known or unknown, who had run their fingers over the gaps and broken edges of ancient Greek remains in hopes of solving the problems that mute archaeological ruins placed before them. At the same time, Eva's startling words of renunciation leave a lingering sense of her work's archaeological charge: she was prepared to talk to archaeologists, confident in her knowledge, yet ready to grant them mastery of their realm and to locate herself outside it.

In the staging of *Prometheus Bound*, both the artistic and the archaeological dialogue are evident. The direction of the chorus, in particular, developed elements Isadora had concentrated on decades before: the dress; poses drawn from visual sources; mobilization of the poses; chorus of native talent; singing of a musical line of church music; attention to ancient sites and adjustment of the body's movements to precepts drawn from the open-air scenic space. The effort went into bringing all this together, to render the integrity of music, dance, words, and stage setting in an emotionally overpowering work. Thus, the desire to create Greek movement reviving a mythical story of high emotional impact follows a traceable line from Isadora Duncan's "multiple oneness" to Eva Sikelianos's circular configurations of many young Greek women dancing and singing in the ancient theater.

The choreography, however, is not a simple continuation of Isadora's work. Instead it involves both influence and dissent, leading to a bold revision of her ideas of Greek-inspired movements. Eva followed certain elements of Isadora's approach, then swerved in another direction. Like Isadora, she concentrated on developing a movement vocabulary from ancient visual sources. In fact, it was precisely in her attention to those sources, especially the way she selected them and filled in their gaps to create the movement and sound, that she made her artistic mark, introducing crucial distinctions that would ultimately influence other American choreographers in addition to Greek directors.

The most important distinction was her attention to vases of the archaic period (eighth century–480 BCE) as opposed to the classical and Hellenistic eras (480–323, 323–31 BCE). She hired the sculptor Bella Raftopoulou to copy imagery specifically from archaic and older vases in the Greek National Archaeological Museum (figure 4.4).[116] She selected this period in opposition to the later classical materials that Isadora Duncan had copied. Her ostensible reason was that the archaic era was the time of tragedy's invention as a performance genre in Athens. She was thus correcting an anachronism of Isadora. The distinction had a more pointedly ideological bearing. Eva later recalled, "The strong invocation of Isadora's art brought to life a period which was not archaic Greece, not classic Greece, but Greece in a later decadent period. In fact, what we were seeing and raving over was Hellenistic bas-relief, or a Southern Italian vase come to life."[117] Emphasis in the passage falls on the contrast between the "archaic," on the one hand, a historical term naming the era prior to 480 BCE, and the "decadent," on the other hand, an evaluative term denoting decline.[118]

During the interwar years, the "archaic"—already a term of distinction in people's reading of Nietzsche's search for a *different* Greece, a dark, chthonic one in contrast to the classical Greece of sweetness and light[119]—became a code word to distinguish true, pure Greeks from later ones, who were seen to have softened the essence of Greece, contributing to the West's decline. The current archaeological thinking was sketched out as early as 1913 by Ernst Buschor, the very expert who would acknowledge Eva's solution to archaeological problems in 1927. In his view, archaic art had an "unpolished, hidden vigor," "childlike boldness," and "fresh progressiveness";[120] in contrast, late classical works, with their highly decorative style, were "late offshoots."[121] The "late offshoots" of the classical and Hellenistic eras were precisely the Greek sources that had attracted Eva to Greece by way of her attachments to decadence and aestheticism. Their softer lines and ambivalent sexuality were once sources of inspiration. They influenced Swinburne and other poets and artists whom Eva adored.[122] Now everyone from Pablo Picasso to Ezra Pound and theorists of fascism and Nazism was turning to preclassical sources in search of evidence of a time before human history began its relentless movement to the present era of decline and decay, so as to find the archaic seed for the world's regeneration.

Eva's insistence on the "archaic" against the "decadence" of later, classical imagery was thus not only a direct contestation of Isadora's choices but a sign of her work's uncomfortable proximity to archaeological and other lines of thought of her day: specifically what Gonda Van Steen has called "the growing fascist-bourgeois movement of the 1920s and 1930s."[123] In making this point, I acknowledge the "wide range of ideological variations on the theme of cultural regeneration as a way out of otherwise terminal decadence," following Roger Griffin, a historian and theorist of fascism.[124] Fascism's relationship with modernity is indeed "labyrinthine," as Griffin describes it.[125] Many projects judged to be progressive, especially those participating in the "prospect . . . of national rebirth" such as the Delphic Festival, carried a right-leaning agenda "in the supercharged mythopoeic climate of inter-war Europe"[126] that was yearning for a unifying myth. Yet if we consider how the Delphic Festival worked to overturn the impact of European appropriations of Greek cul-

FIGURE 4.4. Pen-and-ink drawing by Bella Raftopoulou from an unidentified vase painting, commissioned by Eva to prepare the choreography of *Prometheus Bound*. Acc. 350, Angelos and Eva Sikelianos Papers. Hellenic Literary and Historical Archive (ELIA).

FIGURE 4.5. Eva Palmer Sikelianos's embodiment of the pose drawn by Bella
Raftopoulou (figure 4.4), in an undated photograph, shows how she developed
her movement vocabulary and also how she exaggerated the cross lateral
movements, with head, shoulders and torso, and hips and legs twisting in
different directions. Acc. 189, Eva Sikelianou Papers, No. 350. Benaki Museum
Historical Archives.

ture and sites, it is possible to see it as a decolonizing cultural project of sorts: an effort to reclaim Greeks' sovereignty over their mind, bodies, industry, and cultural inheritance (regardless of whether or not it is precisely correct to identify these appropriations as strictly colonial). The distinction between the nationalism of dominating colonial powers and nationalism growing from a desire to overthrow subjugation should be made, and projects of the second type have historically defined themselves as struggles for national agency and empowerment without necessarily being fascist.[127] Eva was not an unthinking cog in the ideological machinery of the Delphic Festivals. She was committed to representing the continuity of Hellenism in the coordinated song and dance of beautiful young Greek women's eloquent nationalized, racialized bodies in the chorus of *Prometheus Bound*, and, in the athletic games performed in the stadium, as male athletes were forced by their heavy armor to shake off the mechanical sameness of modern life and regain control of their movements.[128] The fusing of antiquity with the present and of the individual with the corporate body[129]—these ideas were irresistible to the idealist in her. This prospect, and especially her persistently mythopoeic thought, aligned her work with some aspects of the spirit of fascism. But she neither was a fascist[130] nor ever adopted a right-wing agenda. Her investment in individual and group autonomy, belief in a diversity of ways of being, and work to develop techniques of self-expression to help liberate the creative impulse against the crushing uniformity of consumerism conflicted with the more authoritarian strains latent in the Delphic Idea.

Her progressive commitment to matters of social and economic justice is most evident in one small detail of the play's direction in the costuming of a character in *Prometheus Bound*. It is a directorial decision that diverged from Eva's fixation on archaic Greek sources, mixing into the production a piece of India's decolonization movement. A letter from Khorshed Naoroji to Eva reveals that Eva had asked Khorshed to help her acquire a "yoga garment"[131] of homespun cloth for one of the costumes of the play. Writing from Bombay on September 16, 1925, Khorshed enclosed a white and a dyed sample of cloth and a description and drawing of the garment: "a simple long tunic with short sleeves and just above the ankles with two splits at the side." She offered to "have it spun, woven, and dyed" by one of her contacts in the khadi movement, provided that Eva sent her the actor's measurements.

I have not discovered if the "yoga garment" itself reached Greece. I believe it was part of the 1927 performance, whether as the actual garment, spun, woven, and dyed in India, or as the costume made by Eva according to Khorshed's instructions. I conjecture that Eva used the costume for Prometheus, the protagonist selected by Angelos as a mythical figure of human suffering to "embody the idea of the modern Greek nation in chains, revolting against tyranny and preparing for its liberation."[132] The actor in this costume, literally embodying the processes of hand spinning, dyeing, and weaving that were the centerpiece of India's Swadeshi movement for the country's economic independence (and also of Eva's everyday living), added a current, international, politicized dimension to Prometheus's performance of anticipated liberation. By conjuring the contemporary image of Gandhi leading a real national revolution against harsh colonial rule dressed in simple handspun cloth in solidarity with India's peasants, the costume unsettled the mythologizing slippage between archaic Greek archaeological prototypes and living Greek bodies. This was the case even if its precise prototype, let alone masked political message, escaped the notice of most audience members.

Eva's theater was about autonomy—not conformity. This is especially apparent in how she worked with her actors. As Raftopoulou copied the archaic gestures, Eva wrote notes on the significance of each one. She then replicated the poses with her body, studying their expressive range (figure 4.5). From this exercise, she developed the movement vocabulary to be linked with the expressive ideas of the chorus. Initially she planned to have each member of the chorus link the words to gestures and movement: she would teach them the foundations (theory of Byzantine music, gymnastic exercises), and they would select poses to match the meaning of their lines.[133] Thus her work would both activate native talent and give room for individuation within the unity of the chorus. Unlike fascist theater, which aspired to uniformity, Eva remained committed to the principle of differentiation. However, since the members of the chorus would not accept her challenge to choreograph themselves, Eva did the preparatory work, linking the poses with the text and from these fixed points working with chorus members to determine their individual movements. In all there were 285 changes of pose correlated with lines of the play recited by the Oceanides.[134]

I have already mentioned Isadora Duncan's revolutionary shift of the dancing body's center from the line connecting the head, sternum, pubic bone, and heels to the solar plexus, the complex of abdominal muscles that meet below the breast. Eva understood this shift in alignment executed by Isadora as an agent propelling her "Dionysian" movements. In *Upward Panic*, she recalled having "seen Isadora stand[ing] quite motionless before large audiences for quite a long spell, with her hands over her solar plexus. . . . Then, when she gave the sign for starting, she really had 'placed a motor in her soul,' and from then on her dancing gave the impression of being involuntary on her part. It was purely Dionysian."[135] Photographs show Eva contracting the same core muscles as a starting point for movement.[136] But the movements she developed to animate poses drawn from archaic sources had strong, sharp angles with rotated cross lateral flexion, in contrast to Isadora's "soft undulations," perpetual "[flow]," and the "frank . . . straight-ahead"[137] gaze.

For Eva, dance did not exist apart from song. In this choreographic element, too, she worked to revise Isadora's efforts. She criticized both the approach of Isadora's brief experiments with a chorus of Greek singers and her abandonment of those experiments and return to music by the giants of the Western canon. In her view, the genius of Greek art lay in the primacy it gave to words and their meaning. Accordingly, she surveyed traditions of music making in Greece to identify a method for enhancing words with melodies and rhythms that supported their meaning. When she settled on Psachos to write the music according to the method of Byzantine chant, it was not because she believed that Greek Orthodox church hymns represented ancient survivals, as Isadora had thought. Her own anachronism, her "anadromic method," ran against the tide of time in the opposite direction. She learned a difficult tradition of improvised chanting as it was used and recorded in the present day to make ancient words of Greek dramatic poetry the basis of new music (figure 4.6).

To set her archaic sources in motion and connect them with the production of sound, she "isolat[ed the] effect of keeping the head in profile and the chest 'en face.' "[138] She even developed a special exercise program to help the women of the chorus keep this cross lateral rotation as they moved and sang. The effect was unlike Isadora's continuous movement style imitating natural movements such as walking, skipping, and running. While Eva harbored a desire to access certain resources of the unconscious, called by her the "abyss of real being,"[139] she was not after Isadora's natural effect. Her search led her instead to ritual feasts, where people gathered to share traditional poetry, song, and dance with an "upward swing."[140] In directing *Prometheus Bound*, she found that high spirits cannot be forced. Even after the chorus of Oceanides "had become word-perfect, melody-perfect, move-perfect," their singing and was "stilted and mechanical,"[141] until several rehearsals in the round orchestral space of the naturally amplified ancient theater produced a similar upward swing, making their voices "free and strong," their movements "beautiful and powerful."[142]

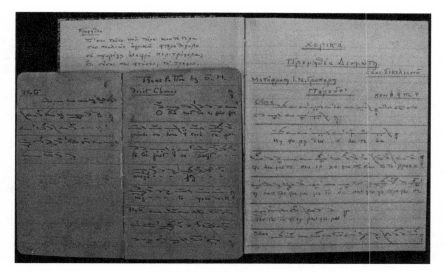

FIGURE 4.6. Eva's handwritten notebooks containing pages with her composi-
tions for the chorus of *Prometheus Bound* in English (left) and Greek (right) in
Byzantine notation, ca. 1940. The one on the left uses Gryparis's demotic Greek
translation and has an oboe accompaniment. The one on the right uses Edith
Hamilton's English translation and has a flute accompaniment. Acc. 189, Eva
Sikelianou Papers, box 22. Benaki Museum Historical Archives.

This close look at Eva's direction of the chorus of *Prometheus Bound*
points to how systematically she built on, yet also revised, prior creative
approaches based on her decades-long practice of theater and study of
archaeological and other sources. Together with the staging techniques
described above, her commitment to amateurism must be recalled, with
all its risks. As with her previous theatrical work, so with this performance,
she directed amateur performers in a noncommercial space both to bypass
the expectation of business profits and to aspire the larger utopian vision—in this case the Delphic Idea of Angelos Sikelianos. She also covered
the festival's expenses. This time, the cost was greater than her inherited
income could support. Eva recognized the necessity of filling the theater
with an elite international crowd. Without it, the booming voice of Prometheus would not reach its intended audience; her "word-perfect,
melody-perfect, move-perfect" chorus would achieve no awe-inspiring effect; and the Delphic Idea of Angelos Sikelianos would pass away. The play
would be no greater than the sum of its systematically devised parts. So
she spent all her inheritance and borrowed one million drachmas against
the value of her houses in Sikya and Delphi to cover the expense of trans-

porting, housing on a cruise ship, and feeding more than one thousand guests. The decision would haunt her for the rest of her life.[143]

Although her dialogue with creative and scholarly interlocutors is traceable now, its enormous machinery disappeared in the actual performance in 1927. When the actors and chorus played to the audience, Mount Parnassus and the ruined Panhellenic sanctuary were never out of sight. The synergy of the setting, the actors' enthusiasm, and the audience's sense of the nearness of ancient Greece attached itself to the highly disciplined production. The range of ideas from which Eva had drawn seemed all to have come from a single source, and the audience received the production as a convincing likeness to ancient drama. The prevailing feeling was that "the drama has been reborn . . . in the original land of its birth."[144]

THE PERSIANS AT JACOB'S PILLOW, 1939

As news of Greek drama's "rebirth" at Delphi traveled across the Atlantic through an American publicity machine that never forgot Eva the wealthy New York heiress, it reached Ted Shawn, the dancer and choreographer later recognized by his troop of Men Dancers as "Papa Shawn" or "the father of American dance."[145] Shawn's collaboration with Eva in 1939 is the final moment in this genealogy of performances in dialogue with archaeology leading to and from Delphi. This cultural moment more than any other shows how Eva's amateur forays into archaeology influenced the movement vocabulary of the generation of modern dance after Isadora Duncan in ways that have yet to be acknowledged.

Before he became acquainted with Eva's work, Shawn performed hero-prophet roles in Denishawn productions, the dance company he cofounded with Ruth St. Denis in 1915. Greek-inspired dances were part of the group's repertoire, which aimed to make dance a vehicle for expressing transhistorical, global, emotional, and spiritual truths. The "Dance Pageant of Egypt, Greece, and India" performed at the open-air Greek Theater at Berkeley in 1916, for example, included the "Bacchanale" with Shawn's student Martha Graham.[146] Typically, Denishawn's Greek pieces, such as the "Bacchanale," were more like well-outfitted tableaux, punctuated with vaudeville-inspired acts of singing and dancing, than tragic drama with a singing and dancing chorus. In contrast to Isadora Duncan, who performed only in the theaters of high art, Denishawn took its internationally styled pageants such as the "Dance Pageant" or Ruth St. Denis's "From a Grecian Vase" on vaudeville tours, where they reached a broad audience—

another reminder that Greek culture appealed to nonelites in addition to the elite educated upper class.[147]

Shawn increasingly relied on Greek themes to introduce new performance ideas as he grew more interested in Isadora Duncan's approach. His sculpture plastique "Death of Adonis,"[148] a controlled, slow-moving piece danced naked with just a fig leaf, deals with the pictorial and sculptural elements of the body. It also tests the audience's tolerance for Greek-style nudity. On this point, Shawn acknowledged the influence of Isadora in a lecture entitled "Dancing and Nudity," recognizing that she had "so absolutely an idea about the art of dance and about the rightness of the naked human body that [she] dared to discard . . . clumsy, awkward, and ugly clothes . . . and appeared in the simple tunic of Greece."[149]

After 1927, Shawn's work entered into dialogue with Eva's production of *Prometheus Bound*. He performed his own Prometheus dance mime in 1929, choreographed to Alexander Scriabin's experimental composition "Prometheus: Poem of Fire." According to Pantelis Michelakis, who compares film versions of Shawn's and Eva Sikelianos's choreographed Prometheus myth, there are shared "aesthetic and artistic preoccupations" in the two artists' work a good decade before they actually collaborated in 1939.[150] Like Isadora and Eva, Shawn turned to Greece as an origin for modern dance, in this case because he "wanted to restore *male* dancing to the dignity he believed it possessed in ancient Greece."[151] Another work, "Kinetic Molpai," which was premiered on October 5, 1935, in Goshen, New York, and performed widely in the United States, takes as its theme the motive that gave birth to dance in Greece. It is an all-male piece in which cowboys in the American West use the expressive range of the gestures of silent film. Shawn choreographed it for his Men Dancers with himself as the *koryphaios*. The program notes, written by Shawn, give the meaning of the *molpe* (ancient song), glossed by classicist Gilbert Murray,[152] and consider how this ancient form speaks to the modern performer. They refer to its multiple media ("rhythmic movement, instrumental music, singing, poetry, drama") and subjects ("Strife, Death, and Thing Beyond Death"). They then speculate on the artistic "essence" of the form: "the yearning of the whole dumb body to express that emotion for which words and harps and singing were not enough."[153] For Shawn, dance was born when the inarticulate body experienced the kind of human frenzy followed by a near complete depletion. We may contrast this to Eva's notion that dance emerged simultaneously with poetry and song in drama. For her, dance could not exist without sung words. But Shawn's Greek-inspired work before he met Eva subordinated everything to strong athletic, masculine movement.[154] Dance—not poetry or song or drama or any other form that emerged from molpai—was for him the true outgrowth of ancient forms, as well as America's "greatest art expression."[155] As compellingly as the dancers in his "Kinetic Molpai" may have moved—and they did move with energy and drive—they did not speak, and they did not sing.

Shawn might have had the missing song in his mind when he was introduced to Eva Sikelianos after a performance in New York's Washington Irving High School in February 1939. She had come to the performance reluctantly, on the recommendation of Katherine Dreier, a painter and patron of the arts who knew Eva through their shared roots in Stonington, Connecticut.[156] When Shawn heard Eva's name, his words expressed a long-held yearning to meet the artist who could teach him what he did not know about the Greek chorus: "But I have been looking for you for years; where have you been?" he reportedly said.[157]

It is tempting to think that Eva's contribution to Shawn's artistry in their collaboration from 1939 through 1941 involved music, drama, and costumes[158] but had little to do with choreography. Eva was "widely known as a musician, producer, and weaver of fine textiles [who] . . . brought an unusual range of knowledge and experience to her revivals of Greek drama," according to the curator of an exhibition featuring her costumes at the Metropolitan Museum of Art in 1936.[159] While choreography was within her range of knowledge, the *syrtos* and *balos* steps that animated her large tragic chorus of *Prometheus Bound* did not have the artistry of the longer, more complex movement phrases that Shawn interwove in his work. Yet the extant record of their collaboration shows that their dialogue encompassed every aspect of dramatic revivals, particularly the choreography, for which Eva had the benefit of direct contact with archaeological sources.

In May 1939, Eva first worked with Shawn's Men Dancers and students at Jacob's Pillow, the farm near Lee, Massachusetts that Shawn bought as a summer retreat for his company and school. She began teaching the chorus of Aeschylus's *Persians*, using music and movements she had composed in the Byzantine system for a performance she was hired to direct for the Federal Theatre Project (FTP) with playwright Eugene O'Neill as her assignment officer. Eva contributed several more original compositions from the FTP project: a piece based on Isaiah 52:1 ("Awake, awake, put on thy strength, O Zion"); another based on two short poems by Walt Whitman; and two "Pyrrhic dances" from Aristophanes' *Peace*. In the middle of the Pyrrhic dances, Shawn "got up with an exclamation . . .

and . . . taught the choreography of this dance which had sprung from his mind, fully armed, as it were by merely hearing the music. So there were men singing and dancing in an hour's time as if they had done it all their lives."[160] From this contemporaneous account, Eva suggests that even when she had choreographed movements for her music, she deferred to Shawn to make the dance. She stated repeatedly in her letters and other writings of the period, including *Upward Panic,* her confidence in his choreography; she felt for the first time that she was perfectly matched with a fellow performing artist to produce an integrated singing and dancing chorus as she imagined it.

That same summer of 1939, while Shawn was away giving lectures and concerts around the country, Eva worked in a more sustained manner on the dramatic opening scene of *The Persians,* while longing to stage the entire play. She and Shawn planned to prepare the complete play and take it "first to American Universities and other centers in America" and eventually to Delphi to "resume" the Delphic Festivals in 1942.[161] She taught the group to sing and dance their parts with her music and Shawn's choreography. She also brought her loom to Jacob's Pillow to make costumes for the chorus of Persians. Although I have them only in black-and-white photographs, the costumes exist in the Killinger Collection of Denishawn, Ted Shawn, and His Men Dancers Costumes at Florida State University and consist of "a navy blue wrap-around style skirt with a fringed trim, attached sash worn over the shoulder, and a skull cap," according to the description of that collection.[162]

A performance at Jacob's Pillow actually left a visual and sound record. A film and series of photographs from one of the "Friday Teas" in late August or early September 1939 exist in the Jacob's Pillow Archives. There is also an audio recording of Barton Mumaw, the *koryphaios,* singing the entire piece as he remembered it many years later. The translated text, Eva's musical compositions in Byzantine notation, many photographs, and her choreographic notes from FTP preparations are in Eva's papers in BMHA.[163] I compared these sources to synchronize the film and cassette recording and reconstruct a sound and motion picture record of the event.[164] I concluded that the surviving material points to Shawn's having absorbed a series of lessons from Eva's choreography on the circular stage in the open-air amphitheater at Delphi—lessons once again in critical dialogue with Eva's predecessors such as Isadora Duncan.

For most of his career, Shawn had been producing work on a raised stage against a big barn door or another solid background. The proscenium stage functioned like a canvas on which "the audience looking up

FIGURE 4.7. Ted Shawn's dancers and students performing the opening lines of *The Persians* in a collaborative composition by Shawn (choreographer) and Eva Palmer Sikelianos (composer), August–September 1939. A film of the production exists. This photograph captures what happens one minute and sixteen seconds into the film. Barton Mumaw, the *koryphaios* of the chorus of Persians has just finished setting the scene of the war between the Persians and Athenians and now expresses concern about a turn of events: "But how my heart is troubled, for I see the strength of Asia gone" (trans. Joan Vanderpool). The chorus forms a semicircle facing outward, as if on a circular stage. Acc. 189, Eva Sikelianou Papers, No. 532. Benaki Museum Historical Archives; Film 23.2 "The Persians." Jacob's Pillow Archive.

from below could see the dancer's relationships within the space," according to dance historian Gayle Kissing,[165] but not their three-dimensional relationship to each other. Eva's work in the open-air amphitheater, where the stage is a circle and the audience viewed the performance from above, had an entirely different effect.[166] The circular architectural arrangement gave Eva a distinct sense of the audience's ever-present line of vision. Performers did not have to adjust their heads or bodies to face the audience but instead kept the integrity of their poses as they moved about the stage. Portions of the recorded performance of *The Persians* suggest that the dancers were imagining themselves on a circular, amphitheatric stage, without making adjustments for their audience on one side of them (figure 4.7).

FIGURE 4.8. Hand-drawn figures on mimeographed sheets labeled "The Persians: Postures, No. 1 and No. 2" give some of the poses of the chorus. Palmer drew the figures and mimeographed printed sheets for actors in the Federal Theatre Project. Evidently she reused them at Jacob's Pillow, since the figures correspond to positions the dancers actually took in the performance at Jacob's Pillow. Acc. 189, Eva Sikelianou Papers, box 24. Benaki Museum Historical Archives.

Several more elements from Eva's choreographic direction are evident. Eva's papers preserve five pages of what she called "Persian Postures" for her choreography for *The Persians*, analogous to the poses she created from Bella Raftopoulou's sketches to express the range of emotions found in *Prometheus Bound* (figure 4.8). Shawn must have used these as a starting point for the choreography. A study of the frames of the performance registered on film finds that Eva's "Persian Postures" mark every beginning and transition of movement (figure 4.9). Specific poses are aligned with emotions, actions, or notions expressed in the chorus's words. Shawn's dancers also replicated the angularity of the archaic-inspired poses that Eva had created to express the emotional range of Aeschylus's words. They used her principle of "Apollonian movement," in which "the head and feet

FIGURE 4.9. Ted Shawn's dancers and students performing the first chorus of Aeschylus's *The Persians* in a collaborative work by Shawn and Eva. Their poses correspond to figures on five sheets labeled "Persian Postures." Compare the two kneeling figures here with the stick figure in "Persian Postures" no. 1, center right. Acc. 189, Eva Sikelianou Papers, No. 537. Benaki Museum Historical Archives.

are in profile, and the chest or back in full view"[167] (figure 4.9), as the motor guiding their movements. Perhaps Shawn felt he had found in Eva's archaic poses and ritualized movements a tool for his Men Dancers to express a wider range of emotions—anxiety, distress, mourning, loss—than the average American public would receive comfortably if it were realistically delivered.

The intensity of Shawn's efforts to internalize lessons from Eva's archaizing contestation of Isadora Duncan's work is evident also in a series of promotional photographs. Soon after Eva went to Jacob's Pillow to work with his dancers, Shawn wrote to ask her if she might loan him the splendid costume of Hermes from *Prometheus Bound* for a photo shoot.[168] One photograph taken a few days later shows Ted Shawn posing inside the replica of the Parthenon in Nashville's Centennial Park (figure 4.10). As a picture of Shawn in an American replica of the Parthenon, it evokes the photograph of Isadora Duncan, taken in 1920 by Edward Steichen, in the source building in Athens. In Steichen's photograph, Isadora faces the camera straight on and raises her hands directly upward in her gesture of prayer. Shawn pushes against Isadora's pose, à la Eva Palmer. His stance cuts across the Parthenon's interior columns at an oblique angle. He twists

FIGURE 4.10. Ted Shawn posing as Hermes in the full-scale replica of the Parthenon in Nashville, Tennessee, on July, 11, 1939. Acc. 189, Eva Sikelianou Papers, No. 557. Benaki Museum Historical Archives.

his shoulders and torso one way and turns his head the other way. The angular, rotated stance displays the twisted, archaic angularity of Eva's work. In fact, it almost replicates her stance in the photograph taken when she was choreographing the Oceanides (see back to figure 4.5).

The comparison of Ted Shawn posing as Hermes in 1939 with Greek dance poses of Eva and Isadora may be extended in another chronological

direction. Film frames of Martha Graham's ferociously kinetic revival of
the story of Clytemnestra of 1958,[169] an evening-length drama that was
part of her post–World War II work *Hellenic Journey*, show her "etch[ing]
patterns on the space as clear as those that travel around ancient vases."[170]
One photo shot capturing Graham's moving body aligns almost perfectly
with both Shawn's and Eva's twisted, angled torsos—although, in my view,
Graham's twisting contractions and angularity and, indeed, the contorted-
ness of her positions and movements are so much more pronounced that
they give the feeling of being older than history: prehistoric rather than
archaic.[171]

Comparisons such as these tease out from this series of episodes an
argument about lineage in modern dance. Isadora Duncan's "Bacchic
shiver" set a dance revolution in motion; it gave impetus and form to a
new kind of dancing with Greek-inspired works. A variety of other performers, writers, and artists simultaneously sought to give movement and
voice to ancient Greek sources. Of the many who turned to the Greeks to
revitalize modern life, Eva Sikelianos's work is an unacknowledged source
of influence especially on the movement vocabulary of modern dance.
Although she was neither a dancer nor a choreographer, the "enormous
vitality"[172] of her direction of the Greek chorus at the ancient site of Delphi
gave special authority to her revision of Isadora's formula. From her work,
influential creators such as Martha Graham learned how to conduct a
deeper archaeology,[173] to reach down further into the lacunae of archaic
sources to create their prototypes of modern culture.

Eva's unacknowledged role in the history of modern dance is less vital
to this story, however, than the fact that her direction of the Delphic Festival of 1927 and the larger festival of 1930 was devised and received
within a dense intermedial web of texts, photographs, sketches, social
visits, drunken improvisations, amateur efforts, dreams, hallucinations,
life narratives, and rehearsed, staged, and even canceled performances. No
single person or event had absolute priority in articulating the first principles of the project. In addition to the artistic dialogue among people who
knew of one another's work, there were also archaeological discoveries to
contend with. Nothing in the actual or planned performances that I have
been discussing suggests itself as a direct contribution to conventional
archaeology, as the German scholar Buschor thought was the case with
Prometheus Bound in Delphi in 1927. This is precisely the point. The work
of Eva and other performing artists was not one of systematic, scientific
recovery of buried material remains. It did not aim to contribute to historical knowledge. It did not concern itself with past life as it was. Its subject

instead was—in the words of George Cram Cook—"The life / That never was / And shall not be."[174] It fastened its attention on the gap between what "never was" and what "shall not be," looking for missing signs of things that decay in an instant: movements, gestures, sounds, rhythms, and emotions—and there imagining how to fill the ancient space with "life." Yet, true to a principle of scientific investigation, it also treated discoveries of the past as grounds of inquiry, asking questions, contesting others' answers, and building on new styles and directorial choices on the contested ground.

It may be useful to think of the approaches taken to reviving ancient drama as examples of what has been called alternative archaeologies. The term was introduced by anthropologist-archaeologist Bruce Trigger in an influential essay of 1984 reminding readers that "archaeology always operates within a social context,"[175] which in turn bears on the kind of record produced and questions that are asked. Archaeologist Yannis Hamilakis has taken the idea a step further to point to the "many different contexts starting from antiquity [in which] ruins of the past aroused intense interest in people, who invested them with their own memories, meanings, and associations, often incorporated them in their own material and social lives, and produced their own narratives and stories about them."[176] My attention to the extensive engagement with the ruins of Greece's past found in the sequence of scenes of artistic work in the first decades of the twentieth century has brought into view creative contexts outside the formal disciplines of archaeology, where people with peculiar talents and different kinds of learning asked interesting questions about ancient space and the human activities that distributed themselves within it. Attention to the alternative archaeologies existing at an oblique angle to the formal work of collecting and studying past relics also draws into the story of classical scholarship forgotten women such as Eva Sikelianos, who studied ancient sources carefully yet disclaimed scholarly expertise in order to claim an alternative way of knowing Greek:[177] what Bonnie Smith has identified as "expanded cognition . . . beyond the horizon of the professional."[178] The distinct performance language that Eva and her many collaborators and interlocutors developed on the edges of archaeological sites, with its aesthetic, kinetic, ideological, and emotional registers, not only expanded the horizons of archaeology. As Eva's dismissive, though pleased, response to the eminent Ernst Buschor suggests, it challenged, yet sought artistically to meet and transcend the distinction of archaeological correctness.

CHAPTER 5

Writing

Eva was gradually withdrawing from society as her collaboration with Ted Shawn took her from Lee, Massachusetts, to Eustis, Florida, and a series of disappointments made survival a consuming concern. A long string of troubles followed the Delphic Festivals, bringing sources of grief beyond her financial ruin. First, Konstantinos Psachos stopped speaking to her after the festival of 1930. Then he collaborated with Linos Karzis, her assistant director with whom she had multiple disagreements: Karzis used her formula to produce *Prometheus Bound* in the Panathenaic Stadium in Athens on September 21, 1931, claiming the directorial choices were his own. Angelos was enthusiastic, while Eva denounced the production. Moreover, Angelos publicly insisted that all the work of the festivals was his alone. In his words, it was the "fruit of *my* lifetime . . . on which *I* worked . . . *all alone*."[1] He named his deceased sister Penelope as the sole inspiration.[2] He systematically wrote Eva out of the story.

Eva might have sunk into oblivion, the remnants of her life casually tossed or dispersed, if writing had not increasingly replaced the other media in which she worked. From writing *Upward Panic* to exchanging weaving tips, to translating Angelos Sikelianos's work, to becoming a polylingual correspondent with hundreds of people as World War II gave way to the Cold War, Eva made writing the primary medium of her art of living. She found urgency in writing—a clarity of purpose that propelled her into the present in a new way—especially after she received a contraband package of Angelos's wartime resistance poems, the Ακριτικά *(1941–1942)* (*Akritika*, songs or poems of the borders and their guards), on the eve of the Greek civil war in 1944. The urgency of that critical moment thrust her into political action, turning her pen into a tool for anti-imperialist activism in a way that set up her brilliant last act.

UPWARD PANIC

Survival was already a challenge for Eva before she met Ted Shawn. Her overspending on the first Delphic Festival of 1927 and carryover of a debt of one million drachmas led to Eva's impoverishment in the 1930s. She returned to the United States in 1933 to raise cash. She became a working woman for the first time in her life when an opportunity to found a school of Greek drama in California fell through.[3] Before that, during the first six decades of her life, her steady monthly income from the trust set up by her father's lawyers in 1888 gave her the means to live as she pleased. Amateurism was a point of pride: the mark of a woman with the means to pay others to attend to her daily needs while she occupied herself with handiwork, music, and the performing arts without having to satisfy a paying employer. Her first paid labor was her direction of Euripides' *Bacchae* at Smith and Bryn Mawr Colleges in the spring of 1934 and 1935, though the payment just covered her most basic living expenses while she was preparing the play.[4] Those two jobs did not lead to long-term employment directing Greek drama at American colleges, as she anticipated.[5] Her hiring by the Federal Theatre Project in January 1936 brought more steady income, but she received termination papers unexpectedly in August 1937 without ever bringing a Greek play to the stage.

A few months after that work's disappointing end, early in 1938, she began writing a book in hopes of selling the publishing rights to repay her debts and keep creditors from seizing the homes she had mortgaged in Sikya and Delphi. Eva confessed her ambition to her sister May, to whom she was obligated for small gifts of money that pulled her out of emergencies:[6] "I have . . . a kind of ambition to free your mind of worry about me," she wrote, "before my present outer makeup dissolves into something else. Perhaps my book will help. It will either go far or do nothing. It is not a half way book. It is not a middling good egg. It is either rotten or remarkable. Anyway, as old Mamie used to say on occasions good or ill:—Praise be to God."[7]

Eva had been writing for much of her adult life. Writing was part of her art of self, a habitual practice of disciplining the self that involved reading, keeping notes, composing treatises, and receiving and responding to correspondence, by which she renewed and repositioned herself in relation to the surrounding world. She perennially submitted to (in words she borrowed from her father) "a sort of doctrine . . . [of] everlasting striving to be what I should be, in order to properly accomplish the thing I feel worth while."[8]

In an important way, the ethical dimension in Eva's "doctrine . . . [of] everlasting striving" of self in relation to things and people of the world anticipates Michel Foucault's work on ethics in the last decade of his life. In Foucault's usage, ethics refers not to moral philosophy, a doctrine of principles to be applied to the self, but to "an exercise of the self on the self by which one attempts to develop and transform oneself, and to attain a certain mode of being."[9] The convergence of Eva's doctrine of striving with Foucault's exercise of self, four decades later, likely owes something to their shared reading of ancient Greek philosophy from the point of view of the person trying to imagine how to live otherwise within the power-knowledge-truth complex of the present world. This convergence extends to the social dimension of her projects, evident in her lectures on weaving and music discussed in previous chapters. Consistently she proposed oppositional practices—themselves marked with tensions and contradictions—for remaking the material world, reclaiming human industry, retuning the voice and ear, and restructuring power in the face of organized politicoeconomic practices that functioned to control people's lives.

The word "technique" became a recurring theme in the new, longer work that Eva was aspiring to write: a book to explain the unfinished idea at the center of the Delphic project. Eva called the book *Upward Panic*, after Pan, the Greek pastoral half-human half-goat hybrid whose name symbolized the power of nature to spread ruin while planting the seeds for art. Pan was a sign of modern pantheism and neopagan movements for Eva's generation of educated, progressive, white American women. Whether derived from the root *pan*, meaning everything (Pan was associated with everything from sheep to nature to rustic music to sex) or *pa*, meaning guardian of flocks, it is etymologically connected to *panic* (πανικός, literally, that which pertains to Pan). In her brief "Foreword," Eva glossed the book's title as the "opposite" of the techniques of war and politics, which arouse terror and move masses of people to self-destruction in a mad rush of fear. She writes:

> With terror to guide them, men, like the herd of Gadarene swine, now are rushing swiftly down a steep place to destruction. The infusion of this terror into men is an ancient technique, well-known and widely practiced today. But the opposite technique, which can start and sustain panic mov-

ing upwards, is less well-known and is not practiced at all. This book contains a suggestion of what that other technique is.[10]

The idea at the core of the book is that there exists, buried deep in human prehistory yet visible in rare historical moments, a certain technique for creating and sustaining a powerful collective feeling that does not "reduce people to a sort of chain-store uniformity" or obliterate their "precious uniqueness" in the way of modern states, but encourages them instead to exercise "the basic autonomy of every soul, individual, or of a people, united with the knowledge of its infinite sociability."[11] "Upward panic" is the key word naming a technique that works to preserve individual and collective autonomy, the exercise of which occupies Eva's narration. Other words in the book name the same technique: "drama," "tragic drama," "performance," the "Delphic Idea," "Dorian Orthodoxy," "Apollonian Rhythm," and "politics." All but "politics" were terms connected with the revivals of weaving, music, and drama she spearheaded up to the point when she began writing *Upward Panic*. "Politics" is a late addition, one about which I will say more later in this chapter.

Here I want to think further about the kind of book Eva was writing, a book that puzzled me in 1993 when I first took the posthumously published volume in my hands and read it as "The Autobiography of Eva Palmer Sikelianos," as described by its subtitle. Even then—before I encountered her lesbian love letters and wondered how to reconcile their tremulous, confessional voice with the flat, unrevealing one of *Upward Panic*—I felt it was a peculiar autobiography. Years later I determined to study the book's history. I looked for extant manuscript versions and the relevant correspondence and found two archival boxes among the fifty-three that constitute her papers in the Benaki Museum Historical Archives (boxes 12 and 13). The boxes are labeled "Αυτοβιογραφία: Μέρος Α" (Autobiography: Part I; box 12) and "Αυτοβιογραφία: Μέρος Β" (Autobiography: Part II; box 13). The contents of the boxes contradict the labels, however. Each box contains a complete typed copy of the version of the entire manuscript published by John P. Anton. Let us call this version 3. The words "Upward Panic" appear on the title page of this manuscript version without the word "autobiography." Beneath the manuscript in box 13 are two alternative versions labeled Part II.[12] These would have followed a Part I, which Eva elsewhere described as "autobiographical."[13] The first alternate version is entitled "Part II: Music" (referring to all the arts of the Muses). Let us call this version 1. It comprises essays exploring manifold appearances of upward panic: 1. Thing-in-itself; 2. Ancient Greece; 3. Satyrs; 4. Emerson and Apollo; essay 5 is missing; 6. Is Greek music dead?; 7. Krishna and Apollo.

The second alternate version comprises chapters numbered 19 through 24, without chapter headings (following chapters 1–18 in Part I). Let us call this version 2. It is structured as an imaginary epistolary dialogue between Ted Shawn and Eva. While its fictional letters expand on topics that the two actually did correspond on, the issues they raise and the material they cover actually align quite closely with version 1 (figures 5.1 and 5.2). Their subjects follow a different numbering of chapters and are: 19. Thing-in-itself; 20. Satyrs; 21. Emerson's philosophy; 22. The place of music, poetry, and dance in Greek culture; 23. Modern appropriations of the Greek; 24. The dramatic chorus of women vs. men; number 25 is missing; 26. Emerson and Apollo, or the place of drama in the world today. The two alternate versions of the second half of the book align, mutatis mutandis, with chapters 19 through 24 of the published version—19. Thing-In-Itself; 20. The Treaty of Two Great Gods; 21. The Birth of Tragedy; 23. Isadora; 24. Men as Creators)—but stopping short of its four closing chapters: 25. Ted Shawn; 26. American Drama; 27. Architecture; 28. Greece. Those last four chapters were added in 1941 as part of Eva's third writing of the manuscript (version 3), when her vision of the realms of "upward panic" expanded in response to the Axis invasion of Greece, as I discuss below.[14]

What does this manuscript history reveal about the kind of book Eva was writing? Certainly, *Upward Panic* never was and never became an autobiography, even if sections contain life writing. No manuscript version has the subtitle "Autobiography." The word was added by John P. Anton in his posthumous English publication of 1993. (It was not in the title of his Greek translation printed the previous year in 1992; but the word "αυτοβιογραφία" does appear in the new Greek edition published in 2011.) The published use of the word "autobiography" is at variance with the manuscript evidence. Moreover, it is in tension with the book's mode of writing. In all three manuscript versions, "Upward Panic" stops short of narrating the unfolding of Eva's life and instead explores in an expository way the media and aesthetic and philosophical debates in which she sought to master the "technique" of "upward panic."[15] Indeed the disposition to explore artistic and philosophical questions overtakes the narration of the life.

This same tension is evident in Eva's correspondence on the book's revisions. Consistently Eva eschewed expert editorial advice recommending

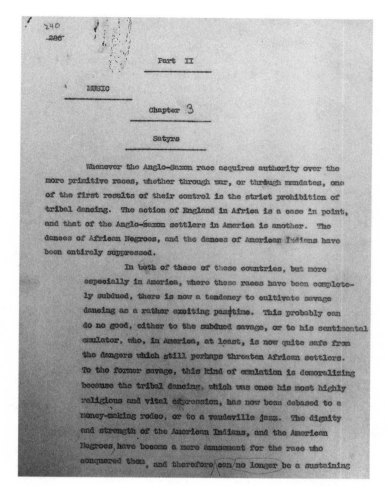

FIGURE 5.1. Manuscript page from *Upward Panic*, version 1, part II, chapter 3, "Satyrs." Acc. 189, Eva Sikelianou Papers, box 13, "Autobiography, Part II." Benaki Museum Historical Archives.

that she either write herself into the book from beginning to end or remove herself from it. For example, James Putnam, assistant to the president of Macmillan Company Publishers, responded to version 1 of the manuscript, submitted for consideration on August 17, 1939. The turnaround was fast, indicating immediate interest in the project. In his rejection letter, dated September 1, Putnam suggested that Eva rewrite the manuscript to address its failed coherence, as identified by one of the book's readers: "This person felt that it was unfortunate that the book fell into two sec-

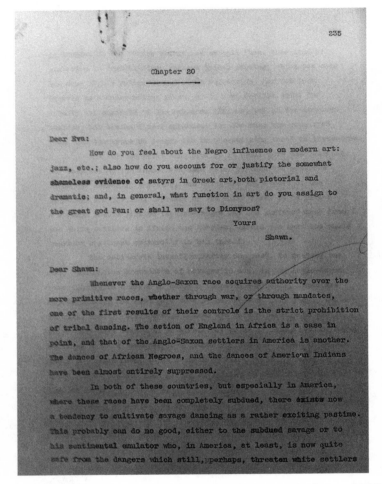

FIGURE 5.2. Manuscript page from *Upward Panic*, version 2, chapter 20. This version has continuous chapter numberings and no headings. The chapters are written as an imaginary epistolary dialogue between Ted Shawn and Eva Sikelianos. Acc. 189, Eva Sikelianou Papers, box 13, "Autobiography, Part II." Benaki Museum Historical Archives.

tions and he, personally, felt the essays, excellent and stimulating as they certainly are, were ill-advised in an autobiographical work, and that the autobiographical material tended to detract from the efficacy of the essays."[16] Lucy Donnelly, a fellow Bryn Mawr student of Eva and retired professor of English at Bryn Mawr College, suggested that she "amplify part I" and "write more freely and comfortably" in part II.[17] From Ellen Dundas Chater, a friend and teacher of English with a passion for Greece, she heard stronger criticism of the second half. Eva's narration was gripping, Chater wrote, but her essays were "just wild. . . . I have read them through and I am honestly in despair. You have such vivid, arresting illuminations, and yet the form of them is quite impossible."[18] She encouraged Eva to step away from the expository portions. Elsa Barker, a professional editor and person of growing importance to Eva in the next decade, gave an even stronger directive. She also told her to change the mode of writing in the "impersonal" parts. In Barker's opinion, these stood in the place of Eva's extending her life story into the present. She encouraged Eva to "realize *at last* that the second part of your book should be autobiographical like the first part. You remember saying that you had written two books instead of one and I am *so glad* you now have the courage to make a unity of the book. I understand your feelings—your shrinking: and it probably was as to say 'an inferiority complex' which made you want the second part to be impersonal."[19]

Eva tried to follow this last piece of advice. In early 1941, she abandoned the two-part structure to introduce moments from her later adult life into the last chapters. To do this, she first tested the epistolary form (version 2), then abandoned it to extend the life story (the posthumously published version 3). She wrote about her frustrations working for the Federal Theatre Project, leading to her illness of double pneumonia, followed by her meeting of Ted Shawn and move to Jacob's Pillow, then Eustis, Florida, to continue their collaboration. Inexplicably, she barely mentioned her Smith and Bryn Mawr productions of Euripides' *Bacchae*, the play that most directly treats the book's two forms of panic: the downward destructive path taken by King Pentheus and the Theban women, and the upward sweep of catharsis experienced by the audience with the play's tragic end. Perhaps this was because she considered the effort "demoralizing," as she felt that the two colleges treated the theatrical revivals as "'recreation' in the modern sense"—a form of entertainment—rather than as "Re-Creation"[20]—a serious work inspiring renewal.[21]

Despite her best efforts, the final version of *Upward Panic* keeps leaving Eva's story behind to return to the mix of subjects that preoccupied her from its first writing. And the tone is impersonal even when it tells her story. For example, the book concludes with the proud moment when Eva heard Americans praise living Greeks. This happened after a small but determined Greek army successfully countered the invading Italian forces in October–November 1940. It was the first defeat of the Axis powers in

Europe. The book quotes from an article in *Time* magazine: "The stuff that myths are made of has been spun out recently in Greece. The Greeks have spoken and acted like a race of giants twenty feet tall, hurlers of thunder-bolts, crushers of men."[22] There's enthusiasm up to this point. Then when the words register Eva's emotional response, the voice is so awkwardly impersonal that the scene almost passes unnoticed: "One's own masked belief was shining on everyone's face. Suddenly one felt the total rapture of having the whole world know what one knows, love what one loves."[23]

Eva's fundamental reticence about herself is striking. Again and again, she makes herself disappear behind her "masked belief," or she disperses herself into the media of her Greek revival projects. Actually, reticence doesn't quite capture the book's absence of interest in Eva's interior life— or even in her external life's course and the many famous people she met. Its strategy of refusal to confess anything requires an interpretive angle to make sense of the many crucial points when it stops short of offering any useful insights about Eva. For example, Eva characterizes Natalie Clifford Barney as "amazingly kind"[24] (against her reputation as "cruel, heartless, and indifferent to the feelings of others"),[25] indicating nothing of the heartache that filled their love letters. And she chooses the arrival of a glaring electric sign advertising Greek products on Lykavittos Hill in Athens[26] as the thing that pushed her to leave Greece rather than any one in a series of Angelos's glaring insensitivities that fractured their relationship. The book's many circumventions of self-revelation deny readers the pleasure of knowing Eva Palmer Sikelianos as a describable, analyzable human subject.

In rereading the book's surviving drafts now, after many years of studying the primary sources of Eva's life, I observe that for much of her adult life her quest to enact another way of being pushed against the impulse to make herself the subject of discourse. The obvious point is that as an actor-director and a queer woman who hid her sexual orientation from society, she had learned to avoid people's probing questions by projecting another self. Eyes were always on her, and she knew it, yet she ignored the gaze in the way of an actor on stage, without ever breaking character or disrupting the authenticity of the performance. The more substantial point is that self-revelation collided with her desire to embody and thus articulate an ethical way of living: to theorize not herself but the art of life she was creating from her daily askesis. While she concealed a central demarcation of her personhood, she participated in the creation of alternative modes of being in dialogue with unconventional sources. Following similar aspirations, the book's attention seems turned quite deliberately on eccentric lessons from the Greeks, both modern and ancient, in the "queer" media that she worked at mastering (Eva referred to Byzantine musical notation as "queer").[27] It gives an account of her perpetual self-exercise of running "anadromically" against the currents of history: the technique of striving to reach an impossible transcendent untimeliness. Having now studied the manuscript history of *Upward Panic*, a book written and revised on the threshold of World War II, I conclude that—despite the advice of editors and friends whom Eva trusted—the writing of the book persistently pushed against the autobiographical function of making Eva Palmer Sikelianos into an introspective record of herself. Instead it embraced an ethical-political function: to articulate the techniques of living in opposition to modern times in order to show people how to redirect the regimes of truth of Western civilization upward—at the very moment when the world was descending into war.

Eva set out to write a book that was not "half way" but "either rotten or remarkable," as she wrote to May in 1941.[28] She had thrown herself into it in the manner in which she did everything. "If it be now, 'tis not to come," she summarized her life's philosophy in a letter to Natalie Barney in the spring of 1939, quoting from Hamlet's late Stoic acceptance of the inevitability of death, which leads to a series of "if" clauses that can never be met and to the more important conclusion: "the readiness is all."[29] "This became a sort of doctrine with me," Eva continued, "that whatever thing I most wished for would come to me, if I myself were only ready for it." Her "doctrine," however, did not offer easy solutions. "This idea of readiness can lead one far afield, for in any objective which is worth following at all, are there not endless byways which one should also be familiar with in order to reach this secret standard of Readiness." Or, putting it another way, she wrote, "I cannot see black at all, but only a luminous gray. This is the one in my Legion who must now be balanced and checked by all the others if I am to find that perilous tight rope equilibrium between them all which will be momentary ecstasy."[30] The book she produced, so filled with byways, so perilously poised between her striving for clarity and "luminous gray," did not solve her problem of survival. She received the rejection from Macmillan in September 1939, then revised the book twice again before setting it aside. Yet the likelihood that she had followed one too many byways in the composition of *Upward Panic*—or in her life, which was bound up with that book—did not disturb her. What mattered was pursuing the many threads of her ideas decisively to their knotted end and facing the consequences calmly, deliberately.

THE LOOM IS THE KEY (AGAIN)

While she was writing and rewriting *Upward Panic*, with money always in short supply, Eva placed herself at the service of friends willing to house her in exchange for her physical labor. The loom was again "the key"[31]—as it had been in Greece but in a way that differed radically from the idea she presented in her lectures on Greek fashion in 1919 and 1921. Weaving was no longer the primary medium of her self-exercise against the dictates of mechanized society. Writing was gradually taking its place, though for a time the two worked in parallel as habitual processes crossing gender lines (writing is historically men's work and weaving the work of women) to fabricate the etymologically related forms of texts and textiles. Now weaving became the means for her to secure her room and board.

First she wove for her friend Mary Crovatt Hambidge, at whose house in Greenwich, Connecticut, she stayed intermittently from 1933 through 1939 and then in Rabun Gap from 1941 to 1944. Eva had met Mary Crovatt when she visited Greece in the 1920s with Jay Hambidge, whose last name she adopted even though he was married to someone else. Jay was a successful industrial artist who sold designs to Tiffany's and Chrysler. He had been commissioned by Yale University Press to write the book *Dynamic Symmetry* (1920), his idea of a natural design methodology found in classical schemes. Like Eva, he approached classical monuments not as a scholar but as an artist looking to recover an ancient process of design. While Jay was measuring the Parthenon and other ancient buildings, Mary was learning to weave from Eva. After his sudden death of a stroke in 1924, she set up a business selling one-of-a-kind dresses, coats, and scarves in New York City, using Raymond Duncan's and Eva's mode of weaving heavy silk warp and a lighter silk weft to produce heavy pleats. Affluent New Yorkers loved the work's "Grecian flair."[32] They lined up to place orders. Mary could hardly keep up with the work. She regularly wrote to Eva to share weaving ideas. Meanwhile she dreamed of returning to Greece to "build a dynamic house beside" Eva's in Sykia, to "weave beautiful garments, make divine pottery, plant flowers, fruits, make jams and everything which is the human expression of God [and] every year put on a festival sometimes ancient Greek sometimes modern, perhaps of Angelo's so that the ideal of beauty will spread everywhere."[33]

When Eva reached the United States in 1933, she took her loom to Mary's home in Greenwich to help her fill those New York orders. In return, Hambidge helped Eva weave one hundred costumes for the Smith

College performance of the *Bacchae* in June 1934. There was reciprocity in this. There was also tension. This is evident in the frequent backhanded compliments in Mary's letters. "From necessity my experience has given me that which you have never had to do. You would have it wonderfully had you ever had to do it whereas if I had had money I would have been an impossible person. I think it is much easier to be big under adversity than prosperity."[34] Their ups and downs are registered in correspondence from Eva's sister May. One day May writes, "Blessing for Mary Hambidge who gives my Boot a home and takes loving care of her."[35] A little later she congratulates Eva for walking out: "I am glad you left anybody—no matter who—and that you are alone with perfect freedom to carry out your own work—as almost all people except real workers are terrible wasters of time."[36] The fight between them, in this case over Hambidge's tendency to go round and round in her complaints about housekeeping, sent Eva out the door six months before the Smith performance of the *Bacchae*. The program notes did not acknowledge Hambidge's labor.[37] Yet Hambidge remained a trusted friend, to whom Eva turned again when she was fired from the Federal Theatre Project. Then near death with double pneumonia, she relied on Hambidge to take her to the Saratoga County Homestead Sanatorium in March 1938, and bring her home again when Eva was released on April 21.

The loom was also the key in Eva's collaboration with Ted Shawn. Between the summer of 1939 and April 1941, Shawn offered Eva room and board, first at Jacob's Pillow, his summer teaching studio, and then in Eustis, Florida, his winter retreat, where the parents of Barton Mumaw, Shawn's lead dancer and partner, lived. In Eustis, the Mumaws gave her a small two-room cottage, with a garden to set up the warp.[38] During those nearly two years when she was working with Shawn, she wove hundreds of yards of material for his costumes: ninety-six yards for new pants for him and his eight dancers in the "Kinetic Molpai,"[39] and hundreds more for the costumes of the *Isaiah* dance and chorus of *The Persians*.

Eva was weaving a special gift for Shawn, a beautifully embroidered silk chlamys, when news reached the world of the Greek victory over the Italians. As already mentioned, this was the first military success of the Allies in Europe. Mussolini, with troops already occupying Albania, made a last-minute decision to invade Greece, thinking that anticommunist, antiparliamentarian Ioannis Metaxas, the general who became dictator on August 4, 1936—the closest Greece ever came to a fascist leader—would give way. Within days of the Italian attack on October 28, 1940, however, the Greek army pushed back hard. The Greeks quickly defeated the

FIGURE 5.3. "Greek soldier," Athens, 1940, celebrating the Greek victory over the invading Italian army in October–November 1940. The photograph by Nelly's (Elli Souyioultzoglou-Seraidary) appeared on the cover of *Life* magazine, December 16, 1940, with the caption "Greek Soldier." Ref. No. ΦA.21. Nelly's © Benaki Museum Photographic Archive.

Italians. *Life* magazine placed a photo of a victorious "Greek soldier" sounding a trumpet in an *evzone* uniform on the cover of its December 16 issue of 1940 (figure 5.3).[40] The world was abuzz, especially when for a second time the Greek army prevented the Italian army's southward drive in March 1941. "Aren't you proud of your Greeks?"[41] a friend wrote to Eva, as if the Greeks were her children.

FIGURE 5.4. Barton Mumaw performing "Hellas Triumphant," in an evzone costume, Carnegie Hall, April 16–17, 1941. He is miming the trumpeter's gesture in the *Life* magazine cover. Acc. 189, Eva Sikelianos Papers, No. 567. Benaki Museum Historical Archives.

Writing to Eva from New York, Barton Mumaw asked her to help him add a "Greek solo" to his first solo performance in Carnegie Hall on April 16–17. Eva secured an evzone costume and found a certain "Miss Vasardaki" to teach him "steps from the Kalamatianos, Kleftikos, and from a Cretan war dance . . . and . . . the Hymn to the Virgin and the Greek National Anthem."[42] Mumaw combined these in a dance he called "Hellas Triumphant" with a visual homage to the *Life* magazine photo (figure 5.4).

He was so ecstatic with the piece's "success, . . . not [as an] encore number but strong and colorful and heartening, I hope,"[43] that he performed it again and again after he was conscripted in the American army, as if to imprint the figure of the triumphant evzone on the imagination of every American soldier.

Meanwhile Eva completed the silk chlamys and sent it to Shawn together with the revised manuscript draft of *Upward Panic* (version 3). Shawn knew the book in the second draft (version 2) with the fictional correspondence between them. He was honored to appear in her expository writing as a luminous sign of the future of performing arts in America. The new version he now read had an entire chapter on him. Eva praised his pioneering work of American dance in 90 percent of the chapter. She recognized him as "one whose gifts and experience were equal to the great new race to be run; whose mind was not fixed in a groove in spite of most varied activities, of which he had always been the center; who was able to consider intelligently an aspect of his own art which he had never thought of before."[44] Then she spent 10 percent of the chapter working through her disagreements with him. One point of difference was over the priority she gave to poetry over the other arts. Eva argued that dance was historically but not aesthetically prior to poetry.[45] The more unsurpassable obstacle to their collaboration—their "bone of contention,"[46] from her point of view—was his pronunciation of the letter R in their collaborative singing-dancing pieces. He refused to roll the R to keep the cavities open as with a vowel rather than to stop the sound by emitting a stop-throat R. She called the latter "guttural manner of the Middle West . . . the grave yard of beautiful English."[47] It was a stopping point in their collaboration.[48]

When Shawn read this, he was stunned. Why the obsession with this small point of difference, he asked in a letter.[49] Eva's response went into even greater detail: the difference was so gravely important that it cancelled their many points of convergence.[50] Shawn was shocked beyond words. He remained silent for nearly two months before acknowledging the letter: "I would have written before, except that your letter . . . depressed me inexpressibly. I didn't know what to say to answer to it, and I still don't, and won't attempt it."[51] The chlamys was hardly compensation for a break he had not anticipated; but it kept him "robed in [Eva's] art and love." He danced in it with "the trunks [he and Barton] made to go with it from one of the pillow covers [she had given him] for Christmas. Everyone loved the dance."[52] Later that year, when he returned Eva's loom and other things she had left behind at Jacob's Pillow, he enclosed a pho-

FIGURE 5.5. Ted Shawn wearing the chlamys that Eva Sikelianos wove for him, with the handwritten inscription, "To Eva the weaver from Shawn the wearer, with gratitude." Shawn sent the photo to Eva with a letter dated August 16, 1941. Acc. 189, Eva Sikelianou Papers, No. 555. Benaki Museum Historical Archives.

tograph of himself in the silk chlamys. His chilly inscription summarized their differences on the basis of that single letter: "To Eva the weaver from Shawn the wearer, with gratitude" (figure 5.5). As "the wea*r*er" versus "the wea*v*er," Shawn cleverly insisted on *his* embodiment of R over Eva's, as if to say that Eva should stick to her weaving. Nevertheless, he remained civil. He would send Eva his "love and gratitude"[53] at regular intervals through the remainder of her life. Eva returned the feelings graciously, without apology, though she had broken up her most promising artistic collaboration in the United States based on the most pesky, unpronounceable English consonant.

After reading Shawn's initial response to her manuscript, when Eva knew she had pushed the relationship beyond repair, she accepted the invitation of Mary Hambidge to join her craft community in Rabun Gap, Georgia. Thus, once again Hambidge was offering Eva a place to stay in return for her labor. Rabun Gap was a property on six hundred acres of wilderness stretching from the crest of the Blue Ridge Mountains to a ravine below. Hambidge had purchased it to create an artist residency program in the memory of Jay. On a high point, she built the Rock House from stones on the property. She added cabins to house recent high school graduates whom she took in to train, and she built the Weaver's Shed to house the looms and serve as a workshop and exhibition area. With the help of those high school graduates, she continued fulfilling orders taken in her New York shop, now called "Rabun Studios," on Madison Avenue. The whole operation in Rabun Gap was called the Hambidge Center for the Creative Arts and Science. Eva's job was to help Hambidge weave, teach, and oversee the exhibition of the young women's work.[54]

No doubt she worked hard. Elsa Barker, her editor friend in New York, reminded her to keep in check her tendency to persist without attending to her health: "don't break wheels, or your axle. . . . Don't get too tired with that exhibition of weaving down there."[55] But weaving was Eva's lifeblood, the practice of self she had been cultivating since she crossed into Penelope's world and began striving to make herself Greek in a different way. Now it was entangled in everything including writing, especially with Hambidge, who was always spelling out some new design: "By the way, Gertrude says that thread ought to go in a No. 12 reed—She says you will put it in a coarser one. The weft will pack together and make it like a rug, which I know you wouldn't want—so we are making it 7 1/2 yards long, 18 in. wide and 217 threads in the warp. You may need at least 6 1/2 yards . . . for the coat and this allows plenty for shrinkage."[56] For the first time in her life, Eva was weaving not just to express her philosophical attachment to a particular notion of human labor or to style herself. Now she was weaving to keep a roof over her head (figure 5.6). This fact, a sign of her precipitous fall in economic class, changed the significance of the craft she adopted in 1906 as a self-creative exercise.

More than this, the act of weaving, with its popping levers, thudding peddles, clicking shuttle, and thumping batten, reinforced the hard knocks of Eva's broken universe. Poverty, damaged relationships, old age, and ill

FIGURE 5.6. Eva in front of cabin in Rabun Gap, Georgia, in the 1940s. She is wearing one of her own or Mary Hambidge's handwoven coats. The Hambidge Center for Creative Arts and Sciences.

health cracked Eva's performative façade. She was no longer weaving to produce an art of life, but to sustain her life, and this breakdown reflected a loss of the control she had over other aspects of her life. Angelos was asking for money for rent, new books, his works' publication. Eva could not satisfy his wishes. She had no cash. May sent pocket money but would not help her repay her debts. Courtlandt and Eva barely spoke. The house in Sykia was eventually sold at auction. Glafkos, who was staying there, was forced to move to America with his wife, Frances, and son, Brastias. He and Frances then divorced.

Through the entire period from her return to the United States until the occupation of Greece by the Axis powers, Eva sent Angelos warm, loving telegrams and letters. She expressed her desire to publish his collected works (as she wrote in one telegram, "I AM WORKING CONSTANTLY FOR THE PUBLICATION I AM GOING TO SUCCEED SOON IF YOUR STRENGTH SUPPORTS ME")[57] and her unsuccessful effort to recover their foreclosed houses ("Je ne vois pour les maisons qu'une seule solution [her sister May] . . . et qu'elle a refusé" (I see for the houses only one solution . . . and she refused).[58] Then she reported her failing health ("GRAVE-MENT MALADE EN HOPITAL PNEUMONIE SUIVIE PAR PLEURISIE NE PEUX RIEN EVA" (I am gravely ill in the hospital, pneumonia followed by pleurisy, cannot do anything),[59] to which Angelos responded with his own ("Ἄρρωστος" [Sick]). When she learned that Angelos had found a new love, an old friend of hers, Anna Karamani, she expressed indescribable joy ("CHARA APERIGRAPTI LATREVO")[60] and consent to their union. And to the news of Greece's victory over Italy in 1940, she described her "entire life as a prayer for victorious Greece" and enclosed $100: "Ὅλ' η ζωή μου είνε μια προσευχή για την Ελλάδα νικηφόρα. . . . Ἔστειλα σήμερα μια προσφορά [$100] τον άλλο μήνα δεν ξέρο [sic]."[61] But Angelos's request that Eva annul their marriage[62] went unanswered.

Before Eva took legal steps, if it was her intention to do so, the German army marched forcefully into Greece, occupying first Thessaloniki, then Athens and the entire mainland as well as many islands of Greece. On April 30, 1941, the government of King George II led by Prime Minister Emmanuil Tsouderos fled Athens for Crete, still retaining the machinery of the dictatorship. From there it was evacuated to Egypt by British authorities (May 24). In September, the king and his men moved to London. The so-called Government in Exile (later the Cairo Government, when senior members moved there in March 1943) was the only Greek government recognized by the Allies, although it did not govern Greece but busied itself with the future of the king. In Greece, the occupying forces asserted their iron will through a collaborationist government. Neither the Government in Exile nor the quisling regime did anything to mitigate the devastating effects on the people of Greece of the rule of the occupiers. They did not protect the country's economy, which collapsed when the country was forced to pay for the foreign occupation at the rate of 40 to 90 percent of its GDP; or its infrastructure, which was destroyed; or its food supply, which was confiscated to support the German army and left a quarter of a million people dead and the remaining population severely malnourished by the end of the first winter; or the lives of forty-five thousand Greek Jews who were deported to death camps; or the tens of thousands of others imprisoned, deported, or killed in acts of retaliation.

The moment the Axis forces occupied Greece, Eva lost contact with Angelos. She heard nothing from him through her entire three-year stay in Rabun Gap.[63] During the same period, Barney, with whom she had reestablished warm ties when Barney visited New York City in 1939, disappeared in occupied Europe, though friends had warned her, a quarter Jew, not to return there. Weaving near Mary Hambidge gave Eva a roof over her head in the house of an old friend. But it could hardly soften the blows of her financial fall, diminishing artistic legacy, unpublished book, dead-end collaborations, and the disappearance of the two people she loved most deeply.

"POLITICS"

The Axis invasion of Greece awakened in Eva a strong concern for the political fate of the Greek nation. Throughout her life, the political, that is to say, politics in the broad sense of areas of human dealings pertaining to power, privilege, and social control, informed her activities in various spheres. In the circle of Natalie Barney in the early 1900s, her efforts to create a performance language for Sapphic theatricality participated in sexual and cultural politics. The politics of race, specifically anti-Semitism, supported her argument that Greek women ought to abandon French fashions, an industry supposedly run by Jews, a people unlike Greeks because they did not have roots. A form of race politics also informed her argument for the use of Greek gestural imagery over jazz dancing as a source of inspiration for modern dance. The latter, she argued, as an emulation of the "savage dancing" of "American negroes by the Anglo Saxons who had subdued them," was "not part of the spiritual and physical heritage of the white race," while it also reduced "the dignity and strength of . . . the American Negroes, . . . [to] a mere amusement for the race who conquered them."[64] (Presumably none of this was true of Anglo Saxon appropriations of Greek dancing in which she also participated.) Eva embraced Greek nationalist rhetoric when she used the arguments of nativism and authenticity respectively to promote handcrafted items and the Byzantine and Ottoman modal musical systems, or when she devised a complex system of parallels linking Greek folk culture to archaic Greece in order to represent the continuity of Hellenism in Delphi. In these and many other instances, the political informed Eva's art of living. Yet her relationship to politics was unacknowledged, or, better, obfuscated by her interest in embodying an alternative temporality transcending historical time, which she identified with Hellenism. By all appearances, she stayed away from "politics," referring to institutions of governance in the narrow sense.

Then, unexpectedly "politics" in this narrow sense appears as a synonym of "upward panic" in "Greece," the last chapter of *Upward Panic*. She wrote the chapter during the book's last revision early in 1941, as the Greek army was successfully battling the Italians in southern Albania, before the German army invaded from the northeast. To reckon with this unexpected Greek victory, she used "politics" as another instance of "upward panic" (alongside the Dionysian impulse, Apollonian rhythm, music, theater, the tragic chorus, etc.): another technique directing people's faculties "to noble uses . . . beyond barriers and boundaries . . . into that Panic of insight and love which alone can make man sane."[65]

To be precise, "politics" appears in earlier chapters but with a contrary meaning. It signifies the social machinery that levels people down and reduces them to masses.[66] The Delphic Idea defended forcefully at the center of the book was specifically conceived as an effort to overcome politics. It identified Delphi as "neutral center outside politics."[67] Far from the dehumanizing cities of modernity, the clean air, starkly beautiful mountains, and vistas of sea, olive groves, ruins, and sky would "lift [people's] consciousness above their petty discords, purify them . . . [make them] spiritually clean toward each other, and . . . lead them to one summit: to Charity, which is love."[68]

The context is the book's reckoning with the devastating historical moment when the Axis alliance was overtaking Europe with a goal to wipe out "the precious uniqueness that all these nations have struggled to preserve."[69] This downward-leveling war machine spread fear and paralysis everywhere. Greece was the exception, Eva argued, following American media representations of the event. In Greece, people stared the enemy down. How to make sense of the Greeks' "dar[ing] to stand up when all others had been devastated," she asked rhetorically, although they had "no money, no clothes, hardly any military equipment."[70] "There was no human consideration that made the action of Greece reasonable from any point of view. Yet she won the first victory of the war."[71] The illogic of the act, the triumph of the irrational in an against-all-odds instance of group resistance was precisely her point: the thing that exemplified upward panic.

Upward Panic turns to "politics" to identify the deeper urge present when groups overcome fear to mobilize against the overwhelming forces of destruction. To define the term, Eva first concedes—as if to resolve tensions in her own usage—that politics has been "debased" beyond recognition by common usage. "Like many Greek words of noble import . . . [it] has become a by-word in all nations, expressing the accumulated meanness and despicable self-seeking at the expense of their constituencies in all countries, of many public men, so that the word 'Politics' not only connotes, it actually denotes in common parlance, the egnoble machinations of public officeholders to retain their place in power, or unlawfully to squander public funds."[72] Then, to recover the word's "noble"[73] meaning, she turns to the definition offered by Angelos Sikelianos in an essay on the Delphic Idea. "Here," Eva writes, "is what that word really means" (and she quotes Sikelianos):

> "The basic autonomy of every soul, individual or of a people, united with the knowledge of its own infinite sociability, thanks to which it can find itself in continuous and beneficial relations with all other souls, and with all the Apollonian and harmonious elements of the world, aiding thus, each one, his own separate development, and also the elevation of the psychic and civilizing Apollonian Rhythm of humanity in general."[74]

The juxtaposition of Angelos's articulation of this ideal of "Politics" and the concession that politics is not always so brings attention to the doubleness of politics, which is underscored by the contradictions in *Upward Panic*. Politics has honorable ends and ignoble means. It solves problems and creates them. The practice of politics both affirms and potentially distorts autonomy. The entire section seems to be working almost too hard to recover some purer meaning of politics—"the sub-conscious fathomless ocean of Greek wisdom" lost in the "sea of oblivion"[75] of modern uses and abuses of the Greek word—as if to move politics *out of* the contemporary polis/city.

The contrast of the passage describing the debased meaning of the word and Angelos's hierophantic writing also brings attention to the doubleness of politics from another angle. As esoteric as Angelos's prose may be, it is entirely symptomatic of a nationalist tendency to use cosmic, mythical terms to purify politics. *Upward Panic* participates in this purifying impulse as it moves forward to explain what "kind of politics"[76] the Greek mobilization represents. In the long passage that I quote below, the tendency is to translate this political, military event, with its inevitable doubleness, into the mystical language of religious sacrifice. Indeed, the purity of the event, as the revival of a *"perfectly clean tradition"* (my emphasis), is guaranteed. This purifying impulse is given a theatrical twist, about which I say more below.

> We know today that Greece balances youth and age in immortal equilibrium. We know it from the few words spoken by Mr. George Vlachos[77] on a day when the future seemed completely black: "Greece," he said, "has shown the world how to fight; she will show it how to die." This perfectly clean Greek tradition:
>
> > Tell them in Lakedaimon, passer by,
> > That here obedient to their word we lie.[78]
>
> Repeatedly, during over four thousand years, Greece has sent us such messages. We have heard so many that it is as if Greece herself inwardly must know why she is so lavish with her own life: why, in fact, she never plays safe. It is as if she foresaw the ultimate danger which it is her destiny to face, and had been practicing for this great performance during all the ages. For indeed it would require this age-long preparation of the race through temporal and spiritual victory, then hopeless defeat, rising again to other victories only to know the bitterness of slavery through hundreds of years, and again rising, renewed and young, to teach the world how to fight and die. Dionysos, god of joy, and god of sorrow, torn by the titans, and again reborn: Osiris dismembered, his limbs scattered to the ends of the earth, and again reassembled and renewed; Christ crucified and resurrected: Greece has lived it all. And in her heart, in her great subconscious wisdom, Greece knows her own destiny, knows the ultimate danger that lies ahead. She knows that her victory today over tyranny, whenever it may be completely consummated, and however more glorious it will be than all other mortal victories, will be only another preliminary test of her strength to enter the lists and tilt for the final trophy to be won by man.[79]

The religionationalist elements here are obvious. The passage asserts that the Greeks, identified as a "race," were prepared by the ages for the present event, the replay of a familiar cycle. They rise to the call of their destiny. The cycle is identified as one of initial assent; then a cosmic contest in which the Greek people, always the disadvantaged party, ready themselves for sacrifice; then death or enslavement, and through it, resurrection and victory over tyranny and death—an "ever recurring cycle" of "life, death, and resurrection," as is stated only a few sentences later.[80] In passing through this cycle, the Greeks are compared to the dying-and-rising-gods Dionysus, Osiris, and Christ. Their history becomes a national religious story. Notable is the way the passage uses myth (a syncretic mix of eastern

Mediterranean sacrificial figures headed by Dionysus) also to move from the particularity of Greece as a site of national purification to the world stage where Greece becomes iconic of revival and recreation. The Greeks, like the resurrection deities they embody, are made exemplary for others in a cycle that keeps repeating itself: now again, as "repeatedly, during over four thousand years" in the past, they "[have] sent out messages" to teach the next generation "how to fight and how to die." All this is a version of the Greek national story.

The passage adds to this national discourse a more interesting dramaturgical layer, as if the event were teaching "us," its English-language readers, how to draw lessons about present life from its high classical drama. Let me state this another way: the chapter "Greece" of *Upward Panic* reads the Greek defeat of the Italians as the spectacular performance of a political tragedy on a world stage. The language of performance is evident. We are told that Greece "never *plays* it safe"; it has been "*practicing* for this great *performance* during all the ages"; it is prepared; it "knows *how to* fight and *how to* die." All this language suggests Greece is aware of its self-making: "inwardly [Greece] must know why she is so lavish with her own life." Its act has been rehearsed. The lines have been learned and realized this time as before through the age-old repetition of performance. That it is a tragic performance is suggested not only by the exemplar of Dionysus but also by the pattern given to the political event. The hero, Greece, is battling cosmic forces. "She" is trapped in a course of "ultimate destruction." She recognizes that she has a hard destiny to face. This is the role that she must play, not just for her descendants by race but for the entire world now and for ages upon ages. By knowing how to die this time, as before, her nobility is confirmed, cosmic order restored, and "we" the audience anywhere in the world and anytime are given to re-create and revive ourselves through the example of her tragic story.

I tend to vacillate in my reading of this attempt to recuperate politics in *Upward Panic*. On the one hand, the interpretation is not political in the narrow sense having to do with the institutions of governance. It does not ask a single political question about the Greek counterattack on the Italian army in Albania. How were the friendly relations of Greece's dictator Metaxas with Mussolini converted into a determination to fight the invading Italians? Or what role did King George II's pro-British feelings play in the decision? Or why did the Greek armed forces dedicate the bulk of their military resources to the Italian invasion and leave nothing for the inevitable German attack? Eva's lack of curiosity about the details of this dangerously unfolding political scene is strikingly consistent with a life-

time of viewing Greek history through the lens of myth rather than as a
site of political engagement.

On the other hand, her dramaturgical reading of the Greek political
moment is intriguing. Obviously, drama, not politics, was her forte. Her
underdeveloped understanding of micropolitics handicapped her on numerous occasions, as I have mentioned in earlier chapters: when she was
unable to assess intergroup dynamics to capture the prevailing spirit of the
times or unwilling to compromise with her collaborators in order to
achieve her artistic ends. At the same time, I think her dramaturgic reading
the "play" of current affairs in Greece captures something crucial to the
structure of Greece's place in the modern world. The language of drama
has been deployed frequently by international elites in the analysis of
modern Greek current affairs. Greeks are expected to produce sociopolitical drama, and when they do, their so-called tragedy is compared and
contrasted with ancient Greek theatrical plays.[81] Neohellenes, in response,
have learned to read, live, and even perform much of their history as
drama, exactly as Eva suggests and for the reason she offers. They bear an
exaggerated awareness that people are watching them, as if the entire
country were indeed an open-air theater—as Eva experienced it when she
first traveled there—in which theirs is a tragic role for replay again and
again, while the world looks on. The insight into the modern Greek performance of its tragic destiny is fascinating in its own right. As a piece of
Eva's life story, I see it being tested in writing first here in early 1941 then
set aside as Eva temporarily disengaged herself from interest in the world.

For much of her time in the cabin in Rabun Gap, Georgia, Eva wove
and stoked the wood-burning stove,[82] lamenting as she watched the world
collapse. Her sister May died unexpectedly at the end of 1941 in her hotel
suite in New York. Eva and her surviving brother, Courtlandt, grieved
May's loss for different reasons. Courtlandt was utterly "desolate," as he
wrote to Eva in a moment of rapprochement.[83] He had been living with
May for many years. Courtlandt could not imagine living without her. Eva
returned to New York to comfort him. She too grieved what was for her
the end of a lifelong dialogue. She went through May's things and collected
her letters. Her grief was double because May left her fortune to Courtlandt, who had none of Eva's financial troubles. Her archive of incoming
correspondence in the year following May's death dwindles from 152
letters in 1940 and sixty-four in 1941 to just twenty-three letters the following year. It includes another rejection letter from Macmillan Publishers,
this time of her translation of *Sibyl*, Angelos Sikelianos's tragedy of 1940,
about the Roman occupation of Greece through the lens of the Delphic

sibyl who refused to prophesy to the emperor Nero and suffered his venge-
ful wrath. The play anticipated Greece's dramatic showdown with the Axis
powers. Yet Macmillan thought the book was "not likely to find a large
market in war time."[84] I can only imagine how incomprehension mixed
with Eva's accumulating bitterness.

A letter from Homer W. Davis, executive vice president of the Greek
War Relief Committee in New York City, dated July, 18 1942, revived
Eva's interest in the world when it eventually reached her in New York. It
went first to Eustis, Florida, then to Rabun Gap before turning back. Even
people in her hometown had lost track of her whereabouts.

Eva would have known Davis as the former president of Athens College,[85] Athens's top preparatory school, founded by the Benakis family in
1925. Now he was writing to enlist her help in the emergency response to
dangerous conditions of famine in Greece. The Greek War Relief Committee was an American organization formed to collect money to send food
into Greece. No sooner than it was created, it lost precious time trying to
convince the British government to allow food to pass through its block-
ade of Greece, until it came up with a plan to "channel [money] through
London to Turkey,"[86] and from there to have food delivered to Greece. "It
is too late merely to improve morale or to prevent suffering," Davis informed Eva frankly of the current danger of mass famine. "Unless food
can be sent regularly and in greatly increased quantities, it is doubtful
whether any of the Greek nation of seven million will be alive by the end
of another year. It remains for us to collect money and more money to pay
for the food and shipping." Specifically, Davis asked her to contribute "the
names and addresses of Americans you can think of who might be a friend
of Greece, now—either because he has lived in the country or has travelled
there; because he has been a student of Greek or philosophy, drama or
mythology, archaeology or humanity; or because he is a philanthropic soul
who realizes the immediate crying need of the Greek nation."[87]

Davis's letter shook Eva out of her despondency. The threat of extinc-
tion of the Greek people called for emergency deployment of her cultural
understanding. Here was an invitation to translate a perilous event in the
current geopolitical conflict for an audience with skewed prior knowledge.
But how to persuade Americans with an interest in dead Greeks to support
the survival of the living? How to bring their attention to the present?
From the fall of 1942 to the spring of 1943, Eva tried at least two approaches. One involved sending to friends and acquaintances printed copies of her essay "What Is Great Theatre?" This small booklet of twenty-
four pages (with fifteen of them on the vitality of the Greek musical modes

preserved in ecclesiastical and folk traditions)[88] concentrated exclusively on lessons she had learned in producing Greek drama. Both the classicizing subject and the self-promotion suggest bad judgment, especially since the book makes no reference to contemporary Greece, let alone the food crisis. Was Eva so obsessed with reading the present political situation through the lens of drama that she could not grasp the incommensurability of so-liciting aid for starving Greeks by teaching the world how to stage trag-edy? Yet her approach won over classicists such as Edith Hamilton, the author of popular books on Greece, who was in regular correspondence with Eva from 1935 to the end of her life: "All that you write about the Greek answer to the problem, as acute today, of the individual and the whole, is said so truly and beautifully. . . . I have read with deep interest your *What Is Great Theatre*—Unmusical as I am, I can understand almost all of it."[89] Hamilton encouraged Eva to write more.[90]

Eva's second approach was an open letter, "For Greek War Relief,"[91] in which she sought to win Americans' sympathy for Greeks by drawing parallels with Americans. The letter pivoted on the point of Americans' persistent (though sometimes waxing and waning) interest in Greece of the past. Like Americans, Eva claimed, Greeks of today were "vividly conscious of the greatness of [Greek's] past achievements"—so much so that they did everything they could to preserve not only the Greek lan-guage but also important "human qualities . . . most characteristically . . . a passion for freedom." Indeed, they were more persistent, as history showed that their preservation efforts happened under repeated foreign conquests and threat of destruction, not least of which was their current situation of occupation, when "thousands of these people have died of starvation, or have been destroyed in concentration camps. . . . But the Greeks are seasoned veterans of the art of living which embraces the art of dying." Eva appealed to Americans to support the Greek War Relief so as "to keep some of these people alive, that we may learn from them how they managed to keep their signal virtues strong for several thousand year[s]."

Though the focus of this letter is quite different from the article on theater, Eva's dramaturgical language of the last chapter of *Upward Panic* is evident in the argument here that Greeks' repeated performance of the "art of living which embraces the art of dying" bore lessons for Americans. Here again is the notion that Greece is a stage on which the contest of values—particularly of the autonomy of individuals and nations—is re-peatedly performed for the benefit of others. Eva can be seen just stretch-ing her knowledge of theater to develop, though clumsily still, a political message.

Yet she did not simply rest on what she already knew. At exactly this time, writing to fellow Americans about Axis-occupied Greece propelled Eva to subscribe to as many news releases and bulletins as she could find in the three languages she read fluently (English, French, and Greek). These she carefully archived. Her papers in the Benaki Museum Historical Archives contain copies of items issued by News Letter of the Greek War Relief; Greek Office of Information news service (accompanied by letters signed by George Haniotis, director of the New York branch); Overseas News Agency; Greek American Council, renamed Greek American Committee for National Unity (an antifascist organization); Victor N. Cohen, Ringier Press Service, Zofingen; Royoume de Grèce, Sous-Secretariat d'Etat la Presse et aux Informations; and Bulletin d'Informations Helleniques. Besides these news releases, she was also reading the Hansard records of parliamentary debates in the House of Lords and in the House of Commons.[92] Many of the subscription materials that she collected survived several moves and eventually came with her to Greece in 1952. They are part of her life record.

A regimen of careful analytical reading filled her days. Disentangling knotty reports of developments in Greece in relation to the Axis occupiers and the groups interested in Greece's liberation was her daily exercise. She kept a low profile, corresponding with only a few people, mostly about the reports she was reading. According to Edith Hamilton, who caught up with her in the beginning of March 1943 after losing contact for several years, "You had vanished for so long, and I could learn nothing about you from anyone. . . . It was a surprise to find out you were in Georgia."[93]

TRANSLATING ANGELOS SIKELIANOS'S ACT OF RESISTANCE

Eva gave special attention to news of underground resistance movements that was escaping occupied Greece. Early in the war, when the Axis powers first occupied Europe, Winston Churchill issued the directive to "set Europe ablaze":[94] to spark and sustain mass resistance against the occupying forces, whatever the consequences. In Greece, Eva learned, the mandate encouraged the creation of a milieu of sabotage and subversion—guerilla groups, intelligence networks, covert operations, organized destruction, and nonstop subversive acts—to prevent the restoration of order under the occupiers. The most effective as an organized force was the National Liberation Front, EAM, with its military arm, ELAS, formed by several cooperating leftist political parties in September 1941, including KKE, the

Communist Party of Greece. The EAM was committed to creating a democratic popular front. In addition to the left, it engaged people from the political center, including prewar liberal, antimonarchist politicians. Popular support for EAM was widespread in Greece, and international support was strong, too, as EAM represented for both the United States and the USSR, in very different ways, the democratic/popular future of Greece. EAM worked especially hard to attract cultural elites of various ideological stripes who shared two basic principles: belief in the sovereignty of the Greek people and a resolutely antimonarchist stance. Angelos Sikelianos, once a vocal supporter of King Constantine I, who had broken rank with monarchists late in the Metaxas dictatorship, was one of EAM's early recruits,[95] Eva would learn soon. Together with EAM, two other antimonarchist resistance organizations came into being, both founded by antifascist military officers: the National Democratic Greek Cooperation (EDES), also formed in September 1941, and National and Social Liberation (EKKA) in the fall of 1942.

One day in March 1943, out of the blue, Eva read about a scene of mass resistance in Athens instigated by Angelos. The occasion was the funeral on February 28 of Kostis Palamas, Greece's grand old demoticist poet and Eva's and Angelos's friend from the golden days of Sykia. People learned of the poet's death in the early hours that morning.[96] As soon as the day broke, a Sunday, they spilled into the streets by the thousands. The gathering was star-studded, with a familiar cast of players from Eva's old life. Angelos, Nausika Palamas (Palamas's daughter and Angelos's companion for a decade), Marika Kotopouli (the actress who made her debut reciting Palamas's prologue to the *Oresteia*), and George Katsimbalis (brother of Kalypso, whose unrequited love for Angelos led to her suicide in 1920) were all present. The prime minister of the collaborationist government, Konstantinos Logothetopoulos, was there too, as were Axis dignitaries and armed soldiers of the German occupying forces. Famous and infamous, women and men, old and young, occupiers and occupied all followed Palamas's coffin from his home in Plaka to the First Cemetery about a mile away. Archbishop Damaskinos of Athens and all Greece, known to his compatriots for his opposition to the occupation, conducted the funeral service in the chapel inside the cemetery.

That this mass gathering took place under Nazi occupation was newsworthy in its own right; but it was Angelos's rousing patriotic, theatrical eulogy that set the underground resistance press abuzz. "All of Greece is leaning on this coffin," he declaimed with force, though weak from illness—and he mimetically leaned on the coffin, as if to indicate to the people that he was uttering stage directions. Naming Palamas as the "hero" who "took the people's speech / and raised it to the heights of the firmament," he charged his audience "to share the [poet's] divine luminosity, raise him up in their hands." Meanwhile, in a classicizing flourish, he called on the ghosts of Orpheus, Herakleitus, Aeschylus, and Dionysios Solomos to take Palamas into their midst. In closing, he repeated the following refrain, which now functioned as "a stirring signal for the general charge toward liberation":[97]

> Echo you trumpets . . . Thundering bells,
> Shake the country bodily from end to end.
> Sound the Paean! Terrible flags of Freedom [Λευτεριά],
> Oh Freedom, unfold in the air!"

Sikelianos's "Λευτεριά" (freedom) and the freely unfurling flag directly recalled Solomos's "Hymn to Freedom," the outlawed national anthem. The crowd picked up the eulogy's cues, in defiance of the armed Axis soldiers standing guard. Led by Sikelianos, people "raise[d] Palamas in their hands," lifting his coffin and marching like an ominous horde to the excavated gravesite. According to one eyewitness testimony, the crowd's performance of defiance had a powerful effect: "A German officer proceeded to lay down a wreath on behalf of the conquerors. Terrible swearing from Marika Kotopouli, our renowned tragic actress, answered this unacceptable gesture. And then, led by . . . Katsimbalis, a friend and spiritual supporter of the poet, a thousand voices shook the calm grove of the dead, raised as one in our National Anthem,"[98] the nation's paean to freedom.

This event—the largest up to then (though not the first)[99] antifascist mass demonstration in occupied Greece—was yet another example of Greeks' mobilizing to affirm their autonomy by theatrically staring down the machinery of force, as they had done against the Italians. It was perhaps Sikelianos's finest hour: his greatest performance, combining poetry, theater, and politics in a way that synchronized his ethnoreligious ambitions with the general will. It is to this historical era and more specifically to this moment that we can date the hallowing of his reputation "as a bard of a former age" who was "uncommonly familiar with our land and the peasants," so that people "called [him] simply 'Anghelos,' as if he were one of them. He knew instinctively how to establish a relation between the words and the behaviour of a Parnassus shepherd or a village woman and the sacred world which he inhabited. He was possessed by a divine force made up of the spirits of Apollo, Dionysius, and Christ."[100]

Eva seized on the occasion to bring attention to his work. From the time when she had traveled through Greece with Angelos in the springtime of 1907, she loved him for his Greek and for his poetry. She loved his poetry persistently throughout her adult life, even after his self-centeredness wore her down. She believed he was a great poet, and she bound her fate to his to help him realize his vision. From the beginning of their marriage, she gave him the freedom and means to travel, try new experiences, and stay in places of his own for study and retreat. She appreciated his intellectual powers. His deep knowledge of world poetry, religion, philosophy, and particularly neoplatonism and religious mysticism inspired her, and she admired his verbal fluency. Language flowed from him easily, as if directly from his extensive reading. She knew his sources well: an eclectic mix of foreign and Greek texts (theosophism, Nietzsche, the gnostic gospels, ancient tragedy, the pre-Socratics, the Orphic corpus, late medieval Greek vernacular literature, romanticism, symbolism) that touched on the particularities of reality as she experienced it too.

Within a week, she had written "The Poet Anghelos Sikelianos," an article recycling material from *Upward Panic*, Sikelianos's *Dithyramb of the Rose* (which Ted Shawn printed in English translation in December 1939), and the unpublished *Sibyl*. The article reiterated the theme that Greece of today, a country more rent apart by conquest and destruction than any other, might teach the peoples of the world, more disunited than ever, the sublime art of readiness to self-sacrifice as a step to liberation. As with everything she wrote, the text subtly reflected on her own situation, this time in her readiness to make sacrifices to promote Angelos's work. Eva submitted the article to Demetrios Michalaros, editor of *Athene: The Quarterly American Magazine of Hellenic Thought*.[101] When "The Poet Anghelos Sikelianos" appeared in the magazine's December 1943 issue,[102] the cover featured the drawing of a bust of Angelos framed by a classical pediment supported by two Doric columns (figure 5.7). Eva immediately sent copies of the article to a long list of acquaintances and old friends.[103]

Though largely repeating points she made in *Upward Panic*, there are some subtle differences worth dwelling on. First, the article places Angelos at its center. He is named in its title, his image appears on the front cover, and the entire article concentrates on his writing, in which is found the "foreboding of the calamities into which the world was [presently] plunging."[104] Beginning a few years before the war, Eva had expressed her desire to make Angelos's work better known by publishing his complete works both in Greek and in English translation. She was able to accomplish neither, as she did not have the money or adequate sway in New York pub-

THE POET ANGHELOS SIKELIANOS

Vol. IV - No. 9   DECEMBER, 1943 $3.00 per Year
                                                 This Copy $1.00 Each

FIGURE 5.7. Bust of "The Poet Anghelos Sikelianos" set within a classical frame, cover of *Athene: The American Magazine of Hellenic Thought* 4, no. 9 (December 1943). The issue included an article by Eva Sikelianos introducing the poetry of Angelos to English readers.

lishing establishments; yet she kept the project in her line of vision. It was one piece of her larger effort to control her legacy, for example, by writing *Upward Panic* to clarify the technique she had been pursuing. Now, with Angelos's sudden reappearance at the funeral of Palamas—after two years' silence—she made him a much larger figure in her art of life: the god-prophet "search[ing] for a true exodus from the long purgatory that he knew was ahead for all the world,"[105] inspiring upward panic.

Second, as a translation for an English-speaking audience, the article makes Eva a mediating figure who renders Greece and Angelos's words transparent. In the first paragraph, Angelos is quite incomprehensible. A young child rising in the middle of the night, he "write[s] the verses that awakened him"[106] while his mother looks on, refusing to interrupt him. "The torrent of song . . . [passes] through him as wind through a reed."[107] The scene is in medias res and disorienting. But Eva assists her readers by standing in their place, expressing the confusion of herself when she heard his verses recited in Greek by Penelope in Paris. Quickly she leads readers into Greece through the door of Angelos's poetry. "These poems were the propelling force that first got me to Greece. This does not mean that I was not aware of ancient columns and statues, of Greek air and Greek light: but up to that time these things were, for me, as near and as distant as ancient heroes and demigods: they were part of my consciousness, but not part of the outside world."[108]

These two points should be kept in view as this life story proceeds, since the assemblage, translation, and publication of Angelos's work will become a dominant activity for Eva, next to which she positions herself as the mediating figure. Meanwhile, "Politics" lingers at the edges of this piece, as it did in *Upward Panic*, coming up almost as an afterthought. For example, when summarizing Angelos's Delphic vision, Eva lays out the same six principles she summarized in *Upward Panic*, the fifth of which is "Politics," much to Eva's surprise. She writes: "The Principle of the Basic Autonomy of Every Soul, individual, or of a people, united with the knowledge of its own infinite sociability. . . . And this principle is the one which, when transferred to action, was called in Dorian orthodoxy *(who would believe it?)* Politics."[109] Her parenthetical interjection of disbelief requires comment, particularly because Eva wrote the article when she had been paying close attention to political developments in Greece already for one year, but before she dedicated herself to influencing the course of American foreign policy. In this introductory presentation of Angelos's work in 1943, Eva was still quite amazed that politics was a piece of her belief system—that the quest for autonomy when pursued as action *was* politics. Up to this point, the Greek passion for freedom—including her own embrace of freedom as a piece of the Greek life—made sense to her poetically and mythically. It was part of her national imaginary as a philhellenic American. It was not yet a site of political engagement.

While weaving and writing in her mountain hideaway in the months after Palamas's funeral, Eva followed developments in Greek politics closely. At a basic level, she worried that Angelos's inspirational public stand had made him vulnerable to German reprisals. As Elsa Barker observed, Angelos's stepping forth as "principal speaker at the funeral of Palamas . . . [meant] that he was alright at the time. But, as you say, it has another side, and leaves him at the mercy of the enemy reprisals. So we have to think of him as in the hands of God, who 'moves in mysterious ways His works to perform.' "[110]

Besides this immediate threat, Eva worried that the complicated dynamics among various groups were creating new strains, endangering the lives of Angelos and others who were connected with one or another resistance movement. Churchill's call for resistance activities happened early in the war without regard for the political fallout that was certain to come when competing visions for postwar Greece clashed. Specifically, the Allies did not take steps to anticipate the conflict between antimonarchists resistance forces, which were in the majority, and powerful elites who were determined to bring back the king, or when the Soviets, currently allies of the British and Americans in the war, sought to gain the upper hand in determining Greece's postwar future. Britain actually stoked the flames by acting on behalf of King George, who was staying in London.

Divisions were not slow to come. In the late fall of 1943, as Eva was anticipating the publication of the article on Angelos, she learned that a delegation of EAM leaders had traveled to meet with the Cairo Government that September. When she asked one of her interlocutors what the delegation was seeking, she received a summary of its positions printed in the progressive Greek American newspaper *To Βήμα* (The Tribune). In its own words, EAM was setting itself apart as the "real, moral and political NATIONAL UNITY," in contrast to "the differentiation between the [Cairo] Government and the People during the continuation of the struggle in Greece." Its first condition was to put an end to "the lack of coordination between the internal struggle [for the liberation of Greece by EAM-ELAS] and the war effort abroad. . . . There is but one struggle, as there is but one liberty. There cannot be two Greeces."[111] The second condition was that the king's return after the war should be subject to a popular referendum.

The mission returned to Greece empty handed. By March 1944, rather than a single government, Greece had three: the puppet government in Athens; the Cairo Government; and the new Provisional Mountain Government, or PEEA (Political Committee of National Liberation), formed by EAM-ELAS in central Greece after it liberated that area. The stated goal of the latter was "to intensify the struggle against the conquerors . . . for full national liberation, for the consolidation of the independence and integrity of our country . . . and for the annihilation of domestic fascism and armed traitor formations."[112] It claimed popular support and was the first government of Greece to grant universal suffrage. Its leaders were tied to Moscow. The Cairo Government was itself divided between republicans and royalists dedicated to the prewar order. In Greece, violence had broken out between EAM, on the one side, and, on the other side, the formerly republican, noncommunist resistance organizations now infiltrated by royalists. Each side suspected that the other was seeking to gain a monopoly on power. To add fire to the tinder, the current leader of the puppet regime, Prime Minister Ioannis Rallis, created the Security Battalions, a paramilitary force "armed and clothed by the Germans, comprising mostly local ideological fascists and Nazi sympathizers, royalists, and criminal convicts . . . to fight the Communist partisans and reduce the strain on the German army."[113] The Security Battalions reached their peak in the spring of 1943 with some twenty thousand German-armed and German-uniformed Greek men causing general mayhem.

"God's mysteries," in Elsa Barker's words, may have preserved Angelos from the occupiers' reprisals, but they did not save Greece from its downward spiral.

ANGELOS'S *AKRITIKA* THRUSTS EVA INTO POLITICS

The sudden arrival of the *Akritika*, a collection of resistance poems by Angelos Sikelianos smuggled to Eva in March 1944, marks a turning point in Eva's life, when the recovery of Greece—for so many years a goal with aesthetic content—became a call to political action. For most of her life, she had worked reviving Greece through the creation, preservation, or promotion of particular forms of art. Beginning now, she was fervently committed to having a say in politics. The conversion of her interest in Greece into tangible political involvement was as complete as it was sudden. It gives reason to pause, to recall previous encounters in Eva's life that brought about a sudden change. The pattern is most clearly evident in the effect on her of Penelope's appearance. Penelope fell into the middle of Eva's world in Paris, and suddenly the Sapphic Eva Palmer was a married woman in Greece. The suddenness of Penelope's arrival was half the key. The other half was the misery Eva was feeling in the company of Barney. Now the human misery was broader, touching something greater than Eva's poor, lonely, broken self. A world war lasting already half a decade was threatening to drag Greece into another war pitting neighbor against neighbor, destroying every progressive element, undermining the recovery of political society. Through her efforts to translate Angelos's work for Americans after his appearance at Palamas's funeral, Eva vicariously experienced the misery of those people whose sovereignty was being disrespected. She would now dedicate herself to questioning the geostrategic reasoning that was aggravating old divisions and leading to new waves of political exclusion. Over the next five years, she would send thousands of letters to American politicians on every level of government, from the president to local leaders, protesting each step that the United States took, following Britain, to determine Greece's postwar military, economic, and political direction.

A letter from George Seferiadis,[114] director-general of the Hellenic Department of Information in Cairo, was the catalyst. Eva knew him as the poet George Seferis. In 1930, he made heads turn with his Στροφή (Strophe), a collection of poems announcing the poetic turn of a new generation. The group of poets was leaving behind Angelos Sikelianos, among others, to embrace a cosmopolitan modernist vision. Seferis visited Angelos in Delphi while Eva still lived there but happened to be absent.[115] After her departure, he befriended Angelos. An accomplished diplomat as well as a poet, he befriended many people, and he would go on to win the first Nobel Prize in Literature for Greece in 1962.

With his letter, written to her in Greek and dated March 22, 1944, Seferis wished to enlist Eva's help in publishing a bilingual edition of a book of poems by Sikelianos. It was the Ακριτικά (1941–1942): five poems of resistance written to keep the Greeks' spirit alive at a liminal moment during the brutal first winter of the occupation, the "period of slavery," as Seferis called it. Despite his alignment with a new generation of poets, Seferis expressed nothing but the deepest respect for Sikelianos. "All of Greece was talking about" Sikelianos's poetic output during the occupation, Seferis informed her. In Cairo, Seferis had heard rumors of two poems printed in underground literary magazines: "The Greek supper with the dead," and "The fable of Solon"; "but [his] hopes of reading the poems themselves were few" until the collection reached him. This was the gift he wished to share, both to tell the world about the struggles of occupied Greece and to honor the poet who was standing by the people's side.

That the poems had national significance was evident from the title, *Akritika*, taken from a cycle of medieval songs about the exploits of *akritai*, men who guarded the Byzantine Empire's eastern edges (*akra*) against Islamic Arabic incursions in the seventh to twelfth centuries. As poetry written down as early as the twelfth century in a vernacular language very near to demotic Greek, the older *Akritika*, or Akritic songs, also straddle the line between ancient and modern Greek. In the Greek national imagination, they signify, by their apparent modernity, the antiquity of *modern* Greek. The straddling of historical linguistic forms by songs about the guards of the empire's frontier thus makes the *Akritika* fertile ground to explore the transcendence of borders. *Digenis Akritas*, the best-known romance in the tradition, canonized as the first work of modern Greek literature, relates the exploits of the strongest, most heroic border guard (nicknamed Digenis because he is bi-ethnic), who even defeated Charon, the ferryman of death. Recalling this rich national tradition and knowing Angelos's work, Eva could anticipate that this was a collection of epic poems about the Greek nation in a cosmic struggle for its survival. This time, rather than fighting Muslims on the eastern imperial border, Greeks were in a deadlock with the Axis occupiers, who after crossing its borders were using the machinery of war to threaten their existence.

The collection's materiality as an object crossing borders of media, space, and time becomes an especially potent agent in Eva's life story. Already in Seferis's letter, the details of the collection's textual manifestations are prominent. The poems originally circulated in one hundred manuscripts[116] handwritten in medieval script illustrated with woodcut prints by artist Spyros Vassiliou. "This too is a sign of the era," Seferis states, suggesting that the medieval handwriting captures a backward movement, but adding that it also represents an exquisite craft—and craftiness—that bypassed censors. One of those handwritten copies secretly crossed several well-guarded borders of occupied Europe to reach Switzerland, a neutral country. From there a photograph of the manuscript traveled to Egypt and was used to make printing plates. Seferis was now printing the book in Cairo in 135 exact copies[117] to convey the "material look in which the book first appeared." A photostat of the photocopy of the handwritten manuscript was the copy Seferis sent to the Greek embassy in Washington with instructions that it should be forwarded to Eva. Now he was asking Eva to fetch the copy, then to translate, publish, and disseminate it in a bilingual edition "in the free world." Already before reaching Eva's door-step, the *Akritika* had changed media several times. It had crossed two major bodies of water and passed through four capital cities—Athens, Geneva, Cairo, and Washington—and three diplomats' hands. Moreover, it had acquired semiotic force as a desirable underground object that was maneuvering its way from oppression to freedom.

Adding another layer of complexity was the secretive stance of the agents who brought the object to new audiences, Seferis included. The invisible hand of the person(s) who copied it one hundred times and the hidden identity of the person(s) who smuggled it to Switzerland marked this copy of the *Akritika* as a forbidden object in occupied Europe. Then Seferis, who was working on supposedly free ground, also insisted on hiding his involvement, both in the Cairo publication and in the copy that reached Eva. He explained, "[In the version prepared in Cairo,] I avoided mentioning the official Greek offices and the details of how the *Akritika* reached us. Even though the poems were published in periodicals in Athens, as I have been informed, it is better for you to say that your publication is based on the Cairo book, which was sent to you by a friend." He also requested that she wait to print the book from the photographic plates of the Cairo edition that would soon reach her. The next line in the letter is particularly obscure: "Προτιμότερο να μη δώσουμε την εντύπωση ότι τα Ακριτικά γίνονται αντικείμενο επίσημης προπαγάνδας" (Better that we not give the impression that the *Akritika* have been made an object of official propaganda). By what logic does the letter move from Seferis's desire to make known to the "free world" patriotic poems defending the value of Greeks' life in the face of the violent occupiers to his insistence on hiding the involvement of the Greek Office of Information of the Cairo Government behind the mask of aversion to "official propaganda"? Granted that Seferis was under pressure at this moment in the Cairo Government, and the decision to have his name associated with an illegally circulating Greek resistance text was not easy. Was he intentionally obscuring his role more out of fear or believing genuinely that the poems would be better received if they could not be read as government propaganda?

I leave it to researchers of Seferis's life and work to explain this erasure of agency in the transnational dissemination of the *Akritika*,[118] as it rubs against his meticulous effort to archive every piece of evidence proving his involvement.[119] What concerns me here is the message that his two-faced gesture of openhandedness encoded in the dispatched object. The provisions for the publication of the *Akritika* either indicate that Seferis would not publically acknowledge his support for Sikelianos's work or that his office was avoiding association because it might be perceived as the wrong sort of patriotism. One or the other or both explanations may stand. Whatever the case, the manuscript Eva retrieved from the Greek Office of Information in Washington—an object moving through space to free itself from the restrictive forces of the occupation—was again subject to censorship, this time imposed for vaguely stated reasons representing unnamed forces. Treachery was imminent in the circle of international players surrounding and including Seferis.

Eva recognized that she was being drawn into a divisive centrifuge. She adjusted her steps. We know this because she did not follow all of Seferis's instructions to the letter. On the one hand, she respected his wish not to be named as the agent of the book's transatlantic dispatch. She made no mention of him or his office anywhere in the manuscript's American publication. Following Seferis's example, she even hid herself. The publication names Paul Nord (penname of Nikos Nikolaidis, who also signed his work Νίκος Λαΐδης and Πωλ Νορ) as the editor and translator. Nikolaidis/Nord was a longtime friend with a proven facility in writing. He worked as a journalist, writer of satirical theater, and translator. Yet I have found no evidence, apart from his name on the cover of the book, that he actually translated the poems or wrote the introduction. Likewise, I cannot say for certain that he did not. What I do know is that in December 1950 he forwarded to Eva a letter from the Irish poet Padraic Colum challenging the translation of the word *andreia* in the poem. Eva responded to explain the choice, as if it was hers.[120] Certainly, Eva oversaw the work from beginning to end, and she and Elsa Barker edited it together. Neither of the two women's names appears on the cover pages. Reference is made just to the "wife of the poet," who received the copy of the poems sent to the United States after they "made their way to the Greek people, and were passed along from one to another through the underground."[121] Perhaps on this occasion, as at other times in her life when Eva used masks, costumes, actors, or other people's names, such as Angelos Sikelianos's, to carry on work better done under cover, she hid behind the unfamiliar, masculine name of Paul Nord to give Angelos and the "Greek people" a more direct say.

On the other hand, Eva ignored Seferis's advice on the publication's timetable. He asked her to begin translating the poems forthwith but to publish the work only after she received from him the photographic plates. He expected her to "do much more beautiful things" than the book he was preparing. Instead, Eva moved quickly, as if pressured by the object. As it was an object moving through time, having left the hand of the copier in

Athens in the winter of 1942 and reached Eva in New York City in the spring of 1944, I believe the arrival of the *Akritika* altered the temporal underpinnings of Eva's creative existence—eliciting an upward panic that brought her fully into the present.

Two years had passed since the one hundred copies were disseminated. In those two years, the social system around the manuscript's distribution and consumption had changed. When it first circulated, it was part of the system of underground resistance acts that resonated with the feeling of popular unity. The collection of poems represented the desire of all Greeks and their allies to overthrow the occupiers. That unity of purpose was now dissolving, as Eva already knew. Things were moving treacherously in a downward panic in the weeks since Seferis had composed his letter. In anticipation of the Axis powers' collapse, a large contingent in the free Greek armed forces stationed in the Middle East rose up against the Cairo Government, demanding that it distance itself from King George II. Moreover, it called for recognition of the Provisional Mountain Government, which the Soviets were rumored to be running. The Cairo Government suppressed the mutiny and imprisoned thousands of soldiers. Meanwhile the British were preparing to dispatch the king, who had stayed in London for the duration of the war. In Greece, the Security Battalions were attacking EAM-ELAS members with anticommunist frenzy, and EAM-ELAS was striking back in all directions. It captured, killed, and beheaded Colonel Dimitris Psarros, the leader of the antimonarchist resistance organization EKKA, on Easter Sunday, April 17. Sikelianos was known to be a member of EAM. The manuscript version of the *Akritika* left no doubt that he had been secretly circulating resistance literature. As long as the world was at war and EAM-ELAS was a US-recognized player in planning the future of Greece, Sikelianos's patriotism would not be questioned. Through his eyes, Americans might still "see Greece as a stalwart comrade in the fight for human freedom."[122] But time was short for this generous reading. The mood of the world was hardening.

Immediately upon receiving Seferis's letter, Eva moved back to New York. She gathered friends to celebrate her return.[123] She held another party in June to read some of Sikelianos's poems.[124] That same month, the thirty-one-page *Akritan Songs* appeared in print, self-published with a simple off-white, card-stock cover, like a political tract. The inside cover replicated one of the manuscript's handwritten pages. The short introduction, attributed to Paul Nord and dated June 3, 1934, was followed by the five poems in Greek and English but none of the original's gorgeous woodcuts. A biographical note on Anghelos Sikelianos topped off the volume.

Though carefully edited and without errors, this was a "hurried"[125] job, as Eva explained to Seferis when she sent him several copies in August 1944. She put none of the care of Seferis in the details of the publication. For Eva, the object that reached her by its circuitous route propelled her to pay attention with precision to historical time: "It seemed important to get this out as best we could before the road to Greece is opened," she wrote to Seferis. "At first I meant to wait for the plates from Cairo which you promised to send, but I found their delay might lengthen out immeasurably, and I wanted to make it evident that the poems were written during the German occupation, and secured in a neutral country through underground means."[126]

The *Akritan Songs* marks the moment when Eva was thrust into present time in a new way. For much of her life, she operated within a conception of time in which the present had breadth, containing within it fragments of the past that she was called on to re-collect in creative work. She thrived in the condition of holding to a circular line of continuity in the midst of accumulating ruins, moving round and round the same grounds to breathe into them new desires that had not yet found ground for expression, in order to recreate them anew. Ideally there would be no more ruins, only people with the courage to inhabit past ground creatively to recapture its living potential. Put another way, she made herself untimely as a way to transcend the impermanence of a progressive modern temporality.

This time, holding this collection of poems in her hands in observance of the firm request that she should make it known to the free world, she saw the thick plane of the present diminished to a knife's edge. The significance of the poems, with their call to keep the human spirit turned upward against the drag of the occupying Axis forces, was on the verge of decay in the face of Germany's immanent retreat from Greece.

Time was of essence in a qualitatively different way from the kind of temporal structures she habitually inhabited. The present time of rapidly evolving political events was a sliver of opportunity that followed fast on what came before and led to what would come after unless people collectively intervened. Eva now faced a perilous moment in which she felt called on to act, with knowledge that time was slipping from her hands. This knowledge, besides pushing for the poems' "hurried" publication, set Eva on a course of political action. Her writing on Greece now turned political. She sent thousands of letters—some very long letters—protesting each step that the United States took, following Britain,[127] anticipating the destruction that would follow, and pointing to the ensuing damage she had previously predicted. Already on January 12, 1945, *PM*, a New York daily tabloid, reported that "Mrs. Eva Palmer Sikelianos" had sent at least "two thousand letters on Greece . . . in her single-handed campaign to educate Americans about her adopted country."[128]

Her archive from this period, a carefully selected record of her incoming and outgoing correspondence, shows that she was in dialogue with hundreds of people besides politicians on matters of politics and culture. There were Greek Americans of all walks of life who wrote in response to her open letters, articles, and radio appeals, including a small group that approached her to preside over the Greek American Council, perhaps the first Greek American lobbying organization, formed to pressure the American government against acquiescence to British actions in Greece and later against American aid to the government fighting the communist insurgency.[129] There were people of the theater, literature, and the arts, from Paul Robeson to W.E.B. Du Bois, who identified themselves with the anti-imperialist movement in the United States and wrote to Eva in solidarity asking her to take part in the convening of the "American People's Congress for a lasting peace and in support of a firm alliance of the United Nations."[130] There were writers and translators of modern Greek (Rae Dalven, Kimon Friar, Philip Sherrard); authors of books on contemporary Greece (Henry Miller); archaeologists (Leslie Shear); classicists and historians (L. S. Stavrianos); composers and performers of non-Western music (Ravi Shankar); and poets, translators, and populizers of ancient Greek literature and culture. The list is broad and extensive. Many shared a belief that solidarity was important. Irrespective of the specific cause, people were called on to come together. Eva became a kind of node in a network of crisscrossing groups who viewed America's postwar emergence as a world power from angles other than the official one, and who felt pressed to speak an authoritative language of knowledge to power.

Consider just this brief summary of Eva's first long letter "on the Greek situation" sent to the president of the United States and other politicians, journalists, and power brokers on September 9, 1944.[131] The letter describes the United States at a political crossroads, ready to enter an "era of American influence in the world," while poised to make its first big mistake in Greece, which would "nullify essential objectives for which the Allies are fighting and undermine the ideals Americans have always professed." The president is presented with two possible paths in relation to Greece. He could recognize EAM and the Provisional Government of the Mountains as the official government of Greece. The leaders of EAM "have fully organized government machinery. . . . [They] represent all the old political parties, and their leaders include many scholars and university professors, many priests, and two bishops. . . . EAM is the whole Greek people," she reported with conviction. The other path would be to follow the plan of the British government to eviscerate EAM with the help of German collaborators and to return to Greece the remnants of the prewar dictatorship under Prince Paul, brother of King George, who was seen making the "fascist salute . . . two days before Germany declared war on Greece." Speaking as both "an American of post-Revolutionary stock" and a person with knowledge of Greece, Eva strongly advised the president to choose wisely to allow Greeks to freely determine their future state and so "establish a just peace" in accordance with US commitments.

There's something of the madwoman in Eva the letter writer single-handedly committed to revealing the injustice of American foreign policy. Her "performance of defiance," as Natalie Clifford Barney called her behavior in the streets of Greece in 1906,[132] had long since become a comfortable role. Now Eva described herself as "belong[ing] to what sometimes is called 'the lunatic fringe.' "[133] Her guise was never more eccentric. Her hair, still red, was cut shorter and braided in two pigtails over her ears; her handwoven Greek clothes, aged like her, hung loosely over her slight, shrunken body. Those looking on her thought "she was genuinely oblivious to people's curious glances."[134] Yet she recognized the theater in it all—not just in her role but in that of Greece on the world stage. Now the logic of her thinking about Greece was reversed. The world was turning Greece into a tragedy, in a sort of dry run for performances across the globe:

> The motives which have made Greece a victim are the same as those which have brought misery to India, China, Indochina, etc. But Greece is smaller, nearer home, better known, more easily coped with than these vast countries. Greece, as always, is a testing ground: and recent events have made it clear that the Greek tragedy actually is the venomous center of the detestable imperialist tangle. Thus, when the name and fame of this country will have been restored, the way will have been blazed for establishing permanent human relations with all exploited countries.[135]

A prototype for her strategy may be found in "Solon's Apologue," or the fable of Solon, the least fabulous of Sikelianos's poems. The last poem in the *Akritika* (figure 5.8), it retells a story from Plutarch's *Life of Solon*, in which Solon, the legislator and poet-seer, late in life, recalled the role he played when he witnessed Athens changing its laws so as not to fulfill a prior commitment and threatening to punish anyone who tried to with the death penalty. To resist, Solon put on the mask of a madman. He placed

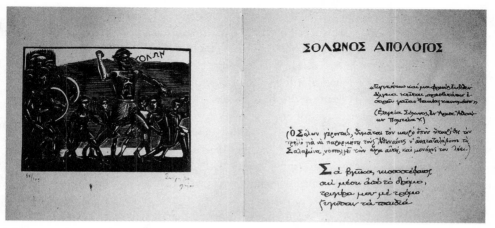

FIGURE 5.8. Solon feigning madness to urge Athenians to follow their principles, in a woodcut by Spyros Vassiliou (left), facing the first page of the poem "Σόλωνος Απολογία" (Solon's Apologue) (right), Angelos Sikelianos and Spyros Vasileiou, *Akritika (1941–1942)*, pp. 36–37. Courtesy Kostas Bournazakis.

an ivy crown on his head. In a madman's voice, he dared to tell his fellow citizens to ignore the laws. Children followed him down the street laughing. And in the end, the Athenians listened and rescinded the bad law. The force of Solon's discourse lay in its unpredictability, because he wore the mask of madness. The poem asks how a citizen can effectively speak the language of resistance in dangerous times. Solon's performance of the madman captures the anarchic, political revolutionary energy that disrupts aspects of lived experience to make visible political issues through public action. Here the technique of upward panic—an idea in which theatricality is inherently present for Eva—encounters politics and turns it into a means of dealing directly with the present moment.

Within weeks, Eva's predictions began to fall into place; unlike Solon's performance, Eva's campaign did not influence the direction of her country's politics. As she anticipated, Britain was working behind the scenes to determine Greece's postwar government. Nazi troops were in retreat. The arrival of the British troops delivered the symbolism of liberation, although British forces did not actually liberate Greece. Their real mission was to install a provisional government marginalizing EAM, as secretly agreed with the Cairo Government, and to prepare for the return of the king. People barely had time to celebrate the evacuation of Nazi troops as their former collaborators began policing the streets in the uniforms of Greek gendarmes and soldiers. Then on December 2, EAM-ELAS was ordered to disarm. The next day, a massive EAM-organized protest of one hundred thousand people entered Syntagma Square in Athens, carrying the flags of the Allies—Greek, British, American, and Soviet—to recall the unity of the wartime allies. Within minutes, police shot into the crowd, killing twenty-eight civilians and injuring hundreds within a few minutes. Suddenly Athens exploded into a battleground between EAM members and British soldiers (numbering seventy-five thousand) supported by the Greek police, National Guard, and the reconstituted Security Battalions. The fighting of the *Dekemvriana*, as these December events are known, continued in Athens through January 6, 1945. When the fighting ended, EAM and its allies withdrew. British authorities arrested twelve thousand suspected leftists and shipped the majority to camps in the Middle East and East Africa. EAM-ELAS took fifteen thousand civilian hostages to camps outside Athens.[136]

When the dust settled, EAM-ELAS was "transformed from victim to oppressor" in "a right-wing backlash."[137] A year of white terror followed, then came the corrupt referendum that brought back the king, topped by the civil war (1946–49) between the Greek government and the Democratic Army of Greece, the reconstituted communist core of EAM-ELAS. With crucial American support under the Truman Doctrine, the government won the war. The casualties were immense: one hundred thousand dead, seven hundred thousand displaced, twenty-five thousand evacuated to Eastern bloc countries, several thousand filling Greece's prisons and islands of exile, half a million Greeks of all political stripes emigrating abroad, and Nazi collaborators tried and freed of their culpability and returning to positions of power.

Eva paid a price, too, for her outspokenness. She was blacklisted by the Committee on Un-American Activities in the US House of Representatives. One document listed her name four times on suspicion of campaigning to "disarm and defeat the United States."[138]

"GREEK HOME-COMING YEAR"

Twenty-two years after Eva began her search for American funding for the Delphic Idea, she found a big supporter. Or rather, the US government found her.

The year was 1950. Under the Economic Recovery Program, or Marshall Plan, the United States was investing money in Greece to promote industry, restore currency, and stimulate growth. The anticommunist anxiety of the Truman Doctrine propelled the project. The idea was to help stabilize the economy in order to secure the alliance of Greece with the United States. Tourism assumed an important place, not only for its expected economic benefits but to affirm the presence of Americans in the so-called free world. To this end, the US ambassador in Athens "prompted the King" to "proclaim 1951 as the 'Greek Home-Coming Year,' "[139] part of a larger "Return to Greece" campaign to encourage Greeks in America to visit Greece, to make America's presence felt while revitalizing the country's economy.

Reviving the Delphic Festivals was consonant with this agenda. In fact, the office of the embassy, with strong input from Trevor Christie, an official for the Marshall Plan's Travel Development Section, and Anne Gault Antoniades (Anthony), vice-consul in the American embassy in Greece, wished to "have Angelo and Eva take over the direction of the Homecoming year."[140] They seemed the perfect model of Greek-American cooperation, and their Delphic Idea combining ancient drama, athletics, and handicrafts in ancient sites was potentially profitable. Moreover, Eva, a loyal philhellene, could be counted on to get the job done. She was still remembered as a wealthy heiress of New York, and she had regained prominence through her promotion of the work of Angelos, the man who had raised the spirits of starving Athenians in the bleakest hour of the Nazi occupation. The fact that she was also blacklisted for her advocacy of the cause of Greek self-determination was somehow not common knowledge.

Eva was not easily convinced. So much had happened in the past decade. Things she once cared about, like publishing *Upward Panic*, were increasingly alien to her. What she wanted from life was more basic. Natalie Clifford Barney had disappeared even longer than Angelos—from May 1940 to 1945. When Eva learned her harrowing tale of hiding in plain view of German soldiers billeted in Romaine Brooks's villa in Florence,[141] she expressed just this simple wish: "I would like to sit with you quietly,— and perhaps talk a little. I am glad you are alive."[142] As for the Home-Coming Year and Delphic revival, she could not trust the American government to see through her new ideas. She had long dreamed of restaging *Prometheus Bound* with Paul Robeson—another blacklisted comrade—in the title role: "His speaking and his surging voice are unequalled—and he is black, which a Titan should be."[143]

Old friends rallied to convince her. Angelos was enthusiastic, though in fragile health. Angeliki Hatzimihali, the folklorist who organized the very successful handiwork exhibitions of the first two festivals, was on good terms with the current government and prepared to work. Antoniades herself seemed really to believe that the Home-Coming Year should not function as just another tourist venture; it needed Eva's signature to create conditions for a real reunion, she argued. With pressure coming from her vast network, which now included not just Greeks, Hellenists, and popularizers of ancient Greece, but a new generation of scholars and activists interested in modern Greece and the Balkans, Eva started to make plans. To Antoniades, she listed her demands, which included passage to Greece and funding for a two years' stay to prepare for the event. She penned a mission statement, "Return to Greece," with Angelos's signature.[144] In December 1950, she applied to the Greek embassy in the United States for a visa, anxious to get started to meet the barely surmountable challenges. As she sat waiting, she found "astonishing satisfaction . . . in letters which . . . came from Greece since word was circulated that perhaps [she would] return,"[145] counteracting her perception that she was confined to the margins of postwar American society.[146]

Months of silence followed before she learned, thirdhand from Antoniades in April of the next year, that the visa was denied because she had signed a manifesto calling the king and queen of Greece fascists and seeking their removal. Eva was expected to sign a renunciation. Again the chorus of friends weighed in, especially Hatzimihali, shocked that this might be true, anticipating a quick corrective: all Eva had to do was sign. Eva dug in her heals. She declared that she could not clarify her position if she was not told directly by a government official how exactly she had proven herself disloyal. "I would have thought that my work on Delphi would be sufficient testimony of the fact that my sole objective in life is to bring the Greek people to an awareness of their own high capacity to match and even exceed their own great tradition."[147] Her intransigence had the effect of bringing attention to her. The situation became unsettled. The dramatic tension grew. People were waiting to see what would happen next. Facing the unexpected drama, she was calm and cool: prepared to prolong the delay. It was as if Eva had prepared herself for a lifetime for this role of suspended homecoming.

To complicate matters more, a series of distressing events for Eva followed in rapid succession. Angelos, plagued by bad circulation, sent his domestic servant Katina to the pharmacy for medication. She returned with the wrong bottle. What he drank proved fatal. He suffered internal bleeding, then died on June 19, 1951. Eva made it clear that she could not oversee the Home-Coming Year without him. Her interrupted return to Greece, intensifying the country's mourning of Angelos, came to represent the cancellation of something much greater. Could Greece experience recovery without Eva's homecoming? The European Recovery Plan then supported a production of Sophocles' *Oedipus Rex* by the Greek National Theatre in the theaters of Delphi and Epidaurus that summer of 1951 and planned a third Delphic Festival the following spring with four performances of *Prometheus Bound* directed by Linos Karzis, Eva's rival. Pieces of the Delphic Idea were popping up here and there without the coherence of the original project. The era of Eva's sojourn in Greece filled her old supporters, now growing in number, with intense nostalgia. Her absence increasingly represented the loss of an unfulfilled vision.

In December of that same year, Eva's brother Courtlandt died. Eva had repaired relations with him a little before the visa fiasco. He still spoke disdainfully of Angelos. "If I told you what I think of Angelos Sikelianos it would be anything but pleasant reading for you—I will spare your feelings," he responded heartlessly to news of Angelos's death.[148] Eva bit her tongue. Upon his death, Courtlandt "bequeathed her the sum of $250,000 . . . IN TRUST, NEVERTHELESS, to invest and reinvest the same, collect the income therefrom and pay over the net income in periodic installments to my said sister for and during her life."[149] $250,000 in trust was the amount she and each of her siblings had inherited in 1888 after the death of their father. Now Eva could live comfortably again and even travel to Greece, if she had reason to return there.

With the support of friends and, this time, acceptance of her visa application, Eva flew to Greece in late April 1952. As if the weird intersection of life events and brand names was not already overwhelming, initially she was to sail on the *Homeland*, but when the boat did not arrive, she booked a flight. It appears that her primary goal was to assemble the papers of Angelos and oversee their publication.[150] Eva had this project in mind for almost ten years. She was not Angelos's literary executor; that role fell to his second wife, Anna, but friends were confiding that they did not trust Anna to handle his literary legacy: She was a "menace,"[151] destroying rather than preserving his work.[152] Eva was also thinking about her posthumous legacy. Evidence of this interest is clear. A few years earlier, Elsa Barker responded to her question of how to select her papers in anticipation of her death. The letter exists as a fragment, as it was itself selected for content. Here is one point that survives and has been underlined in red pencil: "P.S. About papers. I have only one inflexible rule, to destroy anything which could embarrass other people after my departure, indiscreet letters, for example, or somebody's too sharp criticisms of somebody else. Most people have little honor with regard to the dead, who are probably more alive than we are, and may or may not care what is going on here."[153]

Elsa's advice did not convince Eva to destroy everything. Before leaving for Greece, she itemized for Mary Hambidge the things she sent separately by cargo:

150 records of Courtlandt's and his good phonograph
2 small boxes of food for Angelos's cousin in Old Phalero
4 small trunks of books
2 small trunks of papers
(The rest are clothing and I don't remember what else, things that
    seemed important when I was packing.)
bed-spread from Mary Hambidge, hand made[154]

After visiting friends in Athens for two weeks, Eva made her way to Delphi. She stayed in a villager's home, as her airy stone house was uninhabitable. EAM guerrillas had used it as a vantage point, placing machine gun bases on its roof and removing its furnishings. Its condition was not a shock to her, as Anne Antoniades had described seeing it the year before.[155]

The festival began with a *panigyri* (celebration) on the threshing floor, with regional folk songs and dances performed to honor her return after so many years of war. People from five surrounding villages themselves went native for Eva, self-consciously putting on regional costumes to complement her tunic and sandals (figure 5.9). "We haven't worn these in 12 years," they said to her, "and we've been waiting for you even longer than that.' "[156] The four performances of Aeschylus's *Prometheus Bound* followed.

On the festival's final day, she insisted on attending the last performance, though she did not feel well. The weather was bad. Her body was worn out from days of traveling and years of excessive work. After the play, she returned to the village home where she was staying. Someone lit a fire to warm her. She curled up in bed. The next morning, she was found half-paralyzed. A doctor diagnosed a stroke and drove her to the Evangelismos Hospital in Athens, where she lived another five days.

Her funeral picked up the cues of those last living days of theater. Through coincidentally good timing, she had staged one last dramatic act with herself as a mythical hero. Now a powerful collective feeling was in the air. Large crowds gathered at the Cathedral of Athens to pay their last respects to the Greek-dressed philhellene. A busload of friends from the city met hundreds from the villages of Mount Parnassus at modern Delphi's entry point. Several women approached the open casket. Each "came to sing a dirge, with a small floral offering in her hand, which she laid in

FIGURE 5.9. Eva Sikelianos (seated, left) with villagers from Delphi and the surrounding area in a *panigyri* of music and dance near the threshing floor of Delphi, May 1952. Acc. 189, Eva Sikelianou Papers, No. 585. Benaki Museum Historical Archives.

on the corpse."[157] The crowd now processed ceremoniously through the town, passing by Eva's ruined house. A special Byzantine choir from Athens "sang the old Byzantine funeral service, on which . . . Eva herself had done some significant research."[158] When they reached the cemetery, someone placed a pomegranate in one hand and a blade of wheat in the other: symbols of the ancient Greek underworld and the Christian resurrection. Following a custom known from ancient literary sources, not present-day practice, another friend put a gold coin under Eva's tongue for the ferryman Charon. She received the last rights of the Greek Orthodox Church.[159] Then, under a tree at the cemetery's edge in a grave between her mother-in-law, Harikleia, and George Cram Cook, with her feet pointing to the ruined ancient theater and her head nearer to the house, she was laid to rest.

But not quite.

Recollecting a Life

After Eva's burial, her life's possessions gradually acquired the value of relics that would shape her afterlife. For the next forty years, their handling would contribute to the production of a sanitized version of Eva Palmer Sikelianos's life.

The process was set in motion almost immediately. A few hours after her death, it was discovered that five of the fifteen cases listed in her bill of lading were found to be "no longer in existence."[1] This information came from a report to Eva's lawyer in New York by Anne Antoniades, the foreign service officer in the American embassy in Athens who oversaw Eva's return to Greece and would become the executor of her estate. Meanwhile, Greek law did not recognize Eva's marriage to Angelos because it had not taken place in a Greek Orthodox Church. This meant that their son, Glafkos, had no grounds to claim her property in Greece. In the village of Delphi, Eva's friends personally guarded the villa from Angelos's cousin Nikos Proestopoulos. According to her creditors, however, the house was no longer hers because she never repaid the loans taken out against it to fund the first Delphic Festival in 1927.

Perhaps because she owed so much, or because her status under Greek law posed a challenge to the handling of her things, the ten remaining cases of her personal effects went into the possession of the US consul. They were officially sealed in anticipation of an inventory by the Greek state. Antoniades was present when the justice of the peace arrived. She sent this account to Eva's lawyer in the United States:

> The Justice of the Peace brought with him a clerk to take the inventory of the estate, who sat himself at the desk with all the pomp of a Greek civil servant and the air of one about to witness a revelation. As each piece of baggage was opened and the men saw Eva's motley assortment of worn chlamyses and chitons; her sandals and her funny little homemade shoes

of leather, silk, and wool; a whole trunkful of odds and ends of shoemakers' materials, worn gloves, stockings, and underwear of a style and quality unknown these days; the scattered mass of letters, papers, and books mixed up with towels, wash cloths, and toothbrushes, they wondered why they had gone to such trouble to protect the interests of the non-existent Greek heirs. They just couldn't believe their eyes and kept saying, "But she was such a rich woman, surely there must be something of value in these trunks."[2]

If those same objects had been found in an archaeological trench in Delphi, the "chlamyses and chitons, . . . sandals and . . . funny little homemade shoes of leather, silk, and wool" would have been taken for ancient artifacts, testimony to lives lived twenty-five hundred years before. Instead, the things appeared for what they were: the leftover clothes and props of a deceased actor, rumpled remnants of her brilliant performance. Without the actor to animate them, people wondered if they had been fooled by the original act. "So reluctantly they marked it all 'No Value,' " Antoniades' report continued, "and departed, puzzled, and looking as though they strongly suspected someone had pulled their collective leg."[3]

Yet the remnants of Eva's undeniably broken life were not casually tossed. A group of Eva's friends, with Antoniades working at the forefront, determined to save her materials. With the aid of Glafkos in the United States, they gathered more things in Greece: "2–3 more trunks of manuscripts, books, charts, letters, etc. in NY having to do with her work in Greece."[4] Over time and with persistent effort, they collected whatever they deemed valuable to create an official archive, which would offer proof that Eva existed and that her life had value for Hellenism. On July 15, 1954, the Benaki Museum accepted one trunk of her woven handiwork. Six years later, the museum had acquired forty-one costumes from the Delphic Festivals. It placed these in storage until the issues surrounding Eva's estate could be resolved. Eva's expressed wish was to turn her house in Delphi into a museum and library, and the Benaki Museum anticipated that it would display the costumes in the house, along with other items from Eva's life with Angelos. Eleven years later, in 1965, while the house still remained vacant, the Benaki Museum accessioned Eva's papers in its historical archives. Around this time, the Hellenic-American Union in Athens exhibited her artifacts and photos, and the popular cultural magazine ΗΩΣ (EOS) published a double issue on Angelos and Eva Sikelianos—both in advance of the forty-year anniversary of the Delphic Festivals.

Not all these efforts met with unalloyed success. To realize the international element of Angelos's Delphic Idea, foundations were laid on March 28, 1966, for the reception hall of a proposed European Cultural Center of Delphi, funded by the Greek government with a grant from the European Council.[5] King Constantine II and Queen Anna Maria of Greece participated in the ceremony. Constantine was the son of King Paul and Queen Frederica, whom Eva publicly denounced as fascists in the 1940s. As far as I know, no one expressed outrage that the king and queen attended, despite Eva's strong disapproval of the Greek monarchy. Perhaps she rested more easily in her grave, less than a mile from the reception hall, when Greeks voted to end the monarchy in a national referendum eight years later, in December 1974. The Greek government then revisited its plan to create a European Cultural Center of Delphi[6] in 1975 and established the center two years later. The restoration of the Sikelianos house and its conversion into the Museum of the Delphic Festivals took another decade.[7] Meanwhile, Eva's book manuscript remained unpublished until 1992, half a century after its writing, while the piles of Eva's love letters, some in Natalie Barney's archive, others brought by Octave Merlier from Barney's apartment in Paris to Athens in 1969—with the promise to Barney that he would microfilm them—lay buried for many more years. They were neither microfilmed nor returned, but instead hidden in the stacks of the Center for Asia Minor Studies, with access to them and to many other materials of Eva Palmer Sikelianos's life strictly forbidden out of respect for the wishes of Anna Sikelianos.

The protracted archiving process—marked by fragmentation, equivocation, and delays of more than half a century—was counteracted by the swift production of a life narrative: a story appropriating Eva's contribution to Greece for the Cold War era. America had emerged from World War II with enhanced power, especially after its military intervention in Greece succeeded in keeping that country in the Western alliance. It began to see itself in the role of ancient Athens: the savior of the free world from a powerful Eastern enemy, this time not Persia but the USSR. The United States, a relatively new country, sought out a clear connection with the Greek past, specifically its status as birthplace of democracy, to establish its authority as the leader of the free world. In the words of Despina Lalaki, Hellenism became a byword for "the American postwar modernization project emphasizing democratic tutelage, economic liberalism, and individual humanism."[8] As a beautifying image, it represented all that America held dear about itself, while it covered over the political reality that America was mobilizing Hellenism to keep Greece and other countries within its sphere of influence. For modern Greece, the stepchild of Hellenism weighed down by the world's greater respect for its past, America's support affirmed its national culture and kept it on the right (Western-oriented, free market, anticommunist) track of modernization.[9]

In multiple publications, from the EOS articles to published accounts in newspapers, Eva's postwar story was made to signify American-Greek relations in this free world alliance. It played out at the imaginary juncture of American-Greek mutual support. Eva and Angelos personified all that was good about the alliance. The account evolved as a kind of romantic morality tale, in which the lone bright thread of falling in love abroad dominates the rich fabric of a woman's existence, overpowering many other strands. By this account, Eva, the beautiful American woman of good pedigree and noble feelings, longed for deep learning and freedom. She entered Bryn Mawr College to study Greek and Latin. She also performed on the stage. In New York and Paris, she lived among rich and famous people. Then, for a time, she lost her way in the (unspecified) excesses of fin de siècle Paris. The turning point was her encounter with Penelope Duncan, a Greek woman also of a fine pedigree, married to an American. When Penelope met Eva, she "sensed that she had found a match for her brother."[10] So she took Eva to Greece to introduce her to Angelos Sikelianos, and from that moment "the lean young American with the long braid of red hair and the tall, handsome Greek poet recognized that they were meant for each other."[11] Thus formed a significant American-Greek partnership. Angelos, a god in Eva's eyes (this is a salient recurring theme), "[led] her with surety to her destination, which was Hellenism."[12] She gave him her unfaltering support. Her generosity extended to all of Greece with the Delphic Festivals. In this collaboration, "Angelos gave the inspiration, and Eva insisted that his was the most important contribution."[13] Her excessive liberality impoverished but also purified her. When she returned to Greece in 1952, she seemed otherworldly, if not saintly. At Delphi during her last days, her body matched the condition of the surrounding ruins, while her clear gaze, looking beyond the camera to an infinite point on the horizon, suggested that she had achieved transcendence (see back to figure I.4 in the introduction).

The narrative also pointed to Eva's contribution to the development of Greek national culture. When Koula Pratsika, leader of the chorus of Oceanides in *Prometheus Bound*, recollected on the Delphic Festivals in the EOS volume, she pointed to a collective discovery of "an unknown Greece, the existence of which we hadn't imagined, a Greece of our own and for ourselves."[14] The sense that Greeks might recover their national heritage through the staging of live performances in ancient theaters contributed to the founding of annual summer festivals in Athens and Epidaurus in 1954–55.[15] To produce new work, several of Eva's younger collaborators built on her respect for the traditions from all the layers of the Greek past to create a popular aesthetic of high Greek art. In the first Athens Festival, the now world-famous maestro Dimitri Mitropoulos, Eva's fellow Athens Conservatory student who set Angelos's poetry to music, directed the New York Philharmonic Orchestra in a performance of an orchestral suite of *Thirty-Six Greek Dances* by Nikos Skalkottas, another fellow student of Eva's who was working to develop high art from traditional music. A few years later, Eva's collaborator Yannis Tsarouchis—the visual artist who had assisted her with scenery and costumes at the Delphic Festival of 1930—worked with theater director Karolos Koun and choreographer Zouzou Nikoloudi, a student of Pratsika, to produce the *Birds* by Aristophanes in a style they called "Greek Folk Expressionism." When the chorus of birds moved confidently about the stage to the Greek rhythms and modes jazzed up by composer Manos Hadjidakis, their bodies drew playful lines of connection from classical to present forms, affirming the continuity of Greek identity.

The high aesthetic of the Delphic Festivals generated not only the structures of Greece's postwar cultural production but an entire industry of splendidly handcrafted objects. For years now, cotton tunics, textiles, leather goods, and gold and silver jewelry in traditional designs have been swaying on the display stands of Greece's endless tourist marketplace. Tourists buy them, introducing to Greece another form of foreign exchange. When they move through ancient sites such as Delphi in their gauzy tunics and sandals, they seem to be giving new life to Eva's still remains. She is the haunting presence behind Greece's postwar reconstruction: the most influential philhellene after Lord Byron.

That was the Eva Palmer Sikelianos I had encountered when leafing through my parents' Greek books many decades ago. Then, the publication of *Upward Panic* in 1993 introduced me to Eva's several inscrutable guises; and the publication in 1995 of 163 of her lesbian love letters by Lia Papadaki suggested that the romantic tale of Eva finding her perfect match in Angelos was yet another mask. Through my research, I would eventually learn that while the postwar narrative of Eva Sikelianos touched on several obvious elements of her life, it covered over many unspoken or obscured but essential details. Missing were Eva's polyamorous relationships with women and her explorations of Sapphic life and performance. The upending effect of her meeting with Penelope, an event that brought her to a state of crisis, was folded into the love story with Angelos. All that was awkward about her marriage to Angelos, including his excessive demands and hurtful disregard, was eclipsed. Her poignantly unrealistic efforts to revive weaving and replace the piano keyboard with a Byzantine organ were rendered folkloric. The direction of the Delphic Festivals, which drew on revival techniques developed in women's colleges and other circles of women outside Greece, came to signify the continuity of Greek national culture through Angelos's claims to being its source. Even Eva's impoverishment became a sign of her patriotic sacrifice for Greece. Her insecurities, rigidity, biases, and disagreements all disappeared. Lost, too, was her theatricality and marvelous self-positioning on "the lunatic fringe." And her political campaign late in life to protest American imperialism, with its grave personal cost, was swept aside.

Missing were all the parts that made Eva so very relevant today. Everything countercultural, subversive, "lunatic," or just complicated in her confrontation of the present world and encounter with the Greeks was smoothed over—all those untimely elements that were culturally illegible in the years after the war. Now the Cold War was over, and a new order was rushing in to replace it, creating new opportunities and dangers. The anachronism of Eva's untimely aspects made them timely for me. I sensed that a textured interpretation of her life might serve as a meditation on questions of our times, precisely because of her willful anachronism.

To locate the missing parts required a different approach to the sources of her life—one that would attend to an expanded archive of her material traces in ways that considered how identities and relationships formed and dissolved around them. This necessity became clear to me when in 2005 a group of artists and scholars gathered at the University of Michigan for the workshop "Eva Palmer Sikelianos: Past, Present, Future Directions" to propose new approaches to Eva's life and work. There was a flash of excitement as Mary Hart, associate curator of antiquities at the Getty Museum, brought out a piece of Eva's miraculously woven cloth for us to handle. The cloth was like no textile I had ever touched: substantial, durable, yet soft and pliant. Then dancer and scholar Ann Cooper Albright jumped up and wrapped herself in it, simultaneously turning her head and lowering her chin in the gesture of the chaste Aphrodite. She suspended the movement. The cloth swayed and fell into Tanagra-like folds. Albright looked like a statue. She took another pose, formed another statue. Gasps of wonder. The rest of us jumped up to play at putting on the cloth in various attitudes. The folds fell over each body differently, forming a different dress. The joyous exchange of our modeling the cloth to create many dresses and attitudes prepared me to explore the changing textures of a woman's work when her work and life are inextricably bound together.

This idea guided me each time I journeyed to study Eva's official archive in the Benaki Museum Historical Archives in Kifissia, a suburb of Athens. More than one hundred times between 2007 to 2017, I walked fifteen minutes from my residence in downtown Athens to Omonoia Square to take the green metro line one hour each way to the terminal stop in Kifissia—past Eva's once stately old neighborhood of Kato Patissia (now a congested area of Athens filled with apartment buildings), past the Athens 2004 Olympic village—then walked for another twenty minutes to the aristocratic home where the Benaki Historical Archives are housed. As often as I followed this route, the operation of my passing from one point to another was never the same. The boom years of the Olympics gave way to the interminable years of economic depression. Stores closed. Apartments emptied. Economic immigrants could be seen embarking on buses returning them to their homes. Refugees arrived, homes abandoned and destroyed, with no promise of return. I took time to observe patterns of dwelling and selling, from the emptying of apartments and stores downtown to the swelling of Victoria Square with refugees. My purse bulged with tissues and pens purchased from beggars. I observed the stress of hard economic times as the archive reduced its hours and staff.

As the conditions surrounding my work changed, so did the project. This was especially true in my negotiations with archivists and directors of collections that led to adjustments in the handling of particular remains of Eva's life. Eva's letters in the Center for Asia Minor Studies underwent the biggest change, since the collection was inaccessible for decades before I received permission to consult the letters for two weeks in the summer of 2009. When I arrived that summer, I was handed two large blue archival folders with the name ΕΥΑ ΣΙΚΕΛΙΑΝΟΥ and words ΜΗ ΠΡΟΣΙΤΑ (not accessible) written on the spine in black marker. I opened one box, then gingerly took out the first folder in the box. Bundles of randomly organized letters, some bound with ribbons from the early 1900s, stole my breath (figure E.1). There were even signs of dried mud from that rainy day when Eva threw the bundles on Natalie Barney's doorstep (as I learned in the correspondence). I returned to the archive in the summer of 2016 and renegotiated my permission. My request for the archive to be opened, supported by my argument that the letters are valuable for an international readership, raised the matter of the status of the archive for the consideration of the board of directors. In the spring of 2017, with the

FIGURE E.1. Dossier 1, folder 1 of the inaccessible letters in Eva Sikelianou Papers, Center for Asia Minor Studies, as it appeared when I opened it in July 2009 and captured it on May 15, 2017. Photo by Elias Eliadis with Artemis Leontis.

permission of the members of the board and support from my home institution, I worked at capturing in photographs my initial experience of reading the letters (figure E.2). Then I completely dismantled the bundles in the two blue folders (figure E.3) to reorganize, catalog, and digitize their contents. I learned of the existence of ten more boxes as I turned in my all but completed work twelve months later. My role in constructing an archive of Eva Palmer Sikelianos became direct, marked, felt, and unexpectedly prolonged.

I followed other routes, too: to places of residence in Corinth, Delphi, Leukas, Paris, Jacob's Pillow, and New York City. In Athens, I walked the streets where Eva regularly passed. I experienced distances and upward and downward inclines; I listened to the sounds, smelled the smells, interacted with different people at discrete moments. I made—and, sadly, also lost—friendships I deeply valued. These many routes brought me to junctures where I found openings into Eva's work in its mesh with life.

My research, begun eleven years ago, leaves me now with this book and three insights on the approach I have pursued. They concern the ways that gender asymmetries, nonspecialist cultures of reading, and structures of power matter in the entanglement of the Greeks in modern living.

FIGURE E.2. Dossier 2, folder marked "EVA fond Natalie Barney" (EVA, archive of Natalie Barney), Eva Sikelianou Papers, Center for Asia Minor Studies, containing letters from Natalie Barney, photographed on May 15, 2017. Photos by Elias Eliadis with Artemis Leontis.

FIGURE E.3. All the bundles of letters from dossiers 1 and 2, Eva Sikelianou Papers, Center for Asia Minor Studies, dismantled, stacked, and photographed on May 15, 2017. Photo by Elias Eliadis with Artemis Leontis.

My first point has to do with Eva's fifty-year project of interweaving art and life. Eva regularly returned to reading Plato and Nietzsche, two thinkers who influenced many of her contemporaries and continue to attract readers pursuing the ethical question of how to practice a transformative art of living. A comparison of Eva to more famous readers, mostly male thinkers and writers,[16] calls attention to her difference. Eva was a queer female performer for whom writing was just one of several exercises of self. It was subsumed under the hybrid art of performance, which she chose to pursue over writing, even though she knew that Natalie Barney demeaned performance as a "reproductive," "effeminate" art as opposed to the "virile" art of writing.[17] She produced no well-known body of work but pursued questions of how to live practically through a living performance, anticipating a feminist epistemology of situated knowledge. Early in their adult years together, Natalie Barney lovingly declared: "Life has been your art—you have set yourself to music, your days are your sonnets."[18] When Eva moved to Greece, she had already disagreed with Barney on the relative importance of performance over writing. Now Barney revised her assessment of the way that Eva was living her art, calling it a deliberate, unfashionable "performance of defiance."[19] The latter statement summarizes, in Barney's typically brilliant turn of phrase, both the performative element of Eva's art of life and the confrontational nature of her life of art: her enactment on a daily basis of the will (after Nietzsche) to confront inherited knowledge and to plant in herself a new habit, a new instinct, a second nature, so that her first nature would wither away.[20]

It was a wonderfully superficial project. I do not use this phrase lightly. The idea that new bodily exercises, performed habitually and with self-awareness, may alter the field of possibilities of an inherited world considered to be restrictive is supported by the positions of some of the aforementioned writers and philosophers. For them, identities were not innate to individuals but performed through the vocabularies, gestures, and objects recognized by society. This counter-Enlightenment position was tested by a small group of people who identified with the aestheticist movement of Eva's era. Given a new spin in the late twentieth century by Foucault and some of his interpreters such as Alexander Nehamas, David Halperin, and Judith Butler, it has been ascendant in the early twenty-first. Millions of people today work at being themselves by becoming otherwise: by changing their names; crossing gender lines; changing their sex; tattooing their bodies; drawing on ancient traditions and distant sources to transform their consciousness; and rejecting conventional ties of association to create new groups and notions of belonging. While some are celebrities, most live their lives in relative obscurity. They aspire, somewhere, somehow, to change the social order through their alteration of the field of possibilities defining themselves.

A precursor of the present movement, Eva's difficult negotiation of the twists, turns, and ultimate precarity of her life have helped me better to recognize the gap between philosophical ideas of the art of transformative living—with their explorations of the power of irony and other figures of thought—and the "performance of defiance" that claims surface truth while struggling to absorb the shocks that the sustained defiance of conventions may bring on. Philosophers did not write the script for Eva's performance. There is no one script for the art of living, only exercises of readiness to face the unexpected.

My second point concerns the archive of modern classicism, by which I mean the body of source materials used for studying the presence of the ancients in modern life. In writing this book, I became aware of undervalued communities of nonspecialists who have had a hand in interpreting ancient Greek sources for the present era. It is a function of archives to enable observers to construct the categories through which we approach a topic. The expanded archive of Greek learning consulted for this book foregrounds Hellenism in the eyes of people who sought a collective, embodied experience of otherness. The circle of Sapho 1900 is one case in point. A group of white, upper-class women who wished to invert the heterosexual norms that pressed hard against their bodies, they consulted the fragments of Sappho to learn how to live collectively a different life. Their performance of Sappho on and off the stage is just one coordinated reinterpretation of the Greeks treated in this book. Another example is the effort by Psachos and his cohort of church musicians to reintroduce non-Western modal music to the Greek Orthodox Church of Greece in order to counter the recent invasion of Western music and ultimately to affirm Greek nationhood. In each case, contact with ancient sources endowed a collective project with the prestige of classical learning. The group located the origin of the work with which it identified itself in these inaudible, immovable ancient sources. It operated in a temporal disjunction, and its backward glance sought to connect elements of the present with the lost past. In the ancient sources, the group also found its "hermetic idiom," as Vassiliki Kolocotroni calls it: a special language requiring special knowledge to unleash it.[21] Case studies such as the ones I have presented here help us to identify the nonspecialist readers of ancient sources who drew on Greek antiquity to imagine their communal alterity. Moreover, we recognize the contribution of these undervalued creators to cycles of renewal that continue to make Greek sources relevant to new generations.

My third point has to do with the power/knowledge clashes that are part of the history of Hellenism, an inherently dynamic, politically charged idea in the modern era. Following the entanglements at different stages in

Eva's encounter with Greece has offered me a sense of just how complex the cultural terrain can be. Hellenism operates on an assimilative model. It is constantly absorbing new snippets of memory from many different cultures as if they were original to its existence. The process can set off conflicts between groups that vie to infuse the Greek past with their culture of knowledge.[22] Indeed cultural interchange, appropriation, and the dominance of one group over another are imprinted in the history of the idea of Hellenism. The complexity increases when people such as Eva—endowed with the power of Western institutions and invested in the transcendence of the Greek past—meet living Greeks in the crucible of Greece and become enamored of the new Greece that they discover.

For decades now, scholars in modern Greek studies have been following the dynamics between self-identifying ethnic Greeks and people who come to Greece "bearing the gifts of classicism, romanticism, philhellenism, orientalism, and a desire for self-regeneration"[23] within a narrow vision of the Greek landscape. But we have been talking mostly to ourselves.[24] The need is urgent for a broader conversation on Hellenism, Orientalism, colonialism, and imperialism. The point is to bring together people who study the Greek past and its reception in the West with those who study its presence in the Balkans, the eastern Mediterranean, northern Africa, and western Asia, in order to better confront the mechanisms that cut short the kinds of exchanges and mixtures that give Hellenism its dynamism.

Eva's performance of the Greek life in the crucible of Greece offers itself for just this kind of multisided conversation. Even her life's end drew on the resources of people on both sides of the Atlantic to determine the handling of her legacy. On that occasion, people who cared about her reputation in Greece and America sought to tame the contrary aspects of her life in order to identify an ideal worthy of imitation in the era of Cold War Greek-American relations. They sanitized her story. They made her one-dimensional. They turned her into an icon of classicism. The constraining of her legacy imitated the processes that have worked to control Hellenism. But Hellenism is not one idea: it is many, and argumentation and differentiation keep them in circulation. Rather than taming her legacy, this book offers not one Eva but many guises of a self that formed and dissolved identities several times, even as she lived her adult life as a Greek revival. She is the Sapphic performer, weaver, director, composer, writer, wife, lover, church musician, reorienting orientalist, nationalist, believer in and skeptic of historical authenticity, advocate and challenger of

Greece's tourist development, fringe lunatic, and political radical. Sometimes alien, sometimes utterly familiar in her vulnerability and discomfort, her otherness solicits us to think further about those guises and the boundaries of modern life—and of the West's vision of Hellenism—that she adopted yet pushed insistently against.

Appendix: Cast of Characters

Abbe, Catherine (also Catherine Amory Bennett, Catherine Palmer) (1843–1920). Eva's mother and a social activist who supported women's suffrage and was a founding member and president of the City History Club of New York.

Abbe, Robert, Dr. (1851–1928). Eva's stepfather, resident surgeon at St. Luke's Hospital, New York. He was the first in America to use radium for treating cancer.

Antoniades (Anthony), Anne Gault (d. 1982). US foreign service officer in the American embassy after 1949 who oversaw Eva's return to Greece in 1952 and became the executor of her estate.

Archbold, Anne Mills (1873–1968). Contemporary of Eva's and heir to an oil fortune who lent the terrace of her Bar Harbor cottage for Eva to stage Swinburne's *Atalanta* in 1905.

Barker, Elsa (1869–1954). American editor and author of spirit-communicated literature best known for three books of *Letters from a Living Dead Man* (1914, 1915, 1919). She was Eva's friend from 1938 to the end of Eva's life.

Barney, Albert Clifford (1848–1902). Rich industrialist from Cincinnati who moved his family to Washington. The father of Natalie Clifford Barney, he left a large inheritance in 1902, which gave Barney the means to live freely.

Barney, Alice (Laura). See Dreyfus-Barney, Laura.

Barney, Alice Pike (1857–1931). Mother of Natalie Barney married to Albert Clifford Barney and a painter, director, and performer who worked to make Washington a center for the arts. She painted a portrait of Eva.

Barney, Natalie Clifford (1876–1972). Multimillionaire writer famous for her weekly salons and openly lesbian life. She met Eva in the 1890s in Bar Harbor and was her lover and collaborator until Eva married Angelos in 1907 and was friend her for life.

Benakis, Antonis (1873–1954). Collector and founder of the Benaki Museum who encouraged Eva to produce the second Delphic Festival, offering funding from Greek benefactors. His support for Eva contributed to the decision of the Benaki Museum to collect her papers and artifacts from the Delphic Festivals including her costumes.

Bernhardt, Sarah (1844–1923). French actor, part of Barney's circle in the early 1900s, who planned to stage Maeterlinck's *Pelléas et Mélisande* with Eva as Mélisande in New York City in December 1905, at Eva's expense, but cancelled the event.

Burlin, Natalie Curtis (1875–1921). American ethnomusicologist and family friend of Eva's whose study of Native American music (producing musical transcriptions in notation and on an Edison cylinder recorder) was an inspiration to Eva.

Buschor, Ernst (1886–1961). German archaeologist who directed the German archaeological institute in Athens from 1921 to 1929. He was skeptical of the Delphic revivals when Eva asked for his support but attended the 1927 festival and enthusiastically approved of her work from an archaeological standpoint.

Calvé, Emma (1858–1942). Famous French female opera singer of the belle époque who sang regularly at the New York Metropolitan Opera House and was a friend of Eva's family. She and Eva corresponded and were frequently together from 1904 to 1905.

Campbell, Mrs. Patrick (1865–1940). British stage actress who auditioned Eva in 1903 and offered her an opportunity to act. Eva refused her condition that she cut ties with Barney and her circle in Paris.

Christie, Trevor (d. 1969). Travel writer and official for the Marshall Plan's Travel Development Section who advocated for Eva and Angelos Sikelianos to take over the direction of the Greek "Home-Coming Year" in 1951.

Cleyrergue, Berthe (1904–97). Housekeeper of Natalie Barney from 1927 onward who welcomed Octave Merlier in 1969 and allowed him to take to Greece over six hundred letters from Eva's correspondence to microfilm them for an archive and museum that he was creating.

Colette (Sidonie-Gabrielle Colette) (1873–1954). French novelist, actor, and journalist who was part of the circle of Natalie Barney in Paris in the early 1900s and performed with Eva in at least two plays.

Cook, George Cram (1873–1924). Classicist who studied at Harvard, became professor of English at the University of Iowa and at Stanford, and was a founding member of the Provincetown Players. He left for Greece with his wife, Susan Glaspell, in 1922 and died in Delphi in 1924. His efforts to organize communal theater at Delphi inspired the first Delphic Festival.

Cook, Nilla (1908–82). Daughter of George Cram Cook who traveled to Greece in 1923 and met the Sikelianoses. Glafkos fell in love with her and followed her to the United States. She returned to participate in the first Delphic Festival and married Nikos Proestopolous, cousin of Angelos Sikelianos, then left him to become a follower of Gandhi.

Delarue-Mardrus, Lucie (1874–1945). Prolific French writer who was part of Barney's circle in Paris in the early 1900s and wrote love poems to her.

Donnelly, Lucy Martin (1870–1948). Fellow student with Eva at Bryn Mawr College who became a professor of English. She corresponded with Eva over the years and offered editorial advice on *Upward Panic* in the 1930s.

Doolittle, Hilda (H. D.) (1886–1945). American poet and writer who studied Greek at Bryn Mawr College a few years after Eva and was fascinated with Greek literature all her life. She visited Greece in 1920 and recorded her own "Delphic vision."

Dragoumis, Ion (1878–1920). Greek diplomat, writer, and intellectual whose efforts to find common ground among nationalism, socialism, demoticism, and an anti-Western stance fed Angelos's imagination, especially after Dragoumis was assassinated in 1920 by Venizelists.

Draper, Ann Mary Palmer. Eva's aunt, who left her $25,000 in 1914.

Dreier, Katherine (1877–1952). American artist and patron of the arts from Stonington, Connecticut, who introduced Eva to Ted Shawn.

Dreyfus-Barney, Laura (1879–1974). Sister of Natalie Barney who participated in some of her performances and handled her and her mother's estates and legacies.

Duncan, Isadora (1877–1927). American dancer who revolutionized dance by making its movements seem more free and natural. She was especially drawn to Greek prototypes and traveled to Greece several times. She knew Eva from Barney's circle in Paris and remained in intermittent contact until her death.

Duncan, Menalkas (1905–69). Son of Penelope and Raymond Duncan.

Duncan, Penelope Sikelianos (1882–1917). Sister of Angelos Sikelianos, married to Raymond Duncan in 1903, who met Eva in Paris in the spring of 1906 when Menalkas was an infant and invited her to Greece that summer. She died of tuberculosis in Davos.

Duncan, Raymond (1874–1976). Brother of Isadora Duncan, married to Penelope Sikelianos, who built the first loom on which he, Penelope, and Eva learned to weave. He was a craftsman, artist, choreographer, and performer who created several schools to teach a technique of living based on the academy of Plato.

Fuller, Loie (1862–1928). American actor, dancer, and choreographer, who created the *Serpentine Dance* by combining twirling movements with

long skirts and multicolored lighting. Her performance in the Panathenaic Stadium in Athens in 1914 brought thousands of spectators.

Glaspell, Susan (1876–1948). American playwright, founding member of
the Provincetown Players who traveled with George Cram Cook to
Greece in 1922. After his death in 1924, she wrote *The Road to the
Temple* (1926) as a tribute to him but neglected to mention Eva and
Angelos, with whom they had spent extended time.

Graham, Martha (1894–1991). American modern dancer and choreographer, student of Denishawn, well known for choreographing pieces
based on Greek mythology and especially tragedy.

Gryparis, Ioannis (1870–1942). Greek symbolist poet whose translation
of *Prometheus Bound* into modern Greek was used in the Delphic
Festivals.

Hambidge, Jay (1867–1924). Canadian artist and designer, author of the
theory of dynamic symmetry based on principles found in Greek arts,
who traveled with Mary Crovatt Hambidge to Greece in the early
1920s and met Eva.

Hambidge, Mary Crovatt (1885–1973). American performer who learned
to weave from Eva during her trip to Greece with Jay Hambidge in the
1920s and created the Hambidge Center craft community in Rabun
Gap, Georgia in the late 1930s. She helped Eva on many occasions,
giving her housing and tending to her health.

Hamilton, Edith (1867–1963). Internationally known American author,
translator, popularizer of classical texts, and educator who graduated
from Miss Porter's School and Bryn Mawr College. She and Eva corresponded from 1935 to the end of Eva's life on drama, translation, and
the significance of Greece for the modern world.

Harrison, Jane Ellen (1850–1928). Cambridge-educated British classicist
who taught at Newnham College. She used archaeological evidence and
anthropological methods to expose the more primitive, matrilinear
roots of Greek culture beneath its classical surface. Eva's work exhibits
multiple connections.

Hatzfeld, Marie de, princess of Hohenlohe, Austria, "Baby" or "Bébé (?).
American woman who became a princess of Austria and was Eva's lover
from 1903 to 1905.

Hatzimihali, Angeliki (1895–1956). Greek folklorist who organized the
exhibit of handiwork at the Delphic Festivals and became Eva's close
friend. Eva stayed with her when she returned to Athens in 1952.

H. D. See Doolittle, Hilda.

Kalomiris, Manolis (1883–1962). Composer from Smyrna who founded
the Greek national school of music. He accepted Angelos's invitation

to compose the music for the chorus *Prometheus Bound*, then yielded to Eva's choice of Psachos.

Kanellos, Vassos (ca. 1895–1985). Greek dancer and choreographer who saw Isadora Duncan dance in Greece when he was a student at the School of Fine Arts and turned to creating Greek dance-drama. He and his wife, Tanagra, staged a mime-representation of the Septeria (the battle between Apollo and Python) as the closing event of first Delphic Festival.

Katsimbali, Kalypso (d. 1920). Sister of George Katsimbalis, who fell in love with Angelos in 1918 and committed suicide in 1920 when he did not reciprocate.

Katsimbalis, George (1899–1978). Greek literary critic who became Henry Miller's guide in Greece and the hero of Miller's book *The Colossus of Maroussi*.

Kazantzakis, Nikos (1883–1957). Greek writer of international fame and close friend of Angelos from 1914 to 1922. They traveled together to sites of religious or spiritual significance in Greece. They cut ties in 1922 over cultural and political differences.

Lounsbery, Grace Constant (1876–1974). American playwright who crossed paths with Eva at Bryn Mawr College, graduating in 1898. She was part of Eva's circle in the early 1900s, and the two corresponded throughout life.

Magnus, Maurice (1876–1920). An American author and traveler who was briefly Isadora Duncan's manager and followed her to Greece in 1915. He escorted Penelope Sikelianos to a sanatorium in Davos and paid her expenses.

Merlier, Octave (1897–1976). French scholar of Greek literature and director of the French Institute in Athens from 1938 to 1960. He married ethnomusicologist Melpo Logotheti and came to know Eva through their shared musical interests. In the 1960s and 1970s he worked to create an archive and museum of the Delphic Festivals.

Miller, Henry (1891–1980). American prose writer who traveled to Greece in 1939 and wrote *The Colossos of Maroussi* about his time there with George Katsimbalis, George Seferis, and Lawrence Durrell. He nominated Angelos Sikelianos for the Nobel Prize for Literature in 1946.

Mistriotis, Georgios (1840–1916). Professor of ancient Greek at the University of Athens and founder of the Society for the Instruction of Ancient Greek Dramas, supporting the performance of Greek drama in ancient Greek. His students protested a production of the *Oresteia* in 1903 and inspired Isadora Duncan's staging of the *Suppliants*.

Mitropoulos, Dimitris (1896–1960). Greek composer and conductor of world fame who met Eva when he was a student at the Athens Conservatory. He composed music for several of Angelos's poems while staying with the Sikelianoses in Sikya the summer of 1924.

Mumaw, Barton (1912–2001). American dancer and choreographer who joined Denishawn and later Shawn's Men Dancers. He was leader of chorus of *The Persians* choreographed by Shawn and Eva and later incorporated Greek dances in his Carnegie Hall solo debut in April 1941.

Naoroji, Khorshed (b. 1893). Granddaughter of Dadabhai Naoroji from Bombay, who studied piano at the Sorbonne University in Paris. She traveled to Greece with Eva in 1924 to study Byzantine music, then, returning to India, joined Gandhi's movement.

Nikolaidis, Nikos (Nord, Paul) (1899–1981). Greek poet, journalist, and publisher credited as the English translator of Angelos's *Akritan Songs*.

O'Neill, Eugene (1888–1953). Major American playwright connected with the Provincetown Players. He was Eva's assignment officer for the Federal Theatre Project from 1936 to 1937.

Orozco, José Clemente (1883–1949). Mexican muralist who painted Prometheus at Pomona College. Eva promoted his work in her Delphic Studios, a gallery she set up on Washington Square, Manhattan, in 1928 with Alma Reed. Orozco painted her portrait.

Palama, Nausika (b. 1890s). Daughter of Kostis Palamas who had an affair with Angelos from 1915 to the mid-1920s.

Palamas, Kostis (1859–1943). Major Greek poet, father of Nausika, who promoted Sikelianos's work. International reports of his funeral during the German occupation in February 1943, at which Angelos had given a stirring eulogy, inspired Eva to publish an article in the American literary magazine *Athene* on Angelos's work.

Palmer, Catherine. See Abbe, Catherine.

Palmer, Courtlandt, Jr. (1871–1951). Eva's brother and a concert pianist and composer. He studied with Ignacy Paderewski and had a concert career.

Palmer, Courtlandt, Sr. (1843–88). Eva's father, heir to a fortune made in the hardware business and real estate. He was trained as a lawyer but occupied himself with public matters. Progressive in his politics and a freethinker, he was the founder and president of the Nineteenth-Century Club, a debating society that met in his home in Gramercy Park.

Palmer, May Suydam (1872–1940). Sister of Eva and a painter. She lived from the early 1900s to the late 1930s with their brother Courtlandt in Europe.

Palmer, Robert (1867–1927). Eva's oldest brother. He lived a life of leisure in France until his wife Marion had him committed for alcoholism, physical abuse, and insanity in 1910.

Pasagianni, Eleni Sikelianou. See Sikelianou, Eleni.

Pasagiannis, Kostas (1872–1933). Greek writer and travel essayist, brother of Spelios, who encountered Eva Palmer when she first arrived in Athens. His sister Falitsa was in love with Angelos around 1906.

Pasagiannis, Spelios (1874–1910). Greek writer and judge, brother of Kostis and Falitsa, who was married briefly to Eleni Sikelianou and performed in Nea Skini.

Pratsika, Koula (1899–1984). Dancer and choreographer who studied with Mary Wigman and became an influential figure in Greece. She was the leader of the chorus of Oceanides *Prometheus Bound* at the Delphic Festivals and "high priestess" in the first Olympic torch-lighting ceremony at ancient Olympia in 1936.

Proestopoulos, Nikos (1899–1968). Greek writer and translator who was Angelos Sikelianos's cousin and married briefly to Nilla Cook. He sought to take possession of Eva's home in Delphi after her death.

Proestopoulou, Katina (?). Cousin of Angelos, sister of Nikos Proestopoulos, who was a servant in the Sikelianos house and Angelos's mistress for many years.

Psachos, Konstantinos (1866–1949). Professor of Byzantine music at the Athens Conservatory who became Eva's teacher and wrote the music for the choruses of *Prometheus Bound* (1927) and the *Suppliants* (1930) performed in the Delphic Festivals. Eva supported his scholarly work and efforts to preserve and teach Byzantine music.

Raftopoulou, Bella (1902–92). Greek sculptor and artist whose copies of poses and gestures from ancient Greek art gave Eva the expressive language for her choreography of plays at Delphi.

Reed, Alma (1889–1966). American journalist who supported the Delphic Idea briefly, translating part of Angelos's work and running with Eva a small gallery and salon in an apartment they shared in Manhattan in the late 1920s, which they called an "ashram" in honor of Mahatma Gandhi.

Robeson, Paul (1898–1976). American actor and bass-baritone singer, part of the Harlem Renaissance. As a political activist, he corresponded with Eva in the 1940s about their shared criticism of US foreign policy. She planned to stage *Prometheus Bound* with him as Prometheus.

Seferis, George (George Seferiadis) (1900–1971). Greek diplomat and modernist poet who won the Nobel Prize for Literature in 1963. He sent Eva a copy of Angelos's *Akritika* in March 1944, asking her to translate and circulate it in a bilingual Greek-English publication.

Shawn, Ted (1891–1972). Pioneer dancer and choreographer. After the breakup of Denishawn, his school and troupe with Ruth St. Denis, he formed the Men Dancers and founded a performance center at Jacob's Pillow. He collaborated with Eva from 1939 to 1941 with the intention to produce singing and dancing choruses following the techniques of Greek drama.

Sikelianos, Angelos (1884–1951). Greek poet and playwright whose work explored national and spiritual matters. He spearheaded the revival of the Delphic Festivals. He was married to Eva Palmer (1907) and Anna Karamani (1940).

Sikelianos, Eleni (b. 1965). American poet and professor of creative writing at Brown University, great-granddaughter of Eva and Angelos Sikelianos and literary executor of Eva Palmer Sikelianos.

Sikelianos, Frances. See Waldman, Frances Lefevre.

Sikelianos, Glafkos (1909–ca. 1994). Son of Eva and Angelos, father of Mark (Brastias) by his first wife, Frances Lefevre, and, by his second wife, Marion Tryon, father of Chris, John, Melitsa, and Poppy, and grandfather of Eleni Sikelianos. He worked as a boat builder and designer and in the merchant marine.

Sikelianos, Ioannis (1831–1910). Father of Angelos and his siblings, Hector, Menelaos, Eleni, and Penelope. He was a high school teacher of French at the gymnasium of the town of Leukas.

Sikelianou, Anna Karamani (1901–2006). Second wife of Angelos Sikelianos, who married him in 1940, survived him for more than half a century, and lived by managing his literary estate and weaving and selling her goods. She reportedly asked that Eva Sikelianou's papers in the Center for Asia Minor Studies be inaccessible to the public until 2020.

Sikelianou, Eleni (Pasagianni, Eleni; also Hélène and Helen) (?). Sister of Angelos, briefly married to writer Spelios Pasagiannis. She acted in the troupe Nea Skini and in Raymond Duncan's *Electre*.

Sikelianou, Harikleia Stefanitsi (1847–1926). Mother of Angelos and his siblings and wife of Ioannis. She received a good education in the Arsakeion girl's school and encouraged education in her household. She is buried in Delphi next to Eva.

Sikelianou, Penelope. See Duncan, Penelope Sikelianos.

Strauss, Richard (1864–1949). Major German composer known especially for his operas and songs. He stayed with Eva and Angelos in their house in Delphi during his visit to Greece with his architect Michael Rosenhauer in 1926, when they were searching for a place to build an opera house.

Tagore, Rabindranath (1861–1941). Bengali writer, composer, and artist who became the first Asian to win the Nobel Prize for Literature (1913). He knew the Sikelianoses through Khorshed Nairoji and likely met them during his trip to Greece in 1926. His ideas shaped Angelos's vision to create a center of international scope at Delphi.

Tarn, Pauline. See Vivien, Renée.

Thomas, M. Carey (1857–1935). Scholar of English, feminist, and president of Bryn Mawr College from 1894 to 1922. She admitted Eva in 1896, suspended her in 1898, and was present when she directed the *Bacchae* with students in 1935.

Vanderpool, Joan Jeffery (1910–2003). Photographer of archaeological excavations in Greece who married archaeologist Gene Vanderpool and settled permanently in Greece in the 1930s. Eva used her English translation of *The Persians* and corresponded with her.

Venizelos, Eleftherios (1864–1936). Liberal politician who was elected prime minister of Greece eight times and between 1910 and 1920 and 1924 and 1933, clashing with the monarchy on several occasions. He and his wife, Helena Schilizzi, a major benefactor of Greece, were friends of Eva and supported the second Delphic Festival.

Vivien, Renée (born Pauline Mary Tarn) (1877–1909). British poet who wrote decadent verse in French. She translated Sappho and wrote about lesbian desire, including her relationship with Barney. Eva introduced her to reading Greek in 1900 and was a model for at least one character in her work.

Waldman, Anne (b. 1945). American poet in the tradition of the beat poets and Walt Whitman and the daughter of Frances and John Waldman. In her early life, she knew Eva and has shared memories of her on many occasions.

Waldman, Frances Lefevre (b. 1910). First wife of Glafkos and mother of Brastias (Mark), then Carl and Anne by her second husband, John Waldman. She assisted Eva with preparations for the second Delphic Festival, weaving and making masks, and remained close to her. She is the translator of Angelos's *Dithyramb of the Rose* and *Border Guards* (a translation of the *Akritika*).

Yardley, Virginia Greer (1878–1971). A modernist painter from Delaware who fell in love with Eva at Bryn Mawr College and visited her in Greece in 1906. She lived and painted in Europe for nearly three decades and corresponded with Eva for several years.

Notes

INTRODUCTION

1. BMHA 189/32 Letter Beatrice B. Beecher to Eleanor Roosevelt, December 28, 1934.

2. Eva Palmer is listed in *The Social Register, New York* under her stepfather and mother's name (4) and with two siblings (*Social Register*, 323). The family's assets, which she inherited, are sketched out in her father's obituary ("Courtlandt Palmer Dead," *New York Times*, July 24, 1888, 5) and included real estate (the Hotel Churchill, Union Square Hotel, and other properties on Broadway), her father's private fortune of $250,000, and her grandfather's estate, valued at over $4 million.

3. This was true especially after he petitioned for the commutation of the death penalty for anarchists convicted in Chicago's Haymarket Affair, discussed in Avrich, *Haymarket Tragedy*, 341.

4. BMHA 189/33 Letter Eleanor Roosevelt to Eva Palmer Sikelianos, January 16, 1935. SCMS has a copy of Eva's undated letter accepting Roosevelt's invitation to "talk over with you the subject of hand weaving and of home industries in general." The meeting is reported in Elizabeth Young, "Abundant Life Plan Unfolded by Poet's Wife," *Washington Post*, January 30, 1935, 13.

5. Souhami, *Wild Girls*, 52, and Pougy, *Idylle saphique*, 215.

6. Colette and Phelps, *Autobiographie tirée des oeuvres*, 116.

7. Corovilles, "Tragedies of Angelos Sikelianos," 5.

8. EOS, 384.

9. EOS, 8.

10. National Museum of American History, "Original Kodak Camera, Serial No. 540."

11. "Sapphic" (or the lowercase "sapphic") was becoming a term of self-ascription naming a specifically modern understanding of female same sex desire (Doan and Garrity, "Introduction," 5) and referring to women who desired women with awareness that the ancient poetess Sappho wrote about female same-sex love. The word "Lesbian" names a person from Lesbos, the birthplace of Sappho, and was not used with clear connotations of the woman with intimate attachments to women before the 1920s, with rare exceptions. Barney calls the woman who dares to become a creator after the "virile" Sappho a "Lesbian" (BLJD NCB 12 9995 Nos. 44–50, discussed below). The lowercase "lesbian" became a positive term of self-ascription in the 1960s, when it also acquired strong in-group associations. When not attentive to period self-ascription, I use "lesbian" to denote female same-sex desire and "queer" or LGBTQ for persons not subscribing to normative sexual or gender identities. On several occasions, I

have found myself at a loss because the words available to me do not align with identities or acts of a given moment.

12. DeJean, *Fictions of Sappho*, 282.

13. Kantsa, "'Lesvia,'" 29.

14. M. Reynolds, *Sappho Companion*, 291–92.

15. Freeman, *Time Binds*, especially p. 9.

16. UP, 51.

17. BLJD NCB 12 9995 Nos. 230–34 Letter NCB to EP January 8, 1907, Paris to c/o Jean Siciliani Ile de St. Maure (les Ionienne), Greece.

18. The newness to which contemporary modernists were devoted is epitomized by this phrase from Ezra Pound's canto 53. "Make it new, day by day, make it new" is Pound's phrase in full, and the antecedent of "it" is old material (Chinese, Japanese, Greek, Latin, Italian, French, Anglo-Saxon) that Pound considered to be worth reviving. Moreover, "day by day" may be taken as the medium in addition to the temporal frame for this achievement. Eva Palmer's working at transforming herself and the world by reviving the old "day by day" was therefore not opposed to Pound's meaning.

19. Doan and Garrity, "Introduction," use the term "Sapphic modernities" to establish a link between cultural theories of modernity and "sapphism," a word connecting Sappho exclusively with same sex desire in English in the 1890s (3) and bearing connotations of modern urban life (8).

20. UP, 22.

21. Prins, *Ladies' Greek*.

22. UP, 78.

23. Payne, *Splendor of Greece*, 102, quoting the actor.

24. Goldhill, *Who Needs Greek*, 121, describes the "nervousness" in people's reception of Eva Palmer's dress.

25. Nietzsche, "On the Uses and Disadvantages of History for Life," 60.

26. Porter, *Nietzsche and the Philology of the Future*, chapter 4, "Inversions of the Classical Ideal" (167–224), carefully follows the challenge Nietzsche faced in trying to develop a critical perspective on a kind of facile classicism that he located in Germany. Readers of Nietzsche extended the critique to other countries, including Greece and the United States.

27. Hanink and Fletcher, "Orientation," points to many creative forms of biographies—third-person nonfiction narrative, creative nonfiction, fiction, poetry, and drama—and to their classical prototypes. Several trends are apparent in recent Greek writing inspired by the Sikelianos story. Chomenidis, *Ο φοίνικας* (The phoenix), a newly published novel "inspired by the love of Eva Palmer and Angelos Sikelianos but not tied to real events" (back cover), is a recent creative biography. Gerardis, *Τα κομπολόγια* (The worrybeads), a novel interweaving the lost Evion Panharmonium into an adventure story about the blackmarket trade in Byzantine manuscripts, shifts attention to the cultural biography of things and their relationships to people.

28. Beard and Henderson, *Classics*, 101, make a related point but in universalizing terms. See Hamilakis, "Fragments of Modernity and the Archaeologies of the Future," 56, on the proximity of archaeology and daily life, and Hamilakis, *Nation and Its Ruins*, chapter 4, "The Archaeologist as Shaman," exploring how Greek

archaeologist Manolis Andronikos came to embody national identity through his direct, sensory relationship with the soil, artifacts, and history of Greece.

29. Essays in Holmes and Marta, eds., *Liquid Antiquity*, explore liquidity (in contrast to monumentality) as a feature of Greek and Roman antiquity's operation as a tradition.

30. See Fotou and Brown, "Harriet Boyd Hawes (1871–1945)"; Morrow, "Edith Hayward Hall Dohan (1879–1943)"; and Mellink and Quinn, "Hetty Goldman (1881–1972)," on some of the first women to become field archaeologists and lead expeditions in Greece.

31. Prins, *Ladies' Greek*, points out that Harrison's professional career was "circuitous" (16) even though she became one of the most famous classicists of her era. Two biographies of Harrison appeared in 2002. Robinson, *Life and Work of Jane Ellen Harrison*, gives a detailed account of an extraordinary life and career, whereas Beard, *Invention of Jane Harrison*, deconstructs the life narrative that has made her extraordinary.

32. See Fox, *Riddle of the Labyrinth*, on Alice Kober's work preparing the ground for the decoding of the Linear B, for which Michael Ventris received credit.

33. Kourelis, "Flights of Archaeology," discusses the parallel case of Georg Vinko von Peschke (1900–59), the Austrian artist on the staff of the American School excavations at Corinth who "brought archaeological practices into a direct conversation with modernist poetics that sought to incorporate old historical landscapes with new and radical conceptions of the self" (723).

34. For a study documenting how classics has served as a meeting ground where women's professional relationships extend into private spaces, see Pounder, "Blegens and the Hills," on the complex interplay of public and private in the relationship of archaeologists Ida Thallon Hill and Elizabeth Pierce Blegen, mentor-student, companions, and wives of the more famous archaeologists Bert Lodge Hill and Carl Blegen, who collaborated all together on projects and regularly entertained the broader archaeological community in the mansion they shared on Ploutarchou Street in Athens.

35. I discuss several cases and sources in chapter 2.

36. I borrow the idea that biographical writing may offer a "tactic" for moving through multiple histories and communities from Herzfeld, *Portrait of a Greek Imagination*, 1.

37. Hodder, "On Absence and Abundance," proposes that biographical research can be a "sampling device . . . to navigate the abundant archive" (453).

38. I use the first name, Eva, throughout the book except where I wish to make a point about the distinct identity of Eva Palmer and Eva Sikelianos, or Eva Palmer Sikelianos, in which case I use the full name. I also refer to Angelos Sikelianos and Penelope Sikelianos Duncan as Angelos and Penelope, and to Isadora Duncan and Raymond Duncan as Isadora and Raymond. The reason is not to suggest familiarity but to keep the subjects clear when several people share the same family name. Additionally, this spares me the trouble of specifying the maiden, married, or hyphenated name, unless there is a point in using these, as in this and the following paragraph.

39. EOS, 384.

CHAPTER 1: SAPPHIC PERFORMANCES

1. I discuss my use of "Sapphic" and other terms of self-ascription in the introduction.

2. The phrase "Sapho 1900" comes from a portrait of Renée Vivien in Billy, *L'Époque 1900*, published in 1951, describing her as "Sapho cent pour cent . . . L'autre Sapho, celle de Lesbos" (One hundred percent Sappho . . . The other Sappho, the one of Lesbos) (227). According to Elaine Marks, the phrase "[implied] that Renée Vivien was the exclusively lesbian poet of the belle epoque" (Marks, "'Sapho 1900,'" 176). Sappho's name appearing with one p was a common spelling in French from the seventeenth century (see Scudéry, *Story of Sapho*, 8). Since then it has been applied repeatedly to the group of women writers including Vivien, Barney, Lucie Delarue-Mardrus, and Colette, who crossed paths in Paris at the turn of the century. Joan DeJean argues that Billy's branding of Vivien is not as affectionate as it appears, since he eventually shows "that the writers really were 'Sapho 0%,' because they never understood 'the other Sapho, the one from Lesbos' at all" (DeJean, *Fictions of Sappho*, 285).

3. Vicinus, "Adolescent Boy," 92. Vicinus draws attention to the fin de siècle period to trace how men and women writers "who were part of recognized homosexual networks . . . recuperated and refashioned common images and character stereotypes" that were being simultaneously formulated by medical writers "in order to confirm its own culture" (92).

4. The coding of female same-sex love that uses the Greek names of Sappho and Lesbos overlaps with the coding of male same-sex as Greek love or *griechische Liebe*, *socratische Liebe*, and *platonische Liebe* in British and German literature, respectively. See Dowling, *Hellenism and Homosexuality in Victorian Oxford*, on the Victorian coding of same-sex male sexuality; see Potts, *Flesh and the Ideal*, and Gustafson, *Men Desiring Men*, on the parallel set of tropes in German classicism.

5. Ray and Barney, "Decadent Heroines or Modernist Lovers," 47. See Albert, *Lesbian Decadence*, for an encyclopedic view of turn-of-the-century reinscriptions of lesbianism that takes into account literary and nonliterary sources.

6. Jaloux, *Les saisons littéraire 1904–1914*, 100, and Colette, *My Apprenticeships, and Music-Hall Sidelights*, 112. See also Ofek, *Representations of Hair in Victorian Literature and Culture*, 84, on turn-of-the-century cross-generational manipulations of the hair sign system in the Pre-Raphaelite Brotherhood's work.

7. In reader-response criticism, "implicate" is used to measure the reciprocal interdependence of readers and texts. For Kuiken, Miall, and Sikora, for example, readers are "implicated" in texts through different kinds of "expressive enactment": performative reflections that fold words into experience, making the old written words of others do new things ("Forms of Self-Implication in Literary Reading," 177). In classical reception studies, "implication" indicates, in the view of Charles Martindale, the two-way "process of understanding, backwards and forwards" (Martindale, "Reception," 171), or the dialogue of modernity with antiquity (Martindale, "Introduction," 5). A competing view is that of Simon Goldhill, for whom reading Greek texts is simultaneously "an act of self-formation"

(Goldhill, *Who Needs Greek*, 297) or "self-fashioning" (as he argues throughout). My use of "implicate" builds on Goldhill's analysis, as well as on studies of the presence of Sappho's fragments in Victorian images and writing in Prins, *Victorian Sappho*. See also duBois, *Sappho Is Burning*, DeJean, *Fictions of Sappho*, and M. Reynolds's introduction to *The Sappho Companion*.

8. According to Birdwood, "Etymology and Meaning of 'Pleached,'" there are "two Latin words, plecto, the first, meaning 'I strike' (cf. plectrum), . . . and the second meaning 'I braid,' 'intertwine'" (282).

9. According to Porter, "What Is 'Classical' about Classical Antiquity," 40, the classical was in the Roman period primarily the kind of knowledge that was sensible (seen, felt, and heard) but barely articulated because it was widely received as a model that people wished to re-create. This conception of the classical is the legacy of the West.

10. The line-drawn version of the vase painting was published in Dumont and Chaplain, *Les Céramiques de la Grèce proper*, 358, with the description on 360.

11. The S. S. *Sappho* ferried people to Mount Desert Island for more than a decade until the gangplank broke between the wharf and the steamship on August 6, 1899, and at least twenty people drowned ("Twenty Drowned Near Bar Harbor; Two Hundred Excursionists Fell in a Mass into the Water," *New York Times*, August 7, 1899, 1).

12. Wickes, *Amazon of Letters*, 46 gives the earliest account of this often recounted story. I have not located the original.

13. Yatromanolakis, *Sappho in the Making*, follows this ancient history, arguing that "the ideological paradigms and polarities that conditioned the reception of Sappho in antiquity (outside the island of Lesbos) were constantly different from those that shaped the ancient understanding of the poetry of Pindar, Arkhilokhos, Alkaios, and the Homeric epics" (167).

14. See fragment 1, Oxyrhynchus papyrus 1800, in the collection of "Testimonia vitae atque artis" (Accounts of art and life) about Sappho in Campbell, *Sappho and Alcaeus*, 2–3.

15. The phrase is found in Porphyrio commenting on the "mascula" and "Saffo" in Horace's *Epistles* 1, 19, 28, and quoted in Campbell, *Sappho and Alcaeus*, 19.

16. In antiquity, verbal play on the ambiguities of Lesbian identity is found in Anacreon fragment 358, though the meaning and authenticity of the text are disputed. As David M. Halperin points out, "the transformation of 'lesbian' into the proper name of a particular sexual orientation, into a conceptual shorthand for 'female homosexual,' took a very long time. Neither the island nor the people of Lesbos associate with 'lesbianism' in our sense of the term before the second century A.D." ("First Homosexuality?," 231).

17. "Lesbian" acquires strong in-group associations in the late 1950s. See Valentine, "Lesbians Are from Lesbos," on the history of the Daughters of Bilitis, one club that started in San Francisco and spread across the United States, using the name of Sappho of Lesbos as a discursive "space where one could remove her mask and live happily as a lesbian" (152).

18. Prins, *Victorian Sappho*, 174–75.

19. Prins, 60. The generative qualities of Sappho's poetry continue. A recent

example is Ruth Salvaggio's *Hearing Sappho in New Orleans*, a book inspired by the author's discovery of a volume of Sappho's poetry while sifting through the ruins of her flooded home in the aftermath of hurricane Katrina. The discovery inspired her to look for Sappho in the interface of poetry, music, and desire in the history of that city.

20. UP, 32.

21. D. D. Palmer and B. J. Palmer, *Science of Chiropractic*, 52–53.

22. Ingersoll, "Tribute to Courtlandt Palmer," 338–39.

23. *Appleton's Annual Cyclopaedia and Register of Important Events*, 236.

24. Courtlandt Palmer, *New Education*, 12.

25. Palmer, 6.

26. See Goldhill, *Who Needs Greek*, on the "three stage structure of thought" in critical cultural conflicts about Greekness (296–99): first, the identification of Greece as a missing homeland, which is then followed by efforts to draw lines of affiliation with the absent Greek past and then the implication of the self through acts of self-formation. To this structure my book adds another complicating "stage": the encounter with Greece and living Greeks.

27. Spivey and Squire, *Panorama of the Classical World*, 169.

28. Richard, *Greeks and Romans Bearing Gifts*, 49.

29. Maynard, "Greek Revival: Americanness, Politics and Economics," 132. Maynard suggests that the Americanness of Greek revival architecture may have been an early twentieth-century reinterpretation of the movement.

30. Fox-Genovese, *Mind of the Master Class*, 42. Agard, "Classics in the Midwest Frontier," makes a similar point (103–4).

31. UP, 29.

32. Bar Harbor's historical museum bears Robert Abbe's name for the large collection of artifacts he donated.

33. UP, 29.

34. They were Mrs. Henry F. Dimock, George Dorr, Henry Lane Eno, and George W. Vanderbilt.

35. Johnson, "Building of the Arts at Bar Harbor," 678.

36. Bar Harbor Historical Society, "Building of the Arts."

37. Johnson, "Building of the Arts at Bar Harbor," 676. There were additional plans for a "Greek amphitheater . . . near-by against the slope of the hill . . . to give open-air performances of Greek and Elizabethan drama, as well as frequent festivals by the choral society of the village" (676).

38. Shelley, "Preface" to *Hellas* (1822), in Shelley, Leader, and McNeill, *Percy Bysshe Shelley*, 549.

39. Johnson, "Building of the Arts at Bar Harbor," 678.

40. Winterer, *Mirror of Antiquity*, 201.

41. Winterer, 201.

42. "Eva Palmer finished Miss Porter's School with the class of 1891" (Ann Craig Befroy, email message dated January 24, 2012). Befroy is director of archives, Spanish teacher, and head diving coach at Miss Porter's School. I use this quote with her permission.

43. BMCSC, Eva Palmer Transcript. Eva Palmer passed entrance examinations in June and September 1896, with conditional entry in Latin and algebra. She

studied Latin her freshman year (1896–97), probably at an advanced intermediate level as there was no elementary Latin, and she passed the Latin "condition" in February 1897, with a test in composition and translation of prose and poetry passages at sight. Her sophomore year she studied elementary and intermediate Greek during the fall and winter semesters (1897–98), including composition and Plato's *Apology*, Sophocles' *Antigone*, and Homer's *Odyssey* in the fall and Euripides' *Medea*, Herodotus, and Homer's *Iliad* in the winter. Although Greek was on her transcript in the winter, she interrupted her studies in May 1898 for reasons I discuss later. She did not receive grades that semester. I am grateful to Eleni Sikelianos for granting me permission to read the transcript. I note that Mortimer Earle was Eva's professor. Besides teaching her Greek, he remained a presence in Eva's life decades after his death in 1905: Eva bought beachfront property in Sikya in 1910, a coastal settlement about ten miles from the theater of Sicyon, which Earle had excavated, and a few years later built a villa there. She was lifelong friends with his wife, Ethel Earle.

44. Horowitz, *Power and Passion of M. Carey Thomas*, 395.

45. Blankley, "Sappho's Daughters," 11. Winterer, *Mirror of Antiquity*, states that "as president of Bryn Mawr College, Thomas looked rather to Sappho to define the educated woman" (88).

46. M. C. Thomas, "Education of Women," 345.

47. Wharton, "Preface to Second Edition," in Sappho and Wharton, *Sappho, Memoir, Text, Selected Renderings and a Literal Translation*, vi.

48. Catullus 35, 16–17.

49. UP, 25. According to Palmer's academic record, between fall 1896 and winter, she took four semesters of general English, which included six courses on the English essay (BMCSC). On Gwinn's expertise in Swinburne, see Horowitz, *Power and Passion of M. Carey Thomas*, 149–51.

50. Swinburne, *Notes on Poems and Reviews*, 8–9.

51. Benstock, *Women of the Left Bank*, 173, discusses the meanings and performances of "inversion" as a term indicating a reversal, or "conversion" (178) of socially expected gender roles.

52. BLJD C2 2920 No. 275 (Papadaki, 87), Letter EP to NCB [August 1902] from Hotel de l'Europe Luzern. She wrote this to Barney after seeing Mounet Sully's performance of *Oedipus Rex* for a second time.

53. "Inversion" is the term Ellis and Symonds use in 1897 to characterize the same-sex "impulse," identified by them as a "'sport' or variation" (*Sexual Inversion*, 133) as well as a "disease" and an "abnormality" (128).

54. Yardley, who attended Bryn Mawr without matriculating yet mysteriously appears in the class book of 1901 (BMCSC), confessed her "crush on Eva Palmer" to her former English professor Mary Gwinn Hodder, with whom she had a significant exchange of letters. See MGAH C0450, Letter Virginia Yardley to Mary Gwinn Hodder, Postmarked October 26, 1910, New York City to Baltimore, Maryland: "In the Bryn Mawr days . . . a horror to me . . . , beside my puppy dog devotion to her, was my taste for all that she seemed to me to stand for. . . . I supposed I appeared to the world at large simply a tiresome little girl with a crush on Eva Palmer, & possible social aspirations."

55. BMCSC, MC Thomas Correspondence, Reel 148, Letter M. C. Thomas to EP, July 28, 1898.

56. Jane Ellen Harrison states this was a commonplace belief in a passage in which she describes her own "dear delight of learning for learning's sake a 'dead' language for sheer love of the beauty of its words and the delicacy of its syntactical relations, . . . the rapture of reconstructing for the first time in imagination a bit of the historical past" ("Scientia Sacra Fames," in *Alpha and Omega*, 117).

57. See Winterer, *Mirror of Antiquity*, 202.

58. Harrison found in the Greek-derived word "heresy" an "eager, living" side of learning: a "personal, even passionate" side, freed from "traditional faiths and customs, *qua* traditional" ("Heresy and Humanity" [1912], reprinted in *Alpha and Omega*, 27). Fiske, *Heretical Hellenism*, situates Harrison among several learned women who "used Greek knowledge to assert authority in the male-dominated fields of scholarship and publishing, to express subjectivities and sexualities disallowed by conventional Victorian gender ideologies, and to challenge the authoritative structures of knowledge represented by Newman, Arnold, and other prominent male writers" (17).

59. "Dr. and Mrs. Robert Abbe are enjoying their remodeled home, Brook End. Miss Eva Palmer and Courtlandt Palmer, daughter and son of Mrs. Abbe, are with them" ("Bar Harbor," *New York Times*, July 15, 1900, 14).

60. The earliest reference I have found linking Eva Palmer and her family to Bar Harbor is in the *Bar Harbor Record*, June 21, 1894, 8, which names "Abbe, Mrs. Robert, Miss Palmer, Miss Eva Palmer, Mr. Courtlandt Palmer, New York," as renters of the "Italian Villa, Eden Heights," on Mount Desert Island. Eva's recollection in a letter to Barney dated 1930 (UW Renée Lang EPS letter to NCB April 27, 1930, Athens to Paris) looks back "about 35 years ago" to the time when Barney refused to "[leave her] alone" and so corroborates 1894 or 1895 as the start date of their relationship.

61. Eva wrote that she and Barney "had known each other from childhood, especially during American summers in Bar Harbour [*sic*] when we used to go horse-back riding all over the island of Mt. Desert" (UP, 37). Barney made a similar claim (*Souvenirs indiscrets*, 64–65; see Rodriguez, *Wild Heart*, 57). While I do not doubt Eva's or Barney's memory of their youth, I generally look for evidence to support autobiographical recollection. From all I have gathered, Eva spent her childhood summers in Stonington, Connecticut, at her uncle Charles Phelps Palmer's estate (Slosberg, "An Oracle of Delphi," 5), and at Lake Dunmore in Vermont, where her father died in 1888, then in Bar Harbor after her mother remarried.

62. Souhami, *Wild Girls*, 23.

63. BLJD C2 2920 Nos. 1–2 (Papadaki, 1) Letter EP to NCB July 28, 1900, Bar Harbor.

64. Dr. Robert Abbe was a member of the committee on the scope and plan of the medical and surgical facilities of the new hospital.

65. Barney's recollection of the event is in her unpublished manuscript "Mémoires secretes," archived in BLJD and recounted in Rodriguez, *Wild Heart* (56–59). It contains several unconfirmed elements, including the temporal setting of 1893, when Natalie would have been seventeen and Eva nineteen.

66. The *World*, another New York newspaper, published "Alice in Bar Harbor" (August 30, 1900, 3), covering the theatrical event and drawing attention to the closing scene of "several charming tableaux, including Sappho, by Eva Palmer."

67. Pauline Tarn was the birth name of Renée Vivien.

68. "Bar Harbor Social Season," *New York Times*, August 30, 1900, 7.

69. "Bar Harbor Social Season," *New York Times*, August 26, 1900, 14. "Miss May Palmer" was Eva's sister; "Miss Alice Clifford Barney" was Natalie Clifford Barney's sister, also known as Laura.

70. "Bar Harbor Social Season, *New York Times*, August 26, 1900, 14.

71. Prins, "Greek Maenads, Victorian Spinsters," 46.

72. Preston, Modernism's *Mythic Pose*, 36.

73. Hains, "Greek Plays in America," 28, mentions that "Radcliffe College brought out a series of 'Homeric Pictures' " in 1894.

74. Montrose Moses, critic of the *Theatre*, thought the revival of *The Trojan Woman* performed in the stadium of the City College of New York in 1915 "looked like a picture"—precisely the pictorial effect director Granville Barker aspired to create. See Hartigan, *Greek Tragedy on the American Stage*, 16.

75. Many versions of Sappho existed, indications both of the nineteenth-century "Sappho craze" (Ehnenn, *Women's Literary Collaboration, Queerness, and Late-Victorian Culture*, 18) and of the ambiguity in her reception. She was the "great poetess" (Prins, *Victorian Sappho*, 54); the teacher surrounded by dedicated pupils; the spurned heterosexual lover whose love for Phaon sent her over the Leukadian cliff; the ancient courtesan; and the same-sex lover. Goldhill, "Touch of Sappho," discusses several artistic renderings of Sappho as both attempts and failures to control female desire. I list a sampling of modern depictions of Sappho in Leontis, "Eva Palmer Sikelianos before Delphi," 62–63n15.

76. "Eva Palmer" appears in announcements, playbills, and programs of theatrical performances beginning in 1897, when she played the part of Pollie with Frank Daniels in " 'The Idol's Eye,' a New Operetta, by Smith and Herbert, at the Broadway Theatre" ("New Theatrical Bills," *New York Times*, October 26, 1897, 7). On March 12, 1898, she produced and played Rosalind in *As You like It*, the Bryn Mawr College freshman play presented to the class of 1901 (BMCSC 9VP/1900 *As You Like It* printed program; UP, 26).

77. "Dinner to George Vanderbilt," *New York* Times, August 15, 1899, 7.

78. "Cholly's Chimes: The Critic of Gotham's Four Hundred Rings a Few Changes," *Ironwood Times*, December 8, 1894, 4: "Mrs. Robert Abbe . . . and her daughter, Miss Eva Palmer, are going on a visit to George Vanderbilt at Asheville, N.C. The Palmers, who are all learned and studious, and George Vanderbilt, who is extremely bookish, are old friends, and nothing could be more natural than the proposed visit. Yet one of those infernal busybodies who make it their business to start false rumors sees in this visit a positive determination on the part of the youngest Vanderbilt to marry Miss Palmer. . . . Of course there is not a word of truth in it."

79. BLJD NCB L2 9995 Nos. 329–30 Letter NCB to EP [late in 1907?]: "Let your thoughts come back with me to the beginning of it all—when you first came to me and made me love you— . . . it is you who have never been mine utterly, who

have been undecided and unhappy all these months, been unhappy because of your old love, and weak. . . . It was you who kept me waiting who did not often come at all—who left me perplexed and bewildered in my faith and love for you."

80. BLJD C2 2920 Nos. 1–2 (Papadaki, 1) Letter EP to NCB July 28, 1900, Bar Harbor.

81. BLJD C2 2920 Nos. 1–2.

82. BLJD C2 2920 Nos. 1–2.

83. BLJD C2 2920 Nos. 1–2.

84. BLJD C2 2920 Nos. 238–42 (Papadaki, 21) Letter EP to NCB n.d., Bar Harbor: "But Socratic ideals are far from you, you are not moved by the thought of one's own mind being outside of and beyond all passions and desires."

85. In Barney's words, "Eva was as retiring as Renée; they managed to spend their evenings together so that they could continue to study Greek while I went to all the society functions, as my parents wished, in order to silence certain rumors which were being spread about me from Washington right up to the Bar Harbour [sic] peninsula" (Barney and Livia, Perilous Advantage, 33). Benstock, Women of the Left Bank, 277, reckons that Palmer knew Greek best and shared her knowledge of Sappho's Greek with Vivien and Barney. Eva probably read Wharton's 1895 third edition (as did, H. D. another Bryn Mawr student—see Gregory, H. D. and Hellenism, 154), with its introductory "memoir" and simultaneous presentation of the Greek text and multiple English translations. When Vivien returned to France in late 1900 with a copy of Wharton, she owed her first Greek lessons to Eva, as Goujon rightly suggests (Tes blessures sont plus douces que leurs caresses, 142–43). A careful reading of Eva and Barney's correspondence shows that Eva guided Barney in her Greek learning. Barney repeatedly belittled Eva's learned reserve yet acknowledged her "ignorance" next to Eva (CAMS Dossier 2 Letter NCB to EP October 6, 1900, Bryn Mawr to New York City).

86. Rodriguez, Wild Heart, 57.

87. Rodriguez, 56.

88. CAMS Dossier 2 Letter NCB to EP March 1, 1901, from France: "Your wonderful hair that drew me to you, and so when I was near you bound it around me and I felt it tight about me pulling me back. You hold me from around the sea; you hold me to you forever."

89. Vivien, Woman Appeared to Me, 46.

90. Bartholomot Bessou, L'imaginaire du féminin dans l'oeuvre de Renée Vivien, uses the term "exhumation intellectual" (42) for the reclaiming of formerly buried female figures, and she attributes this type of exhumation especially to Renée Vivien.

91. CAMS Dossier 2 Letter NCB to EP February 15, 1902, Paris to New York: Barney uses the word "inverse" to describe her attraction to women.

92. BLJD C2 2920 Nos. 138–40 (Papadaki, 3) Letter EP to NCB n.d., Bar Harbor: "Je suis follement amoureuse de toi ce soir."

93. BLJD C2 2920 Nos. 323–24 (Papadaki, 15) Letter EP to NCB n.d., Bar Harbor. Papadaki suggests a date of the summer of 1901; but the letter fits into the sequence of events in the late summer of 1900 when Barney discovered Duck Brook with Eva.

94. The photographs appeared posthumously in Vivien, Barney, Palmer, and Goujon, *Album Secret*.

95. Her residence probably consisted of a sitting room with a fireplace, desk, more than one table, and couch in addition to her sleeping quarters.

96. BLJD NCB 12 9995 Nos. 6–9 Letter NCB to EP October 15, [1900], Bryn Mawr to Boston c/o Mrs. Robert Abbe, Somerset Hotel, Boston, MA.

97. BLJD NCB 12 9995 Nos. 6–9.

98. See K. Thomas, " 'What Time We Kiss,' " for a discussion of the parallel case of "Michael Field," the aunt-niece Sapphic couple who wrote poetry after Sappho, seen through "contemporary queer theoretical preoccupations with temporality" (328).

99. Freeman, "Introduction," 163.

100. CAMS Dossier 1 Letter EP to NCB undated.

101. BLJD C2 2920 Nos. 81–82 (Papadaki, 122) Letter EP to NCB undated, from Brook End.

102. Eva's correspondence from the mid-1920s to the end of her life is abundant in her archive in BMHA, while nothing exists there of her letters prior to 1907. The later correspondence, which Eva selected to survive her, reveals little of what we might call a private self, whereas the earlier correspondence, which she delivered to Barney to hide, is self-revealing.

103. BLJD NCB 12 9995, the letters of NCB to EP, consists of 330 pages; BLJD C2 2920 the letters of EP to NCB, consists of 430 pages/169 letters, and several letters from EP to others (Liane de Pougy, Renée Vivien). CAMS has over six hundred letters and more than double the number of pages, including 127 letters from NCB to EP, fifty-six from EP to NCB, sixty-seven from "Bébé" or "Baby," who was Marie de Hatzfeld, princess of Hohenlohe and EP's lover from 1903 to 1905, fifty-four from Emma Calvé, twenty-eight from Ilse Deslandes, eleven from Constant Lounsbery, five from Virginia Yardley, and more from Colette, Georgette Leblanc, Henriette Rogers, "Lil," Nina Russel, Wanda Landowska, Marguerite Moreno, and other lovers in addition to her family members.

104. BLJD C2 2920 Nos. 174–75 (Papadaki, 39) Letter EP to NCB [1901, New York].

105. M. Reynolds, *Sappho Companion*, 291. The phrase "Sappho presided" summarizes the "complicated uses to which Barney and her circle put their image of Sappho" (291). Reynolds refers specifically to gatherings that would have taken place in the garden of Neuilly, her home in Paris from the early 1900s to 1909; but she conflates Neuilly with Barney's better-known salon in the "Temple à l'amitie" at 20 rue Jacob, her home on the Left Bank from 1909 until her death in 1972. Thus she creates an anachronistic scene combining people who never crossed paths. She also mistakenly associates Eva Palmer with the "Huntley and Palmer biscuit empire" (292), a common error.

106. BLJD C2 2920 Nos. 107–8 (Papadaki, 39) Letter EP to NCB August 21, 1907, in Neuilly.

107. BLJD NCB 12 9995 Nos. 241–44 Letter NCB to EP "1st of February."

108. Barney published her sketch of the Temple à l'Amitié as the frontispiece for *Aventures de l'Esprit*. See Winning, "Dorothy Richardson and the Politics of Friendship," 99, for a high-resolution reproduction.

109. UP, 51.

110. The correspondence is in CAMS Dossier 3 Folder 2, entitled "Mme Berthon correspondance et traduction, lettres Shawn, etc."

111. I was allowed to read the files for two weeks in 2009, then given full access in 2016.

112. In chronological order, here are some early references to the erotic relationship of Eva and Barney: Rubin, "Introduction to *A Woman Appeared to Me*," 91; Wickes, *Amazon of Letters* (1976), 91, 95, 217; Chalon, *Portrait of a Seductress* (1979), 11; Vivien, Barney, Palmer, and Goujon, *Album Secret* (1984); Jay, *Amazon and the Page* (1988), 13–16.

113. Longinus, *On Sublimity*, quotes the poem (and so preserves it for posterity) in a framework that medicalizes not just this poem but "Sappho's display of excellence." For her excellence lies, according to Longinus, in "choos[ing] the emotions associated with love's madness from the attendant circumstances and the real situation" (Campbell, *Sappho and Alcaeus*, 79), as if she were a medical doctor giving a report.

114. Prins, *Victorian Sappho*, 17.

115. Prins points to the large number of translations of Sappho fragment 31 and suggests that the "broken tongue" of Sappho "lends itself to perpetual translation, in many different tongues . . . demonstrating not only the differences between languages but the internal disjunction—the *glossa eage*—within every language" (41). Barney and Eva's correspondence offers examples of such translations, but it also points to forms of proliferation that exceed linguistic translation as they spill out onto bodies and their effects.

116. BLJD C2 2920 Nos. 148–49 (Papadaki, 4) Letter EP to NCB [1900], Brook End to Ban-y-Bryn, suggests that Eva declared her love for Barney while championing her love for someone else: "C'est assez drôle qu'hier soir dans ta lettre que je viens d'oublier de t'apporter, je t'ai dit que j'étais amoureuse de toi au point d'être capable presque d'être jalouse si tu en aimais une autre!! Et voici que j'ai fait mon mieux pour te donner un autre amant, amante, que dirai-je?" (Isn't it funny that last night in your letter that I just forgot to bring you, I told you that I was in love with you to the point of being able to be almost jealous if you loved someone else!! And here I have done my best to give you another lover, a mistress—what shall I say?)

117. Rodriguez, *Wild Heart*, 161.

118. BLJD C2 2920 Nos. 174–75 (Papadaki, 39) Letter EP to NCB [1901]: "Yesterday I saw Radcliffe. He is in love with you, as you know, but deeply, madly, passionately, what you will, almost beautifully. So much in love that he crazily expects to glean your spirit by gathering mine, to feel your hands by holding mine, to touch your body by kissing mine. He quite ingeniously looks on me as a mirror which is to reflect you, as a window which is to let you through like fresh air and sunlight. I am for him a medium, a messenger, with no more human interest than a telegraph wire which serves to transmit the shock."

119. BLJD C2 2920 Nos. 150–51 (Papadaki, 30) Letter EP to NCB [1901, Bar Harbor]: "Yes Marguerite may see us if you think that she has eyes to see. I have no modesty as you know, as long as I feel sure of the eyes that are looking;—if they are clear enough to find beauty in the human body that is strained and bound and

held by desire, to find purity in passion, to realize why white flowers of all flowers have the heaviest odor, they would merely add to the marvel of having you touch me."

120. BLJD NCB 12 9995 Nos. 26–29 Letter NCB to EP n.d.: "There is a beautiful little witch called Lady Anglesey. . . . She—the remembrance—has hair the colour of yours—is that why I first adored her and why when she took it down I was first disappointed in her."

121. Calvé was a "cultural icon of lesbian opera fans" (Haggerty and Zimmerman, *Encyclopedia of Lesbian and Gay Histories and Cultures*, 1: 558) for her role as Fanny Legrand in Massenet's opera *Sapho* and for her voice and stage persona, which registered as "Sapphonic" (Wood, "Sapphonics," 40).

122. Dorf, "Dancing Greek Antiquity in Private and Public," analyzes Duncan's place in Barney's community of performers, and his *Performing Antiquity* follows the trail of Greek inspirations from Paris to Delphi. Barney herself listed "Isadora" as a potential player in an amateur women's theater that she planned to have Eva direct. See CAMS Dossier 2 Letter NCB to EP dated "Tuesday," which I have elsewhere situated in the fall of 1905 (Leontis, "Eva Palmer Sikelianos before Delphi," 48n41).

123. Papadaki identifies this "Lily" whom Eva mentions in several letters to Barney dating from 1901 to 1903 (see BLJD C2 2920 Nos. 67–69, Papadaki, 109) as Lilian Florence Maud Anglesey, also known as "tante Minnie" (Papadaki, 65n1). She is not Elizabeth "Lily" de Gramont (duchesse de Clermont Tonnerre), since Barney did not meet that Lily before 1909.

124. Yardley, a woman of class who inherited no wealth, was the most attentive of Eva's lovers to issues of money and class as they influenced relations in the group. Her painfully beautiful correspondence with Palmer and Mary Gwinn Hodder, found in CAMS, MGAH, and other archives, has many keen observations on power relations in the group. I am grateful to Michael Prettyman for sharing his valuable discovery of Yardley's letters and helping me to make sense of her five letters in CAMS.

125. Tryphe, "Cinq petits dialogues grecs," 1.

126. Tryphe, "Cinq petits dialogues grecs," "Prologue," 2.

127. BLJD NCB 12 9995 Nos. 44–50 Letter NCB to EP December 20, 1901, Washington, DC, to New York City. The quotes in this paragraph are all from this letter.

128. BLJD NCB 12 9995 Nos. 60–62 Letter NCB to EP February 6, 1902, Washington, DC, to New York City.

129. BLJD C2 2920 No. 237 (Papadaki, 82) Letter EP to NCB (Papadaki, 82) 11 W. Fiftieth Street to Washington, DC. The date is approximately May 1902, when Eva was twenty-eight and Barney twenty-six.

130. BLJD C2 2920 No. 237 (Papadaki's transcription, my translation). The quotes are from this letter.

131. In BLJD NCB 12 9995 Nos. 51–53 Letter NCB to EP December 3, 1901, Washington, DC, to New York City.

132. Vicinus, *Intimate Friends*, 180.

133. Vicinus, 180.

134. BLJD C2 2920 Nos. 150–51 (Papadaki, 30) Letter EP to NCB [1901, Bar

Harbor] tells of Eva's search for *three* similar dresses: "If you prefer to take a safer way and leave the choice to me, I will hunt about to see what can be gotten here. Do you want both dresses just alike and as near like mine as possible, or a bit varied?"

135. BLJD NCB 12 9995 Nos. 44–50.

136. BLJD NCB 12 9995 Nos. 44–50.

137. BLJD NCB 12 9995 Nos. 44–50.

138. BLJD C2 2920 Nos. 15–19 [Papadaki, 61] Letter EP to NCB January 30, 1902, from 11 W. Fiftieth Street.

139. BLJD NCB 12 9995 Nos. 65–73 Letter NCB to EP April 21, 1902, from Washington, DC.

140. BLJD C2 2920 Nos. 9–14 (Papadaki, 53) Letter EP to NCB [December 1901].

141. BLJD C2 2920 Nos. 9–14.

142. I discuss some of these composers in chapter 3.

143. BLJD C2 2920 Nos. 420–23 (Papadaki, 149) Letter EP to NCB [1907].

144. MGAH Letter Virginia Yardley to Mrs. Alfred Hodder, Postmarked Boston, MA, November 9, 1910, and New York City, November 11, 1910, sent to East Mount Vernon Place, Baltimore Maryland. According to Yardley, Eva also said, "'Men are far more spiritual than women.' . . . What she most missed [at Bryn Mawr] was not having men to work with, 'it is when [Courtlandt] is practicing away,' that I can work.' 'He plays all day till I shut the piano down on his fingers. I am what Cory's music has made me.'"

145. BLJD C2 2920 Nos. 29–35 (Papadaki, 68) Letter EP to NCB [March 7, 1902, New York] reports Courtlandt's harsh words to Eva in 1900 and her sorrow over their damaged relations: "In Bar Harbour [*sic*] two years ago he said things to me that made our old relationship go up in smoke. Since then we have said very little to each other and written not at all, but he is dear to me as nothing in the world is except you, I felt then and I do still that all explanations were useless." In CAMS Dossier 2 Letter EP to Courtlandt Palmer January 1, 1906, Eva calls on Courtlandt to explain his behavior: "Will you tell me before I leave why you have acted as you have toward me? . . . I chose friends whom I thought worthy. Through some years of hardship and difficulty I have proved them to be so,—and you ask me to give them up, or at least you seem to ask me by your avoidance and your apparent hatred of me." After Courtlandt's death on December 16, 1951, David McK. Williams, Courtlandt's self-appointed "oldest friend," referred vaguely to "his illness" and its symptoms: "he seemed to shun us who loved him so very much" (BMHA 189/49 Letter David McK. Williams to EP [December 1951–April 1952]), Cuernavaca Mexico to New York City. There's not enough evidence to explain Courtlandt's aggressive behavior toward Eva. Why was he so possessive of her and disapproving of her lovers? Why was he hard on her almost to the end of his life, and what was "his illness" to which McK. Williams referred?

146. See, for example, BMHA 189/45 Letter from "C" to EPS July 3, 1951, from the Stanhope Hotel, responding to the obituary of Angelos Sikelianos: "If I told you what I think of Angelos Sikelianos it would be anything but pleasant reading for you—I will spare your feelings; only please do not send me any more translations of this newspaper trash."

147. I deduce these dates from letters in which Eva mentions her vocal music lessons to Barney.

148. "Latest News from Europe," *Sun* (New York), June 1, 1890, 1, http://chroniclingamerica.loc.gov/lccn/sn83030272/1890-06-01/ed-1/seq-1/.

149. CAMS Dossier 2 Letters May Palmer to EP August 10, 1904; Catherine Abbé to EP August, 18, 1904; and Courtlandt Palmer to EP August 27, 1904, all addressed to Thonon-les-Bains hotels in Haute-Savoie, France.

150. UP, 13.

151. BLJD C2 2920 Nos. 29–35 (Papadaki, 68) Letter EP to NCB March 7, 1902, from New York refers to this plan.

152. BLJD C2 2920 Nos. 29–35.

153. BLJD C2 2920 Nos. 339–40 (Papadaki, 54) Letter EP to NCB December 9, 1901, from New York reports that Eva sang in pianist Christine Baker's salon, and Madame Ludwig Breitner "said with apparent sincerity that my work was beautiful, judged as an artist and not as an amateur." BLJD C2 2920 Nos. 355–60 (Papadaki, 74) Letter EP to NCB [March 1902, New York] reports that Baker offered to collaborate with her.

154. Borchmeyer, *Richard Wagner*, 360.

155. CAMS Dossier 2 Letter NCB to EP March 1, 1901, Paris.

156. CAMS Dossier 2 Letter NCB to EP March 1, 1901, Paris.

157. BLJD C2 2920 Nos. 222–23 (Papadaki, 41) Letter EP to NCB [late fall 1900, New York].

158. BLJD C2 2920 Nos. 199–200 (Papadaki, 47) Letter EP to NCB [late fall 1900, New York].

159. BLJD C2 2920 Nos. 224–27 (Papadaki, 52) Letter EP to NCB [1901, New York] my translation of the original French.

160. BLJD C2 2920 Nos. 211–19 (Papadaki, 72) Letter EP to NCB [March 1902, New York].

161. BLJD C2 2920 Nos. 211–19. Rodriguez, *Wild Heart*, 68, states that Barney developed a love for Wagner's work from the time of her European tour in 1894.

162. BLJD C2 2920 Nos. 355–60 (Papadaki, 74) Letter EP to NCB [March 1902, New York].

163. BLJD C2 2920 Nos. 183–88 (Papadaki, 37) Letter EP to NCB [1901, New York City].

164. BLJD C2 2920 Nos. 382–83 (Papadaki, 137) Letter EP to NCB June 10 [1906, Neuilly].

165. BLJD C2 2920 Nos. 83–87 (Papadaki, 127) Letter EP to NCB October 5, 1905, Bar Harbor to Neuilly.

166. BLJD C2 2920 Nos. 83–87.

167. BLJD C2 2920 Nos. 382–83 (Papadaki, 187) Letter EPS to NCB June 10 [1907, Neuilly]: "-et encore plus ta tendresse et ton amitié!"

168. Barney expressed this wish in the opening sonnet of her "Cinq petits Dialogues Grecs (Antithèseset parallèlles)," published under the pseudonym "Tryphé": "Lesbos, belle Lesbos, de tes lèvres blèmies / Réveille la beauté de tes amours célèbres, / Leur volupté défuncte et leur gloire outragée / . . . / Écoute ma chanson du lit bleu de l'Égée / Et souris-mois, Sapho, du fond de ténèrbres." The translation is from Reynolds, *Sappho Companion*, 292.

169. Wickes, *Amazon of Letters*, 94.

170. Sappho epigram from the Palatine Anthology 158D. The epigram drew the attention of other American women too. In 1918, Edna St. Vincent Millay wrote a poem following its lines of inspiration. See Merriam, "Rewriting Grief," 98.

171. Crane, "Mapping the Amazon's Salon," 157.

172. Barney, *Equivoque*, 80.

173. Dorf, "Dancing Greek Antiquity in Private and Public," 9, identifies Penelope on the "harp" and possibly Eva Palmer as the "singer and orator" above her; but neither characterization seems to withstand close scrutiny: Penelope is listed as the flute player in the published play, and Eva's costume in all the other photographs does not match that of the "singer and orator."

174. Barney, *Equivoque*, 66–67.

175. CAMS Dossier 1 Letter Robert Abbe to EP August 8, 1906: "You borrowed $750 / June 14th $404=$1154, June 29th pd $525, balance due $629. It seems a cruelly big sum—and I don't need it . . . , yours truly Robert Abbe."

176. I discuss the event and its effects in detail in chapter 3.

177. APB Box 5 Correspondence Letter EP to Alice Pike Barney undated: "I have temporarily adopted the Duncan family:—Isadora's brother, his wife who is Greek, and their baby who is too small to be amusing. But Raymond and Penelope you would find paintable."

178. The characterization is Eva's projection: CAMS Dossier 2 Letter EPS to NCB [summer 1907, Neuilly]: "Penelope is coming to stay with me a little, so for now I am strictly proper."

179. BLJD NCB 12 9995 Nos. 205–7 Letter NCB to EP July 18, 1906: "Will you and the Duncans come? All of you? Or will you remain in Paris?"

180. BLJD NCB 12 9995 Nos. 208–10 Letter NCB to EP July 28, 1906.

181. BLJD NCB 12 9995 Nos. 203–4 Letter NCB to EP July 14, 1906, Villa Corneille Luchen.

182. BLJD NCB 12 9995 Nos. 213–15 Letter NCB to EP August 6, 1906, from Bayreuth to Paris: "Tu as décidé que parce que je m'oppose à la 'voie' que tu as choix . . . que je suis non amical" (Papadaki's transcription, my translation).

183. BLJD C2 2920 No. 417 (Papadaki, 138) Letter EP to NCB [August or September of 1906, Athens to Neuilly].

184. BLJD C2 2920 Nos. 282–87 (Papadaki, 133) Letter EP to NCB no date.

185. BLJD C2 2920 Nos. 282–87.

186. BLJD C2 2920 No. 417 (Papadaki, 138) Letter EP to NCB [August or September 1906], Athens to Neuilly.

187. CAMS Dossier 1 Letter EP to NCB undated.

188. BLJD C2 2920 Nos. 424–25 (Papadaki, 140) Letter EP to NCB [fall 1906], Athens to Neuilly.

189. Sappho fragment LP 34. (The numbering of the fragments was standardized by Edgar Lobel and Denis Page and bears their initials, LP.)

190. BLJD C2 2920 Nos. 424–25.

191. BLJD C2 2920 Nos. 424–25.

192. UP, 70. The addresses on Eva's incoming correspondence from 1906 to 1907 show that she left Athens for Leukas before December 13, 1906, when a letter from Catherine Abbe was forwarded to "Santa Maura" (the Italian name for

Leukas) (CAMS Dossier 1). Having traveled with Angelos in the Ionian Islands early in January, she came to write to Natalie, "j'aime Angelo" (BLJD C2 2920 Nos. 103–6 [Papadaki, 144] Letter EP to NCB January 22, 1907, Corfu). I surmise that Angelos took Eva to Sappho's promontory just before January 8, 1907, when Natalie Barney responded derisively to Eva's letter describing a visit to a site in "Leukade" of great importance to her: "Evalina, Evalina, . . . how unfeelingly you rob the dead of their mystery by this . . . tourist love of sites developed in you by, it can be nothing else, a most alarming lack of imagination" (BLJD NCB 12 9995 Nos. 230–34 Letter NCB to EP January 8, 1907, Neuilly to St. Maura).

    193. UP, 70.

CHAPTER 2: WEAVING

    1. Letter Kostas Pasagiannis to his brother, Spelios Pasagiannis (brother-in-law of Angelos Sikelianos), dated June 1907, quoted in AS Chronography, 37.

    2. The photo is widely available and can be found in Lebrecht Music and Arts, "Lillian Gish in Delphos Dress."

    3. Koda, Goddess, 19. The himation is a rectangular piece of cloth of heavier fibers worn as a cape or shawl.

    4. The phrase is from Harrison and Murray, Themis, xii. I discuss the case of Jane Harrison below.

    5. BLJD C2 2920 Nos. 420–23 (Papadaki, 149) Letter EP to NCB [fall 1907, Greece to Neuilly]. This letter, written a year later, described her feelings of the previous two years using metaphors of dress.

    6. "A Play for Bernhardt," Washington Post, January 9, 1906, 5. BLJD C2 2920 No. 379 (Papadaki, 106) Letter EP to NCB [spring 1906] suggests that Eva kept tabs on Barney's alligator and another pet named "Albertine" (after Barney's father) when Barney was away: "The alligator has disappeared and Albertine is in a horrible freeze."

    7. CAMS Dossier 2 Letter May ("Boota") to EP September 27, 1905, Paris to W. Fiftieth Street, New York, NY.

    8. UP, 46.

    9. On the strike, see Shorter and Tilly, Strikes in France, 118–19.

    10. UP, 46.

    11. UP, 47.

    12. Winterer, Mirror of Antiquity, 123.

    13. Jowitt, Time and the Dancing Image, 95.

    14. Eva's mother reported this comment in a letter she wrote after Eva saw Duncan perform in Bayreuth in August 1904. See CAMS Dossier 1 Letter Catherine Abbe to EP September 1, 1904: "Mrs Douglas . . . says she saw her dance at Lambach's studio—but apparently was not attracted toward her because she felt that she not [only] had bare feet and legs, but believed she only wore one garment—and she seemed to feel as if she were on the ragged edge of shameless exposé, which to her took away from the gracefulness of her posing."

    15. Sladen, "On the Collecting of Greek Terra-Cotta-Statuettes," 89. On the influence of Tanagrine figures on turn-of-the-century dancers and visual artists, see

Albright, "Tanagra Effect," and Florman, "Gustav Klimt and the Precedent of Ancient Greece," 318.

16. Dykes, "Documentation of a Mariano Fortuny Delphos Gown," 26: "No one knows, even today, how Fortuny created the pleats on the Delphos gown. He never told any of his assistants."

17. Dykes, 24.

18. FIDM Museum and Galleries website, "Mariano Fortuny."

19. Carrara, "Mariano Fortuny," 352: Duncan was the "first to wear" Fortuny's "Knossos scarf."

20. Fortuny's Delphos dresses cost around $125 in 1907 at a time when a tailored suit cost about $10 (Dykes, "Documentation of a Mariano Fortuny Delphos Gown," 29); in 2018 the asking price for the vintage dresses on eBay began at $5,000.

21. See Potts, *Flesh and the Ideal*, 222–53, on the link modern thinkers forged between classical Greek (especially male nude) sculpture and human freedom.

22. Both Nike of Samothrace and Marianne, the romantic figure of revolutionary France, were popular figures of female liberation. A few years after Palmer and the Duncans began their experiments in Greek weaving, Isadora Duncan found inspiration in both Nike of Samothrace and Marianne for her dance dedicated to the Marsellaise (1915). See Preston, *Modernism's Mythic Pose*, 169–70.

23. Koda, "Classical Art and Modern Dress."

24. See Pointon, "Liberty on the Barricades," 42.

25. Cf. Hiram Powers's statue *The Greek Slave* (1844), an immensely popular work based on the Venus de Medici, depicting a nude Greek woman in chains. The statue's female nudity no less than her shackled hands place her in opposition to statues of women in free-flowing Greek dresses representing tyranny's broken chains.

26. UP, 48.

27. UP, 48.

28. UP, 48.

29. Mary Hart described her reconstruction of the process thus in a paper she presented at the Modern Greek Studies Association Symposium in 2007 entitled "Ancient Form to Modern Expression," 5. I am grateful to her for sharing her expert understanding of the process.

30. UP, 51. Liberty and Company was founded by Arthur Lasenby Liberty in London in 1875 "in response to the Aesthetic Movement's mania for all things Japanese" and promoted "textiles, particularly Chinese, Japanese, and Indian coloured silks, as a key area of its merchandise" (Jackson, *Twentieth-Century Pattern Design*, 23). A. A. Vantine and Company in New York called itself an "oriental store" and was an importer of goods from Japan, China, India, Turkey, Persia, and the East. Neither store sold actual Greek fabrics, but Liberty's did sell Greek-style fabrics, and dress reformers and artists like Palmer bought both stores' goods to recreate ancient Greek styles.

31. Duncan, *My Life*, 93. The house currently stands at 34 Chrisafis and Dikearchou in the municipality of Vyronas in Athens and houses the Isadora et Raymond Duncan Centre de Recherche sure la Danse. See the Isadora et Raymond Duncan Dance Research Center website.

32. Duncan, *My Life*, 97.

33. Duncan, 105.

34. Corrigan, *Dressed Society*, 74–75.

35. Rowbotham, *Dreamers of a New Day*, 41.

36. Stein, "Autobiography of Alice B. Toklas," 40.

37. On Raymond meeting Penelope, see the newspaper article "Back to Grecian Costume. Barelegged and Wearing a Toga an American Returns," *Kansas City Times* 72, no. 292 (December 7, 1909): 6: "It was while dwelling on the island of Leucad, from which mythology says the unhappy Sappho leaped into the sea, that he met Mrs. Duncan. As Miss Penelope Sikelianos she was a kindred spirit of the unusual American, and they were married."

38. "Society Attracted by Grecian Dance; Miss Florence Fetherston Believes It Will Become Popular Here," *Philadelphia Inquirer* 161, no. 159 (December 6, 1909): 6.

39. Stein, "Autobiography of Alice B. Toklas," 41, mentions that Raymond was broke when they arrived and Penelope was pregnant with Menalkas.

40. Besides their archaizing dress, Eva later recalled that the Duncans ate "archaic fashion, each on his own couch, with our long narrow tables nicely spread before us" (UP, 60).

41. CAMS Dossier 1 Letter Catherine Abbe to EP August 20, 1906, Bar Harbor to Neuilly with note "please forward to Kopanos."

42. The theme of "eccentricity" comes up in a letter from Catherine Abbe and another from Eva's Parisian friend Nina: "I am wondering whether I might tell you the report has got about you are eccentric. . . . Do as you think right. . . . Forgive me for telling you, we should ignore scandal but avoid it. I've not discussed it with Natalie but it seems to me I should like you to know" (CAMS Dossier 2 Letter Nina to EP [August/September 1906, Paris to Kopanos]).

43. UP, 54.

44. BLJD C2 2920 Nos. 235–36 (Papadaki, 141) Letter EP to NCB [winter 1906–7]: "And I love being alone, here or almost anywhere,—perhaps someday even in Neuilly."

45. CAMS Dossier 2 Letter Nina to EP [August/September 1906], Paris to Athens: "I heard it yesterday only you have got [mixed up with] Isadora I suppose." CAMS Dossier 2 Letter "Cousin Polly" to EP September 21, 1906, Paris to Athens: "I heard that you had arrived and also what the Greeks themselves think of the Duncans so I hope you won't linger on with them long and also that you find it too cold weather for your Greek clothes and have gotten into your nice pretty warm ones."

46. The first written reference I have found is in Georgios Papandreou's letter of September 21, 1910, and is excerpted in AS Chronography, 51–52, from which these quotations are taken and translated. A note by editor Kostas Bournazakis explains that the letter was shown to him by Freddy Germanos (AS Chronography, 288n15).

47. UP, 58.

48. UP, 66.

49. BLJD C2 2920 Nos. 426–27 (Papadaki, 140) Letter EP to NCB [winter 1906–7], Phaleron (Athens) to Paris (Papadaki gives the date August 1906, but I

have found no evidence that Eva traveled to Leukas before December). This and the next comment appear in a long letter Palmer wrote to Barney from Leukas and then from Phaleron near Athens over the course of at least a week. She may have traveled to Leukas in December, then returned to Athens briefly to see Angelos off to Rome, then traveled again to Leukas in the early spring and stayed into the summer.

50. BLJD C2 2920 Nos. 426–27.

51. BLJD C2 2920 Nos. 426–27.

52. BLJD C2 2920 Nos. 103–6 (Papadaki, 144) Letter EP to NCB January 22, 1907, "Santa Maura, Ionian Islands," Corfu: "il est le seul être qui m'ait jamais fait penser à toi, en resemblance je veux dire. Souvent je reste saisie en écoutant non pas seulement tes idées, mais presque tes mots" (he is the only person who ever made me think of you, I mean in resemblance. I am often struck in hearing not only your ideas, but almost your words).

53. CAMS Dossier 2 Telegram EP to NCB September 4, 1906, Athens to Neuilly: "Je vais aussi bien que l'on peut sans toi" (I am as well as I can be without you).

54. BLJD C2 2920 Nos. 103–6: "et puis d'ailleurs tu seras hereuse de savoir qu'il n'aime pas plus que toi mes robes d'à présent!" [sic] (and then besides you will be happy to know that he does not like my dresses any more than you do!), words Barney repeated in CAMS Dossier 1 Letter NCB to EP February 14, 1907 ("what a Valentine"), "since Angelo does not like the Greek [dress] for you."

55. In Penelope Sikelianos's hand I have seen only a few notes, all of them published. One sent to Angelos from Paris in 1911 is filled with figurative expressions granting him power over her ("my love, my . . . Muse, my soulmate . . . my fortress") while still placing herself in a protective role ("be careful of your health . . . don't go missing me") (AS Chronography, 54, my translation). These published notes do not clarify what Penelope's intentions were when she introduced Eva to Angelos. Yet her sisterly caretaking role makes evident that she was at least thinking about her brother's interests. Her own marriage to Raymond Duncan did not bring her wealth or stability, however.

56. Papadaki asserts that Penelope sought to make Eva a patron of Angelos's work when she saw Eva's practice of producing Natalie Barney's plays (L. Papadaki, Γράμματα της Εύας Πάλμερ Σικελιανού στη Natalie Clifford Barney, 20).

57. BLJD NCB 12 9995 Nos. 239–40 Letter NCB to EP July 25, 1907, hand-delivered to rue de Longchamps: "Eva darling, I am disappointed . . . that you have again saddled yourself with people who impose and abuse your hospitality—Penelope will always encourage your marriage to her ridiculously affected and quite unworldly brother."

58. BLJD NCB 12 9995 Nos. 230–34 Letter NCB to EP January 8, 1907, Paris to c/o Jean Siciliani Ile de St. Maure (les Ionienne), Greece.

59. BLJD NCB 12 9995 Nos. 216–21 Letter NCB to EP October 27, 1906, Neuilly to Athens.

60. See chapter 1 on their visit to "Sappho's promontory."

61. AS Chronography gives details about several relationships.

62. AS Chronography, 77.

63. AS Chronography, 97, 103, 105.

64. AS Chronography, 37–38.

65. CAMS Dossier 2 EP to NCB letter August 3 [1907], Pavillon Georges: "Can't we agree to disagree until you like him, or I cease to like him?"

66. BLJD NCB 12 9995, Nos. 230–34 Letter NCB to EP January 8, 1907, care of Jean Siciliani Il de St. Maure (les Ioniennes), Greece.

67. CAMS Dossier 2 Letter EP to NCB June 1 [1907], Leukas [to Neuilly]: "so that my coming may not be an annoyance to you, tell Aline to prepare clothes for me to wear and see me afterwards. That is, if you still dislike these as much as before. I, unfortunately, still prefer them but I don't think I hate proper clothes much more than I used to."

68. BLJD NCB 12 9995 Nos. 239–40 Letter NCB to EP July 25, 1907, 56 rue de Longchamps.

69. CAMS Dossier 2 Letter EP to NCB hand-delivered letter [summer 1907]: "I found the beautiful flowers."

70. BLJD C2 2920 Nos. 107–8 (Papadaki, 145) Letter EP to NCB August 21 [1907], Neuilly.

71. CAMS Dossier 2 Letter EP to NCB [summer 1907, hand-delivered in Neuilly]: "Yesterday Angelo was for going away for good. His despair reminded me of Courtlandt. . . . The memory and because I'm fond of him too made me keep him, and in the evening, still wretched because of 'the cause, the cause,' because of you, I didn't ward him off walking across the garden, sympathetic for his unhappiness. . . . I'm too tired to think."

72. VGY/MTP from Mary Gwinn and Alfred Hodder Papers (C0450) Princeton University Firestone Library, Letter Virginia Yardley to Mary Gwinn Hodder dated "Monday."

73. BLJD C2 2920 Nos. 107–8.

74. And to Barney she wrote, "I lied to him, and told him I cared more for him than for you" (BLJD C2 2920 Nos. 107–8).

75. BLJD C2 2920 Nos. 420–23.

76. BLJD C2 2920 Nos. 107–8.

77. "Angelo" is another inflected form of Άγγελος (Angelos in my usage, the nominative form of the name) and Eva's preferred transliteration of the name in English. She also uses "Anghelos." Throughout the book, I transcribe her and other people's English spellings faithfully without regularizing them.

78. BLJD C2 2920 Nos. 107–8.

79. BLJD C2 2920 Nos. 107–8.

80. "Woman Scorns Hosiery and Frills. Single Garment and Sandals Suffices Devotee," La Bellingham Herald, Bellingham, WA, September 6, 1907, 1, America's Historical Newspapers, SQN: 114D524250E2D870. Goldhill, Who Needs Greek, to uches on Palmer's "transgress[ion of] Edwardian mores" (121) on that transatlantic journey.

81. "Miss Palmer Weds Ancient Philosopher, Angelo Sikelianos, Whom She Met in Greece, Followed Her Over Seas," Special to the New York Times, September 10, 1907, 7.

82. "Looked Like Greek Goddess: Miss Palmer Landed in Classic Costume," New York Times (1857–1922), September 1, 1907, 1.

83. "Her Attire Creates a Stir. Liner's Passenger Wears Sandals and Loose Flowing Robe." *Washington Post*, September 2, 1907, 1.

84. Rowbotham, *Dreamers of a New Day*, 42: a "revolt against the conventions of appearance and behavior" in Palmer's day "meant putting oneself into an unprotected space."

85. "Social Gossip: A Budget of Interesting Personalities in the Realm of Fashion, from Various Exchanges," Special to the *Washington Post*, September 2, 1907, 7.

86. "Social Gossip," 7.

87. "Her Attire Creates a Stir, 1.

88. The *Washington Post* "Social Gossip" column of September 2, 1907, appeared under the more sensational title "New Dress Reform Shocks Fifth Avenue. Miss Palmer's Toga and Sandals Startles New York. Was Newport Belle. Young Woman of Wealth and Social Position Has Strange Ideas," in the *Lexington Herald*, September 5, 1907, 9.

89. "No Hose, No Frills for Her: One Garment Enough for This Rich Girl; Preaches New Cult. Startling in a Breeze. What's Immodest in Bare Nether Limbs If Bare Arms Are All Right, She Asks," *Chicago Daily Tribune*, September 1, 1907, 1.

90. "No Hose, No Frills for Her," 1.

91. "Devotee of One-Garment Costume Who Startled Passengers on Ocean Liner," *Chicago Daily Tribune*, September 2, 1907, 5. The story is retold in UP, 80.

92. "Miss Palmer Weds Ancient Philosopher," 7.

93. "Miss Palmer Weds Ancient Philosopher," 7.

94. "Dressed in Greek Costume. Picturesque Wedding of a Rich American Girl," *Bemidji Daily Pioneer*, September 11, 1907, 2.

95. "Miss Palmer Weds Ancient Philosopher," 7.

96. BLJD C2 2920 Nos. 107–8.

97. Catherine Abbe was reported in Vichy at the end of May 1910. See Marconi Transatlantic Wireless Telegraph, "Americans at Vichy; Season Awakening Slowly, but Weather Has Been Delightful," *New York Times*, May 29, 1910, C3.

98. UP, 84.

99. UP, 84.

100. Catherine Abbe died Saturday, September 25, 1920. See "Mrs. Catherine Amory B. Abbe," *New York Times*, September 28, 1920, 10.

101. "Going native" refers to the gesture of the Western traveler who, experiencing some form of alienation at home, upon entering a culturally distinct place, for complex reasons and with equally social and political effects, undergoes a transformation, adopting the other's costume and ways. On the complex politics of "going native," see Huhndorf, *Going Native*, 5–7.

102. See Goldhill, *Who Needs Greek*, on Greek "self-fashioning" as learning "how to walk, talk, think, and act Greek, and how to take up your role in Greek social institutions and rituals" (82). Goldhill's case studies are Lucian of Samasota—the second-century satirist who lived in present-day Syria and wrote exclusively in Greek—and, sixteen centuries later, in Nietzsche's "a constant and active reconstruction by participation of classical tradition" (297).

103. BLJD C2 2920 Nos. 407–12 (Papadaki, 15) EP to NCB New Year's Day [1909], Leukas.

104. Woolf, "Dialogue upon Mount Pentelicus," writes of the "tough old riddle of the modern Greek and his position in the world today" (65). See Leontis, *Topographies of Hellenism*, 109–13, for a discussion of Woolf's story and the riddle.

105. UP, 49.

106. OM, 42.

107. UP, 113.

108. UP, 108.

109. UP, 109.

110. UP, 109.

111. UP, 109.

112. UP, 219.

113. UP, 218.

114. UP, 219.

115. UP, 219.

116. UP, 219.

117. Nietzsche, "On the Uses and Disadvantages of History for Life," 60.

118. Wagner, "What Is German?," 155–56.

119. OM, 75.

120. OM, 44.

121. OM, 70–71.

122. The edited volume of Cohen and Joukowsky, *Breaking Ground*, brings attention to the range of approaches particular to twelve women archaeologists and their structural relationship to the discipline of archaeology in sites in the eastern Mediterranean and Near East between 1851 and 1985. It highlights, for example, the diplomatic skills of Harriet Boyd Hawes; the invisibility of Edith Hall; Hetty Goldman's segue into the Red Cross and relief work during World War I; and Winifred Lamb's skill in identifying vase paintings. See also Diaz-Andreu and Sørenson, *Excavating Women*.

123. Crowfoot, "Grace Mary Crowfoot (1877–1957)," 6.

124. Crowfoot, 8.

125. Crowfoot, 11.

126. An example of experimental replications in the margins of classical studies today, which uses "reverse engineering" to follow the "internal logic" of a lost process and bring it back "to life," is Schwab, "Caryatid Hairstyling Project."

127. Carrell, "Replication and Experimental Archaeology," 4.

128. Carrell, 4.

129. Diaz-Andreu and Sørenson, in *Excavating Women*, point to a division of labor in archaeology along gender lines and relate it both to the exclusion of women from field work and the academy and to women's "easier access" to museum posts and managerial jobs (9). These differences of labor and access prompted a shift in "archaeological thinking," with women such as Harriet Boyd Hawes giving greater weight to "the function of artifacts (household objects, domestic utensils, and stone and clay implements" (9–10) than to monumental discoveries. Hudson, *Social History of Archaeology*, relates women's early twentieth-century

presence in the margins of the field of archaeology to "the rise of social and local history" over "military/political history" (19–20).

130. B. Smith, *Gender of History*, 165, 166.

131. B. Smith, 18.

132. UP 109, as quoted above. Her idea of the "Greek" suggested here may have drawn on ancient Greek sources such as the compositional principle for the speeches Thucydides wrote in his *History*, which aimed to render what was "opportune for the moment" (τὰ δέοντα μάλιστα) rather than accurately to reproduce words that cannot be recovered (*History*, 1.21.2). I am grateful to Netta Berlin for this observation.

133. Harrison and Murray, *Themis*, 12.

134. Pollock, "Sacred Cows," 21.

135. Freeman, *Time Binds*, ix–xiv.

136. Her phrase, "the absolute right of each person . . . to choose whatever is right for his/her soul" (OM, 72), is most representative of her idea of freedom as an individual right of choice, something she claimed to have inherited from her father.

137. UP, 76.

138. BMHA 189/28 Letter EPS to May Palmer September 17–30, from Upper Agoriani Parnassos.

139. UP, 76.

140. Letter Mary Berenson to Isabella Stewart Gardner May 13, 1923, from Sparta, Greece, in Berenson and Gardner, *Letters*, 658.

141. VGY/MTP letter Virginia Yardley to Mrs. Alfred [Mary Gwinn] Hodder November 9, 1910, Boston, MA, to Baltimore, MD.

142. UP, 69.

143. Letter Mary Berenson to Isabella Stewart Gardner May 13, 1923, Berenson and Gardner, *Letters*, 658–59.

144. Letter Mary Berenson to Isabella Stewart Gardner June 21, 1923, from I Tatti, in Berenson and Gardner, *Letters*, 660: Angelos "sat opposite a mirror, before which he arranged and re-arranged himself in a Pythian Apollo pose. He spoke a sonorous French, smelling strongly of garlic (metaphorically speaking) and had an invariable reply to any interrogation—delivered with rolling eyes and chest thrown out—C'est une question tr-r-r-ès pr-r-r-o-fonde!" We all thought him an unmitigated ass."

145. The phrase describing Angelos has been printed so many times that it is hard to identify the source.

146. Georgios Papandreou's letter of September 21, 1910, is excerpted in AS Chronography, 51–52, from which these quotations are taken and translated. A note by editor Kostas Bournazakis explains that he was shown to him by Freddy Germanos (AS Chronography, 288n15).

147. UP, 61.

148. BLJD C2 2920 Nos. 407–12 (Papadaki, 15) EP to NCB New Year's Day [1909], Leukas.

149. BLJD C2 2920 Nos. 407–12.

150. UP, 87.

151. VGY/MTP Letter Virginia Yardley to Mrs. [Mary Gwinn] Hodder November 5, 1911, rue M. le Prince.

152. AS Chronography, 57. The source of the report is not given in this book. I can only guess that this may be thirdhand information to the author by Anna Sikelianos, Angelos's second wife.

153. Letter Mary Berenson to Isabella Stewart Gardner June 21, 1923, I Tatti, Berenson and Gardner, *Letters*, 660–61: "Poor Eva! But they are seldom together: And it cannot be denied that in spite of her inspired spouse she is a happy and contented woman." Ironically, after the death of Angelos and Eva, people commented on their inseparability. See, for example, Dimopoulos, "Ο ποιητής και η Εύα" (The poet and Eva), 101.

154. Letter Mary Berenson to Isabella Stewart Gardner May 13, 1923, Sparta, Berenson and Gardner, *Letters*, 658–59.

155. Ruyter, *Cultivation of Body and Mind in Nineteenth-Century American Delsartism*, 59.

156. Preston, *Modernism's Mythic Pose*, 239.

157. UP, 76.

158. Pangalo, "'Right' According to Whom?," 228. Pangalo's article is critical of Palmer Sikelianos's advocacy of Greek dress because, she argues, by dressing as an ancient Greek, Pangalo argues, Palmer Sikelianos completely ignored the social codes of contemporary Greece.

159. UP, 87.

160. Zamir, "Population Statistics of the Ottoman Empire in 1914 and 1919," 87.

161. Mary Berenson reported that Palmer was "still beautiful" when she saw her in Greece four years later on May 13, 1923. See Berenson and Gardner, *Letters*, 658.

162. Nirvanas, "Ωραία Ματαιωπονία," 21.

163. The lectures were published that year as *Τρεις διαλέξεις: Η μόδα εις την Ελλάδα; Το μαγαζί; Η Ελληνική μουσική* (Athens: Estia, 1921) and again in 2005 in OM.

164. OM, 32, 33.

165. OM, 33.

166. See "Arts and Crafts Movement."

167. OM, 40.

168. UP, 76.

169. OM, 37.

170. OM, 37.

171. OM, 36–37.

172. OM, 38.

173. OM, 36.

174. OM, 37.

175. Sorin, *Time for Building*, 53.

176. UP, 5.

177. See Matalas, "Οι διαδρομές του φυλετισμού του Πέτρου Βλαστού," especially the discussion of a series of lectures on the subject of racial eugenics delivered by Petros Vlastos in 1914 to the Εκπαιδευτικός Όμιλος (Educational Association, of

which Angelos Sikelianos was a member) and to the Lyceum of Greek Women (227–30), and of their influence on Sikelianos (234–36).

178. Fleming, *Greece—a Jewish History*, 101.

179. The bibliography on Gandhi's readings in Ruskin is substantial. A good starting point is McLaughlin, *Ruskin and Gandhi*, 1974.

180. See Rowbotham, *Dreamers of a New Day*, 43, quoting the father of suffragist Margery Corbet Ashby: "If you want to change anything else, do not reform your clothes."

181. One urban weaver was Anna Karamani, Angelos Sikelianos's second wife. People in Athens have related to me how they would see her weaving as they passed her home in the exclusive neighborhood of Kolonaki.

182. AHC MH-JH Box 5 Folder 7 Letter Muriel Noel to Mary Hambidge April 21, 1921: "My scheme for the 'Society for the Preservation of Old Egyptian Crafts' not yet formed but thinks it would include weaving, pottery, baskets, copper and brass work, etc." On another occasion Noel expressed frustration on "[seeing] 'the natives wearing nasty cheap turbans woven with the commonest Swedish designs. . . . I feel someone ought to study the lost weaving before it becomes a lost art" (Alvic, *Weavers of the Southern Highlands*, 98, quoting letter Muriel Noel to Mary Hambidge March 28, 1921, from the Jay and Mary Crovatt Hambidge Papers, Smithsonian Archives of American Art).

183. AHC MH-JH Box 5 Folder 7 Letter Muriel Noel to Mary Hambidge May 20, 1921: "I think I may get a Greek one [loom] made in Athens by the man who made your[s] and have it adapted for using loom weights."

184. AHC MH-JH Papers Box 5 Folder 7 Letter Muriel Noel to Mary Hambidge April 21, 1921: "Please give my kindest regards to Madame Siklianou [*sic*]. You are lucky to have her as a teacher."

185. Remington, "Notes," 282.

186. Nirvanas, "Ωραία Ματαιοπονία," 22.

187. Nirvanas, 23.

CHAPTER 3: PATRON OF BYZANTINE MUSIC

1. "Greek Orthodox Church" refers to the branch of the Eastern Orthodox Christian Church that conducts its services in Koine Greek. The church calls itself a continuation of the Apostolic Church (Ware, *Orthodox Church*, 217) based on the line of descent of its hierarchy and its continued use of Koine Greek and other ancient eastern Mediterranean languages. "Greek" in this case signifies the liturgical language, not ethnicity or nationality. The "Greek" in "Greek Orthodox" additionally became an ethnic-national marker with the rise of national movements in the Balkans, when in 1833 the monarchy of Greece declared the Church of Greece independent of the Patriarchate of Constantinople and part of the Greek nation-state. The easy slippage between the ecumenical and national meaning of "Greek" is crucial to the subject of this chapter.

2. Here I activate the punning potential of "reorient." This verbal play borrows from a trend in postcolonial studies, found, for example, in *REORIENT*, the online magazine that "provide[s] a fresh and modern perspective on topics related

to the arts and culture of the Middle East, and positively change[s] the way people—including Middle Easterners themselves—view this vast, diverse, and culturally-rich region" (*REORIENT*).

3. Bennett Zon suggests that the kind of self-reflexive othering that I consider to be evident in key moments of Eva's study of Byzantine music may be a piece of ethnomusicological research when a scholar works to "disaggregate questions of race from the study of non-Western musical cultures" ("Disorienting Race," 26).

4. Bruno Latour writes of the "matters of concern" in several contexts, including "Why Has Critique Run Out of Steam?"

5. See Erol, "'Musical Question' and the Educated Elite of Greek Orthodox Society in Late Nineteenth-Century Constantinople," on the emergence of the question.

6. The *oktoechos* identifies the system of composition used in Eastern-rite church chant since the Middle Ages. The conventional translation of *-echos* is "tone," referring to something roughly equivalent to a scale in Western musical theory. Byzantine theory has eight (*okto-*) tones, whereas Western theory has just one for all major and minor scales. Each of the eight tones is made of eight ascending notes completing a cycle on the eighth note; but unlike the fixed notes of Western scales (do re mi, etc.), the intervals between notes are different in each Byzantine tone and form eight different melodic types. Musicologists agree that the eight-tone system is closer to Near Eastern makam than to Western scales, since they function as melodic types comprising a series of important notes, habitual phrases, and tendencies of melodic development rather than a ladder of fixed notes related harmonically to one another. The eight-tone system was modified in the thirteenth and nineteenth centuries by John Glykys and John Koukouzeles and by Chrysanthos of Madytos respectively. The latter codified the Neobyzantine system under debate here, which is the system that Eva learned. It is known in pedestrian terms as Byzantine music, and I refer to it thus except where it is important to make a historical distinction, when I use the term Neobyzantine.

7. Anastasiou, "Η τρισύνθετος γλυκυφωνία της ψαλτικής κατά τριπλή εκδοχή των τριών μουσικοδιδασκάλων Ιωάννου Σακελλαρίδου, Κωνσταντίνος Ψάχος, Σίμωνος Καρά," 30.

8. Romanou, *Εθνικής μουσικής περιήγησις, 1901–1912*, 40.

9. Romanou, 45.

10. Samson, *Music in the Balkans*, 256.

11. Samson, 211.

12. Dragoumis, "Constantinos A. Psachos (1869–1949)," 77. For biographical information, see also Anastasiou, "Κωνσταντίνος Ψάχος," Dragoumis, "Κωνσταντίνος Α. Ψάχος," and Romanou, "Ένας Έλληνας δάσκαλος."

13. Mackridge, *Language and National Identity in Greece, 1766–1976*, 2.

14. This is a point made by Van Steen in "'You Unleash the Tempest of Tragedy.'"

15. Van Steen, "'You Unleash the Tempest of Tragedy,'" 365.

16. Macintosh et al., *Agamemnon in Performance*, 368, and Van Steen, "'You Unleash the Tempest of Tragedy,'" 364.

17. Papazoglou, "Between Texts and Context," points out that Paul Schlenther's Viennese production had "very little music" (212).

18. See Dibble, "Stanford, Sir Charles Villiers."

19. Van Steen, "'You Unleash the Tempest of Tragedy,'" 365.

20. Quoted in Chatzipantazis, "Στη βαριά σκιά της Κλυταιμνήστρας," 17–18.

21. Georgiou, "Modern Greek Theatre and National Cultural Identity."

22. Georgiou, 5, quoting a review in the Greek newspaper Νέον Αστύ, November 7, 1903.

23. Arkoumanea, "Ο Αγαμέμνων στο ταψί, η Κασσάνδρα στο φορείο."

24. Van Steen, "'You Unleash the Tempest of Tragedy,'" 367.

25. Siopsi, "Music in the Imaginary Worlds of the Greek Nation," 33.

26. Antoniou, "Acting Tragedy in Twentieth-Century Greece," 30. For example, Mistriotis directed Sophocles' Elektra in 1899 in the Municipal Theatre of Athens with new music by Ioannis Sakellaridis, a composer who also wrote Greek Orthodox Church music and lectured on the continuity of ancient music transmitted through traditional Greek religious and secular music. On that performance, see Constantinides, "Classical Drama in Modern Greece," 21.

27. Siopsi, "Music in the Imaginary Worlds of the Greek Nation," 31.

28. Siopsi, 30.

29. Van Steen, "'You Unleash the Tempest of Tragedy,'" 363. It is notable that the play was performed in katharevousa, with just the prologue in demotic Greek. Other ancient plays performed in demotic Greek such as the Antigone performed by the troupe Nea Skini that same month did not incite Mistriotis's wrath. Antoniou argues that Mistriotis's opposition to the Oresteia had to do with the production's location in the Royal Theatre: "It was a politically driven act of opposition to the king" (44). Papazoglou, "Between Texts and Contexts," points to the criticism of playwright Grigorios Xenopoulos, who, in an essay of 1903, called revivals of Greek drama "far too 'archaic'" a dramatic instrument "to captivate a modern audience" (214).

30. Van Steen, "'You Unleash the Tempest of Tragedy,'" 364.

31. Mackridge, Language and National Identity in Greece, 1766–1976, 229.

32. On her and Raymond Duncan's first meeting, see chapter 2.

33. Duncan, My Life, 114.

34. It has been asserted that Penelope was also part of Nea Skini, but I have not found evidence to support this.

35. The poster of Antigone with Eleni Pasagianni as Jocasta may be found on Vanikioti, Giotas, and Gana, "Θεατρικές παραστάσεις της Αντιγόνης στον εικοστό αιώνα," slide 4. See also Georgiou, "Modern Greek Theatre and National Cultural Identity," 3.

36. The years he taught were 1867–85, 1886–95, and 1897–1905. See IAEN Ιστορικό Αρχείο Ελληνικής Νεολαίας, "Η μέση εκπαίδευση στην Λευκάδα," Ιωάννης Σικελιανός.

37. The Gymnasium where her father taught was not open to girls.

38. For example, Ioannis Vilaras (1771–1823), a prerevolutionary proponent of literary demoticism from Epiros, was an "important pioneer of the demotic movement" (Horrocks, Greek, 348).

39. Angelos Sikelianos, "Πηνελόπη Σικελιανού," 52.

40. Romanou, Εθνικής μουσικής περιήγησης, 1901–1912, 63–64.

41. See Palamas, "Τα Τραγούδια μας εις τα ξένα," 1.

42. Lambelet, "Η εθνική μουσική"; Rentzeperi-Tsonou, "Το 'ελληνικό στοιχείο' σε έργα φωνητικής μουσικής των Ελλήνων συνθετών της Εθνικής Μουσικής Σχολής Μ. Καλομοίρη και Μ. Βάρβογλη," 1–2.

43. Angelos Sikelianos, "Πηνελόπη Σικελιανού," 53. Efthalia Papadaki, who spent decades meticulously researching the life and work of Angelos and Eva Sikelianos, reports that Penelope studied the flute with her aunt Aspasia Verykiou (E. Papadaki, "Αναζητώντας μια ελληνική ευτοπία," 55).

44. Angelos Sikelianos, Πηνελόπη Σικελιανού, 53.

45. Glytzouris, "'Resurrecting' Ancient Bodies," 96, gives further details. I discuss the choreography of this performance in the next chapter.

46. Duncan, My Life, 95.

47. Duncan, 113.

48. UP, 185.

49. Glytzouris, "'Resurrecting' Ancient Bodies," 108n60.

50. Duncan, My Life, 114.

51. AS Chronography, 31.

52. "Glytzouris, "'Resurrecting' Ancient Bodies," 108n60, with reference to numerous newspaper articles of the time.

53. Duncan, My Life, 113.

54. Duncan, 115.

55. Duncan, 95.

56. UP, 186.

57. Vlagopoulos, "'Patrimony of Our Race,'" gives the most up-to-date account of Bourgault-Ducoudray's musical transcriptions, harmonizations, and notation and of the cross-fertilization of his collection and ideas with the national school of music in Greece.

58. See Samson, Music in the Balkans, 227–28, and Romanou and Barbaki, "Music Education in Nineteenth-Century Greece," 68.

59. Samson, Music in the Balkans, 228.

60. Samson, 228.

61. Samson, 228.

62. I discuss the influence of Emmanuel's La danse grecque antique d'après les monuments figurés in the next chapter.

63. CAMS Dossier 1 Letter Catherine Abbe to EP September 13, 1904.

64. Burlin, Songs of Ancient America, iii.

65. Burlin, iii.

66. Burlin, iv–v: "I have in nowise changed the melodies, nor have I sought to harmonize them in the usual sense, nor to make of them musical compositions. I have merely tried to reproduce the actual sound of the grinding, and to add enough harmony to give, as it were, background to the picture ... disregarding all prescribed harmonic progressions. My one desire has been to let the Indian songs be heard as the Indians themselves sing them."

67. Burlin, iii.

68. Burlin, iii.

69. CAMS Dossier 1 Letter Catherine Abbe to EP December 7, 1906, to c/o R. Duncan Kopanos.

70. CAMS Dossier 2 Letter Catherine Abbe to EP May 17, 1904.

71. CAMS Dossier 1 Letter Catherine Abbe to EP, May 8, 1907, to EP Leukas, Greece.

72. UP, 46.

73. BMHA 189/9 Articles by Eva Sikelianos, "Concerning Greek Music," unpublished ms. [1928]. The quotes in this paragraph are from the longer quote that follows.

74. See Gonzalez, *Plato and Heidegger*, 253.

75. BMHA 189/9 "Concerning Greek Music," 4–5, 10–13.

76. See chapter 2. Her most extensive elaboration of *syntrimmata* is the lecture on "Ελληνική μουσική" (Greek music) delivered in sequence in February 1921 following her lecture on Greek fashion and a second one entitled "Το μαγαζί: Προτάσεις προς λύσιν ενός εργατικού προβλήματος" (The shop: Proposals for a solution to an employment problem). The three lectures, first published in 1921, appear in OM.

77. UP, 94.

78. "Society Attracted by Grecian Dance: Miss Florence Fetherston Believes It Will Become Popular Here," *Philadelphia Inquirer* 161, no. 159 (December 6, 1909): 6.

79. "Raymond Duncan's Lecture: Large Audience Greets Exponent of the Seven Rhythms," *Philadelphia Inquirer* 161, no. 174 (December 21, 1909): 6. See also "Greek Music and the Folk Songs of Hellas."

80. "Raymond Duncan's Lecture," 6.

81. "Duncan Dances in 'Elektra': Trips Lightly in His Besandled Feet—Mrs. Duncan as Elektra," *New York Times*, April 12, 1910, 11.

82. "Duncan Dances in 'Elektra.'"

83. In February 1910, the Duncans led a gathering at the Evangelismos Greek Orthodox Church on West Thirtieth Street in New York to protest the performance of Richard Strauss's *Elektra* at the Manhattan Opera House "as a defamation of the work of the classic Greeks." See "Elektra Defames Classics, Say Greeks: In Church Meeting Denounce the Opera," *New York Times*, February 10, 1910, 7. Goldhill, *Who Needs Greek*, 116–21, discusses the controversy from the point of view of the Duncans' dress.

84. BMHA 189/28 Letter EPS to Catherine Abbe June 24. An archivist penciled in [1914] as the probable year, but I think the date is inexact. Psachos was photographed in the field with an "Edison" in 1910 (Eustathios Makris, "Ηχογραφήσεις του Κωνσταντίνου Α. Ψάχου σε κυλίνδρους Edison," 74). Might not this be the "Edison" Eva purchased for him? If so, the letter must predate the photo, as it states that Psachos was anxiously awaiting the Edison. In the same letter, Eva mentions her preparation of a book of poetry, referring either to her luxury edition of *Αλαφροΐσκιωτος* printed in 1909 or the first volume of *Πρόλογος στη Ζωή* (1915). I suggest the former.

85. BMHA 189/28 Letter EPS to Catherine Abbe June 24.

86. RD, 1: 23, "Illustration 3 February 1912: M. Raymond Duncan et son école." The Akadémia later moved to 31 rue de Seine.

87. RD, 1: 3, George-Michel, "L'Homme nu et les spectacles Grec."

88. Sophocles, *Elektra*, line 380, translated by Sir Richard Jebb (1894).

89. "Duncan Gowns for Paris. Rue De La Paix Modistes Seek Designs by Tunic Wearing American," *Kansas City Star* 32, no. 174 (March 10, 1912): 7.

90. UP, 94.

91. According to Piliouras, "Ο Σικελιανός δεν μένει πια εδώ," the Sikelianoses purchased the property with a small house in 1910 and constructed the villa between 1914 and 1918 (140).

92. Pratelle, "Rescuing Epirus," 423.

93. "Dancer Pacifies Albania: Raymond Duncan Opens Communal Bakeries in New Kingdom," *Washington Post*, April 19, 1914, 16.

94. Pratelle, "Rescuing Epirus," 424.

95. "The Divine Gift," *Washington Post*, July 9, 1913, 4.

96. "Finding Work for War's Refugees: They Overcrowd Greece and Raymond Duncan Has Organized Relief Plan," *Trenton Evening Times*, July 4, 1915, 5.

97. "Idol of Greeks May Be Returned to Cabinet," *Wilkes-Barre Times-Leader*, June 9, 1915, 5.

98. Angelos sided with the royalists in 1916, according to Karalis, "Βιο-εργογραφία," 114. I do not know if Eva took a position.

99. F. Reynolds et al., *Story of the Great War*, vol. 7, 2190.

100. Clogg, *Concise History of Modern Greece*, 85–86.

101. "Greece Soon Will Vote upon Return to Power of Ministry Whose Program Includes War," *Trenton Evening Times*, June 8, 1915, 1.

102. "Isadora Duncan Fails to Arouse Enthusiasm for Venizelos in Athens," *Musical America* 22, no. 25 (October 23, 1915): 28.

103. Wright, *Maurice Magnus, a Biography*, 76.

104. Wright, 97.

105. The quotes that follow are from Bournazakis, "Έξι γράμματα της Πηνελόπης Σικελιανού," 275, 276, and 277 respectively.

106. BMHA 189/9 Articles by Eva Sikelianos, "An Appeal to Musicians," unpublished, handwritten ms. [1924]. What recommended Psachos to her was his effort to "preserve traditional forms of Byzantine psalmody" and "defend the integrity of the received tradition of chanting" and folk music "in the face of Westernization" (Lingas, "Tradition and Renewal in Contemporary Orthodox Psalmody," 351).

107. Remington, "Notes," 282. Dragoumis, "Constantinos A. Psachos (1869–1949)," 80, confirms that Eva was conferred the "highest certificate" in Byzantine music.

108. Psachos's contribution to the study of Greek music was substantial, and much of the work lies beyond my expertise. A good starting point is the volume edited by Evangelos Karamanes, *Κωνσταντίνος Ψάχος*.

109. AS Chronography, 59.

110. Angelos Sikelianos, "Αρίστος Καμπάνης."

111. Kambanis, "Πρόσωπα και πράγματα," n.p.

112. F. Reynolds, *Story of the Great War*, vol. 9, 2704.

113. Kambanis would later become the chief editor of *Neon Kratos*, a government publication of the Metaxas dictatorship. See Petrakis, *Metaxas Myth*, 17.

114. Kambanis, "Πρόσωπα και πράγματα," n.p.

115. Kambanis, n.p.

116. Kambanis, n.p.

117. See Erol, "'Musical Question' and the Educated Elite of Greek Orthodox Society in Late Nineteenth-Century Constantinople," 154.

118. The issue remains generative to this day.

119. Psachos, *Η παρασημαντική της Βυζαντινής μουσικής*, 7.

120. Kambanis, "Πρόσωπα και πράγματα," n.p.

121. Kambanis, n.p.

122. Kambanis, n.p.

123. Kambanis, n.p.

124. Kambanis, n.p.

125. Makris, "Ηχογραφήσεις του Κωνσταντίνου Α. Ψάχου σε κυλίνδρους Edison," 74.

126. Ρωμαίικος, *romeic*, is the adjective from Ρωμιός (*romios*, the self-appellation of Greek speakers in the Byzantine and Ottoman eras) adopted by demoticists with positive connotations to designate the unofficial dimensions of neohellenism, in contrast to *Hellenic*, a word that increasingly bore high cultural, Western connotations.

127. "Συναυλία με έργα Καλομοίρη: Η πρώτη συναυλία; Αναβίωση της πρώτης συναυλίας με έργα Μανώλη Καλομοίρη όπως δόθηκε ακριβώς στο Ωδείο Αθηνών στις 11 Ιουνίου 1908" (Concert with music by Kalomiris: Revival of the first concert with works by Manolis Kalomiris exactly as given at the Athens Conservatory on June 11, 1908), Odeion Athinon website, http://www.odeionathinon.gr/content/view /267/1/, accessed January 26, 2016; this link is no longer available.

128. *Nea Estia*, nos. 1481–85: 531.

129. "Konstantinos Psachos."

130. Psachos's cultural politics did not fit neatly into the Greek *katharevousa*-demoticist camps. He wrote in *katharevousa* yet assumed the evolving continuity of the Greek culture during the Byzantium and Ottoman periods. The complexity of his position stemmed from his close association with the ecumenical patriarchate of Constantinople, which both represented the continuity of Byzantium in the Ottoman Empire and opposed demotic Greek.

131. The collection was published by 1908 by Spyridon Kousolinos and reprinted in 1998 by Koultoura, both in Athens. Greek collections of Ottoman and Near Eastern music had been published before in Constantinople but not in Athens. See Plemmenos, "Η 'θελξίθυμος' μούσα της Ανατολής," 110.

132. Ottoman Greeks distinguished "ψαλτική μουσική" (chant music) from "εξωτερική μουσική" (secular music). The key distinction of religion versus worldliness also contains a secondary distinction. The church's Koine Greek stood in contrast to the many languages heard in secular music, which was performed in the vernacular language(s) of its audience. But when Greek elites sought to promote religious unity under the aegis of the Orthodox patriarchate, they grouped together folksongs of Albanians, Bulgarians, Turks, Vlachs, and Greeks with "local traditions of Orthodox ecclesiastical music" in order to prove the shared Greek roots of secular music among Eastern Orthodox Christians.

133. Plemmenos, "Η 'θελξίθυμος' μούσα της Ανατολής," 112.

134. Pennanen, "Nationalization of Ottoman Popular Music in Greece," points out that "recordings of Ottoman popular music which Greek musicians made in

the Ottoman Empire . . . are nowadays regarded as a part of Greek national music. . . . Conversely in the 1930s Ottoman-Greek music was often classified as Oriental and thus non-Greek by the educated classes of Greece" (15). Psachos and his colleague, Smyrna-born classical composer Kalomiris, were exceptions in calling this music Greek and "stating that [it] stemmed from ancient Greece" (15).

135. Psachos made these arguments in the lecture in articles he published in his journal Φόρμιγξ (Phorminx). See Romanou, Εθνικής μουσικής περιήγησης, 61–62.

136. Romanou, 61–62.

137. Psachos's friend Dimitrios Peristeris, a medical doctor also transplanted from the Ottoman East to Greece, used the adjective "γλυκυτέρπνος" (sweetly pleasing) to describe the music's therapeutic effects on any "ψυχικήν αδυναμίαν" (weakness of the spirit). See Plemmenos, "Η 'θελξίθυμος' μούσα της Ανατολής," 108, quoting from a letter written by Peristeris to Psachos dated October 12, 1907.

138. Kambanis, "Πρόσωπα και πράγματα," n.p.

139. Kambanis, n.p.

140. Kambanis, n.p.

141. Kambanis, n.p.

142. "Konstantinos Psachos": "He was interested in the political situation, more so regarding the Liberal Party, and was personally acquainted with Eleftherios Venizelos and the King Constantine."

143. Fitzpatrick, *Liberal Imperialism in Europe*, 225.

144. Letter Angelos Sikelianos to Ion Dragoumis, November 24, 1912, from the archives of Markos Dragoumis, reprinted in *Kathimerini*, July 6, 1997. Today advocates of the Greek Nazi party Χρυσή Αυγή (Golden Dawn) quote the phrase to claim Sikelianos as a predecessor. See the Golden Dawn website, http://www .xryshaygh.com/enimerosi/view/aggelos-sikelianos-eimai-tetrakathara-ethnikisths -63-chronia-apo-to-thanato, accessed June 21, 2018.

145. BMHA, "Appeal to Musicians," ms. p. 3.

146. BMHA, "Appeal to Musicians," ms. p. 9.

147. BMHA 189/28 Letter EPS to May Palmer September 17–30 from Upper Agoriani Parnassus.

148. I discuss this letter in Leontis, "American in Paris, a Parsi in Athens." For details on the monastery and its history during the Greek War of Independence, see "Ιερά Μονή Παναγίας Δαμαστάς Φθιώτιδος" (Monastery of Panagia Damasta Phthiotis), Monastiria.gr, http://www.monastiria.gr/sterea-elada/nomos-fthiotidas /iera-moni-panagias-damastas/, accessed June 21, 2018.

149. Quatremère de Quincy, *Le Jupiter olympien*.

150. Danos, "Culmination of Aesthetic and Artistic Discourse in Nineteenth-Century Greece," 75.

151. Kourelis, "Byzantium and the Avant Garde."

152. UP, 82. Kourelis, "Byzantium and the Avant Garde," 391–93, reproduces the interior of the Tiffany chapel and discusses the Byzantine influences.

153. Psachos, Η παρασημαντική της Βυζαντινής μουσικής, 7.

154. Psachos, 10.

155. "Barney and Brooks were in a league of their own, totally independent and financially responsible" (Langer, *Romaine Brooks*, 4).

156. Elliot and Wallace, *Women Writers and Artists*, 19.

157. "Courtlandt Palmer Dead," *New York Times*, July 24, 1888, 5.

158. Records of her correspondence with the lawyers and trustees from the time of the Delphic Festivals to the end of her life exist in BMHA.

159. CAMS Dossier 1 Letter Robert Abbe to EP August 8, 1906 (quoted in chapter 2).

160. Kazantzakis, *Selected Letters of Nikos Kazantzakis*, 106.

161. Dragoumis, "Constantinos A. Psachos," 83.

162. Romanou, "Ένας Έλληνας δάσκαλος," n.p.

163. Samson, *Music of the Balkans*, 257.

164. BMHA "Appeal to Musicians," 18.

165. I discuss three below: "Η Ελληνική μουσική" (1921, published in OM); "An Appeal to Musicians: A New Organ" (ms. 1924), and "Concerning Greek Music" (ms. 1928).

166. BMHA "Appeal to Musicians," 18.

167. Tillyard, *Byzantine Music and Hymnography*: "All the types of Byzantine mode so far described, whether chromatic or not, can be played with sufficient accuracy on our modern keyed instruments, and sung without difficulty by western singers" (44).

168. BMHA, "Appeal to Musicians," 19.

169. BMHA, "Appeal to Musicians," 21–22.

170. The two smaller organs have two two-octave keyboards, one Western, the other Byzantine. The Center for the Study of Greek Folklore of the Academy of Athens has one of the organs, donated by Eleni Dalla, goddaughter of Psachos. For a description and photographs, see Makris, "Παρουσίαση του μικρού Παναρμονίου."

171. Karas, "Η μεγάλη ιδέα της Εύας," 276.

172. OM, 83.

173. OM, 82.

174. OM, 81.

175. OM, 83.

176. OM, 87.

177. OM, 91, following *Will to Power* no. 419.

178. OM, 92.

179. BMHA "Appeal to Musicians," 1, 23, my emphasis.

180. BMHA 189/28 Letter EPS to May Palmer September 17–30, my emphasis.

181. OM, 92, my emphasis.

182. Trubeta, *Physical Anthropology, Race, and Eugenics in Greece (1880s–1970s)*, 158.

183. Rummel, "Statistics of Turkey's Democide."

184. Glaspell, *Road to the Temple*, 280.

185. Glaspell, 280.

186. Angelos Sikelianos, "Δελφικός λόγος: Λόγος σπερματικός."

187. Burke, "Angelos Sikelianos," 119.

188. BLJD C2 2920 Nos. 114–15 (Papadaki, 155) Letter EPS to NCB 4 July 1924, written "going to Corinthia, Sykia, Greece."

189. AS Chronography, 121.

190. BLJD C2 2920 Nos. 114–15.

191. BLJD C2 2920 Nos. 396–402 (Papadaki, 110) Letter EP to NCB [1903], from Avila, Spain.

192. BLJD C2 2920 Nos. 396–402.

193. BLJD C2 2920 Nos. 396–402.

194. BMHA "Appeal to Musicians," 2.

195. BMHA "Appeal to Musicians," 16.

196. By 1930, when Eva faced impoverishment and wondered what had made her turn her back on American social norms, she attributed some of her unconventionality to Barney: not to the example of Barney but to the pressure Barney placed on Eva to become different. She wrote to Barney, "You are almost bourgeoisie in your utter steadiness—and one sees how through all the changes . . . you have simply been immovable and that your mission has quite clearly been to make others change. . . . No one has done this as heroically as you, with such clear disdain of those who fail. . . . Looking back, I wonder what would have happened if, about 35 years ago, you had left me alone. Would I have ever found my own open road where I follow my soul leaping and racing as your grayhound used to leap and race around your carriage? . . . Yet perhaps there were in me American needs of respectability growing downwards which might have pushed up if you had not violently uprooted and transplanted the whole sapling. Would my tree-top have ever [grown] so freely if you had not twisted me into a knot of pain for—how many years? Were you the mystic and only gate which led to my distant mountain?" (UW Renée Lang EPS letter to NCB dated April 27, 1930 from Athens to Paris).

197. BMHA "Appeal to Musicians," 2.

198. BMHA 189/9 Articles by Eva Sikelianos, "Concerning Greek Music," unpublished, handwritten ms. [1928], 80. Khorshed's letters with the return address at "3 Pl. de la Sorbonne" support the view that she was a student at the Sorbonne University. See Patel, "Gandhi and the Parsis," 27. The intercultural collaboration of Eva and Khorshed may be compared to others analyzed in Leela Gandhi, *Affective Communities*.

199. Patel, "Gandhi and the Parsis, 3.

200. Patel, 4.

201. UP, 97.

202. Khorshed calls herself "a woman of 31" in BMHA 189/29 Letter Khorshed Naoroji to EPS December 20, 1924, Paris, so she was born in 1893, the year Ardeshir Naoroji died.

203. Grover and Arora, *Great Women of Modern India*, 205.

204. For example, in 1907 Khorshed was listed as passing the "preparatory division" of students of music tested in Bombay for Trinity College of Music, London (Edgar Faulkner, "Trinity College, London: Bombay Musical Successes, Associate Pianist Certificated," *Times of India*, November 18, 1907, 4, ProQuest Historical Newspapers), and in 1911 she came in third "with honors" in the junior division in singing ("Trinity College of Music: Bombay's Exam Passes, *Times of India*, November 20, 1911, 10, ProQuest Historical Newspapers).

205. BMHA 189/9 "Concerning Greek Music," 77.

206. BMHA 189/29 Letter Khorshed Naoroji to EPS December 1, 1924, Paris.

207. BMHA 189/29 Letter Khorshed Naoroji to EPS 1925, "Paris Sunday."

208. BMHA 189/29 Letter Khorshed Naoroji to EPS December 20, 1924, Paris.

209. BMHA 189/29 Letter Khorshed Naoroji to EPS n.d., [Sikya].

210. BMHA 189/29 Letter Khorshed Naoroji to EPS 1925, "Paris Sunday."

211. BMHA 189/29 Letter Khorshed Naoroji to EPS January 2, 1925, Paris.

212. After Angelos's death in 1951 Khorshed brought up the uncomfortable household scene in Sikya again, without mentioning the details of incidents still troubling her twenty-five years later: "I shall try accepting some of the incidents at Sikya when Mitropoulos was there but as you rightly said we each had our own [unintelligible]. . . . It seems so long ago, but life has brought to me peace so I might look back on only the incidents that matter" (BMHA 189/45 Letter Khorshed Naoroji to EPS June 24, 1951).

213. BMHA 189/29 Letter Khorshed Naoroji to EPS January 2, 1925, Paris.

214. UP, 98.

215. BMHA 189/9 "Concerning Greek Music," 80–81.

216. BLJD C2 2920 Nos. 114–15 Letter EPS to NCB July 4, 1924, "going to Sykia, Corinthia, Greece."

217. UP, 19.

218. UP, 188, gives this brief history of the moonstone. I have reconstructed the dates.

219. UP, 98.

220. Nirvanas, quoted in OM, 23.

221. BMHA 189/29 Letter Khorshed Naoroji to EPS December 20, 1924, Paris.

222. No one source describes Khorshed's circle. I have pieced her network together through extant correspondence in the Eva Sikelianou archive in BMHA, for example, her letter to Eva dated December 1, 1924, in which she describes her discussion about Greece with members of the Hindustan Association in Paris: "You can't imagine how enthusiastic young India is about young Greece. Bagchi suggests that I should concentrate an entire article on Greece as sun for the spiritual side and that he'll have it published in the Modern Review of India" (BMHA 189/29 Letter Khorshed Naoroji to EPS December 1, 1924, Paris).

223. On March 24, 1928, "Khurshed Banoo A. D. Naoroji" performed at the Excelsior Theatre in Bombay a program of "old modal songs and dances adapted from the Ajanta frescoes" (*Times of India*, March 22, 1928, 3).

224. Du Bois, *Souls of Black Folk*, 7.

225. BMHA 189/29 Letter Khorshed Naoroji to EPS 1925, "Paris Sunday."

226. BMHA 189/29 Letter Khorshed Naoroji to EP March 1925, Ss. Pilsna Brindisi.

227. BMHA 189/29 Letter Khorshed Naoroji to EPS December 20, 1924, Paris.

228. BMHA 189/29 Letter Khorshed Naoroji to EPS April 3, 1925, 30 Napeer Sea Road, Bombay. More evidence on her musical activities.

229. BMHA 189/29 Letter Khorshed Naoroji to EPS January 2, 1926, Paris.

230. Dinyar Patel email message, January 12, 2008: "I wonder how Dadabhai's figuring with the institutions and ideals of democracy (through the British Parliament and his advocacy of steady reform leading to self-government) colored his granddaughter's impressions while traveling to the birthplace of democracy." Quoted with permission.

231. BMHA 189/29 Letter Khorshed Naoroji to EPS November 25, 1924, Sykia to Athens.

232. Du Bois, "Strivings of the Negro People."

233. E. Papadaki, "Αναζητώντας μια ελληνική ευτοπία," 129–31, discusses Angelos's choice of *Prometheus Bound*, referring to Sikelianos's "Δελφικός λόγος: Η πνευματική βάση της Δελφικής Προσπάθειας, 1927" (112). In her view, fascism, one of several "revolutionary movements based on the traditional values of the people," interested him (118–19).

234. Trotter, *Priest of Music*, 34–35, writes that Mitropoulos studied at the conservatory between 1910 and 1916. Eva was there from 1914 to 1919. BMHA 189/29 Letter Dimitri Mitropoulos to Eva June 1, 1924, from Berlin displays the warm, familiar terms of their interaction.

235. Sakallieros, *Dimitri Mitropoulos and His Works in the 1920s*, 113–16, discusses Mitropoulos's stay in Sykia and the significance of the compositions he produced.

236. Kourelis, "Thalero," maps out "how close Sikya and Delphi are."

237. BMHA 189/29 Letter Khorshed Naoroji to EPS April 3, 1925, Bombay to Athens: "I shall give my ultimatum to the family that I begin my work in Indian music with a view to a profession as soon as I can grasp it. If not I want to try yoga. I do not wish to begin to try to begin an Academy of European music before we have a good one of purely Indian music. I won't go against my principles. I daresay I shall find my way out."

238. BMHA 189/29 Letter Khorshed Naoroji to EPS September 16, 1925, Bombay to Athens.

239. Van Steen, "'World's a Circular Stage,'" 377.

CHAPTER 4: DRAMA

1. The translation was by Ioannis Gryparis, a poet who, in the 1930s, became director of the National Theatre of Greece.

2. See Fournaraki, "Bodies That Differ," on "the close collaboration of the Lyceum with Eva Palmer-Sikelianos" (81n89). See also Anastasopoulou, *Καλλιρρόη Παρρέν*, 271–72, on Eva's early collaboration with the Lyceum in 1910.

3. Glytzouris, "Resurrecting Ancient Bodies," 93–94, analyzes these choreographic choices.

4. Van Steen, "'World's a Circular Stage,'" 383.

5. Porter, "What Is 'Classical' about 'Classical' Antiquity?," discusses how "feeling" and "sounding classical" (43) are pieces of socially conditioned experiences (40).

6. Van Steen describes some scathing reviews in "'World's a Circular Stage,'" 377. The reviews from the 1927 festival were generally more positive than those of the festival of 1930.

7. Pratsika (1899–1994), a student of Mary Wigman and major figure in Greek dance, carried the revivalism of the Delphic Festivals through a lifetime of performance. She was "high priestess" in the first torch-lighting ceremony at ancient Olympia in 1936 (MacAloon, "'My Programme Became Very Strict,'" 101) and founded and directed Greece's State School of Dance for decades. See Savrami, *Ancient Dramatic Chorus through the Eyes of a Modern Choreographer*, 8–17,

and 68n14, and Hassiotis, "Commentary from the Documentary, 'A Century of Contemporary Dance in Greece.' "

8. Pratsika, "Αναμνήσεις από τις πρώτες Δελφικές Εορτές του 1927," 127.

9. UP, 113.

10. I discuss this in chapter 5.

11. UP, 51.

12. UP, 61.

13. UP, 113–14. I discuss this in detail later in this chapter.

14. Glytzouris, " 'Resurrecting' Ancient Bodies," 86.

15. Glytzouris, " 'Resurrecting' Ancient Bodies," 96, discusses Isadora Duncan's *Suppliants* of 1903, the Anthistiria (May Day) celebration by the Lyceum of Greek Women in the Panathenaic Stadium in 1911, Loie Fuller's performance in the same stadium in 1914, and Vassos and Tanagra Kanellos's work in the United States after 1919. These precedents supported the idea of a continuous line of transmission from ancient to modern Greek dance. Eva's "major contribution" to these American efforts was significant: in Glytzouris's words, she brought many Greek "elements together as a whole for the first time in performances of ancient tragedy, offering a unified theatrical experience" (97). Pantelis Michelakis casts a wider net in his comparison of the choreography of *Prometheus Bound* by Eva Sikelianos in 1927 and 1930 and Ted Shawn in 1929 by situating their work "within and against the wider social and cultural history of dance and the reception of Prometheus in the 1920s" ("Dancing with Prometheus," 225).

16. The bibliography is immense. See, for example, Van Steen, " 'World's a Circular Stage," for its study of the Delphic Festivals' use of theatrical space, enlarging on Nietzsche's principle that dramatic performances should convey collective emotion.

17. Michelakis, "Theatre Festivals," 155–59.

18. Glytzouris, " 'Resurrecting' Ancient Bodies," touches on this, while Van Steen, "Myth, Mystique, Nietzsche, and the 'Cultic Milieu' of the Delphic Festivals, 1927 and 1930," faces it head on.

19. Duncan, *My Life*, 42, 45, names the British Museum, and 53–54 names the Louvre.

20. Boone, "Bliss Carman's Pageants, Masques, and Essays, and the Genesis of Modern Dance," points to a line of succession from "Henrietta Russell Hovey to Bliss Carman and Mary Perry King, and thence to Ted Shawn, Denishawn and the dance of today" (178).

21. Cunningham, *Reforming Women's Fashion, 1850–1920*, 144.

22. Banaji, "Womanly Eloquence and Rhetorical Bodies," 157.

23. Wilbor, *Delsarte Recitation Book*, 462.

24. Preston, *Modernism's Mythic Pose*, 75. I discuss Delsartean beliefs and practices more thoroughly in chapter 2.

25. Preston, 153.

26. Although the parallels of Isadora's choreography and Emmanuel's study were observed in her lifetime, I first read of the connection and subsequent links to the Delphic Festivals in Tsoutsoura, "Το ιστορικό βάθος στην προβληματική και την αισθητική της αναβίωσης του χορού στις 'Δελφικές Γιορτές,' " 37.

27. Emmanuel, *La danse grecque antique d'après les monuments figurés*, title page, my translation. The Greek quote is from Athenaeus 629 b.

28. Albright, *Traces of Light*, 173, comparing Duncan's to Fuller's work, argues that Fuller also "incorporated the contemporary cultural evocations of 'nature' and 'Greek' in her stagings of what were essentially modernist theatrical landscapes" while contesting Duncan's claim on Greece. Whereas Duncan was "imitating movements of dancers as represented on Greek vases," Fuller aspired to go deeper to achieve "the original natural expression and movements which inspired the Greeks when they made their vases."

29. Holst-Warhaft, "In the Wake of the Greek Classical Moment," 8, lists the equation of moral rectitude as one of the effects of the "classicizing process" in modern forms.

30. Duncan, "Dancer of the Future," 173.

31. Dyson, *In Pursuit of Ancient Pasts*, 191.

32. Marchand, *Down from Olympus*, shows that Ernst Buschor, like other Weimar archaeologists, wished "to use the revival of Greece to regenerate mankind," archaeology to conquer history (336).

33. Steichen took more than one photograph. See, for example, Edward Steichen, *Isadora Duncan in the Parthenon, Athens*, gelatin-silver chloro-bromide print, 1921, displayed in the Toledo Museum as part of an exhibit on Degas and Dance in 2015–16, "January 8 Art Minute," Toledo Museum website, http://www .toledomuseum.org/2016/01/08/jan-8-art-minute-edward-steichen-isadora -duncan-in-the-parthenon-athens/, accessed February 9, 2018.

34. Duncan, "Parthenon," 64–65.

35. See the photograph "Duncan in a Dionysian Mode," in Franko, *Dancing Modernism/Performing Politics*, 19, figure 4, taken from the Isadora Duncan Collection, San Francisco Performing Arts Library and Museum.

36. See Raymond Duncan's photograph of Isadora Duncan dancing in the Theater of Dionysus in 1903, Jerome Robbins Dance Division, New York Public Library Image ID ps_dan_cd3_38, "Duncan, Isadora 10," New York Public Library Digital Collections, http://digitalcollections.nypl.org/items/8606fc41-c48c-dba9 -e040-e00a18065db5, accessed December 20, 2016. The synaesthetic interplay of the visual arts and dance and the absorption of musicality evident through a comparison of the drawing from composer Maurice Emmanuel's book and the photograph of Isadora Duncan's dance are evidence of the "aesthetic cross-breeding" that features in the story of modernism retold in Jed Rasula's *History of a Shiver* (42).

37. Duncan, *My Life*, 306. "Nietzsche created the dancing philosopher" is another iteration (Duncan, "I See America Dancing," 49).

38. Nietzsche, *Birth of Tragedy and the Case of Wagner*, 42.

39. Nietzsche, 51.

40. Duncan, *My Life*, 120.

41. Franko, *Dancing Modernism/Performing Politics*, 18.

42. Duncan, *My Life*, 116.

43. T. J. Smith, "Reception or Deception?," 89.

44. UP, 46.

45. CAMS Dossier 2 Letters: May to EP August 10, 1904; Catherine Abbé to

EP August, 18, 1904; and Courtlandt to EP August 27, 1904, all sent to Thonon-les-Bains hotels in Haute-Savoie, France.

46. Davidson, "Bayreuth Revisited," 255, writes about the performance.

47. UP, 105.

48. UP, 105.

49. BLJD C2 2920 Nos. 323–24 (Papadaki, 15) Letter EP to NCB [1901, Bar Harbor].

50. UP, 105–6.

51. Gosse, *Life of Algernon Charles Swinburne*, 110.

52. Swinburne's Wagnerian affinities are elaborated in Sypher's "Swinburne and Wagner," and McGann, "Wagner, Baudelaire, Swinburne."

53. Swinburne's identification with Sappho has been debated since Zonana, "Swinburne's Sappho," argued that his adoption of Sappho as Muse recovers a suppressed "female creativity and female sexuality" (48). As mentioned in chapter 2, Swinburne is credited for introducing to England the "lesbian" Sappho he discovered in Baudelaire.

54. "What Is Doing in Society," *New York Times*, July 22, 1905, 7, reports that "Dr. Robert Abbé, Mrs. Abbé, and the latter's children, Miss Eva Palmer and Cortlandt [*sic*] Palmer, have arrived at their Bar Harbor cottage, Brookend."

55. Although "Archbold Cottage" burned down in Bar Harbor's great fire of October 21, 1927, surviving pictures confirm this description. See Bryan et al., *Maine Cottages*, 210–11, quoting from the *Bar Harbor Record*.

56. CAMS Dossier 1 Letter EP to "Natalie my beloved" [1905].

57. See CAMS Dossier 1 Letter Constant Lounsbery to EP September 19, 1904, sent from the Adirondack Mountains Loon Lake House, Loon Lake, New York, to 16 W. Forty-Seventh Street, New York.

58. UP, 45. See Albright, *Traces of Light*, 150, and Dorf, "Dancing Greek Antiquity in Private and Public," 9, for discussions of this performance.

59. BLJD C2 2920 (Papadaki, 127) Nos. 248–49 [September 1905], Brook End [to Neuilly].

60. See Pluggé, *History of Greek Play Production in American Colleges and Universities from 1881 to 1936*, on the 1889 Smith College *Electra* (the first Greek play revived at a women's college): "The members of the chorus . . . as a whole seem to have reacted in a more or less formalized manner to the dramatic situations presented on the stage. . . . The movements of the dance were described as slow and solemn, consisting chiefly of body swaying, without much change in position. Gesture and facial expression constitute the important elements of this dance" (97–98).

61. Pluggé, 99.

62. Daly, "Natural Body," 290.

63. UP, 47.

64. BLJD C2 2920 Nos. 248–49.

65. UP, 93.

66. UP, 172.

67. The website "Dumbarton Oaks" gives this history.

68. CAMS Dossier 2 Letter EP to NCB undated.

69. CAMS Dossier 2 Letter NCB to EP "Tuesday" [1905]. The quotes from Barney in this paragraph are all from this letter.

70. Michelakis, "Theater Festivals," 152.

71. Papadaki, 85n1.

72. UP, 44.

73. AS Chronography, 103.

74. AS Chronography, 111.

75. AS Chronography, 119.

76. Angelos Sikelianos, Δελφικός λόγος: Αρχά των αρίστων (1927).

77. Angelos Sikelianos and Reed, *Delphic Word* (1928). *Upward Panic* gives a different time line. Eva has Sikelianos speak about the Delphic Idea the morning after their first meeting in August 1906 (63). She quotes him holding forth on both Delphi and drama as a "bridge" or "causeway" to "spiritual understanding" (65–66). I have not found independent evidence that Sikelianos developed a Delphic vision before 1919 or aligned it with the performance of theater before George Cram Cook inaugurated his "Delphic Players" in the fall of 1923.

78. AS Chronography, 71, my translation.

79. AS Chronography, 99.

80. Hirst, "Christ and the Poetic Ego in the Poetry of Palamas, Sikelianos, and Elytis," 245.

81. Hirst, 249.

82. AS Chronography, 113.

83. H. D. and Tryphonopoulos, *Magic Ring*, 247.

84. Collecott, *H. D. and Sapphic Modernism*, 131.

85. Gregory, *H. D. and Hellenism*, 36.

86. Preston, *Modernism's Mythic Pose*, 191.

87. Sword, *Engendering Inspiration*, 164.

88. Sword, 164, quoting H. D.'s *Magic Ring*.

89. Ioannidou, "Toward a National *Heterotopia*," states this in absolute terms: "Sikelianos was not interested in the revival of Greek drama" (393). L. Papadaki, *Το εφηβικό πρότυπο και η Δελφική Προσπάθεια του Άγγελου Σικελιανού*, 82–90, maps out stages in the evolution of the Delphic Idea from 1921 to 1930, suggesting that the revival of ancient drama is almost an afterthought, explained after the fact in Sikelianos's "Plan général du mouvement delphique" in 1930.

90. Glaspell, *Road to the Temple*, 392.

91. Chansky, *Composing Ourselves*, 42.

92. Glaspell, *Road to the Temple*, 241.

93. Glaspell, 311.

94. Cook, *My Road to India*, 18.

95. Glaspell mentions visiting Sykia (without naming Angelos or Eva) to explain how she acquired Theodora, an Asia Minor refugee working in the household who became her "servant" (*Road to the Temple*, 37). Eva mentions George Cram Cook as the lost translator of Angelos's poetry (UP, 71). The silence of each woman about the other is resounding.

96. Glaspell, *Road to the Temple*, 349.

97. Glaspell, 388.

98. Glaspell, 332.

99. Glaspell, 388.

100. Glaspell, 266.

101. Hains, "Greek Plays in America," 25. At the opening of his paper, which he prepared as a report on the "history of the rendition of Greek plays in American" (39) read at the Classical Association of the Midwest and South (CAMWS) in 1910, Hains states that he sent out queries "to considerably more than a hundred institutions" to collect reliable data "in regard to every Greek and Latin play that has been staged in the United States" (24), and he found that the practice in American institutions of higher learning was unexpectedly widespread. See Fisher, "Theater Department at Wabash College," for a longer view of the place of Greek drama in staged performances at one midwestern American college.

102. Glaspell, *Road to the Temple*, 409.

103. Glaspell, 261. Interest in "music composed in imitation of ancient Greek modal scales" became a feature of several American college productions of Greek drama from 1907 to 1919, beginning with the 1907 revival of *Iphigenia at Taurus* at the University of Iowa (where Cook taught from 1895 to 1899), for which modal music deemed to be Greek was composed (Pluggé, *History of Greek Play Production in American Colleges and Universities from 1881 to 1936*, 92).

104. Ben-Zvi, "George Cram Cook's *Road to the Temple*, 97–101, 110–12, draws lines of comparison between Cook and Isadora Duncan and Eva Sikelianos respectively.

105. Glaspell, *Road to the Temple*, 246.

106. Chansky, *Composing Ourselves*, 26.

107. Glaspell, *Road to the Temple*, 407.

108. Glaspell, 246.

109. Glaspell, chap. 49, "The Play Begins," describes the steps in Cook's collaboration with villagers in Delphi.

110. Glaspell, 405.

111. E. Papadaki, "Αναζητώντας μια ελληνική ευτοπία," 91–93, and Vogeikoff-Brogan, "'Going Native,' detail this sequence of events.

112. "Greek Drama to Be Given Again at Ancient Delphi," *New York Times*, October 11, 1925, X8.

113. "Modern Greeks to Evoke Life of Classic Times," *New York Times*, January 16, 1927, X20. Nilla Cook, who had a part in the 1927 festival, wrote that the athletic games were dedicated to her father (*My Road to India*, 60).

114. UP, 113.

115. UP, 113–14.

116. Glytzouris, "Δελφικές Γιορτές," 152–57, gives a fuller account of Raftopoulou's role and the process of composition on the basis of her drawings.

117. UP, 182.

118. I remind readers of Eva's ambivalence to decadence in Barney's circle, discussed in chapter 1.

119. Many of Eva's contemporaries developed the sense that the ancient Greeks were "unimaginably different" (MacNeice, *Autumn Journal*, 39) from accepted notions of them, particularly those received "within the prescribed boundaries of doctrinal Christianity" (Fiske, *Heretical Hellenism*, 152). Among them were anthropologists, art historians, dancers, philosophers, poets and writers, and psychia-

trists. They joined archaeologists in excavating beneath the classical surface to reach the darker, blinder strata (Dodds's concern in *Greeks and the Irrational*) and, by a sleight of hand, hailed prehistoric Greece as "protomodern" (Gere, *Knossos and the Prophets of Modernism*, 11). Theirs was a renewal of pagan antiquity seized from the tempering effects of Christianity.

120. Buschor, *Greek Vase-Painting*, 63.

121. Buschor, 155.

122. See Jeffreys, *Reframing Decadence*, for a marvelous exploration of the painterly and literary tradition of decadence in dialogue with Hellenistic and Roman sources.

123. Van Steen, "Myth, Mystique, Nietzsche and the 'Cultic Milieu' of the Delphic Festivals, 1927 and 1930," 55. Dimitris Plantzos points to the "influence of body-fascist ideals" in the Delphic Games, particularly in the display of half-naked men in ancient army gear who revived war dances in the ancient stadium ("Glory That Was Not," 162–63).

124. Griffin, "Modernity, Modernism, and Fascism," 10.

125. Griffin, 19.

126. Griffin, 19.

127. Jusdanis, *Necessary Nation*, chap. 1, works to find the line distinguishing many forms of nationalism from extreme right-wing expressions of collective unity such as fascism.

128. See Glytzouris, "'Resurrecting' Ancient Bodies," 87.

129. Witt, *Search for Modern Tragedy*, x.

130. BMHA 189/33 Copy of letter EPS to Mary Hambidge September 4 [1935], 63 Belvedere Road, Montreal (care Mrs. H. I. Rutherford), to Greenwich, CT: "I am not, au fond, a pacifist, I mean the following: that if the issues involved could ever be clarified so that one could live up the true principles of education, justice and economy and the people who really represent these things on one side, and all the morons on the other, headed by Mussolini and Hitler—I think my instinct would certainly be to fight."

131. BMHA 189/29 Letter Khorshed Naoroji to EP September 16, 1925, Bombay to Athens. All the quotations in this paragraph are from this letter.

132. Prins, *Ladies' Greek*, chap. 2.

133. UP, 109.

134. Glytzouris, "'Resurrecting' Ancient Bodies," 91. Copies of the poses with the matching lines from *Prometheus Bound* exist in CAMS dossier 7.

135. UP, 183.

136. More photographs of Eva exist showing this contraction, for example, Nelly Sougioutzoglou-Seraidare's photo of "Eva Sikelianou in Delphi," found on the *Art Topos* website ("Nelly Sougioutzoglou-Seraidare: Eva Sikelianou in Delphi").

137. UP, 182.

138. UP, 182. A series of photographs appearing in Eleni Sikelianos, "Lefevre-Sikelianos-Waldman Tree and the Imaginative Utopian Attempt," illustrate the angularity of movements in the choreography of *Prometheus Bound*.

139. UP, 168.

140. UP, 150.

141. UP, 114–15.

142. UP, 115.

143. On July 25, 1937, Eva wrote to her friend Vliamo Nikolaidis, "The question of how I might save the houses at Delphi and Sykia . . . tormented me" every day from the moment of the first festival's end (AS-EP Letters, 288).

144. UP, 118. The quotation, capturing the words of "Gabriel Boissy, Editor-in-chief . . . and others," more or less summarizes the message of much of the international coverage.

145. Terry, *Ted Shawn, the Father of American Dance*, 13. Shawn encouraged his students to call him "Papa," according to the *Jacob's Pillow* website, http://www.jacobspillow.org/exhibits-archives/ted-shawn, accessed December 20, 2016.

146. See Jerome Robbins Dance Division, NYPL, Image ID DEN_0387V "Ruth St. Denis, Ted Shawn, and company in Bacchanale from the Greek section of the Greek pageant, San Diego performance" (1916), http://digitalgallery.nypl.org/, accessed December 20, 2016.

147. See Jerome Robbins Dance Division, NYPL, Images ID DEN_0444V through DEN_0448V "Ruth St. Denis in From a Grecian Vase, Orpheum," from the Orpheum vaudeville act based on the Greek Theatre pageant of 1916.

148. See Jerome Robbins Dance Division, NYPL, Images ID: DEN_1521V through DEN_1526V "Ted Shawn in Death of Adonis."

149. JRDD-NYPL-TS Box 65, Folder 27, Ted Shawn, "Dancing and Nudity."

150. Michelakis, "Dancing with Prometheus," 225.

151. Hanna, "Patterns of Dominance," 36, my emphasis.

152. Murray, *Classical Tradition in Poetry*, chap. 2, treats the subject of "Molpê" just eight years before Shawn choreographed *Kinetic Molpai*.

153. JRDD-NYPL-TS Box 89 Folder 2 "Programs 1930–1939" Program notes for *Ted Shawn's Men Dancers: O! Libertad: An American Saga in Three Acts*, performed February 22, 1939, at State Teachers College, Millersville, Pennsylvania.

154. See Foulkes, *Modern Bodies*, 99–101, for a detailed description of the *Kinetic Molpai*.

155. JRDD-NYPL-TS Program notes for *Ted Shawn's Men Dancers: O! Libertad*.

156. Slosberg, "Oracle of Delphi," 8, identifies Katherine Drier's Stonington roots.

157. UP, 201.

158. UP, chap. 25, "Ted Shawn" (199–214), Shawn's extant correspondence with Eva in BMHA, and JRDD-NYPL-TS contain references to costumes from the 1927 *Prometheus Bound* that Eva loaned to Shawn and new costumes that Eva designed and wove for *Kinetic Molpai* and for *Isaiah 52:1*.

159. M.E.M., "Costume in Revivals of Greek Drama," 134.

160. UP, 203.

161. BMHA 189/37 Letter EPS to Katherine Dreier May 17 [1939].

162. Young, *Killinger Collection*, 24.

163. UP, 204, mentions the event.

164. Norton Owen helped me to track down these resources in the Jacob's Pillow Archives and gave me the equipment to piece together the visual and sound

record. His essay "Ted Shawn's Moving Images" helped me to read the archived film and sound files.

165. Kassing, *History of Dance*, 187.

166. See Van Steen, " 'World's a Circular Stage,' " for a rich analysis of Eva's use of the amphitheatrical configuration.

167. UP, 223.

168. BMHA 189/37 Letter Ted Shawn to EPS July 10, 1939: "tomorrow afternoon I am going to have a session of photographs at the Nashville Parthenon—the head of the Park Board having given orders the building is to remain closed while I am using it! And I will either bring or send the results."

169. See the photograph "Paul Taylor and Martha Graham performing in Graham's 'Clytemnestra' in 1960," *New York Times*, "From the Archives: Martha Graham and Her Dancers," http://www.nytimes.com/slideshow/2016/04/01/arts /dance/from-the-archives-martha-graham-and-her-dancers/s/03GRAHAMSS -slide-9L2J.html?_r=0, accessed December 26, 2016.

170. Jowitt, "Martha Graham's *Clytemnestra* Lives to Kill Again."

171. Malnig et al. call the movements of Clytemnestra "very archaic" ("Clytemnestra and the Dance Dramas of Martha Graham," 8), and Graham wrote that her path to making dances followed "ancestral footprints" (*Blood Memory*, 13, 14). "Prehistoric" is my term to underscore Graham's efforts to construct a dance language representing myths from a woman's point of view *before* men canonized their versions of the stories. See Yaari, "Myth into Dance," on Graham's interpretation of Greek myth and tragedy.

172. M.E.M., "Costume in Revivals of Greek Drama," 135.

173. On Graham as a "brilliant archaeologist," see Deborah Jowitt, "The Monumental Martha," *New York Times*, April 29, 1973, 125.

174. Quoted in Glaspell, *Road to the Temple*, 351.

175. Trigger, "Alternative Archaeologies," 357.

176. Hamilakis, "Fragments of Modernity and the Archaeologies of the Future," 56.

177. Mahn, "Romance in Ruins," states that early women ethnographers in Greece "used their oblique purchase of the classics to figure new kinds of national and sexual identities" and so discovered "another access point to a larger engagement with the difficulty of not knowing Greek" (17).

178. B. Smith, *Gender of History*, 171–72. Prins, *Ladies' Greek*, 19, uses Smith's observation to make a related point about Jane Harrison's scholarship.

CHAPTER 5: WRITING

1. AS Chronography, 116, my emphasis. The attribution of full credit for the festivals to Angelos and concomitant erasure of Eva happened with the festival of 1930. See for example, "The Delphic Festivals Begin," *New York Times*, May 2, 1930, 8, which credited the theatrical performances' "faithfulness to type in acting and costume . . . to 20 years of study by Angelo Sikelianos."

2. Angelos Sikelianos, "Το πρόβλημα της μουσικής και του χορού στο αρχαίο δράμα," 309.

3. UP, 144–45.

4. BMHA 189/33 Letter Mrs. J. Chadwick-Collins to EPS July 13, 1935, Bryn Mawr to Saratoga Springs, NY, shows that Eva was given room and board in the deanery. The *Bacchae* at Bryn Mawr ran a deficit of $603.50. Prins, *Ladies' Greek*, chap. 5, writes extensively about Eva's work translating the play into movement in the context of the two women's college performances.

5. BMHA 189/31 Letter Ed Perkins to Mrs. Sikelianos. Perkins, an agent who worked for the Los Angeles Greek Theatre in 1933, invited Eva to create a Greek drama school in the theater, then rescinded the offer, suggesting that she would do better to look to "eastern colleges, such as Bryn Mawr or Smith," for interest in staging Greek drama.

6. BMHA 189/31 Letter May Palmer to EPS December 9, 1933, Lausanne to New York City.

7. BMHA 189/39 Letter EPS to May Palmer October 24, 1941, Rabun Gap to Lausanne. Eva retrieved her letters to May upon May's death.

8. BLJD C2 2920 Nos. 120–23 (Papadaki, 156) Letter EPS to NCB May 8, 1939, from Greenwich, CT, to Plaza Hotel, New York City.

9. Foucault, "Ethics of the Concern for Self as a Practice of Freedom," 282. I acknowledge here the influence of Halperin, *St. Foucault*, on my reading of Eva's ongoing striving to transform herself.

10. UP, 1.

11. UP, 233–34.

12. Anton does not report the existence of these variant endings. In his appendix to the "Introduction," subtitled "The Manuscript of *Upward Panic*," he refers to "an outline of Eva's plan for an autobiography . . . in the Library of Performing Arts, Dance Collection at the New York Public Library," in which she "had divided the book into two major parts, preceded by a Preface, Part I: *Autobiographical*, and Part II: *Music*" (UP, xxi). But he acknowledges only *one* version of the manuscript in two copies ("A1 and A2," UP, xxii) in the BMHA.

13. She writes in a letter to an unidentified correspondent who must have been encouraging her to write a memoir, "As a matter, I wrote such a book about ten years ago. About half of it was autobiographical, and then there seemed to me to be sort of commentaries on the first part" (CAMS Dossier 3 Folder 1, "Εύα Σικελιανού Upward Panic").

14. BMHA 189/39 Letter EPS to May October 24, 1941, Rabun Gap to Lausanne refers to her revision of the manuscript.

15. Anton makes this point: "Ultimately, *Upward Panic* is more the biography of an idea than the autobiography of a person, of an idea that swept the person in a steady course toward self-realization" (UP, xii).

16. BMHA 189/37 Letter James Putnam to EPS September 1, 1939, New York City to Lee, MA.

17. BMHA 189/36 Letter Lucy Donnelly to EPS December 5, 1938, Bryn Mawr, PA. See also SC MS 295 Letter EPS to Peggy Murray November 28, 1938, Greenwich, CT, to New York City.

18. BMHA 189/37 Letter Ellen D. Chater to EPS Undated notes on *Upward Panic*.

19. BMHA 189/39 Letter Elsa Barker to EP January 31, 1941, New York City to Eustis, FL. The emphasis is Barker's.

20. UP, 148.

21. See Prins, *Ladies' Greek*, 221–31, for a marvelous discussion of Eva's Smith and Bryn Mawr College productions.

22. UP, 229, quoting *Time*, March 17, 1941.

23. UP, 229.

24. UP, 41.

25. UP, 39.

26. UP, 142.

27. UP, 101.

28. BMHA 189/39 Letter EPS to May Palmer October 24, 1941, Rabun Gap to Lausanne.

29. *Hamlet* 5.2.232–34: "We defy augury. There's a special providence in the fall of a sparrow. If it be now, tis not to come; if it be not to come, it will be now; if it be not now, yet it will come: the readiness is all."

30. BLJD C2 2920 Nos. 120–23 (Papadaki, 157) Letter EPS to NCB March 27, 1940, Eustis, FL, to Paris. Eva is responding to a most tender, loving letter from NCB (Papadaki, 164).

31. OM, 40.

32. Alvic, *Weavers of the Southern Highlands*, 100.

33. BMHA 189/29 Incoming Correspondence 1925 Mary Hambidge to EPS November 7, 1925, Greenwich, CT, to Serifou Street, Athens.

34. BMHA 189/29 Mary Hambidge to EPS November 7, 1925.

35. BMHA 189/31 Letter May Palmer to EPS "Nov. 6 [1933]" Beau-Rivage-Palace Lausanne to Greenwich, CT.

36. BMHA 189/31 Letter May Palmer to EPS, Postmarked December 13, 1933, Beau-Rivage-Palace Lausanne to Greenwich, CT.

37. SC 1934 Box 2054 folder 1, "The Bacchae" playbill back page credits Jane Henle '34, Mrs. Hudson, and Kay McDermott as "assistants in weaving" and Menalkas Duncan for designing and making the fawn skins but not Mary Hambidge.

38. UP, 208.

39. UP, 207.

40. *Evzones* are special elites of the Greek armed forces, thus named for their well-girt (ευ-ζων-, *eu-zone*), kilt-like costume that has evolved from the distinctive dress of Greek revolutionary fighters.

41. BMHA 189/39 Letter Tantine to EPS February 11, 1941. "Tantine" is Josephine MacLeod, whom Eva knew as a disciple of Swami Vivekananda through her circle of friends inspired by American transcendentalism and other Western esoteric movements.

42. BMHA 189/39 Letter Barton Mumaw to EPS March 23, 1941.

43. BMHA 189/39 Letter Barton Mumaw to EPS December 18, 1941.

44. UP, 202.

45. UP, 211–12.

46. UP, 213.

47. UP, 213.

48. UP, 213–14.

49. BMHA 189/39 Letter Ted Shawn to EPS April 12, 1941, Hotel Sevilla, 117 W. Fifty-Eighth Street, New York City to Eustis, FL.

50. JRDD-NYPL-TS Letter EPS to Ted Shawn, April 15, 1941, Eustis. A copy of the letter is in BMHA 189/39.

51. BMHA 189/39 Letter Ted Shawn to EPS July 3, 1941, Jacob's Pillow to Rabun Gap "c/o Mrs. Hambidge."

52. BMHA 189/39 Letter Ted Shawn to EPS August 16, 1941.

53. BMHA 189/39 Letter Ted Shawn to EPS July 3, 1941.

54. BMHA 189/39 Letter Elsa Barker to EPS April 17, 1943, New York City to Rabun Gap.

55. BMHA 189/39 Letter Elsa Barker to EPS April 17, 1943.

56. BMHA 189/39 Letter Mary Hambidge to EPS "Thursday [1942]" Rabun Gap to New York [just after her sister May Palmer's death].

57. BMHA 193/32 No. 918 Telegram EPS to AS March 15, 1937, New York City to Elpidos 4, Athens, translated from French.

58. BMHA 193/32 No. 922 Letter EPS to AS July 27, 1937, 108 E. Seventeenth Street, New York City.

59. BMHA 193/32 No. 929 Telegram EPS to AS April 5, 1938, sent to 23 Dionysiou Areopagytou.

60. BMHA 193/32 Telegram EPS to AS November 9, 1940 Eustis, FL, to 4 Elpidos, Athinai.

61. BMHA 193/32 Number 944 Letter EPS to AS November 10, 1940, Eustis, FL.

62. AS-EP Letters, 163–67 Letter AS to EPS May 12, 1939, Athens.

63. JRDD-NYPL-TS Letter EPS to Ted Shawn January 18, 1945, reports that Eva read in one of "the routine telegrams from Athens published every day in the Greek National Herald" an item stating that "Sikelianos and Kazantzakis had been chosen for a special diplomatic mission in Washington." The next telegram reported that "Sikelianos was too ill to travel"; then another that "his health was improving. Since then no more news about him. This, in fact, is the only personal news of him that has come through since the beginning of the German occupation."

64. BMHA 189/13 Autobiography Part B version 2 chap. 20, 235–36.

65. UP, 193.

66. UP, 79.

67. UP, 46.

68. UP, 146.

69. UP, 233.

70. UP, 229.

71. UP, 229.

72. UP, 234.

73. UP, 233.

74. UP, 234.

75. UP, 233.

76. UP, 235.

77. She is quoting from the open letter of Georgios Vlachos (Γ. Α. Βλάχος) to Adolf Hitler, published in the Greek newspaper *Καθημερινή*, March 8, 1941.

78. This is the epitaph by Simonides for the Spartan dead (Diel no. 92), and it was inscribed on the tomb at Thermopylai. The translation is "attributed to various hands" and has become standard. See Vance, "Classics and Modern War," 594.

79. UP, 235.

80. UP, 234.

81. Examples of stories and cartoons in the popular media that portray the Greek economy as tragic are too numerous to cite. Hanink, *Classical Debt*, tracks a number of them in chaps. 6 and 7, "Classical Debt in Crisis" and "We Are All Greeks?"

82. BMHA 189/39 Letter Elsa Barker to EPS April 17, 1943, from New York City.

83. BMHA 189/39 Telegram Courtlandt Palmer to EPS December 27, 1941: "My darling. May died suddenly. Today I am desolate."

84. BMHA 189/39 Letter Theodore M. Purdy J., Associate Editor, to EPS May 1942?

85. "Homer W. Davis, 88; Ex-Greek College Chief," *New York Times*, August 31, 1984, D14. Athens College is the premier preparatory school in Greece, founded by Emmanuel Benakis.

86. Mazower, *Inside Hitler's Greece*, 47.

87. BMHA 189/39 Letter Homer W. Davis to EPS July 18, 1942, Greek War Relief Association Inc., 730 Fifth Avenue, New York City, to Eustis, FL, forwarded to Rabun Gap then to the Stanhope Hotel, New York City.

88. BMHA 189/9 Pamphlet *What Is Great Theatre? A Gift to the Greek War Relief Effort from Eva Sikelianou*, twenty-four-page, 4 1/4" × 16 1/2" booklet. Eva sent the publication and a cover letter to friends and acquaintances.

89. BMHA 189/39 Letter Edith Hamilton to EPS March 9, 1943, from 133 E. Seventieth Street, New York City, to Rabun Gap.

90. BMHA 189/39 Letter Edith Hamilton to EPS March 9, 1943: "I wish you would write more." BMHA 189/40 Letter Edith Hamilton to EPS October 20, 1944: "And as I read—and reread—what you say, I wonder all over again why you do not write—why you—I will not say, waste yourself on me; you stimulate me, excite my mind, but why do you not think of the audience you might have. I *wish* you would."

91. BMHA 189/9 Article "For Greek War Relief," April 1943 from Columbia, SC, page 6 (marked 5) of six typed manuscript pages.

92. BMHA 189/40 Copy of letter EPS to N. J. Cassavetas September 21, 1944.

93. BMHA 189/39 Letter Edith Hamilton to EPS March 9, 1943.

94. Multiple sources give this quote without an original published citation. See, for example, Charmon, "Hugh Dalton," 61.

95. Aristoula Ellinoudi (Αριστούλα Ελληνούδη), "ΑΓΓΕΛΟΣ ΣΙΚΕΛΙΑΝΟΣ: ᾽Πάντα ανοιχτά, πάντα άγρυπνα τα μάτια᾽ της ποίησής του 50 χρόνια από το θάνατό του, 117 από τη γέννησή του," *Ριζοσπάστης*, Sunday, June 17, 2001, 4. AS Chronography, 207, states that he joined EAM in November 1941.

96. A death notice was posted outside Eleftheroudakis bookshop. See Mazower, *Inside Hitler's Greece*, 117.

97. Rigopoulos, *Secret War/Μυστικός Πόλεμος*, 100.

98. Rigopoulos, 101. See also Mazower, *Inside Hitler's Greece*, 117–18.

99. Rigopoulos, *Secret War/Μυστικός Πόλεμος*, 90, reports on an earlier demonstration of October 28, 1942, the second anniversary of the failed Italian invasion of Greece. The demonstration was orchestrated throughout Athens in defiance of German and Italian forces stationed across the city by the Axis occupiers.

100. George Seferis Nobel speech, http://www.nobelprize.org/nobel_prizes /literature/laureates/1963/seferis-lecture.html, accessed June 22, 2018.

101. See Moskos, *Greek Americans*, 84–85.

102. Eva Sikelianos, "Poet Angelos Sikelianos," 32.

103. BMHA 189/40 Letter Demetrios Michalaros to EPS January 13, 1944, from 919 Wellington Street, Chicago, to EPS in Rabun Gap.

104. Eva Sikelianos, "Poet Angelos Sikelianos," 32.

105. Sikelianos, 24.

106. Sikelianos, 23.

107. Sikelianos, 24.

108. Sikelianos, 23, my emphasis.

109. Sikelianos, 26.

110. BMHA 189/39 Letter Elsa Barker to EPS July 20, 1943, from New York City to EPS in Rabun Gap: "I was v. glad to learn that Angelo was the principal speaker at the funeral of Palamas, b/c it means that he was alright at the time."

111. BMHA 189/39 Copy of typed manuscript, English translation of EAM statement issued on September 15, 1943, and published in the *Greek-American Tribune* on December 3, 1943.

112. Panourgiá, *Dangerous Citizens*, 61.

113. Panourgiá, *Dangerous Citizens* supplementary website, chap. 2, "1936–1944," https://dangerouscitizens.columbia.edu/1936-1944/epitaphios/1/index .html, accessed June 22, 2018.

114. BMHA 189/40 Letter George Seferis to EPS March 22, 1944, Cairo, Egypt. All the quotes below are from this letter.

115. AS Chronography 146–47. Seferis visited Angelos at Delphi while serving as the guide for the French politician Édouard Herriot, who was three times prime minister of France and a leader in the center-left Radical Party. After Eva left Greece, he and Angelos traveled in the same literary circles. He states in his letter that he regretted never having met her.

116. A note opposite the title page of the Athens 1942 publication states this, and Seferis repeats it in his letter to Eva.

117. Angelos Sikelianos and Spyros Vassiliou, *Ακριτικά*, note on unnumbered page after the last poem of the Cairo 1944 publication.

118. The Cairo edition looks like a faithful copy of the manuscript, as if made by no intervening hand, while the proofs show Seferis's detailed notes to the printer. Its introduction, signed "Οι Εκδότες" (the publishers), does not acknowledge Seferis as its author, even though his notes show that he wrote it.

119. Beaton, *George Seferis*: 227–28; 458–59n34.

120. BMHA 189/50 Draft of letter EPS to Predraic Colum December 1950.

121. Angelos Sikelianos and Nord, *Akritan Songs*, 4–5.

122. This was the opinion of F. W. Bradley, dean of University of South Carolina,

who wrote to Eva upon receiving a copy of the *Akritan Songs* in June 1944. BMHA 189/40 Letter F. W. Bradley to EPS.

123. BMHA 189/40 Letter Sima to EPS April 11, 1944, refers to a party given by Eva and Helen (Angelos's sister Eleni Sikelianos?).

124. BMHA 189/40 Letter Peggy Murray to EPS, June 20, 1944: "Through the eyes of the poet we can see Greece as a stalwart comrade in the fight for human freedom. Through his eyes also we can see them as a people meriting the acclaim of the world for their stout resistance"; Letter Miss Irma Richter to EPS June 21, 1944, thanks Eva for party at Stanhope and "two Akritan songs."

125. Gennadius Library, Papers of George Seferis, Letter EPS to Seferis August 14, 1944.

126. Gennadius Library, Papers of George Seferis, Letter EPS to Seferis August 14, 1944.

127. BMHA 189/50 Draft of Letter EPS to Robert T. Leicester, Executive Secretary of the Win the Peace Conference, January 24, 1946.

128. "One Woman's Drive for the Greeks," *PM*, January 12, 1945, 13.

129. BMHA 189/42 Letterhead of the Greek American Council [1946–47] shows the address 152 W. Forty-Second Street, New York City, and the officers: President Eva Sikelianos; Treasurer Stephen Leondopoulos; Secretary Michael Mands (Mandelakis); Vice Presidents Dr. George Karaflos, Costas N. Laskaris, Dr. L. S. Stavrianos. The group of Americans was formed in 1945 to lobby against American acquiescence to British actions in Greece and eventually American aid to the right-wing Greek government.

130. BMHA 189/41 Letter Bartley C. Crum, Jo Davidson, Julius Conspark, and Paul Robeson to EPS November 20, 1945.

131. BMHA 189/40 Draft of letter EPS "on the Greek situation" September 9, 1944. The quotations in this paragraph is from this letter.

132. BLJD NCB 12 9995 Nos. 230–34 Letter NCB to EP January 8, 1907, Paris to c/o Jean Siciliani Ile de St. Maure (les Ionienne), Greece.

133. BMHA 189/50 Draft of Letter EPS to Edith Hamilton December 1, 1950.

134. Elizabeth Young, "Abundant Life Plan Unfolded by Poet's Wife," *Washington Post*, January 30, 1935, 13.

135. BMHA 189/42 Copy of letter EPS to Robert T. Leicester, Executive Secretary of Win the Peace Conference, January 24, 1946.

136. Voglis, *Becoming a Subject*, 53.

137. Mazower, "Three Forms of Political Justice, 31.

138. Committee on Un-American Activities, "Report of the Communist 'Peace' Offensive," 106, 108, 112, appendix 5.

139. Vogli, "Making of Greece Abroad," 25.

140. BMHA 189/50 Draft of letter EP to Anne G. Antoniades July 25, 1951.

141. Langer, *Romaine Brooks*, chap. 8, pieces together the events.

142. BLJD NCB 12 9995 Nos. 124–25 (Papadaki, 158) Letter EPS to NCB November 28, 1947, from 1088 Park Avenue, New York City, to Studio House, 2306 Massachusetts Avenue, Washington, DC.

143. BMHA 189/50 Draft of letter EPS to Courtlandt October 22 [1950]. The idea comes to her in the early 1940s. She mentions it to Edith Hamilton in 1944, and she brings it up again to Eleanor Roosevelt at the time when she is approached

by Antoniades in 1950 (BMHA 189/50 Draft of letter EPS to Roosevelt, November 19, 1950).

144. BMHA 189/14 "Επιστροφή στην Ελλάδα" in Greek, and "Return to Greece" in English, undated.

145. BMHA 189/50 Draft of letter EPS to Edith Hamilton, January 17, 1951.

146. BMHA 189/50 Draft of letter EPS to Edith Hamilton, December 1, 1950.

147. BMHA 189/50 Draft of letter EPS to Anne Antoniades, May 1, 1951.

148. BMHA 189/45 Letter Courtlandt to EPS, July 3, 1951.

149. BMHA 189/3 Will of Courtlandt Palmer, 4.

150. CAMS Dossier 6 Letter EP to Titsa Chrysochoidou dated January 23, 1952, states, "Κοιμάμαι και ξυπνώ με αυτήν την θεία σκέψη του: μια έκδοση πολυτελή,—σε πολλά αντίτυπα, και σε χαμηλή τιμή, για να μπορέσουν να την έχουν δική τους όλη η νεολαία" (I go to sleep and wake up with this divine thought of his: a luxury edition of his work in multiple copies and at a good price, so that young people will be able to own it).

151. BMHA 189/45 Letter Elsa Barker to EPS October 30, 1951.

152. BMHA 189/8 "Letters to Anne Antoniades and executors of will after Eva's death, 1952–78, Letter Anne G. Antoniades to Richard N. Crockett, June 16, 1952.

153. BMHA 189/39 Excerpted letter Elsa Barker to EPS [1943].

154. BMHA 189/50 Draft of letter EP to Mary Hambidge April 17, 1952, 64 W. Twelfth Street, New York City.

155. BMHA 189/45 Letter Anne Antoniades to EPS May 11, 1951. A description exists also in BMHA 189/8 Letter Richard N. Crockett to Ann Antoniades June 16, 1952.

156. Lekakis, "Επιστροφή στους Δελφούς," 385.

157. BMHA 189/8 Letter Anne G. Antoniades to Richard N. Crockett June 16, 1952, Athens.

158. BMHA 189/8 Letter Anne G. Antoniades to Richard N. Crockett June 16, 1952, Athens.

159. Koula Pratsika, speaking on "Παρασκήνιο, η αναβίωση του αρχαίου δράματος," an episode of the program on ERT television dedicated to Angelos and Eva Palmer Sikelianos, directed by Dimitris Hatzopoulos, researched and directed by Lakis Papastathis, YouTube, http://www.youtube.com/watch?v=NKTa_NX6TJ4, accessed December 31, 2016, starting at 52 minutes.

EPILOGUE

1. BMHA 189/8 Letter Anne G. Antoniades to Richard N. Crockett June 25, 1952, Athens to New York City.

2. BMHA 189/8 Letter Anne G. Antoniades to Richard N. Crockett September 15, 1952.

3. BMHA 189/8 Letter Anne G. Antoniades to Richard N. Crockett September 15, 1952.

4. BMHA 189/8 Letter Richard N. Crockett to Anne G. Antoniades, October 14, 1952.

5. European Cultural Center of Delphi website "Chronology" section, gives most of the information in this paragraph.

6. European Cultural Center of Delphi website, "Chronology: 1975."

7. In 2017, the museum's contents were moved to the newly restored house of Angelos Sikelianos in Leukas.

8. Lalaki, "On the Social Construction of Hellenism."

9. Lalaki.

10. Anthony (Αντωνιάδη), "Ταξίδι στους Δελφούς," 11.

11. Anthony (Αντωνιάδη), 11.

12. Merlier, "Εύα Σικελιανού," 109.

13. Anthony (Αντωνιάδη), 11. Anthony made the point that Eva gave the event its artistic direction in addition to the financial backing.

14. Pratsika, "Αναμνήσεις από τις πρώτες Δελφικές Εορτές του 1927," 127.

15. The story is slightly more complicated than I suggest, but the point is that the festivals "precipitated the systematic use of ancient Greek theaters and the establishment of ancient drama festivals outside Athens" and directly influenced the creation of the Athens and Epidaurus festivals after the war. See Eleftheria Ioannidou, "Toward a National *Heterotopia*," 393.

16. I have in mind Nietzsche, Ralph Waldo Emerson, translator Benjamin Jowett, and Oscar Wilde—all people whom Eva read.

17. BLJD NCB 12 9995 Nos. 44–50 Letter NCB to EP December 20, 1901, Washington to New York City. See discussion in chapter 2.

18. CAMS Dossier 2 Letter NCB to EP March 1, 1901, Paris.

19. BLJD NCB 12 9995 Nos. 230–34 Letter NCB to EP January 8, 1907, Paris to c/o Jean Siciliani Ile de St. Maure (les Ionienne), Greece.

20. Nietzsche, "On the Uses and Disadvantages of History for Life," 76.

21. Kolocotroni, "Still Life," 12.

22. Settis, *Future of the Classical*, 91.

23. Calotychos, "Kazantzakis the Greek?," 189. Gourgouris, *Dream Nation*, and Van Steen, *Liberating Hellenism from the Ottoman Empire*, work through some of the knots in the intersection of Hellenism with Orientalism and colonialism. See especially Van Steen, 147–74.

24. Lambropoulos, "Afterword," makes this point in the closing commentary of the *Cultural Critique* issue "Classical Reception and the Political": "An interest in the Greeks of modernity would be a challenge for classical reception studies since they have been excluded from its tradition" (216). Exceptions are Greenwood, *Afro-Greeks*—especially chap. 2, "An Accidental Homer" (21–68), which considers how several neohellenist conceptions of Hellenism complements and are mutually enriched by reinvention of Greece in the Caribbean (58) in the twentieth century—and Hanink, *Classical Debt*, a critical reading of classical discourse in the modern world with careful attention to scholarship in modern Greek studies.

References

Abbreviations for Works by Eva Palmer Sikelianos

OM   Eva Palmer-Sikelianou, *Ωραία Ματαιοπονία: Τρεις διαλέξεις* [Beautiful futility: Three lectures], edited by Ritsa Fragou-Kikilia. Athens: Ellinika Grammata, 2005.

Papadaki   Lia Papadaki and Eva Palmer Sikelianos, *Γράμματα της Εύας Πάλμερ Σικελιανού στη Natalie Clifford Barney* [Letters of Eva Palmer Sikelianos to Natalie Clifford Barney]. Athens: Kastanioti, 1995.

UP   Eva Palmer-Sikelianos and John P. Anton. *Upward Panic: The Autobiography of Eva Palmer-Sikelianos.* Choreography and Dance Studies 4. Chur, Switzerland: Harwood Academic, 1993.

Primary Sources on Eva Palmer Sikelianos's Life (Archives, Libraries, Public Documents, and Books)

AHC MH-JH   Atlanta Historical Center, Mary Hambidge and Jay Hambidge Papers MSS 962.

APB   Smithsonian Museum Archives, Alice Pike Barney Papers.

AS Chronography   Bournazakis, Kostas. *Χρονογραφία Άγγελου Σικελιανού (1884 1951)* [Chronography of Angelos Sikelianos]. Athens: Ithaka, 2006.

AS-EP   Sikelianos, Angelos, and K. Bournazakis. *Γράμματα στην Εύα Πάλμερ Σικελιανού* [Letters to Eva Palmer Sikelianou]. Athens: Ikaros, 2008.

BLJD   Bibliothèque littéraire Jacques Doucet.

BLJD C2 2920   contains Eva Palmer's letters to Natalie Clifford Barney with the library's numbering of pages of correspondence.

BLJD NCB 12 9995   contains Natalie Clifford Barney's letters to Eva Palmer with the library's numbering of pages of correspondence.

BLJD NCB 2314   contains Renée Vivien's (Pauline Tarn's) letters to Eva Palmer.

BMCSC   Bryn Mawr College Special Collections.

BMHA 189   Benaki Museum Historical Archives, Eva Sikelianou Papers Accession No. 189. The finding aid for the papers is at https://www.benaki.gr/index.php?option=com_collectionitems&view=collectionitem&id=165355&Itemid=0&lang=el (accessed June 27, 2018).

BMHA193   Benaki Museum Historical Archives, Angelos Sikelianos Papers Archive No. 193.

CAMS   Center for Asia Minor Studies, Octave Merlier Archive, Eva Sikelianou Papers.

ELIA   Hellenic Literary and Historical Archive, Angelos and Eva Sikelianos Papers Archive No. 350.

EOS   Papageorgiou, K. Ath. (Παπαγεωργίου, Κ. Αθ.). "Αγγελος Σικελιανός–Εύα Πάλμερ–Σικελιανού: Δελφικές Εορτές" [Angelos Sikelianos–Eva Palmer-Sikelianou: Delphic Festivals]. Ειδικόν αφιέρωμα της επιθεωρήσεως ΗΩΣ [special issue of EOS]. Athens: Papademas, 1998, 2nd ed.

Gennadius Library, American School of Classical Studies in Athens.

Jacob's Pillow Archives.

JRDD-NYPL-TS   New York Public Library, Library of the Performing Arts, Jerome Robbins Dance Collection, Ted Shawn Papers.

KP   Konstantinos Psachos folder, Lillian Voudouri Library, Athens Music Hall.

MGAH   Princeton University Library, Mary Gwinn and Alfred Hodder Papers, CO450.

RD   M. Raymond Duncan et son école, Extraits de Presse 1912–1966, 2 vols., "Arts de spectacle," Richelieu site, Bibliothèques nationale de france, 4°SW 661 (1).

SC MS 295   Smith College, Sophia Smith Collection, Joan and Peggy Murray Papers.

SC 1934   Smith College, Sophia Smith Collection, Class of 1934 Records, 1927–94.

UW   Renée Lang—University of Wisconsin Special Collections, Renée Lang Papers.

VGY/MTP   Letters of Virginia Greer Yardley (1878–1971) compiled by Michael Taylor Prettyman (from the Princeton University, Firestone Library Rare Books and Special Collections, Mary Gwinn and Alfred Hodder Papers, C0450 and miscellaneous other sources, see above MGAH), copyright 2005.

Print and Electronic References Cited

Agard, Walter R. "Classics on the Midwest Frontier." Classical Journal 51 (1955): 103–10.

Albert, Nicole G. Lesbian Decadence: Representations in Art and Literature of Fin-de-Siècle France. Translated by N. Erber and W. A. Peniston. New York: Columbia University Press, 2016.

Albright, Ann Cooper. "The Tanagra Effect: Wrapping the Modern Body in the Folds of Ancient Greece." In The Ancient Dancer in the Modern World: Responses to Greek and Roman Dance, edited by Fiona Macintosh, 57–76. Oxford: Oxford University Press, 2010.

———. Traces of Light: Absence and Presence in the Work of Loie Fuller. Middletown, CT: Wesleyan University Press, 2007.

Alvic, Philis. Weavers of the Southern Highlands. Lexington: University Press of Kentucky, 2001.

Anastasiou, Grigorios G. (Αναστασίου, Γρηγόριος Γ.). "Η τρισύνθετος γλυκυφωνία της ψαλτικής κατά τριπλή εκδοχή των τριών μουσικοδιδασκάλων Ιωάννου Σακελλαρίδου, Κωνσταντίνου Ψάχου, Σίμωνος Καρά." In *Κωνσταντίνος Ψάχος: Ο μουσικός, ο λόγιος, Πρακτικά ημερίδας*, edited by Evangelos Karamanes, 29–48. Athens: Academy of Athens, 2013.

———. "Κωνσταντίνος Ψάχος." *Encyclopaedia of the Hellenic World, Constantinople*, 2008. http://www.ehw.gr/l.aspx?id=11060 (accessed June 8, 2018).

Anastasopoulou, Maria (Αναστασοπούλου, Μαρία). *Καλλιρρόη Παρρέν, η συνετή απόστολος της γυναικείας χειραφεσίας: Η ζωή και το έργο*. Irakleio: Vikelia Dimotiki Vivliothiki, 2013.

Anthony, Anne (Αντωνιάδη, Anne). "Ταξίδι στους Δελφούς." "Angelos Sikelianos–Eva Palmer-Sikelianou: Delphic Festivals," special issue of *EOS*, 1998, 8–15.

Antoniou, Michaela. "Acting Tragedy in Twentieth-Century Greece: The Case of *Electra* by Sophocles." Doctoral thesis, Goldsmiths, University of London, 2011. Goldsmiths Research Online. http://research.gold.ac.uk/6383/ (accessed December 13, 2016).

Appleton's Annual Cyclopaedia and Register of Important Events 12 (1888).

Arkoumanea, Louiza (Αρκουμανέα, Λουίζα). "Ο Αγαμέμνων στο ταψί, η Κασσάνδρα στο φορείο: πως μια τριανδρία σκηνοθετών θεμελίωσε στις αρχες του εικοστού αιώνα την παράδοση της σκηνοθεσίας της αρχαίας ελληνικής τραγωδίας στην Ελλάδα." *Το Βήμα*, September 26, 2010, http://www.tovima.gr/books-ideas /article/?aid=356845 (accessed June 9, 2018).

"The Arts and Crafts Movement." *Current Encyclopedia: A Monthly Record of Human Progress* 2: 1219–23. Cambridge, MA: Harvard University Modern Research Society.

Arwill-Nordbladh, Elisabeth. "Twelve Timely Tales: On Biographies of Pioneering Women." *Reviews in Anthropology* 37, nos. 2–3 (2008): 136–68.

Avrich, Paul. *The Haymarket Tragedy*. Princeton, NJ: Princeton University Press, 1986.

Banaji, Paige V. "Womanly Eloquence and Rhetorical Bodies: Regendering the Public Speaker through Physical Culture." In *Rhetoric, History, and Women's Oratorical Education: American Women Learn to Speak*, edited by David Gold and Catherine L. Hobbs, 154–76. New York: Routledge, 2013.

Bar Harbor Historical Society. "Building of the Arts, Bar Harbor, 1918." *Maine Memory Network*. https://www.mainememory.net/artifact/21194 (accessed June 21, 2018).

Barney, Natalie Clifford. *Equivoque*. In *Actes et entr'actes*, 49–81. Paris: E. Sansot, 1910.

———. *Quelques Portraits-Sonnets de Femmes*. Paris: Ollendorf, 1900.

———. *Souvenirs indiscrets*. Paris: Flammarion, 1960.

Barney, Natalie Clifford, and Anna Livia. *A Perilous Advantage: The Best of Natalie Clifford Barney*. Norwich, VT: New Victoria, 1992.

Bartholomot Bessou, Marie-Ange. *L'imaginaire du féminin dans l'oeuvre de Renée Vivien, de mémoires en mémoire*. Clermont-Ferrand: Presses Universitaires Blaise Pascal, 2004.

Beard, Mary. *The Invention of Jane Harrison*. Oxford: Oxford University Press, 2002.

Beard, Mary, and John Henderson. *Classics: A Very Short Introduction*. Oxford: Oxford University Press, 1995.

Beaton, Roderick. *George Seferis: Waiting for the Angel, a Biography*. New Haven, CT: Yale University Press, 2003.

Benstock, Shari. *Women of the Left Bank: Paris 1900–1940*. Austin: University of Texas Press, 1986.

Ben-Zvi, Linda. "George Cram Cook's *Road to the Temple*." In *Americans and the Experience of Delphi*, edited by Paul Lorenz and David Roessel, 89–117. Boston: Somerset Hall, 2013.

Berenson, Bernard, and Isabella Stewart Gardner. *The Letters of Bernard Berenson and Isabella Stewart Gardner, 1887–1924*. Edited and annotated by Rollin van Hadley. Boston: Northeastern University Press, 1987.

Billy, André. *L'Époque 1900: 1885–1905*. Paris: J. Tallandier, 1951.

Birdwood, George. "The Etymology and Meaning of 'Pleached.'" *Journal of the Society of Arts* 44 (1896): 282.

Blankley, Elyse. "Sappho's Daughters." Review of *The Amazon and the Page: Natalie Clifford Barney and Renée Vivien*. *Women's Review of Books* 5, nos. 10–11 (July 1988): 11. http://www.jstor.org/stable/4020345 (accessed June 21, 2018).

Boone, Laurel. "Bliss Carman's Pageants, Masques, and Essays, and the Genesis of Modern Dance." In *Bliss Carman: A Reappraisal*, edited by Gerald Lynch, 165–80. Ottawa: University of Ottawa Press, 1990.

Borchmeyer, Dieter. *Richard Wagner, Theory and Theatre*. Oxford: Oxford University Press, 1991.

Bournazakis, Kostas (Μπουρναζάκης, Κώστας). *Χρονογραφία Ἀγγέλου Σικελιανού (1884–1951)*. Athens: Ikaros, 2006.

———. "Έξι γράμματα της Πηνελόπης Σικελιανού." *Νέα Εστία* 158, no. 1781 (September 2005): 262–77.

Burke, John B. "Angelos Sikelianos and the Balkan Idea: A Forgotten Response." *Balkan Studies* 16, no. 2 (1975): 119–25.

Burlin, Natalie Curtis. *Songs of Ancient America: Three Pueblo Indian Corn-Grinding Songs from Laguna, New Mexico*. New York: G. Schirmer, 1905.

Buschor, Ernst. "Begriff und Methode der Archäologie" (1932). In *Algemeine Grundlagen der Archäologie: Begriff und Methode, Geschichte, Problem der Form, Schrifzeugnisse; Handbuch der Archäeologie*, by U. Haussmann, 3–10. Munich: C. H. Beck, 1969.

———. *Greek Vase-Painting*. Translated by G. C. Richards. New York: E. P. Dutton, 1921 (German edition, 1913).

Butler, Judith. *Gender Trouble: Feminism and the Subversion of Identity* (1990). New York: Routledge, 2011.

Bryan, John Morrill, Fred L. Savage, and Richard Cheek. *Maine Cottages: Fred L. Savage and the Architecture of Mount Desert*. New York: Princeton Architectural Press, 2005.

Calotychos, Vangelis. "Kazantzakis the Greek? Travel and Leisure, Hunger and Pathos, Localism and Cosmopolitanism in Nikos Kazantzakis's Journeying." *JMGS* Supplement to 28, no. 1 (May 2010): 189–217.

———. *Modern Greece: A Cultural Poetics*. Oxford: Berg, 2003.

Campbell, David Arthur. *Sappho and Alcaeus*. Cambridge, MA: Harvard University Press, 1982.

Carrara, Gillion. "Mariano Fortuny." In *The Berg Companion to Fashion*, edited by Valerie Steele, 351–52. London: Berg, 2010.

Carrell, Toni L. "Replication and Experimental Archaeology." *Historical Archaeology* 26, no. 4 (1992): 4–13.

Chalon, Jean. *Portrait of a Seductress: The World of Natalie Barney*. Translated by Carol Banko. New York: Crown, 1979.

Chansky, Dorothy. *Composing Ourselves: The Little Theatre Movement and the American Audience*. Theatre in the Americas. Carbondale: Southern Illinois University Press, 2004.

Charmon, Terry. "Hugh Dalton: Poland and SOE, 1940–1942." In *Special Operations Executive: A New Instrument of War*, edited by Mark Seaman, 61–69. New York: Routledge, 2006.

Chatzipantazis, Thodoros (Χατζηπανταζής, Θόδωρος). "Στη βαριά σκιά της Κλυταιμνήστρας: Το ελληνικό θέατρο σε αναζήτηση ενός νέου Αισχύλου." In *Πολυφωνία: Φιλολογικά μελετήματα αφιερωμένα στον Σ. Ν. Φιλιππίδη*, edited by Angela Kastrinaki, Alexis Politis, and Dimitris Polychronakis, 9–25. Irakleio: Crete University Press, 2009.

Chomenidis, Christos (Χωμενίδης, Χρήστος). *Ο φοίνικας*. Athens: Pataki, 2018.

Chrysanthos of Madytos. *Εισαγωγή εις το θεωρητικόν και πρακτικόν της Εκκλησιαστικής Μουσικής συνταχθείσα προς χρήσιν των σπουδαζόντων αυτήν κατά την νέαν μέθοδον παρά Χρυσάνθου του εκ Μαδύτων, Διδασκάλου του Θεωρητικού της Μουσικής*. Paris: Rigniou, 1821.

Clogg, Richard. *A Concise History of Modern Greece*. Revised 3rd ed. Cambridge: Cambridge University Press, 2013.

Code, Grant. "Eva Sikelianou: Modern Prophet of Archaic Greece." *Dance Observer* 7 nos. 4–5 (April–May, 1940): 53–54, 66–67.

Cohen, Getzel M., and Martha Sharp Joukowsky, eds. *Breaking Ground: Pioneering Women Archaeologists*. Ann Arbor: University of Michigan Press, 2004.

Colette. *My Apprenticeships, and Music-Hall Sidelights*. London: Secker and Warburg, 1967.

Colette and Robert Phelps. *Autobiographie tirée des oeuvres*. Paris: Fayard, 1966.

Collecott, Diana. *H. D. and Sapphic Modernism, 1910–1950*. Cambridge: Cambridge University Press, 1999.

Committee on Un-American Activities. "Report of the Communist 'Peace' Offensive: A Campaign to Disarm and Defeat the United States." April 1, 1951. Washington, DC: United States House of Representatives. *The Internet Archive*. https://archive.org/details/reportoncommunis00unit (accessed June 20, 2018).

Constantinides, Stratos. "Classical Drama in Modern Greece." *Journal of Modern Greek Studies* 5, no. 1 (May 1987): 15–32.

Cook, Nilla Cram. *My Road to India*. New York: L. Furman, 1939.

Corovilles, Theodora. "The Tragedies of Angelos Sikelianos." *Athene: The American Magazine of Hellenic Thought* 21, no. 1 (Spring 1960): 2–9, 42–43.

Corrigan, Peter. *The Dressed Society: Clothing, the Body, and Some Meanings of the World*. Published in association with *Theory, Culture, and Society*. London: Sage, 2008.

Crane, Sheila. "Mapping the Amazon's Salon: Symbolic Landscapes and Topographies of Identity in Natalie Clifford Barney's Literary Salon." In *Gender and Landscape: Renegotiating Morality and Space*, edited by Lorraine Dowler, Josephine Carubia, and Bonj Szczygiel, 145–60. New York: Routledge, 2009.

Crowfoot, Elizabeth. "Grace Mary Crowfoot (1877–1957)." *Breaking Ground: Women in Old World Archaeology*. http://www.brown.edu/Research/Breaking _Ground/results.php?d=1&first=Grace&last=Crowfoot (accessed June 21, 2018).

Cunningham, Patricia A. *Reforming Women's Fashion, 1850–1920: Politics, Health, and Art*. Kent, OH: Kent State University Press, 2003.

Daly, Anne. "The Natural Body." In *Moving History/Dancing Cultures: A Dance History Reader*, edited by Ann Dils and Ann Cooper Albright, 288–99. Middletown, CT: Wesleyan University Press, 2001.

Danos, Antonis. "The Culmination of Aesthetic and Artistic Discourse in Nineteenth-Century Greece: Periklis Yannopoulos and Nikolaos Gyzis." *Journal of Modern Greek Studies* 20, no. 1 (May 2002): 75–112.

Davidson, Lucretia M. "Bayreuth Revisited." *Theatre Magazine* 4 (1904): 255.

DeJean, Joan E. *Fictions of Sappho, 1546–1937*. Chicago: University of Chicago Press, 1989.

Diaz-Andreu, Margarita, and Marie Louise Stig Sørenson, eds. *Excavating Women: A History of Women in European Archaeology*. New York: Routledge, 1998.

———. "Excavating Women: Towards an Engendered History of Archaeology." In *Excavating Women: A History of Women in European Archaeology*, edited by Margarita Diaz-Andreu and Marie Louise Stig Sørenson, 1–28. New York: Routledge, 1998.

Dibble, Jeremy. "Stanford, Sir Charles Villiers." *Grove Music Online. Oxford Music Online*. Oxford University Press. https://doi.org/10.1093/gmo/97815 61592630.article.26549.

Dimopoulos, Takis (Δημόπουλος, Τάκης). "Ο ποιητής και η Εύα." "Angelos Sikelianos–Eva Palmer-Sikelianou: Delphic Festivals," special issue of *EOS*, 1998, 101–7.

Doan, Laura, and Jane Garrity. "Introduction." In *Sapphic Modernities: Sexuality, Women, and National Culture*, edited by Lara Doan and Jane Garrity, 1–13. New York: Palgrave Macmillan, 2006.

Dodds, E. R. *The Greeks and the Irrational*. Berkeley: University of California Press, 1951.

Dorf, Samuel N. "Dancing Greek Antiquity in Private and Public: Isadora Duncan's Early Patronage in Paris." *Dance Research Journal* 44, no. 1 (2012): 3–27. http://muse.jhu.edu/journals/dance_research_journal/v044/44.1.dorf.html N1 (accessed June 21, 2018).

———. *Performing Antiquity: Ancient Greek Music and Dance from Paris to Delphi, 1890–1930*. Oxford: Oxford University Press, forthcoming.

Dowling, Linda C. *Hellenism and Homosexuality in Victorian Oxford*. Ithaca, NY: Cornell University Press, 1994.

Dragoumis, Markos (Δραγούμης, Μάρκος). "Κωνσταντίνος Α. Ψάχος: Συμβολή στη μελέτη της ζωής και του έργου του." In *Η παραδοσιακή μας μουσική*, vol. 1, 61–69. Athens: Filoi Mousikou Laographikou Archeiou Melpos Merlier, 2003.

Dragoumis, Markos Ph. "Constantinos A. Psachos (1869–1949)." *Studies in Eastern Chant 5* (January 1, 1990): 77–88.

duBois, Page. *Sappho*. London: I. B. Tauris, 2015.

———. *Sappho Is Burning*. Chicago: University of Chicago Press, 1997.

Du Bois, W.E.B. *The Souls of Black Folk* (1903). New York: Simon and Schuster, 2014.

———. "Strivings of the Negro People." *Atlantic Monthly*, August 1897. http://www.theatlantic.com/magazine/archive/1897/08/strivings-of-the-negro-people/305446/ (accessed June 21, 2018).

"Dumbarton Oaks." Cultural Landscape Foundation website. http://tclf.org/landscapes/dumbarton-oaks (accessed June 21, 2018).

Dumont, Albert, and Jules Clement Chaplain. *Les Céramiques de la Grèce proper*. Vol. 1. Paris: Firmin Didot, 1888.

Duncan, Isadora. "The Dancer of the Future." In *The Twentieth-Century Performance Reader*, edited by Michael Huxley and Noel Witts, 171–77. London: Routledge, 1996.

———. "I See America Dancing" (1927). In *The Art of Dance*, edited by Sheldon Cheney, 47–50. New York: Theatre Art Books, 1928.

———. *My Life*. New York: Liveright, 2013.

———. "The Parthenon" (1903 or 1904). In *The Art of Dance*, edited by Sheldon Cheney, 64–65. New York: Theatre Art Books, 1928.

Dykes, Amy Renee. "Documentation of a Mariano Fortuny Delphos Gown." MS thesis, University of Georgia, 2003.

Dyson, Stephen L. *In Pursuit of Ancient Pasts: A History of Classical Archaeology in the Nineteenth and Twentieth Centuries*. New Haven, CT: Yale University Press, 2006.

Ehnenn, Jill R. *Women's Literary Collaboration, Queerness, and Late-Victorian Culture*. Aldershot, England: Ashgate, 2008.

Elliot, Bridget, and Jo-Ann Wallace. *Women Writers and Artists: Modernist (Im)Positionings*. London: Routledge, 2014.

Ellis, Havelock, and John Addington Symonds. *Sexual Inversion: Studies in the Psychology of Sex*. Vol. 1. London: Wilson and Macmillan, 1897.

Emmanuel, Maurice. *La danse grecque antique d'après les monuments figurés*. Paris: Hachette, 1896.

———. *The Antique Greek Dance, after Sculptured and Painted Figures*. Translated by Harriet Jean Beauley, with drawings by A. Collombar and the author. New York: John Lane, 1916.

Erol, Merih. "The 'Musical Question' and the Educated Elite of Greek Orthodox Society in Late Nineteenth-Century Constantinople." *Journal of Modern Greek Studies* 32, no. 1 (May 2014): 133–63.

European Cultural Center of Delphi website. https://www.eccd.gr/en/the-centre/timeline/ (accessed June 21, 2018).

FIDM Museum and Galleries website. "Mariano Fortuny." http://blog.fidmmuseum.org/museum/2011/01/mariano-fortuny.html (accessed June 21, 2018).

Field, Michael. *Long Ago*. London: G. Bell, 1889.

Fisher, James. "The Theater Department at Wabash College." Wabash College Theater website, 2009. Updated by Dwight Watson in 2013. https://www

.wabash.edu/images2/academics/theater/files/Theater%20Department%20production%20history.pdf.

Fiske, Shanon. *Heretical Hellenism: Women Writers, Ancient Greece, and the Victorian Imagination*. Athens: Ohio University Press/Swallow, 2008.

Fitzpatrick, Matthew P. *Liberal Imperialism in Europe*. New York: Palgrave Macmillan, 2012.

Fleming, K. E. *Greece—a Jewish History*. Princeton, NJ: Princeton University Press, 2010.

Florman, Lisa. "Gustav Klimt and the Precedent of Ancient Greece." *Art Bulletin* 72, no. 2 (June 1990): 310–26. http:/www.jstor.org/stable/3045736 (accessed June 21, 2018).

Fotou, Vasso, and Ann Brown. "Harriet Boyd Hawes (1871–1945)." In *Breaking Ground: Pioneering Women Archaeologists*, edited by Getzel M. Cohen and Martha Sharp Joukowsky, 198–273. Ann Arbor: University of Michigan Press, 2004.

Foucault, Michel. "The Ethics of the Concern for Self as a Practice of Freedom." Interview conducted by H. Becker, R. Fornet-Betencourt, and A. Gomez Müller on January 20, 1984. In *Michel Foucault: Ethics, Subjectivity, Truth*, vol. 1, 281–301. Essential Works of Foucault 1954–1984. New York: New Press, 1984.

Foulkes, Julia L. *Modern Bodies: Dance and American Modernism from Martha Graham to Alvin Ailey*. Chapel Hill: University of North Carolina Press, 2002.

Fournaraki, Eleni. "Bodies That Differ: Mid- and Upper-Class Women and the Quest for 'Greekness' in Female Bodily Culture (1896–1940)." In *Sport, Bodily Culture, and Classical Antiquity in Modern Greece*, edited by Eleni Fournaraki and Zinon Papakonstantinou, 49–86. Abingdon: Routledge, 2011.

Fox, Margalit. *The Riddle of the Labyrinth: The Quest to Crack an Ancient Code*. New York: Ecco, 2013.

Fox-Genovese, Elizabeth, and Eugene D. Genovese. *The Mind of the Master Class: History and Faith in the Southern Slaveholders' Worldview*. Cambridge: Cambridge University Press, 2005.

Franko, Mark. *Dancing Modernism/Performing Politics*. Bloomington: Indiana University Press, 1995.

Freeman, Elizabeth. "Introduction: Queer Temporalities." Special section of GLQ: A Journal of Lesbian and Gay Studies 13, no. 2–3 (2007): 159–76. doi:10.1215/10642684-2006-029.

———. *Time Binds: Queer Temporalities, Queer Histories*. Durham, NC: Duke University Press, 2010.

Gandhi, Leela. *Affective Communities: Anticolonial Thought, Fin-de-Siècle Radicalism, and the Politics of Friendship*. Durham, NC and London: Duke University Press, 2006.

Georgiou, Michalis. "Modern Greek Theatre and National Cultural Identity: The Innovative Performances of Ancient Greek Drama in the Nea Skini and the Royal Theatre (1901–1903)." Paper presented at European Society of Modern Greek Studies, February 20, 2011. European Society for Modern Greek Studies website. http://www.eens.org/?page_id=1683 (accessed June 21, 2018).

Gerardis, Takis (Γεράρδης, Τάκης). *Τα κομπολόγια*. Athens: Kedros, 2015.

Gere, Cathy. *Knossos and the Prophets of Modernism*. Chicago: University of Chicago Press, 2009.

Glaspell, Susan. *The Road to the Temple*. New York: Frederick A. Stokes, 1941.

Glytzouris, Antonis. "'Resurrecting' Ancient Bodies: The Tragic Chorus in *Prometheus Bound* and *Suppliant Women* at the Delphic Festivals in 1927 and 1930." In *Sport, Bodily Culture, and Classical Antiquity in Modern Greece*, edited by Eleni Fournaraki and Zinon Papakonstantinou, 86–116. Abingdon: Routledge, 2011.

Glytzouris, Antonis (Γλυτζούρης, Αντώνης). "Δελφικές Γιορτές (1927, 1930): Η αναβίωση του αρχαιοελληνικού χορού στον Προμηθέα Δεσμώτη και στις Ικέτιδες του Αισχύλου." *Τα Ιστορικά–Historica* 22 (June and December 1998): 147–70.

Goldhill, Simon. "A Touch of Sappho." In *Classics and the Uses of Reception*, edited by Charles Martindale and Richard F. Thomas, 250–73. Malden, MA: Wiley-Blackwell, 2008.

———. *Who Needs Greek: Contests in the Cultural History of Hellenism*. Cambridge: Cambridge University Press, 2002.

Gonzalez, Francisco J. *Plato and Heidegger: A Question of Dialogue*. University Park: Pennsylvania State University Press, 2009.

Gosse, Edmund. *The Life of Algernon Charles Swinburne*. New York: Macmillan, 1917.

Goujon, Jean-Paul. *Tes blessures sont plus douces que leurs caresses: Vie de Renée Vivien*. Paris: R. Deforges, 1986.

Gourgouris, Stathis. *Dream Nation: Enlightenment, Colonization and the Institution of Modern Greece*. Stanford, CA: Stanford University Press, 1996.

Graham, Martha. *Blood Memory*. New York: Doubleday, 1991.

"Greek Music and the Folk Songs of Hellas" (review). *Musical Times* 50, no. 799 (September 1, 1909): 577–80.

Greenwood, Emily. *Afro-Greeks: Dialogues between Anglophone Caribbean Literature and Classics*. Oxford: Oxford University Press, 2010.

Gregory, Eileen. *H. D. and Hellenism: Classic Lines*. Cambridge Studies in American Literature and Culture 111. Cambridge: Cambridge University Press, 1997.

Griffin, Roger. "Modernity, Modernism, and Fascism: A 'Mazeway Resynthesis.'" *Modernism/Modernity* 15, no. 1 (January 2008): 9–24. doi:10.1353/mod.2008.0011.

Grover, Verinder, and Ranjana Arora, eds. *Great Women of Modern India: Sucheta Kripa lani*. Great Women of India 6. New Delhi: Deep and Deep, 1993.

Gustafson, Susan E. *Men Desiring Men: The Poetry of Same-Sex Identity and Desire in German Classicism*. Detroit: Wayne State University Press, 2002.

Haggerty, George, and Bonnie Zimmerman. *Encyclopedia of Lesbian and Gay Histories and Cultures*. New York: Garland, 2000.

Hains, D. D. "Greek Plays in America." *Classical Journal* 6, no. 1 (October 1910): 24–39. www.jstor.org/stable/3286760.

Halperin, David. "The First Homosexuality?" In *The Sleep of Reason: Erotic Experience and Sexual Ethics in Ancient Greece and Rome*, edited by Martha Nussbaum and Juha Silvola, 229–68. Chicago: University of Chicago Press, 2013.

———. *St. Foucault: Towards a Gay Hagiography*. New York: Oxford University Press, 1997.

Hamilakis, Yannis. "The Fragments of Modernity and the Archaeologies of the

Future: Response to Gregory Jusdanis." *Modernism/Modernity* 11, no. 1 (2004): 55–59.

Hamilakis, Yannis. *The Nation and Its Ruins: Antiquity, Archaeology, and National Imagination in Greece.* Oxford: Oxford University Press, 2007.

Hanink, Johanna. *The Classical Debt: Antiquity in an Era of Austerity.* Cambridge, MA: Harvard University Press, 2017.

Hanink, Johanna, and Richard Fletcher. "Orientation: What We Mean by 'Creative Lives.'" In *Creative Lives in Classical Antiquity: Poets, Artists and Biography,* edited by Richard Fletcher and Johanna Hanink, 203–28. Cambridge: Cambridge University Press, 2016.

Hanna, Judith Lynne. "Patterns of Dominance: Men, Women, and Homosexuality in Dance." *Drama Review* 31, no. 1 (Spring 1987): 22–47.

Harrison, Jane Ellen. *Alpha and Omega: Women of Letters.* London: Sidgwick and Jackson, 1915.

Harrison, Jane Ellen, and Gilbert Murray. *Themis: A Study of the Social Origins of Greek Religion.* Cambridge: Cambridge University Press, 1912.

Hart, Mary. "Ancient Form to Modern Expression: Costume Design in the Delphi Productions of Eva Palmer Sikelianos." Paper delivered at the Modern Greek Studies Association Symposium, Yale University, New Haven, CT, October 20, 2007.

Hartigan, Karelisa. *Greek Tragedy on the American Stage: Ancient Drama in the Commercial Theater, 1882–1994.* Westport, CT.: Greenwood, 1995.

Hassiotis, Natasha. "Commentary from the Documentary, 'A Century of Contemporary Dance in Greece,' NET" (New Greek Television), January–February 2001. http://sarma.be/docs/162 (accessed June 21, 2018).

Herzfeld, Michael. *Portrait of a Greek Imagination: An Ethnographic Biography of Andreas Nenedakis.* Chicago: University of Chicago Press, 1997.

H. D., and Demetres P. Tryphonopoulos. *Magic Ring.* Gainesville: University Press of Florida, 2009.

Hirst, Anthony. "Christ and the Poetic Ego in the Poetry of Palamas, Sikelianos, and Elytis." *Journal of the Hellenic Diaspora* 27, nos. 1–2 (2001): 243–65.

Hodder, Jake. "On Absence and Abundance: Biography as Method in Archival Research." *Area* 49, no. 4 (2017): 452–59. doi: 10.1111/area.12329.

Holmes, Brooke, and Karen Marta, eds. *Liquid Antiquity.* Geneva, Switzerland: DESTE Foundation, 2017.

Holst-Warhaft, Gail. "In the Wake of the Greek Classical Moment." In *The Classical Moment: Views from Seven Literatures,* edited by Gail Holst-Warhaft and David R. McCann, 1–21. Lanham, MD: Rowman and Littlefield, 1999.

Horowitz, Helen Lefkowitz. *The Power and Passion of M. Carey Thomas.* Champaign: University of Illinois Press, 1999.

Horrocks, Geoffrey. *Greek: A History of the Language and Its Speakers.* London: Longmans, 1997.

Hudson, Kenneth. *A Social History of Archaeology: The British Experience.* London: Macmillan, 1986.

Huhndorf, Shari Michelle. *Going Native: Indians in the American Cultural Imagination.* Ithaca, NY: Cornell University Press, 2001.

ΙΑΕΝ Ιστορικό Αρχείο Ελληνικής Νεολαίας, Εθνικό Ίδρυμα Ερευνών. "Η μέση εκπαίδευση στην Λευκάδα: Διδακτικό προσωπικό 1829–1929: Ιωάννης

Σικελιανός." http://iaen.gr/iaen/teachers.php?class=2&order=1&target=282 (accessed December 13, 2016.).

Ingersoll, Robert Green. "Tribute to Courtlandt Palmer." In *Fifty Great Selections, Lectures, Tributes, after Dinner Speeches and Essays, Carefully Selected from the Twelve Volume Dresden Edition of Colonel Ingersoll's Complete Works*, 338–49. New York: C. P. Farrell, 1920.

Ioannidou, Eleftheria. "Toward a National *Heterotopia*: Ancient Theaters and the Cultural Politics of Performing Ancient Drama in Modern Greece." *Comparative Drama* 44, no. 4/45, no. 1 (2010): 385–403.

Isadora et Raymond Duncan Dance Research Center. http://www.duncandance center.org/en/ (accessed June 21, 2018).

Jackson, Leslie. *Twentieth-Century Pattern Design*. New York: Princeton Architectural Press, 2007.

Jaloux, Edmond. *Les saisons littéraire 1904–1914*. Fribourg: Librarie de l'Université, 1950.

Jay, Karla. *The Amazon and the Page: Natalie Clifford Barney and Renée Vivien*. Bloomington: Indiana University Press, 1988.

Jeffreys, Peter. *Reframing Decadence: C. P. Cavafy's Imaginary Portraits*. Ithaca, NY: Cornell University Press, 2015.

Johnson, Owen. "The Building of the Arts at Bar Harbor." *Century Magazine* 76, no. 5 (September 1908): 676–78.

Jowitt, Deborah. "Martha Graham's Clytemnestra Lives to Kill Again." *Village Voice*, May 20, 2009. https://www.villagevoice.com/2009/05/20/martha -grahams-clytemnestra-lives-to-kill-again/ (accessed February 9, 2018).

———. *Time and the Dancing Image*. Berkeley: University of California Press, 1989.

Jusdanis, Gregory. *The Necessary Nation*. Princeton, NJ: Princeton University Press, 2001.

Kambanis, Aristos (Καμπάνης, Αρίστος). "Πρόσωπα και πράγματα: Ελληνική μουσική." *Εσπερινόν Νέον Αστύ*, February 5, 1916, n.p. Clipping archived in KP.

Kantsa, Venetia. "'Lesvia: (I) A Same-Sex Desiring Woman (II) A Woman Inhabitant of Lesbos Island': The Re-introduction of a Word of Greek Origin into Modern Greece." In *Language and Sexuality (through and) beyond Gender*, edited by Costas Canakis, Venetia Kantsa, and Kostas Yiannakopoulos, 25–42. Newcastle upon Tyne, UK: Cambridge Scholars, 2010.

Karalis, Vrasidas (Καραλής, Βρασίδας). "Βιο-εργογραφία." *Διαβάζω* 424 (December 2001): 114–16.

Karamanes, Evangelos (Καραμανές, Ευάγγελος), ed. *Κωνσταντίνος Ψάχος: Ο μουσικός, ο λόγιος*. Conference proceedings, November 30, 2007. Athens: Academy of Athens, 2013.

Karas, Simon (Καράς, Σίμων). "Η Μεγάλη Ιδέα της Εύας." "Angelos Sikelianos–Eva Palmer-Sikelianou: Delphic Festivals," special issue of *EOS*, 1998, 276–78.

Kassing, Gayle. *History of Dance: An Interactive Arts Approach*. Champaign, IL: Human Kinetics, 2007.

Kazantzakis, Nikos. *The Selected Letters of Nikos Kazantzakis*. Edited and translated by Peter Bien. Princeton, NJ: Princeton University Press, 2012.

Koda, Harold. "Classical Art and Modern Dress." Metropolitan Museum of Art

Timeline of Art History. https://www.metmuseum.org/toah/hd/god2/hd_god2 .htm (accessed June 22, 2018).

———. *Goddess: The Greek Classical Mode*. New York: Metropolitan Museum of Art; New Haven, CT: Yale University Press, 2003.

Kolocotroni, Vassiliki. "Still Life: Modernism's Turn to Greece." *Journal of Modern Literature* 35, no. 2 (Winter 2012): 1–24. doi: 10.1353/jml.2012.0011.

"Konstantinos Psachos." *Εγκυκλοπαίδεια Μείζονος Ελληνισμού, Κωνσταντινούπολη.* http://constantinople.ehw.gr/forms/fLemmaBody.aspx?lemmaid=11407 (accessed December 18, 2016).

Kourelis, Kostis. "Byzantium and the Avant Garde: Excavations at Corinth, 1920s and 1930s." *Hesperia: The Journal of the American School of Classical Studies at Athens* 76, no. 2 (April–June 2007): 391–442.

———. "Flights of Archaeology: Peschke's Acrocorinth." *Hesperia* 86, no. 4 (October–December 2017: 723–82.

———. "Thalero." *Objects, Buildings, Situations: Musings on Architecture and Archaeology*, July 27, 2015. http://kourelis.blogspot.com/2015/07/thalero.html (accessed June 20, 2018).

Kuiken, Don, David S. Miall, and Shelley Sikora. "Forms of Self-Implication in Literary Reading." *Poetics Today* 25, no. 2 (Summer 2004): 171–203.

Lalaki, Despina. "On the Social Construction of Hellenism: Cold War Narratives of Modernity, Development and Democracy for Greece," 1–6. Hellenic Observatory website. http://www.lse.ac.uk/europeanInstitute/research/hellenic Observatory/CMS%20pdf/Events/2011-5th%20PhD%20Symposium/Lalaki .pdf (accessed June 19, 2018).

Lambelet, Georgios (Λαμπελέτ, Γεώργιος). "Η εθνική μουσική" [National music]. *Παναθήναια* 82–90 (1901): 126–31.

Lambropoulos, Vassilis. "Afterword: The Future of the Past Received." "Classical Reception and the Political," special issue of *Cultural Critique* 74 (Winter 2010): 214–17.

Langer, Cassandra. *Romaine Brooks: A Life*. Madison: University of Wisconsin Press, 2015.

Latour, Bruno. "Why Has Critique Run Out of Steam? From Matters of Fact to Matters of Concern." *Critical Inquiry* 30, no. 2 (Winter 2004): 225–48.

Lebrecht Music and Arts. "Lillian Gish in Delphos Dress." Author Pictures at Lebrecht. http://www.authorpictures.co.uk/search/preview/lillian-gish-in -delphos-dress-made-from-satin/0_00299087.html (accessed June 8, 2015).

Lekakis, Mihalis. "Επιστροφή στους Δελφούς." "Angelos Sikelianos–Eva Palmer-Sikelianou: Delphic Festivals," special issue of *EOS*, 1998, 382–88.

Leontis, Artemis. "An American in Paris, a Parsi in Athens." In *A Singular Antiquity, Archaeology, and Hellenic Identity in Twentieth Century Greece*, edited by Dimitris Damaskos and Dimitris Plantzos, 359–73. Athens: Benaki Museum, 2008.

———. "Eva Palmer's Distinctive Journey." In *Women Writing Greece: Essays on Hellenism, Orientalism, and Travel*, edited by Vassiliki Kolocotroni and Efterpi Mitsi, 159–84. Amsterdam: Rodopi, 2008.

———. "Eva Palmer Sikelianos before Delphi." In *Americans and the Experience of Delphi*, edited by Paul Lorenz and David Roessel, 1–50. Somerset Hall, 2013.

———. "Fashioning a Modern Self in Greek Dress: The Case of Eva Palmer Sikelianos." In *Hellenomania*, edited by Katherine Harloe, Nicoletta Momigliano, and Alexandre Farnoux, 213–33. London: Routledge, 2018.

———. "Greek Tragedy and Modern Dance: An Alternative Archaeology?" In *Oxford Handbook of Greek Drama in the Americas*, edited by Kathryn Bosher, Fiona Macintosh, Justine McConnell, and Patrice Rankine, 204–20. Oxford: Oxford University Press, 2015.

———. "Griechische Tragödie und moderner Tanz: Eine alternative Archäologie?" In *Ruinen in der Moderne: Archäologie und die Künste*, edited by Éva Kocziszky, 201–19. Bonn: Reimer Verlag, 2011.

———. *Topographies of Hellenism: Mapping the Homeland*. Ithaca, NY: Cornell University Press, 1995.

Lingas, Alexander. "Tradition and Renewal in Contemporary Orthodox Psalmody." In *Psalms in Community: Jewish and Christian Textual, Liturgical, and Artistic traditions*, 348–56. Symposium Series Society of Biblical Literature 25, edited by Harold W. Attridge and Margot E. Fassler. Leiden: Brill, 2004.

MacAloon, John J. "'My Programme Became Very Strict': A Conversation with Athanassios Kritsinelis." In *Bearing Lights: Flame Relays and the Struggle for the Olympic Movement*, edited by John J. Macaroon, 100–125. London: Rutledge, 2013.

Macintosh, Fiona, Pantelis Michelakis, Edith Hall, and Oliver Taplin, *Agamemnon in Performance*, 458 BC–AD 2004. Oxford: Oxford University Press, 2005.

Mackridge, Peter. *Language and National Identity in Greece, 1766–1976*. Oxford: Oxford University Press, 2010.

MacNeice, Louis. *Autumn Journal*. London: Faber and Faber, 1946.

Mahn, Churnjeet Kaur. "Romance in Ruins: Ethnography and the Problem with Modern Greeks." *Victorian Studies* 52, no. 1 (Autumn 2009): 9–19. doi: 10.1353/vic.0.0305.

Makris, Eustathios (Μακρής, Ευστάθιος). "Ηχογραφήσεις του Κωνσταντίνου Α. Ψάχου σε κυλίνδρους Edison." In Κωνσταντίνος Ψάχος: ο μουσικός, ο λόγιος, edited by the Academy of Athens, 69–78. Athens: Academy of Athens, 2013.

———. "Παρουσίαση του μικρού Παναρμονίου." In Κωνσταντίνος Ψάχος: ο μουσικός, ο λόγιος, edited by the Academy of Athens, 297–304. Athens: Academy of Athens, 2013.

Malnig, Julie, Janet Eilber, Deborah Jowitt, Gay Morris, Bruce Altshuler, and Sharon Friedman. "Clytemnestra and the Dance Dramas of Martha Graham: Revising the Classics." *Dance Chronicle* 33, no. 1 (March 12, 2010): 5–43. doi: 10.1080/01472520903574717.

Marchand, Suzanne L. *Down from Olympus: Archaeology and Philhellenism in Germany, 1750–1950*. Princeton, NJ: Princeton University Press, 1996.

Marks, Elaine. "'Sapho 1900': Imaginary Renée Viviens and the Rear of the Belle Époque." "The Politics of Tradition: Placing Women in French Literature," special issue of *Yale French Studies* 75 (1988): 175–89.

Martindale, Charles. "Introduction: Thinking through Reception." In *Classics and the Uses of Reception*, edited by Charles Martindale and Richard F. Thomas, 1–13. Oxford: Blackwell, 2006.

———. "Reception—a New Humanism? Receptivity, Pedagogy, the Transhistorical." *Classical Receptions Journal* 5, no. 2 (2013): 169–83.

Matalas, Paraskevas (Ματάλας, Παρασκευάς). "Οι διαδρομές του φυλετισμού του Πέτρου Βλαστού." In Efi Avdela (Έφη Αβδελά), et al., *Φυλετικές θεωρίες στην Ελλάδα: Προσλήψεις και χρήσεις στις επιστήμες, την πολιτική, τη λογοτεχνία και την ιστορία της τέχνης κατά τον 19ο και τον 20ό αιώνα*," 215–44. Irakleio: Crete University Press, 2017.

Mazower, Mark. *Inside Hitler's Greece: The Experience of Occupation, 1941–1944*. New Haven, CT: Yale University Press, 1993.

———. "Three Forms of Political Justice: Greece, 1944–1934." In *After the War Was Over: Reconstructing the Family, Nation, and State in Greece, 1943–1960*, edited by Mark Mazower, 24–41. Princeton, NJ: Princeton University Press, 2000.

Maynard, W. Barksdale. "The Greek Revival: Americanness, Politics, and Economics." In *American Architectural History: A Contemporary Reader*, edited by Keith L. Eggener, 132–41. London: Routledge, 2004.

McGann, Jerome. "Wagner, Baudelaire, Swinburne: Poetry in the Condition of Music." *Victorian Poetry* 47, no. 4 (Winter 2009): 610–32.

McLaughlin, Elizabeth T. *Ruskin and Gandhi*. Lewisburg, PA: Bucknell University Press, 1974.

Mellink, Machteld J., and Kathleen M. Quinn. "Hetty Goldman (1881–1972)." In *Breaking Ground: Pioneering Women Archaeologists*, edited by Getzel M. Cohen and Martha Sharp Joukowsky, 298–350. Ann Arbor: University of Michigan Press, 2004.

M.E.M. "Costume in Revivals of Greek Drama." *Metropolitan Museum of Art Bulletin* 31 (1936): 134–35.

Merriam, Carol. "Rewriting Grief: Edna St. Vincent Millay's Recrafting of Ancient Poetry of Grief and Loss." In *Rewriting Texts Remaking Images: Interdisciplinary Perspectives*, edited by Leslie Anne Boldt-Irons et al., 97–106. New York: Peter Lang, 2010.

Merlier, Octave. "Εύα Σικελιανού." "Angelos Sikelianos–Eva Palmer-Sikelianou: Delphic Festivals," special issue of *EOS*, 1998, 109–10.

Michelakis, Pantelis. "Dancing with Prometheus: Performance and Spectacle in the 1920s." In *The Ancient Dancer in the Modern World: Responses to Greek and Roman Dance*, edited by Fiona Macintosh, 224–35. Oxford: Oxford University Press, 2012.

———. "Theater Festivals, Total Works of Art, and the Revival of Greek tragedy on the Modern Stage." *Cultural Critique* 74 (2010): 149–63.

Morrow, Katherine Dohan. "Edith Hayward Hall Dohan (1879–1943)." In *Breaking Ground: Pioneering Women Archaeologists*, edited by Getzel M. Cohen and Martha Sharp Joukowsky, 274–97. Ann Arbor: University of Michigan Press, 2004.

Moskos, Charles C. *Greek Americans: Struggle and Success*. New Brunswick, NJ: Transaction, 1989.

Murray, Gilbert. *The Classical Tradition in Poetry: The Charles Eliot Norton Lectures*. Cambridge, MA: Harvard University Press, 1927, 1930.

National Museum of American History. "Original Kodak Camera, Serial No. 540."

Smithsonian American History. Americanhistory.si.edu/collections/search /object/nmah_760118 (accessed December 30, 2017).

Nehamas, Alexander. *The Art of Living: Socratic Reflections from Plato to Foucault*. Berkeley: University of California Press, 1998.

"Nelly Sougioutzoglou-Seraidare: Eva Sikelianou in Delphi." *Art Topos* website. http://www.artopos.org/main-en.html?artists/nellys/eva-en.html&3 (accessed June 22, 2018).

Nietzsche, Friedrich Wilhelm. *The Birth of Tragedy and the Case of Wagner*. Translated by Walter Kaufmann. New York: Vintage Books, 1967.

———. "On the Uses and Disadvantages of History for Life." *Untimely Meditations*. Translated by R. J. Hollingdale, edited by Daniel Braezeale, 57–123. New York: Cambridge University Press, 1997.

Nirvanas, Pavlos (Νιρβάνας, Παύλος). "Ωραία Ματαιοπονία" [*Estia* newspaper, May 17, 1919]. In Eva Palmer-Sikelianou, *Ωραία Ματαιοπονία: Τρεις διαλέξεις*, edited by Ritsa Fragou-Kikilia, 21–24. Athens: Ellinika Grammata, 2005.

Ofek, Galia. *Representations of Hair in Victorian Literature and Culture*. Farnham: Ashgate, 2009.

Owen, Norton. "Ted Shawn's Moving Images." In *Envisioning Dance on Film and Video*, edited by in Judith Mitoma et al., 61–67. New York: Routledge, 2002.

Palamas, Kostis (Παλαμάς, Κωστής). "Τα τραγούδια μας εις τα ξένα." *Το Αστύ* 2, no. 2192 (December 25, 1896): 1; reprinted in *Άπαντα*, vol. 15, 350–84.

Palmer, D. D., and B. J. Palmer. *Science of Chiropractic: Its Principles and Philosophies*. Davenport, IA: Palmer School of Chiropractic, 1906–10.

Palmer, Courtlandt. *The New Education: Manual (Industrial) Training an Indispensable Department of It; An Essay in Explanation of the Gramercy Park School and Tool-House Situated at 104 East 20th Street, New York*. New York: Printing Department of the Institute, 1885.

Palmer-Sikelianou, Eva (Palmer-Σικελιανού, Εύα). *Ωραία Ματαιοπονία: Τρεις διαλέξεις*. Edited by Ritsa Fragou-Kikilia. Athens: Ellinika Grammata, 2005.

Palmer-Sikelianos, Eva, and John P. Anton. *Upward Panic: The Autobiography of Eva Palmer-Sikelianos*. Chur, Switzerland: Harwood Academic, 1993.

Palmer-Sikelianou, Eva, and John P. Anton (Πάλμερ-Σικελιανού, Εύα, and John P. Anton). *Ιερός πανικός*. Edited and translated by John P. Anton. Athens: Exantas, 1992.

———. *Ιερός πανικός: Αυτοβιογραφία*. Introduction, translation, and notes by John P. Anton, edited by Thanasis A. Vasileiou. Athens: Miletos, 2010.

Pangalo, Léna "'Right' According to Whom? Eva Palmer-Sikelianos and Cross Cultural Dress." In *Anglo-American Perceptions of Hellenism*, edited by Tatiani G. Rapatzikou, 228–40. Cambridge: Cambridge Scholars, 2007.

Panourgiá, Neni. *Dangerous Citizens: The Greek Left and the Terror of the State*. New York: Fordham University Press, 2009.

Papadaki, Efthalia (Παπαδάκη, Ευθαλία). "Αναζητώντας μια ελληνική ευτοπία: Το 'μυστικό' πέρασμα της Εύας και του Άγγελου Σικελιανού από το Δελφικό ομφαλό." Unpublished manuscript, 2015.

———. *Πίσω από το πέπλο της ωραιότητας: Ο μυστικός κόσμος της Εύας και του Άγγελου Σικελιανού*. Athens: Benaki Museum, 2018.

Papadaki, Lia (Παπαδάκη, Λία). *Γράμματα της Εύας Πάλμερ Σικελιανού στη Natalie Clifford Barney*. Athens: Kastanioti, 1995.

———. *Το εφηβικό πρότυπο και η Δελφική Προσπάθεια του Άγγελου Σικελιανού*. Athens: National Hellenic Research Foundation, 1995.

Papageorgiou, K. Ath. (Παπαγεωργίου, Κ. Αθ.). *Άγγελος Σικελιανός–Εύα Πάλμερ-Σικελιανού: Δελφικές Εορτές, Ειδικόν αφιέρωμα της επιθεωρήσεως ΗΩΣ* (Angelos Sikelianos–Eva Palmer-Sikelianou: Delphic Festivals: Special issue of *EOS*). Athens: Papademas, 1998, 2nd ed.

Papazoglou, Eleni. "Between Texts and Contexts: Moderns against Ancients in the Reception of Ancient Tragedy in Greece." In *Re-imagining the Past: Antiquity and Modern Greek Culture*, edited by Dimitris Tziovas, 209–26. Oxford: Oxford University Press, 2014.

Patel, Dinyar. "Gandhi and the Parsis: A Minority Community's Involvement in the Constructive Program for Swaraj." Unpublished paper, 2008.

Payne, Robert. *The Splendor of Greece*. New York: Harper, 1960.

Pennanen, Risto Pekka. "The Nationalization of Ottoman Popular Music in Greece." *Ethnomusicology* 48, no. 1 (Winter 2004): 1–25.

Petrakis, Marina. *The Metaxas Myth: Dictatorship and Propaganda in Greece*. London: I. B. Tauris, 2006.

Piliouras, Nikitas (Πήλιουρας, Νικήτας). "Ο Σικελιανός δεν μένει πια εδώ." *Status*, August 2010, 139–46.

Plantzos, Dimitris. "The Glory That Was Not: Embodying the Classical in Contemporary Greece." *Interactions: Studies in Communication & Culture* 3, no. 2: 147–71.

Plemmenos, Ioannis (Πλεμμένος, Ιωάννης). "Η 'θελξίθυμος' μούσα της Ανατολής: Η Ασίας λύρα του Κωνσταντίνου Ψάχου και το κοινωνικό-ιδεολογικό της πλαίσιο." In *Κωνσταντίνος Ψάχος: Ο μουσικός, ο Λόγιος*, edited by Evangelos Karamanes, 101–34. Athens: Academy of Athens Center for the Study of Greek Folklore, 2013.

Pluggé, Domis E. *History of Greek Play Production in American Colleges and Universities from 1881 to 1936*. Teachers College, Columbia University Contribution to Education 752. New York: Bureau of Publications, Teachers College, Columbia University, 1938.

Pointon, Marcia. "Liberty on the Barricades: Women, Politics, and Eroticism in Delacroix." In *Women, State and Revolution: Essays on Power and Gender in Europe since 1789*, edited by Siân Reynolds, 25–43. Amherst: University of Massachusetts Press, 1986.

Pollock, Griselda. "Sacred Cows: Wandering in Feminism, Psychoanalysis, and Anthropology." In *The Sacred and the Feminine: Imagination and Sexual Difference*, edited by Griselda Pollock and Victoria Turvey Sauron, 9–48. London: I. B. Tauris, 2007.

Porter, James I. *Nietzsche and the Philology of the Future*. Stanford, CA: Stanford University Press, 2000.

———. "What Is 'Classical' about 'Classical' Antiquity? Eight Propositions." *Arion* 13, no. 1 (Spring/Summer 2005): 27–61.

Potts, Alex. *Flesh and the Ideal: Winckelmann and the Origins of Art History*. New Haven, CT: Yale University Press, 1994.

Pougy, Liane de. *Idylle saphique: Roman.* Paris: Des Femmes, 1987.

Pounder, Robert L. "The Blegens and the Hills: A Family Affair. In *Carl W. Blegen: Personal and Archaeological Narratives,* edited by Natalia Vogeikoff-Brogan, Jack L. Davis, and Vasiliki Florou, 85–98. Atlanta, GA: Lockwood, 2015.

Pratelle, Aristides. "Rescuing Epirus." *International Socialist Review* 15 (1914–15): 423–24.

Pratsika, Koula (Πράτσικα, Κούλα). "Αναμνήσεις από τις πρώτες Δελφικές Εορτές του 1927." "Angelos Sikelianos–Eva Palmer-Sikelianou: Delphic Festivals," special issue of *EOS,* 1998, 126–29.

Preston, Carrie J. *Modernism's Mythic Pose: Gender, Genre, Solo Performance.* Oxford: Oxford University Press, 2011.

Prins, Yopie. "Greek Maenads, Victorian Spinsters." In *Victorian Sexual Dissidence,* edited by Richard Dellamora, 43–81. Chicago: University of Chicago Press, 1999.

———. *Ladies' Greek: Translations of Tragedy.* Princeton, NJ: Princeton University Press, 2017.

———. *Victorian Sappho.* Princeton, NJ: Princeton University Press, 1999.

Psachos, K. A. (Ψάχος, Κ. Α.). *Ασίας λύρα, ήτοι συλλογή διαφόρων μελών της Ασιατικής μουσικής.* 2nd ed. Athens: Koultoura, 1998.

———. *Η παρασημαντική της Βυζαντινής μουσικής.* Athens: P. D. Sakellariou, 1917.

Quatremère de Quincy, Antoine Chrysostôme. *Le Jupiter olympien, ou l'art de la sculpture antique considéré sous un nouveau point de vue.* Paris: De Bure Frères, 1815. http://digi.ub.uni-heidelberg.de/diglit/quatremeredequincy1815/0007 (accessed June 10, 2018).

Rasula, Jed. *History of a Shiver: The Sublime Impudence of Modernism.* New York: Oxford, 2016.

Ray, Chelsea, and Natalie Clifford Barney. "Decadent Heroines or Modernist Lovers: Natalie Clifford Barney's Unpublished 'Feminine Lovers or the Third Women.'" "Natalie Barney and Her Circle," special issue of *South Central Review* 22, no. 3 (Fall, 2005): 32–61.

Remington, Preston. "Notes: A Lecture on the Greek Tragic Chorus." *Metropolitan Museum of Art Bulletin* 22, no. 11 (November 1927): 280–83. http://www.jstor .org/stable/3255858 (accessed May 10, 2013).

Rentzeperi-Tsonou, Anna-Maria (Ρεντζεπέρη-Τσώνου, Άννα-Μαρία). "Το 'ελληνικό στοιχείο' σε έργα φωνητικής μουσικής των Ελλήνων συνθετών της Εθνικής Μουσικής Σχολής Μ. Καλομοίρη και Μ. Βάρβογλη." *Muse-e-journal* 2. www.muse .gr/muse-e-journal/A_M_Rentzeperi.pdf (accessed June 10, 2018).

REORIENT. Online magazine, 2012–present. http://www.reorientmag.com/ (accessed June 22, 2018).

Reynolds, Francis J., et al. *The Story of the Great War: With Complete Historical Record of Events to Date.* Vol. 7. New York: P. F. Collier and Son, 1916.

———. *The Story of the Great War: With Complete Historical Record of Events to Date.* Vol. 9. New York: P. F. Collier and Sons, 1916.

Reynolds, Margaret. *The Sappho Companion.* New York: Palgrave/St. Martin's, 2001.

Richard, Carl J. *Greeks and Romans Bearing Gifts: How the Ancients Inspired the Founding Fathers.* Lanham, MD.: Rowman and Littlefield, 2008.

Rigopoulos, Rigas. *Secret War/Μυστικός Πόλεμος: Greece–Middle East, 1940–1945; The Events Surrounding the Story of Service 5-16-5*. Translated by Jesse M. Heines in collaboration with Rigas Rigopoulos and Dionysis Rigopoulos from a draft translation by Eleni Dedoglou. Paducah, KY: Turner, 2003 (1973).

Robinson, Annabel. *The Life and Work of Jane Ellen Harrison*. Oxford: Oxford University Press, 2002.

Rodriguez, Suzanne. *Wild Heart: A Life: Natalie Clifford Barney and the Decadence of Literary Paris*. New York: Ecco, 2002.

Romanou, Katy (Ρωμανού, Καίτη). "Ένας Έλληνας δάσκαλος: Κωνσταντίνος Ψάχος." Review of Konstantinos Psachos, *Η παρασημαντική της Βυζαντινής Μουσικής*, 2nd ed. (1978). *Kathimerini*, August 23, 1979, n.p.

———. *Εθνικής μουσικής περιήγησης, 1901–1912: Ελληνικά μουσικά περιοδικά ως πηγή έρευνας της ιστορίας της νεοελληνικής μουσικής*. Vol. 1. Athens: Koultoura 1995.

Romanou, Katy, and Maria Barbaki. "Music Education in Nineteenth-Century Greece: Its Institutions and Their Contribution to Urban Musical Life." *Nineteenth-Century Music Review* 8 (2011): 57–84. doi:10.1017/S1479409 811000061.

Rowbotham, Sheila. *Dreamers of a New Day: Women Who Invented the Twentieth Century*. London: Verso, 2010.

Rubin, Gayle S. "Introduction to *A Woman Appeared to Me*." In *Deviations: A Gayle Rubin Reader*, 87–108. Durham, NC: Duke University Press, 2012. doi 10.1215/9780822394068-004.

Rummel, Rudolf J. "Statistics of Turkey's Democide: Estimates, Calculations, and Sources. *Statistics of Democide*, 1997. Powerkills website, University of Hawaii Political Science Department. https://www.hawaii.edu/powerkills/SOD.CHAP5 .HTM (accessed June 10, 2018).

Ruyter, Nancy Lee. *The Cultivation of Body and Mind in Nineteenth-Century American Delsartism*. Westport CT: Greenwood, 1999.

Sakallieros, Giorgos. *Dimitri Mitropoulos and His Works in the 1920s: The Introduction of Musical Modernism in Greece*. Athens: Hellenic Music Centre, 2016.

Salvaggio, Ruth. *Hearing Sappho in New Orleans: The Call of Poetry from Congo Square to the Ninth Ward*. Baton Rouge: Louisiana State University Press, 2012.

Samson, Jim. *Music in the Balkans*. Boston: Brill, 2013.

Sappho and Henry Thornton Wharton. *Sappho, Memoir, Text, Selected Renderings and a Literal Translation*. 2nd ed. London: David Stott, 1887.

———. *Sappho: Memoir, Text, Selected Renderings*. London: John Lane, 1895.

Savrami, Katia. *Ancient Dramatic Chorus through the Eyes of a Modern Choreographer: Zouzou Nikoloudi*. Cambridge: Cambridge Scholars, 2017.

Schwab, Katherine. "The Caryatid Hairstyling Project." Fairfield University Media Center. April–September 2009. Video. https://www.fairfield.edu/undergraduate /academics/schools-and-colleges/college-of-arts-and-sciences/programs/visual -and-performing-arts/art-history-and-visual-culture/caryatid/ (accessed June 10, 2018).

Scudéry, Madeleine de. *The Story of Sapho*. Translated with an introduction by Karen Newman. Chicago: University of Chicago Press, 2003.

Settis, Salvatore. *The Future of the Classical*. Cambridge: Polity, 2006.

Shelley, Percy Bysshe, Zachary Leader, and Michael O'Neill. *Percy Bysshe Shelley: The Major Works*. Oxford: Oxford University Press, 2003.

Shorter, Edward, and Charles Tilly. *Strikes in France, 1830–1968*. Cambridge: Cambridge University Press, 1974.

Sikelianos, Angelos (Σικελιανός, Άγγελος). "Αρίστος Καμπάνης· Ἡροσφορά στον Ἥφαιστον.'" *Νέαν Ελλάδα*, September 17, 1914, 1–2; reprinted in EOS, 329.

———. *Δελφικός λόγος: Αρχά των αρίστων*. Athens: Estia, 1927.

———. "Δελφικός λόγος: Λόγος σπερματικός." In *Πεζός Λόγος*, vol. 2, *Δελφικά 1921–1951*, edited by G. P. Savvidis (Γ. Π. Σαββίδης), 13–21. Athens: Ikaros, 1980 (first published in 1921).

———. "Η Δελφική ένωση (ένα προανάκρουσμα)." In *Πεζός Λόγος*, vol. 2, *Δελφικά 1921–1951*, edited by G. P. Savvidis, 323–83. Athens: Ikaros, 1980 (first published in 1931).

———. "Πηνελόπη Σικελιανού." *Πεζός Λόγος*. Vol. 4, *1940–1944*, edited by G. P. Savvidis, 49–56. Athens: Ikaros, 1983 (written 1940–44).

———. "Η πνευματική βάση της Δελφικής Προσπάθειας." In *Πεζός Λόγος*, vol. 2, *Δελφικά 1921–1951*, edited by G. P. Savvidis, 67–118. Athens: Ikaros, 1980 (first published in 1927).

———. "Το πρόβλημα της μουσικής και του χορού στο αρχαίο δράμα." In *Πεζός Λόγος*, vol. 2, *Δελφικά 1921–1951*, edited by G. P. Savvidis, 309–21. Athens: Ikaros, 1980 (first published in 1931).

Sikelianos, Angelos, and Kostas Bournazakis (Σικελανός, Άγγελος, and Κώστας Μπουρναζάκης). *Γράμματα στην Εύα Πάλμερ Σικελιανού*. Athens: Ikaros, 2008.

Sikelianos, Angelos, and Paul Nord. *Akritan Songs (1941–1942)*. New York: Spap, 1944.

Sikelianos, Angelos, and Alma M. Reed. *The Delphic Word: The Dedication*. New York: H. Vinal, 1928.

Sikelianos, Angelos, and Spyros Vassiliou (Σικελιανός, Άγγελος, and Σπύρος Βασιλείου). *Ακριτικά*. Cairo: n.p., 1944.

———. *Ακριτικά (1941–1942)*. Athens: n.p., 1942.

Sikelianos, Eleni. "The Lefevre-Sikelianos-Waldman Tree and the Imaginative Utopian Attempt." *Jacket* 27 (April 2005). http://jacketmagazine.com/27/w-sike.html (accessed June 22, 2018).

Sikelianos, Eva. "The Poet Angelos Sikelianos." *Athene* 4, no. 9 (1943): 23–35, 67–68.

———. *What Is Great Theatre*. Self-published, 1944.

Siopsi, Anastasia. "Music in the Imaginary Worlds of the Greek Nation: Greek Art Music during the Nineteenth-Century's *Fin de Siècle* (1880s–1910s)." *Nineteenth-Century Music Review* 8 (June 2011): 17–39. doi:10.1017/S1479409811000048.

Sladen, Douglas. "On the Collecting of Greek Terra-Cotta-Statuettes." *The Collector, Containing Articles and Illustrations, Reprinted from the Queen Newspaper, of Interest to the Great Body of Collectors, on China, Engravings* 1 (1903): 86–90.

Slosberg, Steven. "An Oracle of Delphi: Evalina Palmer Sikelianos." *Historical Footnotes: Bulletin of the Stonington Historical Society* 49, no. 1 (Winter 2013): 4–8.

Smith, Bonnie. *The Gender of History: Men, Women, and Historical Practice.* Cambridge, MA: Harvard University Press, 2000.

Smith, Tyler Jo. "Reception or Deception? Approaching Greek Dance through Vase-Painting." In *The Ancient Dancer in the Modern World: Responses to Greek and Roman Dance*, edited by Fiona Macintosh, 77–98. Oxford: Oxford University Press, 2010.

Sophocles. *The Electra of Sophocles.* Edited with introduction and notes by Sir Richard Jebb. Cambridge: Cambridge University Press, 1894. http://data .perseus.org/texts/urn:cts:greekLit:tlg0011.tlg005.perseus-eng1 (accessed June 10, 2018).

Sorin, Gerald. *A Time for Building: The Third Migration, 1880–1920.* Vol. 3, *The Jewish People in America.* Baltimore: Johns Hopkins University Press, 1995.

Souhami, Diana. *Wild Girls: Paris, Sappho, and Art; The Lives and Loves of Natalie Barney and Romaine Brooks.* New York: Macmillan, 2007.

Spivey, Nigel Jonathan, and Michael Squire. *Panorama of the Classical World.* Los Angeles: J. Paul Getty Museum, 2004.

Stein, Gertrude. "The Autobiography of Alice B. Toklas." In *Selected Writings of Gertrude Stein*, edited with an introduction by Carl Van Vechten, 1–239. New York: Knopf Doubleday, 2012.

Stroh, Suzanne. "Interview with Artemis Leontis: Life as a Greek Revival." October 31, 2014. http://www.suzannestrohcreative.com/interview-artemis-leontis/.

Swinburne, Algernon Charles. *Notes on Poems and Reviews.* London: John Camden Hotten, 1866.

Sword, Helen. *Engendering Inspiration: Visionary Strategies in Rilke, Lawrence, and H. D.* Ann Arbor: University of Michigan Press, 1995.

Sypher, Francis Jacques. "Swinburne and Wagner." *Victorian Poetry* 9 nos. 1–2 (Spring–Summer, 1971): 165–83. http://www.jstor.org/stable/40001597 (accessed June 10, 2018).

Terry, Walter. *Ted Shawn, Father of American Dance: A Biography.* New York: Dial Books, 1976.

The Social Register, New York. New York: Social Register Association, 1900.

Thomas, M. Carey. "Education of Women." In *Education in the United States: A Series of Monographs*, edited by Nicholas Murray Butler, 319–58. New York: American Book, 1910.

Thomas, Kate. "'What Time We Kiss': Michael Field's Queer Temporalities." *GLQ: A Journal of Lesbian and Gay Studies* 13, nos. 2–3 (2007): 327–51.

Tillyard, H.J.W. *Byzantine Music and Hymnography.* Charing Cross: Faith, 1923.

Trigger, Bruce G. "Alternative Archaeologies: Nationalist, Colonialist, Imperialist." *Man*, n.s., 19, no. 3 (September 1984): 355–70.

Trotter, William R. *Priest of Music: The Life of Dimitri Mitropoulos.* Portland, OR: Amadeus, 1995.

Trubeta, Sevasti. *Physical Anthropology, Race, and Eugenics in Greece (1880s–1970s).* Boston: Brill, 2013.

Tryphe. "Cinq petits dialogues grecs (Antithèseset parallèlles)." Paris: Editions de la Plume, 1902. storage.canalblog.com/34/15/296109/21686514.pdf (accessed June 10, 2018).

Tsoutsoura, Maria (Τσούτσουρα, Μαρία). "Το ιστορικό βάθος στην προβληματική και την αισθητική της αναβίωσης του χορού στις 'Δελφικές Γιορτές.' " *Πόρφυρας* 14 (July–October 1993): 31–45.

Valentine, Jody "Lesbians Are from Lesbos: Sappho and Identity Construction in *The Ladder.*" *Helios* 35, no. 2 (Fall 2008): 143–69.

Vance, Norman. "Classics and Modern War." Review of *Stand in the Trench, Achilles: Classical Receptions in British Poetry of the Great* by Elizabeth Vandiver. *International Journal of the Classical Tradition* 18, no. 4 (December 2011): 593–98.

Vanikioti, Eleni, Vangelis Giotas, and Dimitra Gana (Βανικιώτη, Ελένη, Βαγγέλης Γιώτας, και Δήμητρα Γκανά). "Θεατρικές παραστάσεις της *Αντιγόνης* στον εικοστό αιώνα." Powerpoint slideshow prepared for the Second Alternative High School of Athens, 2008–9. http://slideplayer.gr/slide/2560599/ (accessed June 10, 2018).

Van Steen, Gonda. *Liberating Hellenism from the Ottoman Empire: Comte de Marcellus and the Last of the Classics.* New York: Palgrave Macmillan, 2010.

———. "Myth, Mystique, Nietzsche, and the 'Cultic Milieu' of the Delphic Festivals, 1927 and 1930." In *Americans and the Experience of Delphi*, edited by Paul Lorenz and David Roessel, 51–88. Boston: Somerset Hall, 2013.

———. " 'The World's a Circular Stage': Aeschylean Tragedy through the Eyes of Eva Palmer-Sikelianou. *International Journal of the Classical Tradition* 8, no. 3 (Winter 2002): 375–93.

———. " 'You Unleash the Tempest of Tragedy': The 1903 Athenian Production of Aeschylus' *Oresteia.*" In *A Companion to Classical Receptions*, edited by Lorna Hardwick and Christopher Stray, 360–72. Malden: Wiley-Blackwell, 2011.

Vicinus, Martha. "The Adolescent Boy: Fin-de-siècle Femme Fatale?" *Journal of the History of Sexuality* 5, no. 1 (July 1994): 90–114. http://www.jstor.org /stable/3704081 (accessed October 18, 2016).

———. *Intimate Friends: Women Who Loved Women, 1778–1928.* Chicago: University of Chicago Press, 2004.

Vivien, Renée. *A Woman Appeared to Me.* Translated by Gayle Rubin. Reno, NV: Naiad, 1976.

———. *Une femme m'apparut—: Texte de la première édition datant de 1904, suivi d'une anthologie de poèmes.* Paris: Adventice, 2008.

Vivien, Renée, Natalie Clifford Barney, Eva Palmer, and Jean-Paul Goujon. *Album Secret.* [Muizon, France]: Éditions À l'cart, 1984.

Vlagopoulos, Panos. " 'The Patrimony of Our Race': Louis-Albert Bourgault-Ducoudray and the Emergence of the Discourse on Greek National Music." *Journal of Modern Greek Studies* 34, no. 1 (May 2016): 49–77.

Vogeikoff-Brogan, Natalia. " 'Going Native': The Unusual Case of George Cram Cook." *From the Archivist's Notebook: Essays Inspired by Archival Research in Athens, Greece* website, August 1, 2013. https://nataliavogeikoff.com/2013 /08/01/going-native-the-unusual-case-of-george-cram-cook/ (accessed June 20, 2018).

Vogli, Elpida. "The Making of Greece Abroad: Continuity and Change in the Modern Diaspora Politics of a 'Historical' Irredentist Homeland." In *Diaspora and Citizenship*, edited by Elena Barabantseva and Claire Sutherland, 14–34. London: Routledge, 2012.

Voglis, Polymeris. *Becoming a Subject: Political Prisoners during the Greek Civil War*. Oxford: Berghahn Books, 2002.

Wagner, Richard. "What Is German?" In *Art and Politics*, vol. 4. Translated by William Ashton Ellis, 149–70. Lincoln: University of Nebraska Press, 1995.

Ware, Timothy. *The Orthodox Church*. New York: Penguin Books, 1993.

Wickes, George. *The Amazon of Letters: The Life and Loves of Natalie Barney*. New York: Putnam, 1976.

Wilbor, Elsie M. *Delsarte Recitation Book*. New York: E. S. Werner, 1905.

Winning, Joanne. "Dorothy Richardson and the Politics of Friendship." *Pilgrimages: The Journal of Dorothy Richardson Studies* 2 (2009): 91–121. http://dorothyrichardson.org/journal/issue2/Winning.pdf (accessed June 20, 2018).

Winterer, Caroline. *The Mirror of Antiquity: American Women and the Classical Tradition, 1750–1900*. Ithaca, NY: Cornell University Press, 2007.

Witt, Mary Ann Frese. *The Search for Modern Tragedy: Aesthetic Fascism in Italy and France*. Ithaca, NY: Cornell University Press, 2001.

Wood, Elizabeth. "Sapphonics." In *Queering the Pitch: The New Gay and Lesbian Musicology*, edited by Philip Brett, Elizabeth Wood, and Gary C. Thomas, 22–66. New York: Routledge, 1994.

Woolf, Virginia. "A Dialogue upon Mount Pentelicus." In *The Complete Shorter Fiction of Virginia Woolf*, edited by Susan Dick, 63–68. New York: Harcourt, 1989.

Wright, Louise E. *Maurice Magnus: A Biography*. Newcastle, UK:: Cambridge Scholars, 2007.

Yaari, Nurit. "Myth into Dance: Martha Graham's Interpretation of the Classical Tradition." *International Journal of the Classical Tradition* 10, no. 2 (Fall 2003): 221–42.

Yatromanolakis, Dimitrios. *Sappho in the Making: The Early Reception*. Cambridge, MA: Harvard University Press, 2008.

Young, Tricia Henry. *The Killinger Collection: Costumes of Denishawn and Ted Shawn and His Men Dancers*. Tallahassee: Florida State University Department of Dance, 1999.

Zamir, Meir. "Population Statistics of the Ottoman Empire in 1914 and 1919." *Middle Eastern Studies* 17, no. 1 (January 1981): 85–106.

Zon, Bennett. "Disorienting Race: Humanizing the Musical Savage and the Rise of British Ethnomusicology." *Nineteenth-Century Music Review* 3, no. 1 (2006): 25–43. doi:10.1017/S1479409800000331.

Zonana, Joyce. "Swinburne's Sappho: The Muse as Sister-Goddess." *Victorian Poetry* 28, no. 1 (Spring 1990): 39–50.

Index